English Syntax

English Syntax   C. L. Baker

The MIT Press
Cambridge, Massachusetts
London, England

This book was set in New Baskerville using computer disks provided by the
author, and was printed and bound by Halliday Lithograph in the
United States of America

Library of Congress Cataloging-in-Publication Data

Baker, C. L. (Carl Lee)
   English Syntax

   Includes index.
   1. English language—Syntax.   I. Title.
PE1361.B35   1989   425   88-8252
ISBN 0-262-02287-7

for Andrew and Catherine

Contents

Chapter 3

Chapter 4

Preface

This work is designed to be used as a textbook in a basic course in English syntax at either the undergraduate level or the beginning graduate level. The book is self-contained, presupposing no prior coursework in English syntax or in linguistics.

The approach to English syntax that is followed in this book has its roots in the discipline of linguistics. As with linguistic work in general, the main goal is not so much prescriptive as descriptive. Thus, unlike many traditional school grammars, this book is not primarily concerned with defining proper English usage. Instead, it takes the English language as it is used today and attempts to describe the way in which its sentences are formed. As a consequence of this orientation, virtually no attention is given to sentences such as *Bob was setting on his bed* and *John and me fed the pigeons*, where the usages of individual speakers are not always in agreement. By contrast, a great deal of time will be spent on trying to understand the structure of uncontroversially acceptable sentences, such as *Joe asked Martha to tell him where to put the chair* and *There seems to be a fly in your soup*.

The fact that this book has a descriptive rather than prescriptive orientation is enough to give it a strongly linguistic character. More narrowly, it falls squarely within the spirit of a particular approach to linguistics known as the *generative* approach. This approach, which was pioneered by Noam Chomsky of the Massachusetts Institute of Technology in the middle and late 1950s, has become far and away the most widely followed method for the study of syntax. The central premise is that a person's fluency in a language rests on a largely unconscious knowledge of a vast system of rules that define the well-formed structures of the language. It is then the primary business of the linguist to try to determine what these unconscious rules are for the language that he or she is studying. Applied to the syntax of English, the generative approach has given rise to an enormous explosion of new research and new ideas. The result of over thirty years' work is an increasingly deep and comprehensive idea of what it is that a person knows when he or she knows English.

Although this book follows the generative approach, it does not conform in detail to any of the particular generative theories of syntax that have been developed in recent years—theories such as transformational grammar, lexical-functional grammar, or generalized phrase-structure grammar. Readers who have some knowledge of these theories will see them at work implicitly in various places in the text; for example, the treatment of direct questions and certain special verbal structures is implicitly transformational in character. Those readers who wish to study one or more of these theories, either during their reading of this book or afterwards, can take many of the basic ideas about English syntax presented here and reformulate them in terms of the particular leading theories in which they are interested.

As a result of studying this book, readers should come to understand the most important syntactic rules of English and how they interact in the formation of individual sentences. This understanding should be sufficiently detailed and concrete to enable them to analyze complicated English sentences with a certain degree of confidence and comfort. The following sentence provides an illustration:

> The woman whose daughter wanted to help her decide which design to adopt has already realized that the new kitchen will be much more difficult to keep clean than the old one was.

Before working through this book, many students (especially native speakers of English) will consciously perceive this sentence as little more than a sequence of individual words that somehow make sense together. By the end of the book, the same readers should be able to identify a variety of structural units, including the following :

- the relative clause introduced by *whose daughter*
- the infinitival indirect question introduced by *which design*, with the missing direct object of *adopt*
- the clausal complement introduced by *that*
- the infinitival complement of *difficult*, with the missing object of *keep*
- the comparative construction associated with this adjective phrase.

Beyond this, they should have an idea of the rules that create these individual structures, those that license their use in the larger contexts in which they occur, and those that account for certain basic properties of their interpretation.

For those readers who want to achieve this kind of mastery, doing the exercises is absolutely essential. In addition to making new material more familiar, they provide a constant review of material introduced earlier. Their overall effect is to ensure an understanding of English rules and English structure that is active and specific rather than passive and vague.

Many people have been of enormous help to me in the preparation of this book. When I was just getting started on the project, in the early 1980s, Jim Shay provided me with a good deal of helpful advice and encouragement, among other things convincing me that there was a genuine need for such a book. Since that time, I have received comments and suggestions from a number of colleagues here at the University of Texas, who actually tested various preliminary versions in their courses here. These people include Georgette Ioup, Frank Trechsel, Pat Stanley, Richard Meier, and Sam Epstein. In addition, Irene Heim, Hans Kamp, and Mats Rooth read and commented on individual chapters. Finally, three people—Wayne O'Neil, Carlota Smith, and Dana McDaniel—went over the entire penultimate version of the manuscript and provided both general suggestions and painstaking page-by-page comments on matters of detail. To all of these people I owe a great debt, even though I did not always take their advice.

I would not want to end this preface without adding a special word of appreciation to several people at The MIT Press. Bob Bolick and Larry Cohen, the two linguistics editors with whom I worked during the writing of the book, provided patient help and encouragement at every step of the way. Paul Bethge's thorough and painstaking stylistic refinement of the manuscript helped immensely to improve the readability of the book. Lorrie LeJeune took on the task of preparing a typeset version, a task which involved (among other things) a heroic expenditure of effort on the trees and other illustrations. Incidentally, the elegant 1947 Studebakers that the reader will encounter in chapter 5 are a joint contribution of Paul and Lorrie.

I

Introduction

Chapter 1

The Field of English Syntax

The central purpose of this first chapter is to give a preliminary idea of what we will be doing in this book. In section 1.1 we will see what the field of English syntax is concerned with and how we can proceed to study it. Section 1.2 puts the study of English syntax within the general context of modern linguistics. In section 1.3 we consider the question of how best to understand the different varieties of English that we hear around us. This discussion will provide some helpful background ideas for section 1.4, where we will compare the approach taken here with the approach taken in traditional school textbooks on English grammar.

1.1 The Subject Matter of English Syntax

By the *syntax* of a language, we mean the body of rules that speakers of the language follow when they combine words into sentences. Thus, when we investigate *English* syntax, we will be trying to determine the rules that dictate how *English* speakers combine words to make sentences.

At first glance, it may not be clear how much there is to be said about English rules. In particular, those who have grown up with English as their native language often take it for granted that no special rules are required for success in using English. For example, in an appropriate situation they might utter a sentence such as (1).

(1)   Martha lives in the house that John sold to her.

In producing this sentence, they would typically have the impression that they were not following any rules at all but merely letting the thought to be expressed dictate the choice of words and their arrangement in the sentence. These speakers, then, might find it hard to believe that any special rules of English sentence formation played a role in shaping this utterance. Thus, we need to start our discussion by looking at some reasons for believing that rules of English syntax really exist.

1.1.1 Evidence for Rules of Syntax

We get a first piece of evidence that English sentence formation follows rules when we look at how the thought expressed in (1) might be expressed by a speaker of Japanese. Let us imagine a person whose only knowledge about English consists of some information about English words and their meanings obtained from a Japanese-to-English dictionary. The most likely result of this person's effort to express this thought would be the sentence given in (2), which corresponds word by word to the sentence that would convey the same thought in Japanese.

(2)   Martha John her to sold house in lives.

Even though this imaginary Japanese speaker has a coherent thought to express and knows the necessary English words, he or she clearly does not have the means to construct a successful English sentence. The striking difference in acceptability between (1) and (2) suggests that a person who sets out to construct an acceptable English sentence must also use some rules that dictate allowable English *word order*. (It should be obvious that an English speaker who tried to construct a Japanese sentence without knowing any rules for Japanese word order would have just as serious a problem in making a sentence that was acceptable to fluent Japanese speakers.)

More evidence that knowing some words and having a thought to express are not enough is provided by the following pairs of sentences:

(3)   a.   The mayor gave John some good advices.
       b.   The mayor gave John some good advice.

(4)   a.   This man going to the station.
       b.   This man is going to the station.

(5)   a.   Jack read the book that Marsha bought it for him.
       b.   Jack read the book that Marsha bought for him.

(6)   a.   Anyone didn't see the accident.
       b.   No one saw the accident.

When asked to say which sentence in each of the above pairs is the more acceptable one, fluent speakers of English would invariably pick the (b) sentences. They might describe the (a) sentences as "funny-sounding" or "not normal" or "the wrong way to say it," even though they would find it easy to tell what thought the sentences were supposed to communicate. All the (a) sentences are of types that occasionally occur in the speech and the writing of students who are in the early stages of learning English as a foreign language. Here again, we can see that a knowledge of English words and their meanings is not enough to guarantee that a person with a thought to convey will be able to express it in a sentence that English speakers will consider acceptable.

We thus have some initial evidence to suggest that English speakers follow rules of some kind when they put sentences together. One curious aspect of these rules requires mention right away: People who have learned English in early childhood as their native language and speak it fluently as adults typically are not able to say exactly what rules they followed in arriving at the correct word order in (1), or in choosing the (b) sentences in preference to the (a) sentences in (3)–(6). Beyond not being able to say what the rules are, they are not even aware of following any rules when they create sentences or when they decide which of two sentences sounds better. Thus, if we are to believe that English speakers follow syntactic rules, we must hold that these rules are *unconscious*. The view we get, then, can be depicted as in (7).

(7)

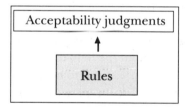

In this diagram, the arrow from the lower box to the upper one indicates that what is in the lower box *determines* what is in the upper one—in this case, that rules determine acceptability judgments. The contrast between the absence of shading in the top box and the presence of shading in the bottom one is designed to mark the difference between what is conscious and what is not. The acceptability judgments that we made in (3)–(6) are "accessible to our introspection": In effect, we can look inside our minds and observe our differing reactions to the sentences in each pair. By contrast, the rules that determine these judgments are "inaccessible to our introspection": We cannot look into our minds and see what the rules are, just as we cannot watch them operating when we are making individual judgments.

Some native English speakers might find it difficult to believe in the existence of rules in their mind of which they have no conscious awareness. They might prefer an alternative view, which could be expressed as follows: "I really don't think that I followed any rules when I picked out the (b) sentences in (3)–(6) as the good ones. Any speaker of English would pick the (b) sentences simply because they are similar to sentences that he or she would have heard before." This view is pictured in (8).

(8)

Acceptability judgments

↑

Previously heard sentences

At first glance, this position may seem to be much more natural than the one diagrammed in (7), which required us to believe in unconscious mental rules. After all, the clearest, most indisputable fact about human language development is that the utterances a person hears in early childhood play an indispensable role in determining what sentences the same person will accept and use at a later stage of life. This fact forces us to acknowledge in some way the contribution of previously heard utterances. The immediate question, though, is whether diagram (8) gives us a reasonable picture of this contribution.

The most important claim that this diagram makes is that previously heard sentences determine judgments *directly*, without the help of mental rules. Before we look at the deficiencies of this view, we need to note that if speakers are to use utterances they have heard in the past to judge sentences offered to them in the present, then they must have some mental record of the past sentences. So we need, at least, to exchange diagram (8) for the slightly more complex diagram (9).

(9)

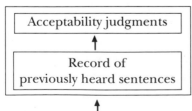

↑

Previously heard sentences

One more change needs to be made in our diagram. Even the person who claims that judgments are based on previous sentences rather than on rules must admit that he or she does not consciously remember any significant number of previously heard sentences and has no awareness of actually using them in judging pairs of sentences like those in (3)–(6). Thus, for the same reason that we shaded the *rules* in diagram (7), we must now shade the *record of previously heard sentences* in diagram (9). The new picture that emerges is shown as (10).

(10)

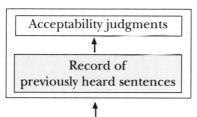

Previously heard sentences

Thus, the basic choice between these two views comes down to a choice between believing in an unconscious set of mental rules and believing in an equally unconscious record of previously heard sentences.

Two basic considerations favor the "rules" view over the "previous sentences" view. The first is that keeping a sufficient record of previously heard utterances would require an immense amount of mental storage. Because of the "mental search" time that would have to be spent in looking for "similar sentences," we would expect acceptability judgments to take much more time than they actually take. The second consideration is that there is a serious problem in saying how the record of earlier utterances would actually be used to judge new ones. The problem hinges on the question of what counts as "similarity." In particular, we need to know when a sentence given to us now and a sentence heard in the past qualify as "similar." For instance, imagine a person who had a mental list of sentences that included (11a). He or she might well conclude that sentence (11b) is "similar" enough to be acceptable.

(11) a. The mayor gave Joe some good suggestions.
b. The mayor gave Joe some good advices.

Thus, if we really judged the acceptability of new sentences by their degree of "similarity" to sentences heard previously, we would almost certainly accept many sentences that in fact we reject.

For these reasons, we will put aside the view represented in (10) and go back to the one represented in (7), in which our judgments are determined by rules. How, though, can we recognize the undeniable connection between sentences heard in childhood and sentences accepted in maturity? The answer is that there is an *indirect* connection: the sentences heard in childhood determine our mental rules, and these rules in turn determine the sentences that we accept in adulthood. This can be pictured as in (12), an expanded version of (7).

(12)

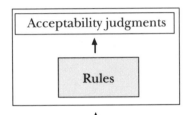

Previously heard sentences

1.1.2 How We Discover the Rules

Suppose now that we accept the idea pictured in (12). We then need to turn to the question of how we find out exactly what the rules are. As was noted above, we cannot look inside our minds and observe them directly. What we can observe, though, are some of the *effects* of these rules. In particular, we can look at judgments of acceptability, of the sort that we have seen several times already. We can then take these observations as hints or clues to the nature of the invisible rules. A concrete illustration of this kind of detective work is given below in the form of a dialogue between a graduate student from France and his American friend. The central project is to determine exactly what rule of English is broken in sentence (3a) (the *good advices* example).

Day 1

Pierre: Yesterday I wrote the sentence "The mayor gave John some good advices," and today it came back corrected.

David: You should have said "The Mayor gave John some good advice."

Pierre: Yes, that's what the teacher wrote on the paper, but I still don't see what rule I violated with the original sentence.

David: I don't know that there's any rule, except that sentences like that just don't sound very good.

Pierre: I know that now, but couldn't you give me a rule that would help me to avoid making the same kind of mistake in the future?

David: What if we just said that the word *advice* is permitted but the word *advices* is not.

Pierre: That looks like the right idea. It allows *some good advice* but rules out *some good advices*.

Day 2

Pierre: I'm still having trouble with the word *advice*. From what you said yesterday, I thought it would be OK to write "The president was hoping for a good advice." But this sentence came back marked wrong, too. So it's not enough just to say that you can't use *advices*.

David: I guess that *advice* follows two rules. One is the rule that we thought of yesterday, and the other is a rule that says that it can't be used with *a* or *an*.

Pierre: Thanks. That's a help.

Day 3

Pierre: Just when I thought things were going better, I had another problem. I've seen sentences where *one* is used as a replacement for a repeated word. For instance, I'm sure that I've seen sentences like "The car that Bill bought was smaller than the one that Martha bought." Does that sound OK to you?

David: It's perfect.

Pierre: Then what's wrong with this sentence: "The advice that Jones got was more helpful than the one that Smith got." I was corrected on that sentence today.

David: I agree that it sounds terrible. Let's just say that the word *one* can't be used in place of *advice*.

Pierre: We now have three separate rules just for *advice*. I hope I don't have to learn this many rules every time I learn a new English word.

David: Don't worry. I doubt very seriously that there are any others as bad as this one.

Day 4

Pierre: Do you think you could help me again? This time I'm having trouble with the word *furniture*. In fact, I made two mistakes in the same composition. I wrote "We had hoped to get three new furnitures every month, but we only had enough money to get a furniture every two weeks."

David: Maybe you could make a list of rules for *furniture*, just like you did for *advice*. It looks as if you can't use *furnitures*, and also that you can't use *furniture* with *a* or *an*.

Pierre: While we're at it, we might see if the third of our restrictions on *advice* is matched by a corresponding rule for *furniture*. How does this sentence sound to you: "The furniture we bought last year was more expensive than the one we bought this year."

David: Terrible! You definitely can't use the word *one* as a replacement for *furniture*.

Pierre: This is really odd. I don't see why *advice* and *furniture* should follow the same rules. I wonder if there are any other words that behave this way.

David: Let's start with a couple of words that are related in meaning to *advice* and *furniture*. How about *suggestions* and *armchair*? Let's see. We can talk about *suggestions* and *armchairs*. Also, it's OK to say *a suggestion* and *an armchair*. Finally, we can use *one* as a replacement for these words: "the first suggestion and the second one"; "this armchair and that one." So these two words are completely different from *advice* and *furniture*.

Pierre: I think maybe I have one that's like *advice* and *furniture*. How do these sentences sound: "We had some corns for supper." "Let me have a corn." "The corn on his plate is larger than the one on my plate."

David: They're all pretty hopeless.

Pierre: What happens with *bean*? Could you say "We had some beans for supper," or "Let me have a bean," or "The bean on his plate is bigger than the one on my plate?"

David: The ideas conveyed by the last two sentences are a little silly, but all three of them sound like perfectly normal English.

Pierre: Each word we've tried is either like *advice* or like *suggestion*. Maybe the simplest thing to do would be to make a list of words like *advice* and a list of words like *suggestion*. Let's call them "group 1 words" and "group 2 words."

David: What are your rules going to say, then?

Pierre: I think they'll be pretty simple, something like this: (1) Only group 2 words can be plural. (2) Only group 2 words can go with *a* or *an*. (3) Only group 2 words can be replaced by *one*.

David: Just out of curiosity, is there anything special that only your group 1 words can do?

Pierre: I don't know offhand. Can you think of any place where *advice* would work but *suggestion* wouldn't?

David: How about after *much*? I can say *too much advice*, but *too much suggestion* and *too much suggestions* both sound bad. Also, *much* goes OK with *furniture* and *corn*, but not with *armchair* and *bean*.

Pierre: So there's at least one rule that allows group 1 words to do something: *much* can be followed by a group 1 word.

David: Wait a minute. What are you going to do with a word like *cake*? You could perfectly well say *cakes*, *a cake*, or *this cake and that one*, all of which seems to put it in group 2. But you can also say *too much cake*, which means that it ought to go in group 1.

Pierre: I don't know any reason why we couldn't just put it in both groups. Then it could undergo all the rules for both groups.

David: Before I forget it, what's the final explanation for why the *good advices* example, which we started with, was bad?

Pierre: It's pretty simple. The one basic fact about *advice* is that it's group 1 but not group 2. So by our first rule for group 2 words, it can't have a plural form.

David: You make it sound easy now. But it was tough going at the beginning.

At this point, the dialogue ends. It has clearly had a happy conclusion: as a result of their unusual persistence and intelligence, Pierre and David have succeeded in rediscovering the traditional grammatical classes of *mass nouns* (their group 1) and *count nouns* (their group 2). In addition, they have found some general rules applying to words in these classes. There are two important respects in which these simple rules are typical of those that will be discussed in the body of this book. First, native speakers of English show total agreement in making the judgments that these rules dictate. Second, they are by and large totally unaware that these rules exist or that they use them in their everyday speech and writing. We have thus discovered some specific examples of the kind of hidden, unconscious rules of English shown in the shaded part of diagram (12).

Even though the "research" that Pierre and David did was conducted in a casual, unsystematic way, their efforts illustrate several aspects of serious syntactic study. The entire project started with a puzzle: Why was a certain sentence not acceptable in English? A first guess was made (the proposal that *advices* was not a legitimate English word), but later clues showed that this guess was too limited in the facts that it accounted for. The investigators did not know at the beginning what the critical clues were going to be; some of them they stumbled onto by accident and others they found by doing little "experiments" that they thought of along the way. When they added to their rules or modified them, they did so for one of two quite different reasons. Sometimes it was from a desire to account for more of the clues that they had found; at other times, it was from a desire to create a simpler, neater system. Each of these desires played a role in their eventual success.

1.2 English Syntax as a Subfield of Linguistics

The approach that will be taken in this book has its roots in the larger field of linguistics. In order to become fully comfortable with this approach, let us look briefly at the history of this relatively new discipline and identify its most basic ideas.

1.2.1 The Development of Modern Linguistics

Although human thinkers had for many centuries been interested in the phenomenon of human language in general and also in particular human languages, the beginning of the nineteenth century saw an explosion of interest in what came to be called *historical and comparative linguistics*. The original fuel for this interest was provided by a small number of European scholars who, in the space of only a few years at the beginning of the nineteenth century, accumulated evidence for an astonishing idea. What they discovered was that a vast array of superficially dissimilar European and Asian languages were actually descended from a common prehistoric language. This family of languages, which included languages as far separated as Irish on the west and Persian and Sanskrit on the east, became know as the *Indo-European* family. Scholars were concerned for the remainder of the century with the enormous project of charting all the relationships among languages in this group and determining the historical changes that had occurred in various branches. Beyond this, especially in the latter part of the nineteenth century and on into the twentieth, they were concerned with a broader project: an attempt to understand the nature of historical change in general.

During this period of linguistics, one particular fact became overwhelmingly clear at an early stage: that all languages are constantly changing.

Even Classical Latin, which earlier scholars had wanted to consider pure and timeless, was now seen to be the result of a sequence of historical changes whose starting point was not even remotely visible. This idea implies that present-day English, by its very nature as a human language, must even now be undergoing a substantial number of changes, and that it would be futile and pointless for anyone to try to freeze it in its present state.

Alongside this interest in language history and language change, increasing attention was given in the early decades of this century to studying the structure of individual languages, and the movement known as *structural linguistics* arose. For many European countries, the native languages in their colonial possessions invited serious study; in the United States and Canada, a multitude of Native American languages offered similar opportunities. In addition to the great wealth of detailed information that was obtained from these projects, both about the individual languages studied and about the workings of human language in general, two very simple but basic truths became apparent. The first was that, contrary to what was widely believed at the time, there are no "primitive" languages. The languages of tribes which by European standards are quite primitive technologically have proved to just as complex as the major European languages, and just as rich in their expressive possibilities. Even though many of these languages had never been written down and had never had grammar books devoted to them, they proved to be governed by coherent systems of rules in exactly the same way that the better-known written languages were. The second basic truth learned in this period was that there was a much wider diversity among different languages that had been suspected. The practical consequence of this discovery was that language scholars abandoned the practice of trying to fit the description of every newly encountered language into the mold provided by the rule systems of Latin and Greek. Instead, they increasingly adopted the view that each language deserved to be described in its own terms.

In the middle and late 1950s, a new movement arose within linguistics; it came to be called *generative grammar*. In many ways this movement represented a natural development out of the structural linguistics of the preceding decades. However, in several respects it was quite revolutionary. The most striking change was its strong psychological orientation, centered around the conviction that the study of language was essentially a study of one aspect of the human mind. The discussion in section 1.1 reflects this idea clearly: What we try to discover when we investigate English syntax is a system of rules that lies hidden in the minds of fluent speakers of the language.

Besides inquiring into the unconscious rules of particular languages, generative grammar has been concerned with an even deeper psychological problem, that of discovering what aspects of human language capacity are determined by our common human genetic endowment rather than by our differing early language environments. The basic idea is that part of what humans know about their language is *innate*—that is, present by virtue of the nature of the human organism rather than by virtue of their early experience with their language. In particular, though all children clearly require help from their language environment in order to learn the rules of their language, there is now much evidence that their minds are provided ahead of time with unconscious principles that dictate what general *kinds* of rules are to be expected. The contribution of these innate principles is illustrated in diagram (13), an expanded version of (12).

(13)

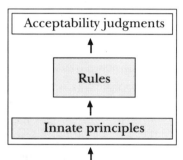

Previously heard sentences

Although the major focus of this book is on English rules rather than on innate principles, particular principles will occasionally be mentioned. In a few cases, we will even use them in our conscious search for the rules of English, just as children use them in their unconscious search for the rules of their language.

Generative grammar thus consists of two related enterprises. One of these is concerned with discovering the rules of particular languages—for instance, English, Chinese, and Arabic. The other is concerned with uncovering the genetically determined principles that make their effects felt in all languages. Just as we speak of English grammar, Chinese grammar, and Arabic grammar when we are talking about the rules of these individual languages, so we can use the term *universal grammar* when we are talking about the genetically determined principles.

1.2.2 Other Areas of English Grammar

Syntactic rules make up only one of several major systems in a fluent speaker's total knowledge of English. In addition to these rules that govern sentence formation, a speaker also knows rules of several other kinds:

morphological rules—rules that regulate the formation of words;
semantic rules—rules that determine interpretations of words and sentences;
phonological rules—rules that determine allowable patterns of sounds;
phonetic rules—rules that determine the actual pronunciation of words and sentences.

For each of these distinct sets of rules for an individual language like English, there is a corresponding component of universal grammar—that is, a distinct system of innate principles that provide a language learner, in advance, with unconcious ideas concerning the exact types of rules to expect in the language to which he or she is exposed.

In the course of exploring these various rule systems individually, generative linguists have discovered a number of interesting respects in which these systems are interdependent. Of especial importance for syntax has been the exploration of the ways in which syntax is related to semantics.

The most basic connection between syntax and semantics resides in the fact that many of the semantic rules that provide interpretations for sentences make reference to the structures that are determined by the syntactic rules. For example, sentence (14) exhibits a special English construction, which will be studied in detail in chapter 9.

(14)   Martha finds John *easy to understand.*

In addition to agreeing on the acceptability of this sentence, fluent speakers of English agree in viewing *John* as the "understood object" of the word *understand*, rather than as the "understood subject." Even if they do not use these traditional terms to describe their intuition, they can tell that (14) implies (15a) but does not imply (15b).

(15)   a.   It is easy for Martha to understand John.
        b.   It is easy for John to understand Martha.

Several interpretive rules play significant roles here. One of these rules makes reference to the special syntactic construction. In describing this construction, then, we will want to go beyond matters that are narrowly syntactic and to offer a brief description of its interpretation. The inclusion of discussions on such interpretive topics follows a long-standing practice of syntacticians, one that is reflected in a wide variety of syntactic works ranging from very traditional studies to the most recent generative studies.

At several points in this book, we will also observe another kind of connection between semantics and syntax: We will see cases in which words with similar interpretations have similar syntactic properties as well. For example, we will see in chapter 3 that words belonging to the semantic class of "personal-care verbs"—words such as *dress, wash,* and *shave*—all may appear in a particular syntactic configuration, and that they are given a special semantic interpretation when they do so. In this and other cases like it, we will note the semantic class in question and the special syntactic behavior that its members share.

1.3 Different Varieties of English

In regard to examples (3)–(6), it was noted that we would find almost total agreement if we were to ask many different English speakers for their judgments. Sometimes, though, we find clear cases in which different speakers do not agree.

1.3.1 Regional Varieties
The following are four sentences that might well give rise to conflicting judgments:

(16)   I'm not sure that Joe loved Alice, but he might have done.

(17)   This car needs washed.

(18)   You might should get a new muffler.

(19)   Joe thinks the Celtics will win tonight, and so don't I.

While virtually all American speakers would find (16) quite strange, a great many British speakers would find it completely normal. With (17), we would find a clear difference of opinion within the United States; residents of the Ohio-Pennsylvania border area would find it perfectly normal, but almost everyone else would find it somewhat strange. In similar fashion, (18) would be accepted principally in the south central states (Texas in particular), and (19) would find its strongest support in Boston and elsewhere in New England.

In discussing differences of the sort illustrated above, we often speak of *regional varieties* or *regional dialects* of English. We can even imagine that what customarily goes under the name "the English language" is actually a collection of closely related sublanguages, one for each geographical area. If we picked the dialects of two particular areas—for example, Pittsburgh and Boston—and set out to write down all the rules of each dialect, we would discover that most of the rules we found were shared by the two dialects, only a small number of relatively minor rules serving to differentiate them.

If we ask ourselves how differences of these sorts are maintained over several generations, the answer is immediately obvious: there are some small differences between the English heard by Pittsburgh children and the English heard by Boston children. Pittsburgh children are exposed to sentences with the "needs cleaned" construction, and they form unconscious rules that allow for it; correspondingly, Boston children hear "so don't I" examples and end up with rules that allow for it. This situation is illustrated in diagram (20).

(20)

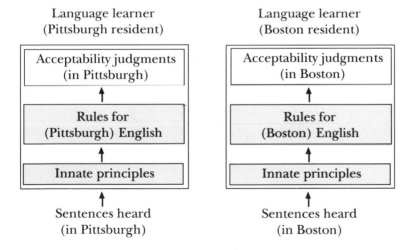

The differences found in the speech of adult Pittsburgh and Boston residents are most plausibly traced to differences in the speech to which members of these two groups were exposed in childhood.

1.3.2 Standard versus Nonstandard English

Let us turn now to another group of examples that give rise to conflicting reactions among different speakers.

(21) a. Joe isn't here.
      b   Joe ain't here.

(22) a. He doesn't live here now.
      b. He don't live here now.

(23) a. They did it themselves.
      b. They did it theirselves.

(24) a. I didn't tell anybody.
      b. I didn't tell nobody.

Many English speakers use the (a) sentences consistently; many others, though, show a definite tendency to use the (b) sentences, at least in their everyday speech.   Both groups of speakers, however, often agree in classifying the (a) sentences as more "correct" than the (b) sentences. The type of contrast shown here is often referred to as a contrast between *standard* and *nonstandard* (or *substandard*) English.

In subsection 1.3.1 it was maintained that all persons exposed to a language in childhood succeed in learning a uniform set of unconscious rules for their language. But the conflicting preferences in (21)–(24) are sometimes seen as supporting just the opposite view—namely, that some children are much more successful than others in the degree to which they master their native language. On this view, a strong and consistent preference for the "correct" (a) examples would indicate successful language learning, and a preference for the "incorrect" (b) examples would be taken as a symptom of unsuccessful language learning.

What could be the source of inaccurate learning of a native language? One initially plausible possibility would be that some individuals are simply less gifted as language learners; perhaps for genetic reasons, their innate principles are either defective or incomplete. This overall idea can be diagrammed as in (25).

(25)

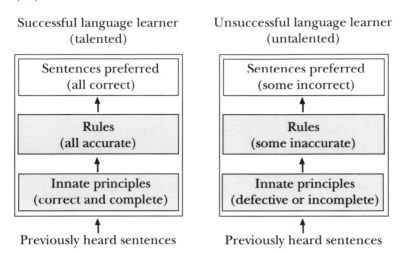

Successful language learner
(talented)

Unsuccessful language learner
(untalented)

Sentences preferred
(all correct)

↑

Rules
(all accurate)

↑

Innate principles
(correct and complete)

↑

Previously heard sentences

Sentences preferred
(some incorrect)

↑

Rules
(some inaccurate)

↑

Innate principles
(defective or incomplete)

↑

Previously heard sentences

Although this idea might seem natural at first, it overlooks a significant fact. What is overlooked becomes clear as soon as we compare in more detail the personal history of a "successful" learner with that of an "unsuccessful" learner. If we had to guess whether the two persons were exposed to the same kinds of utterances in childhood, we would guess right away that they were not, basing this guess on our everyday experience with different kinds of English speech and different individual speakers. The adult who feels completely natural with *Joe isn't here* has almost certainly grown up hearing *isn't* in his immediate social surroundings. By contrast, the person who feels more comfortable with *ain't* has almost certainly grown up hearing *ain't* from family members and friends. Looking at this fact, we might think of a second interpretation of the contrasts shown in (21)–(24): Perhaps the "successful" learner and the "unsuccessful" learner have the same inherent equipment for language learning, and the difference in what they learn should be traced back to differences in the utterances that they heard as children. We are thus moving toward an environmental explanation for the differences in (21)–(24), instead of a genetic explanation.

One possibility is that the first learner has heard sentences that follow rules strictly, whereas the second has heard sentences that do not follow any set rules. Then we might expect the first learner to have a much better chance than the second of arriving at the rules of the language. This idea is pictured in (26).

(26)

Successful language learner   Unsuccessful language learner
(Good language environment)   (Poor language environment)

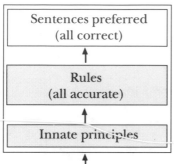

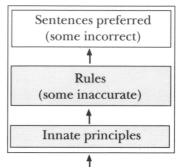

Previously heard sentences   Previously heard sentences
(follow rules)   (don't follow any set rules)

This diagram, like (25), implies that some language learners are more successful than others in learning the rules of their native language. What is new in this diagram is the implication that the deficiencies of the nonstandard speaker are to be attributed to an inferior language environment rather than to an inferior talent for language learning.

But now we need to give some critical scrutiny to the basic assumption that diagrams (25) and (26) share. Is it really true, as they imply, that the speech of some English speakers is not really governed by rules to the same extent that the speech of other speakers is? With this question in mind, let us look again at one of the pairs of sentences with which we started this discussion:

(27)   a.   He doesn't live here now.
       b.   He don't live here now.

For the person who says (27a), the unconscious rule might well be that *doesn't* is a possible alternative way of saying *does not*. For the person who says (27b), a similar rule could be given: *don't* is a possible alternative way of saying *does not*. The second statement looks just as much like a rule as the first statement. (They would share a rule saying that *don't* is an alternative way of saying *do not*.)

Let us also consider another of the sentence pairs presented earlier:

(28)   a.   They did it themselves.
        b.   They did it theirselves.

To see what the difference in the rules is here, it will be helpful to make lists of all of the so-called *reflexive* pronouns for the two varieties of English that we are considering, as follows.

(29)   **Standard**   **Nonstandard**

myself	ourselves	myself	ourselves
yourself	yourselves	yourself	yourselves
himself	themselves	hisself	theirselves
herself		herself	
itself		itsself	

Note that the first two rows are the same for both varieties. For these forms, we can give the following rule:

(30)   To make a reflexive pronoun, use the appropriate possessive form
        (in these instances, *my, your,* and *our*) and attach it to *-self* (singular)
        or *-selves* (plural).

Below the first two rows, the two sides of the chart no longer agree. The right side continues with the same rule: *his, her, its,* and *their* are all possessives; the left side switches to the so-called objective forms (*him, her, it, them*). Thus, not only is the person who says *theirselves* following a rule; he or she is following a more regular, general rule than the person who says *themselves*.

   Careful consideration of these examples, then, suggests that it is a mistake to believe that some English speakers follow rules in their speech and others do not. Instead, it now appear that *all* English speakers are successful language learners: they all follow unconscious rules derived from their early language environment, and the small differences in the sentences that they prefer are best understood as coming from small differences in these rules. Diagram (31) shows the new picture that emerges.

(31)

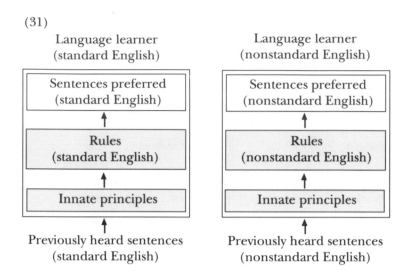

We now have a picture of the differences between a standard speaker and a nonstandard speaker that is completely parallel to the picture, given in (20), of the difference between a Pittsburgh speaker and a Boston speaker. Exposure to slightly different kinds of examples in early childhood leads to slightly differing sets of unconscious rules, which in turn lead to slightly different preferred sentences. The differences of the sort that we are looking at here follow lines of social class and ethnic group rather than geographical lines. Thus, we can speak of *social varieties* or *social dialects*.

We still need to address the question of why the (a) forms discussed above are felt by so many speakers of English to be "better." No linguistic findings of the past century provide any basis for selecting one rule system as inherently superior to another. In fact, it is highly unlikely that a linguist who was given sets of rules for two different varieties of a language could decide just by looking at the rules which one was the variety thought better by speakers of the language.

If what is widely felt as the superiority of standard English over other varieties is not to be found in any characteristics of the rule system, then what could its source possibly be? The answer turns out to be quite simple: a certain variety of speech is often felt to be superior to others because of the fact that the people who happen to speak it have a high degree of power and prestige for reasons having nothing to do with language. When we look for the group in our society to whom the preferred speech we have been talking about is most completely native, it turns out to be roughly the urban, educated, white middle class. As a large group with a high degree of prestige in this society, they have had the good fortune to have their own particular native variety of English enshrined as "standard American English."

If this standard American English is not inherently better than other varieties of American English, then why should we insist on teaching it in schools, colleges, and universities? The answer is simple: the nonstandard constructions of the sort we have been discussing are *stigmatized;* that is, writing them or uttering them in educated middle-class settings can result in one's being considered ignorant, uneducated, or even stupid. Thus, especially for those members of American society who want to spend their lives in middle-class occupations or in the professions, being able to use standard English is at the very minimum a matter of sheer self-defense.

1.4 School Grammar and Modern Syntax

In this concluding section, we will look at the relationship between the way in which English syntax is studied in traditional school grammars and the way in which it will be studied in this book. It will be useful to begin by discussing the central goal of school grammar. Reduced to essentials, it is to provide native English speakers with the rules that they need to know if they are to speak and write "the best English possible." To a certain extent, "the best English possible" means English conforming to the rules of the most prestigious dialect. Thus, for instance, many school grammars will contain rules having the effect of prohibiting *ain't*, or prohibiting *don't* as a contracted version of *does not.*

In some cases, school grammars will also offer arguments purporting to show the inherent superiority of certain rules found in the prestige dialect. One such argument is often given in connection with the contrasting examples given in (24) above:

a. I didn't tell anybody.
b. I didn't tell nobody.

Sentences like (a) are often described as more logical than sentences like (b). The alleged illogicality of (b) resides in the fact that two negative words are used to express an intended meaning that involves just a single logical negation. Such arguments for the superiority of the rules of the prestige dialect always prove to have a fragile foundation. By the argument given above, for instance, we would have to insist that many of the important standard languages of the world, languages such as French and Spanish, are logically deficient and in need of correction. The fact that this charge is never made against French and Spanish suggests that there is no reason to lodge it against nonstandard English. We will see in chapter 15 exactly what the difference is between standard English and nonstandard English in this area of grammar. In the meantime, the point to be remembered is that, in our discussion of the rules of standard English, we will be content to try to discover what the rules are, and will refrain from trying to give arguments for their superiority over the corresponding nonstandard rules in cases where differences exist.

There has traditionally been a second source of rules for "the best English possible." Among these rules are the ones that label the (a) sentences below as correct and the (b) sentences as incorrect.

(32)   a.   It is I
       b.   It is me.

(33)   a.   Father and I went down to camp.
       b.   Father and me went down to camp.

(34)   a.   Whom did you see?
       b.   Who did you see?

(35)   a.   John is taller than I.
       b.   John is taller than me.

These rules owe their place in school grammars to a project that began in the English Renaissance. At that time, it was felt that the best of all possible languages would be one in which the grammatical rules of the language could be identified with the rules of reasoning that humans everywhere use. Classical Greek and Latin appeared to Renaissance thinkers to be the languages that most clearly embodied this ideal. Thus, to the extent that the rules of English as it was then spoken deviated from the rules of these ancient languages, it seemed desirable to change the English rules in order to make English a more "reasonable" language. None of the four rules needed to get the "correct" (a) sentences above were originally native to English; they were all borrowed from Latin and imposed on English by scholars who felt that they were improving the language by doing this. The assumptions on which this project was based have been completely abandoned in modern language scholarship. In particular, Latin and Greek are now seen as neither more nor less logical than any of the thousands of other languages that have been spoken during the history of the human species. In addition, as scholars have increased their knowledge of the way in which individual languages work, the general idea that one language can be improved by borrowing rules from another has fallen into disrepute. Nevertheless, the rules borrowed from Latin live on in traditional school textbooks. What makes this fact unfortunate is that Classical Latin and Early Modern English had markedly different systems of syntactic rules, and the rules that fit quite easily into the Latin system have always constituted an unnatural appendage on the English rule system. Unlike the vast majority of English syntactic rules, which are learned unconsciously in childhood, these rules are not learned by native speakers without the expenditure of a great deal of labor and explicit instruction.

To a large extent, then, school grammars for native English speakers have the aim of "improving" their speech and writing by eliminating or modifying any rules that differ from those found in the prestigious "standard" dialect or that differ from the small collection of rules borrowed from Latin several centuries ago.

The present book has a different aim. Instead of trying to modify the unconscious rules that speakers of English learn in childhood, we will be trying to discover what these rules actually are, following the strategy outlined in subsection 1.1.2. We will assume that, in an overwhelming majority of cases, English speakers know which sentences are good and which are not, and we will try to devise rules that are in conformity with their judgments. In contrast to what is assumed in school grammars, we will assume that any conflicts we find between rules and judgments require a change in the rules rather than a change in the judgments.

One more point needs to be made about the difference between school grammar and the type of grammar we will be pursuing here. Because of their basic aim, school grammars typically cover only a small fraction of English syntactic rules. The reason for this narrowness is that most of the syntactic rules for the standard variety of English are shared with virtually all other varieties of the language. We have already seen two examples of rules that are the common property of English speakers everywhere: the rule that restricts *much* to mass nouns and the rule that requires a noun replaced by *one* to be a count noun. These rules are not discussed in school grammars, simply because every speaker of English uses them correctly without any special instruction.

The result of this exclusive attention to points at which different dialects come in conflict is that the major outlines of English syntax are hardly ever hinted at. In this book, the primary focus of attention will be on just these broad outlines. As a result, we will be giving most of our attention to rules that many readers will not have heard of before. Although many of these rules will seem strange at first, what we will find as we proceed is that they fit together in a very tight, systematic way to tell us exactly what sequences of words count as good English sentences, and what structures these sentences have.

While traditional school grammar and the kind of grammar that we will be considering differ markedly in their general aims and assumptions, there is one area in which they have much in common. Many readers will recall that, in addition to teaching rules of syntax from the prestige dialect of English and from Latin, school grammars also provide a general framework of grammatical concepts. These concepts include "parts of speech" (for example, nouns, verbs, adjectives), grammatical categories (for example, singular, plural, first person, feminine gender), and grammatical relations (subject, direct object, indirect object, predicate). The major reason for including these concepts in school grammars is to make it possible for the learners to understand the rules given to them, many of which refer to one or more of the concepts. For instance, at least some English-speaking children learn in school about the contrast between mass nouns and count nouns. At least one rule found in many school grammars refers to these concepts; it is the rule that states that *less* should not be used with plural count nouns, but only with mass nouns. The inclusion of this rule in school grammars arises from a minor dialect difference among speakers of English: in addition to using *less* in (36a), some speakers would also allow it in (36b), in place of the standard (36c).

(36) a. Joe has less furniture (mass noun) than Fred has.
     b. Joe has less books (plural count noun) than Fred has.
     c. Joe has fewer books (plural count noun) than Fred has.

In order to interpret this rule about *less*, it is clearly necessary to be able to distinguish mass nouns from plural count nouns.

In the syntactic investigations that we will pursue in later chapters, we will use many of the same concepts. To an even greater extent than in school grammars, we will find justification for these concepts in the general rules of English syntax that they allow us to state easily. Just as we have already seen that several rules require a distinction between count nouns and mass nouns, we will also find that several very basic rules require a distinction between nouns and verbs, between common nouns and proper nouns, between singular and plural, and so on. The end result of looking carefully at the rules in which these traditional concepts play a role will be a fuller appreciation of their genuine usefulness.

II
The Syntax of Phrases:
Heads, Complements, and Subjects

Chapter 2

Major English Phrase Types

The goal of the part II of this book, which spans chapters 2–9, is to develop some detailed ideas about English *phrase structure*—about the way in which English sentences are organized into successively smaller units. Chapter 2 is intended to serve two major functions within this larger scheme. The first function, which is the burden of section 2.1, is to offer a preliminary view of what it means to talk about phrase structure, and what kinds of questions arise in studying it. The second function, which is served by the remaining sections of the chapter, is to give a brief overview of a few basic types of English phrases—those that have the most important roles to play in the construction of larger, more inclusive phrases.

2.1 Preliminary Remarks on Phrase Structure

We can get a rough initial idea of what it means to talk about the phrase structure of a sentence by looking at (1).

(1)   The king kept putting his gold under the bathtub.

To the conscious perception of a fluent speaker of English who casually listened to this sentence, it would sound like nothing more than a sequence of individual words following one after another. Yet a traditional grammarian of English would offer something like the following as a guess about how this speaker unconsciously perceived this sentence:

(2)   a.   The word *the* joins with the word *king* to make the phrase *the king.*

     b.   The word *the* joins with the word *bathtub* to make the phrase *the bathtub.*

     c.   The word *under* joins with the phrase *the bathtub* to make the phrase *under the bathtub.*

    d.   The word *his* joins with the word *gold* to make the phrase *his gold.*

    e.   The word *putting* joins with the phrase *his gold* and the phrase *under the bathtub* to make the phrase *putting his gold under the bathtub.*

    f.   The word *kept* joins with the phrase *putting his gold under the bathtub* to make the phrase *kept putting his gold under the bathtub.*

    g.   The phrase *the king* joins with the phrase *kept putting his gold under the bathtub* to make the sentence *the king kept putting his gold under the bathtub.*

Diagram (3) is a graphic representation of this structure.

(3)

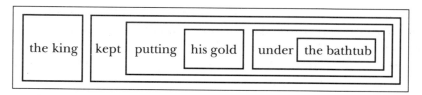

In our discussion of the syntax of a particular phrase, we will find it useful to consider two separate matters. The first concerns the "external syntax" of the phrase, the central question being how the phrase can be used in a larger construction. The second, by contrast, will concern the "internal syntax" of the phrase, the question being how the phrase itself is constructed. For example, if we were studying the phrase *putting his gold under the bathtub* as it is used in sentence (1), a consideration of its external syntax would lead us to ask what rules of English allow it to be used in the position where it appears in (1) and not in other imaginable positions such as those in (4), where the asterisks indicate that the sentences are judged unacceptable.

(4)   a. *The king *putting his gold under the bathtub.*

        b. *The king wanted *putting his gold under the bathtub.*

By contrast, if we want to understand its internal syntax, we must ask what rules allow us to combine the word *putting* with the two phrases that follow it (*his gold* and *under the bathtub*) to make the phrase in question, but not with either phrase alone or with phrases of other types:

(5)   a. *The king kept [putting his gold].

        b. *The king kept [putting under the bathtub].

    c. *The king kept [putting his gold safe].

    d. *The king kept [putting his gold to be under the bathtub].

As was noted above, the remaining sections of this chapter are concerned with giving a brief view of some of the most basic English phrase types. This discussion is intended as preparation for the task of saying how various types of larger phrases are formed. Because of this focus, we will be dividing individual phrases into groups primarily on the basis of properties that affect their external syntax. For example, the phrase in (6a) shares one property with (6b) and shares a different kind of property with (6c).

(6) a.   approves of his brother
     b.   fond of his brother
     c.   seems quiet

The phrases (6a) and (6b) are alike in both ending with *of his brother*, whereas (6a) and (6c) are alike in beginning with the same kind of word. While both kinds of shared properties need to be recognized in a complete grammar of English, only the property that (6a) shares with (6c) will be important in this chapter, because only this kind of shared property carries with it a similarity in external behavior. In the course of this discussion, we will observe some initial examples of the kinds of roles that are played in English syntax by certain traditional part-of-speech distinctions, and by English *verbal inflections* such as past tense, past participle, and present participle.

2.2 Phrases That Serve as Sentence Predicates

A first example of an important class of phrases comes to light as soon as we consider the following rule of traditional English grammar:

(7)   A sentence consists of a subject and a predicate.

The usual school-grammar definition of *subject* is "the thing talked about," whereas the *predicate* is often defined as "the thing said about the subject." Thus, in a sentence like *Irma fed the crocodile*, *Irma* comes out as the subject and *fed the crocodile* comes out as the predicate.

   A natural question to ask is what class of phrases can serve as predicates. We can see immediately that not every kind of phrase can qualify. An initial example of a pair of phrases that differ from one another in this regard is given in (8).

(8)   a.   want to leave the meeting
      b.   eager to leave the meeting

Each of these phrases is well formed in its own right. In addition, they are quite close in meaning. But when we try to join them with a suitable subject, such as *the monkeys*, only the first sentence is acceptable:

(9)   a.   The monkeys *want to leave the meeting.*
      b.   *The monkeys *eager to leave the meeting.*

This difference in acceptability must clearly reside in some difference between *want* and *eager*, since, apart from these two words, the phrases are the same. We find similar contrasts in acceptability with other pairs of phrases that differ from each other only in a single word:

(10) a.   The monkeys *approve of their leader.*
      b.   *The monkeys *fond of their leader.*

(11) a.   The monkeys *know that the President is telling the truth.*
      b.   *The monkeys *certain that the President is telling the truth.*

Evidently the words *want, approve,* and *know* play a central role in determining that the phrases containing them are allowed as predicates of sentences. By the same token, the words *eager, fond,* and *certain* have some property that makes the phrases containing them unsuitable for use as sentence predicates. These examples raise an obvious question: What is it about *want, approve,* and *know* that makes their phrases better as sentence predicates than the corresponding phrases built around *eager, fond,* and *certain?*

A similar question arises when we try to use the following phrases as sentence predicates:

(12) a.   practice medicine
      b.   doctors of medicine

(13) a.   run for office
      b.   candidates for office

(14) a.   oppose the mayor
      b.   opponents of the mayor

Only the first phrase in each pair gives good results:

(15) a.   The men *practice medicine.*
      b.   *The men *doctors of medicine.*

(16) a. Joe's sisters *run for office.*
     b. *Joe's sisters *candidates for office.*

(17) a. The firemen *oppose the mayor.*
     b. *The firemen *opponents of the mayor.*

Thus, the same kind of question arises again: What is it about the (a) phrases in (12)–(14) that makes them better sentence predicates that the (b) phrases? The twelve words that seem to be of central importance in the examples considered so far can be sorted into two groups:

(18) a. want, approve, know, practice, run, oppose
         (acceptable as first word of sentence predicate)

     b. eager, fond, certain, doctor, candidate, opponent
         (unacceptable as first word of sentence predicate)

We get a clear hint concerning the words in (18a) and those in (18b) as soon as we ask how these twelve words would be classified in an English dictionary. One familiar idea of traditional grammar, which was alluded to briefly at the end of chapter 1, is that the words of any language are to be divided into a small number of separate classes called *parts of speech.* This idea is directly reflected in dictionaries: every entry in an English dictionary gives not only an indication of how a word is pronounced and what it means but also at least one part-of-speech classification. If we look up the twelve key words in (18), we will find that those in (18a) are classified as *verbs,* whereas the first three of those in (13b) are classified as *adjectives* and the last three as *nouns.* Let us now adopt the term *head of a phrase* to refer to the single word in the phrase that determines how the phrase as a whole can be used. Then we can summarize our findings in the following simple statement:

(19) Only a phrase headed by a *verb* is permissible as the predicate of a sentence.

This first example of a group of phrases that are relevant for the operation of a grammatical rule has brought out two general points. The first is that whether a phrase qualifies for a certain use depends at least in part on some single key word in the phrase, which we have called the *head.* The second is that a property of the head that is important in this regard is its part-of-speech classification.

2.3 Phrases That Help To Build Subjects

We find an occasion to refer to another traditional part of speech when we examine phrases that can join with the word *the* to make larger phrases that can function as subjects of sentences. Here are some examples:

(20) a.   the *king of Spain*
      b.   the *leader of the army*
      c.   the *heir to the throne*
      d.   the *governor of Texas*
      e.   the *members of the committee*

If we look up the part-of-speech classifications of the four words that come directly after the word *the*, we find that all of them are *common nouns*. Some simple experiments show that this is not just a coincidence. When we try to combine the word *the* with phrases headed by words that are not common nouns, the results are unacceptable:

(21) a.   *the *leads the army* (*leads* is a verb)
      b.   *the *ran the club* (*ran* is a verb)
      c.   *the *fond of the king* (*fond* is an adjective)
      d.   *the *angry at the judge* (*angry* is an adjective)
      e.   *the *serve on the committee* (*serve* is a verb)
      f.   *the *Joe Smith* (*Joe Smith* is a proper noun)

Our result, then, can be expressed roughly as follows:

(22) The word *the* can be combined with a phrase headed by a *common noun*.

We thus have another instance in which the part-of-speech classification of the head of a phrase plays a central role in determining whether the phrase is acceptable in a certain context.

2.4 Phrases Headed by Adjectives

So far, we have a rule that calls for phrases with verbs as heads and a rule that calls for phrases with common nouns as heads. Let us now look at a situation in which phrases headed by adjectives are singled out. The following sentences exemplify one such situation.

(23) a.   *The monkeys seem *want to leave the meeting*.
      b.   The monkeys seem *eager to leave the meeting*.

(24) a. *The monkeys seem *approve of their leader.*
      b.   The monkeys seem *fond of their leader.*
(25) a. *The monkeys seem *know about the bananas.*
      b.   The monkeys seem *certain about the bananas.*

After *seem*, we can apparently have phrases headed by adjectives but not phrases headed by verbs.

   Phrases headed by common nouns also give worse results in this situation than those headed by adjectives:

(26) a.   Vera seems [*fond* of chess].
      b. *Vera seems [*lover* of chess].

(27) a.   Fred seems [*foolish* about moncy].
      b. *Fred seems [*fool* about money].

Thus, when we want to describe the kind of phrases that can come after *seem*, we need to refer to the class of phrases headed by adjectives.

2.5 Phrases Consisting of a Single Word

So far, every phrase we have studied consists of the head word plus other words. Is it ever possible for a phrase to consist just of the head word by itself? We can get an answer by examining the following new examples, keeping in mind the rules developed above.

(28) a.   The monkeys *snore.*
      b.   the *book*
      c.   The monkeys seem *despondent.*

The word *snore* is definitely a verb. If we can also consider *snore* to be a phrase headed by a verb, then (28a) satisfies rule (19), which required that sentence predicates be "phrases headed by verbs." In similar fashion, the word *book* in (28b) is certainly a noun. If we can also count it as "a phrase headed by a noun," then (28b) satisfies the rule that identified the phrases that could be combined with the word *the*. Finally, the word *despondent* in (28c) is an adjective, and if we can consider it "a phrase headed by an adjective," then our rule for what can follow *seem* is satisfied. Thus, if we want the rules developed above to cover as many situations as possible, we have to allow our concept of *phrase* to include instances consisting of only a single word.

Exercises

1. Below are listed several phrases; with each phrase are some example sentences in which the phrase appears. Some of these sentences are acceptable, but others are not. Using the given sentences as your evidence, answer three questions:

   (i)   Could this phrase be a verb phrase?
   (ii)   Could this phrase be an adjective phrase?
   (iii) Could this phrase be a common noun phrase?

In interpreting the evidence, it will be necessary to think about the rough rules developed in the preceding discussion.

   a. *search for money*
       They *search for money.*
       * They seem *search for money.*
       The *search for money* was successful.

   b. *lecture on warfare*
       The politicians *lecture on warfare.*
       *The politicians seem *lecture on warfare.*
       The *lecture on warfare* was hilarious.

   c. *approach the runway*
       The planes *approach the runway.*
       * The planes seem *approach the runway.*
       * The *approach the runway* was carried out smoothly.

   d. *safe*
       * They *safe.*
       The ladders seem *safe.*
       The *safe* was open.

   e. *list of the passengers*
       * They *list of the passengers*
       * They seem *list of the passengers.*
       The *list of the passengers* was long.

2. Below are listed a number of phrases, in each of which the head word is italicized. For each one, devise simple experiments, to answer three questions:

   (i)   Could the phrase be a verb phrase?
   (ii)   Could the phrase be an adjective phrase?
   (iii) Could the phrase be a common noun phrase?

Base these experiments on the rules developed in this section. Be sure to mark with an asterisk examples that seem to you to be unacceptable. Some of the heads may qualify for more than one part-of-speech classification.

    a.   *walk* in the park

    b.   *cross* at the sign

    c.   *appear* in court

    d.   *thought* that all cows eat grass

    e.   *revision* of the manuscript

    f.   *sailor*

    g.   *grief*

    h.   *grieve*

    i.   *run*

    j.   *talk* with their friends

    k.   *tired* of the conversation

2.6 Distinctions among Verb Forms

The previous section gave as a general rule that only a phrase headed by a verb could serve as the predicate of a sentence. This rule has the virtue of accounting for contrasts such as the following:

(29) a.   The monkeys [*know* that the President is telling the truth].

       b. *The monkeys [*certain* that the President is telling the truth].

Nevertheless, a consideration of a broader range of examples shows that it is still too permissive.

2.6.1 Present Tense and Past Tense

Although all the sentences given in (30) have predicates whose head words are verbs, only the first two sentences are acceptable.

(30) a.   The monkeys [*know* everything].

       b.   The monkeys [*knew* everything].

       c. *The monkeys [*knowing* everything].

       d. *The monkeys [*known* everything].

These examples show clearly that our rules need to distinguish between different *inflectional forms* of the same verb. Here we adopt some traditional terminology for English verb inflections and label the four verb forms used above as follows:

(31) a. *know*   present tense

      b. *knew*   past tense

      c. *knowing*   present participle

      d. *known*   past participle

We can now replace our original statement about sentence predicates by a more precise statement:

(32) A phrase headed by a *present tense* or *past tense* verb can serve as the predicate of an independent sentence.

One more kind of restriction still needs to be added, as the following examples show.

(33) a. *The monkey [*know* everything].
     b. The monkey [*knows* everything].

(34) a. The monkeys [*know* everything].
     b. *The monkeys [*knows* everything].

The unacceptability of *know* in (33a) and *knows* in (34b) clearly rests on the fact that the verb phrase is joined with *the monkey* in the first case and with *the monkeys* in the second. A similar contrast is evident in the following pairs of examples.

(35) a. *He [*know* the answer].
     b. I [*know* the answer].

(36) a. He [*knows* the answer].
     b. *I [*knows* the answer].

The rule needed here is one traditionally referred to as a rule of "agreement" between the subject and the verb that heads the predicate:

(37) The verb that heads the predicate of a sentence must agree with the subject in *number* and *person*.

For number, English provides us with two choices:

(38) a. *Singular.* The subject refers to a single individual or is headed by a mass noun.
     b. *Plural:* The subject refers to two or more individuals.

For person, three possibilities are distinguished in English:

(39) a. *First person:* The subject refers to a group of one or more individuals that includes the speaker.
     b. *Second person:* The subject refers to a group of one or more individuals that includes the person or persons being addressed but does not include the speaker.
     c. *Third person:* The subject refers to a group of one or more individuals that includes neither the speaker nor the person(s) being addressed.

By these definitions, the following would be examples of subjects from each of the six possible person-number categories:

(40) a. first-person singular: *I*
     b. first-person plural: *we, John and I, three of us*
     c. second-person singular: *you*
     d. second-person plural: *you, both of you, you three guys, you and Bill*
     e. third-person singular: *he, she, it, the woman, Joan, one of the students*
     f. third-person plural: *they, Alice and Fred, many of them, the students*

We can now say how the forms of *know* depend on the number and person of the subject: All the subjects from the above list go well with *knew*, the past-tense form. Those in the third-person singular group require the form *knows* as their present-tense form. Subjects from the remaining five person-number groups take *know* instead.

The different forms of *know* are typical in the way in which they agree with their subjects. For English verbs in general, there is one past-tense form for all person-number combinations, a special form with *-s* for third-person singular subjects, and a form without *-s* for all five of the other groups. The only verb that shows a greater number of forms than this is the verb *be*, where distinctions for person and number are made in the past tense (*was* versus *were*) as well as in the present tense (*is* versus *are*) and where there is a separate form for the first-person singular of the present tense (*am* instead of *are*).

With all these details as background, we can restate the rule that gives the kinds of phrases that may be used as sentence predicates:

(41) The predicate of a sentence must be a phrase headed by a present-tense or a past-tense verb that agrees with the subject in person and in number.

This restatement needs only one more modification, which will be made in subsection 2.6.5.

2.6.2 Nontensed Verb Forms

We have seen above that present-participial and past-participial verb forms cannot be used as predicates of independent sentences. Let us now look briefly at how they can be used. Examples (42) illustrate two possibilities for the present participle.

(42) a. The monkeys kept [*forgetting* their lines].
       b. We caught them [*eating* the bananas].

In each of these examples, replacement of the present participle by another form of the verb gives bad results, as (43) shows.

(43) a. *The monkeys kept [$\left\{\begin{array}{c} \textit{forgot} \\ \textit{forget} \\ \textit{forgotten} \end{array}\right\}$ their lines].

     b. *We caught them [$\left\{\begin{array}{c} \textit{ate} \\ \textit{eat} \\ \textit{eaten} \end{array}\right\}$ the bananas].

Thus, we have found two situations that require a phrase whose head is not just any verb form, but specifically a present participle. In the next chapter we will consider other situations in which phrases headed by present participles occur, and we will discuss the exact nature of the rules that dictate their use. For now, we will simply observe that a present participle seems to be the only acceptable verb form after *kept* and also after *caught them.*

    Turning now to phrases headed by past participles, we find them used in situations of the sort shown in (44).

(44) The monkeys have [*eaten* the shrimp].

This is the only inflectional form allowed in this context, as we can see by substituting other forms of *eat*:

(45) *The monkeys have [$\left\{\begin{array}{c} \textit{ate} \\ \textit{eat} \\ \textit{eating} \end{array}\right\}$ the shrimp].

For now, we will just say that the context after *have* calls for a phrase headed specifically by a past participle.

Exercises
1. Below are listed several sets of verb forms. Using the statement made in the final sentence of the preceding text, devise some simple experiments to determine which of the forms is the past participle. As in earlier exercises, put asterisks on sentences that you judge unacceptable.

       a. sang, sung, sing   d. bring, brought
       b. watch, watched   e. hang, hung
       c. come, came   f. wrote, write, written

g. say, said   i. has, had, have
h. do, did, done   j. been, be, is, was

2.6.3 The Bare-Stem Form

Another English verb form must be mentioned here, one that is less often discussed than other forms in school grammars. This form is illustrated by examples (46).

(46) a. Joe will [*watch* the monkey].
     b. Fred will make him [*drink* the medicine].

As before, we find that replacing *watch* and *drink* with other inflectional forms gives bad results:

(47) a. *Joe will [$\begin{Bmatrix} watches \\ watching \\ watched \end{Bmatrix}$ the monkey].

     b. *Fred will make him [$\begin{Bmatrix} drank \\ drinking \\ drunk \end{Bmatrix}$ the medicine].

At first glance, the verbs *watch* and *drink* in (46) look like nothing more than present-tense forms. In particular, phrases that look exactly like them appear as the predicates of independent sentences, as in (48).

(48) a. Joe and Fred [*watch* the monkeys].
     b. The monkeys [*drink* the medicine].

Yet we have two good reasons for wanting to say that the verbs *watch* and *drink* in (46) are not present plural forms. The first reason is that, unlike the true present tense forms, they show no agreement with the subject. Even though *Joe* is singular in (46a) and both *Fred* and *him* are singular in (46b), a verb form with *-s* would be impossible:

(49) a. *Joe will [*watches* the monkey].
     b. *Fred will make him [*takes* the medicine].

The second reason for believing that the verb forms in (46) are not present plurals is that there is one particular English verb, the verb *be*, that shows two different forms. The present plural form is *are*, while the form used in the situations we are looking at now is *be*.

(50) a. *Joe will [*are* quiet].
     b. Joe will [*be* quiet].

(51) a. *Fred will make him [*are* quiet].
    b.   Fred will make him [*be* quiet].

For these two reasons, then, we will distinguish a *bare-stem* form, which looks like the present plural except for the one verb *be*. We have just seen two situations in which phrases headed by bare stems are called for: after *will* and after *make him*.

Exercises

1. Assuming the truth of the rule that says that *will* requires a phrase headed by a bare stem, construct experiments that show which of the two words in each of the pairs below is the bare-stem form. Put asterisks on examples that you feel are unacceptable.
    a.   came, come
    b.   do, did
    c.   has, have
    d.   go, gone

2. The sentences given below show verb phrases used as parts of larger constructions that have not yet been discussed. For each of the sentences, determine whether the italicized phrase has as its head a present plural or a bare stem. Do this by replacing the phrase with some phrase headed by *are* and the same phrase headed by *be*, and seeing which one sounds more acceptable.
    a.   We saw them *take the money*.
    b.   Do not *pester the goldfish*.
    c.   We know the monkeys *seem eager to cooperate*.
    d.   Jane isn't sure why the monkeys *try to catch the goldfish*.
    e.   Why not *try to catch the goldfish?*

2.6.4 Infinitival Phrases

The bare-stem form of the verb is actually used in the formation of a slightly more complex type of phrase :

(52) a.   Joe intends *to arrest the monkeys*.
    b.   Jacob forgot *to lock the cage*.
    c.   It is fun *to be noisy*.

We will call phrases of this type *infinitival phrases*; they are formed by adding the special infinitival marker *to* to a bare-stem verb phrase. Sentence (52c), in which *to* is followed by *be*, provides clear evidence that the verb phrase after *to* is headed by a bare stem. Example (53) shows that no other form is possible.

$$(53) \quad \text{*It is fun to} \left\{ \begin{array}{l} \text{am} \\ \text{are} \\ \text{is} \\ \text{been} \\ \text{being} \end{array} \right\} \text{noisy.}$$

2.6.5 "Defective" Verbs: Modals

There is one special group of verbs in English that do not have the variety of different inflectional forms that most verbs have. These verbs, traditionally called *modals*, are *can, could, will, would, shall, should, may, might,* and *must*. As the following examples show, these verbs resemble past-tense and present-tense verbs, in that the phrases they head can serve as sentence predicates.

(54) a. The students [*can* resolve this problem].
     b. The patients [*should* remain in their rooms].
     c. Fred and Harry [*must* have forgotten the beer].

Unlike ordinary verbs, however, modals do not show a singular form in *-s*; they show the same form in the singular as in the plural:

(55) a. The student [can (*cans) resolve this problem].
     b. The patient [should (*shoulds) remain in his room].
     c. Fred [must (*musts) have forgotten the beer].

Also, they do not have past-participial, present-participial, or bare-stem forms. We can see this by comparing *can stand on his head* with *be able to stand on his head*. Although the two phrases have similar meanings, they do not have the same inflectional possibilities. *Be able to stand on his head* has the full range of inflectional forms; these allow it to appear in situations in which *can stand on his head* is impossible.

(56) a. John has [been able to stand on his head].
     b. *John has [can (could) stand on his head].

(57) a. John will [be able to stand on his head].
     b. *John will [can stand on his head].

(58) a. [Being able to stand on his head] is important to him.
     b. *[Canning stand on his head] is important to him.

The one inflectional distinction that several of the modals make is between present tense and past tense. The clearest example of this is that in some circumstances it makes sense to view *could* as a past-tense form and *can* as the corresponding present-tense form:

(59) a.   This year, Sandra *can* whistle the national anthem.
      b.   Last year, Sandra *could* whistle the national anthem.

We will see additional reasons for such a view in chapter 17, when we discuss the rules involved in assigning time interpretations to sentences. However, there are many respects in which the modals do not behave like regular combinations of a verb stem plus a tense but instead act like single units with special meanings. For this reason, we will analyze them, for the time being, as single linguistic units.

In view of the fact that modals can head phrases that serve as sentence predicates, we need to revise our earlier rule concerning such predicates. As a preliminary step, let us give the following definition:

(60) A verb is *finite* if it is present-tense, past-tense, or modal. It is *nonfinite* otherwise. Correspondingly, the phrase headed by the verb will itself be finite or nonfinite.

The rule for sentence predicates can now be stated simply as follows:

(61) The predicate of a sentence must be finite and must agree with its subject in number and person.

2.7 Other Parts of Speech as Heads

So far in this chapter, we have seen several examples in which phrases with the same external behavior have head words belonging to a single part-of-speech class. As a result, several of the rules that we have devised have been of the following form:

(62) Any phrase whose head belongs to part of speech (and possibly inflectional class) *X* can be used in such-and-such a way to form a larger construction.

The traditional parts of speech that we have seen mentioned so far are verb, adjective, and noun. A natural question to ask here is whether the other traditional parts of speech are referred to in rules of this type. The remaining parts of speech are often assumed to be those given in (63), where some examples of each part of speech are given in parentheses.

(63) a.   prepositions (*in, on, about, to, around*)
      b.   pronouns
           i.   definite pronouns (*I, you, him, them*)
           ii. indefinite pronouns (*something, anyone*)

    c. conjunctions
        i. coordinating conjunctions (*and, or, nor, but*)
       ii. subordinating conjunctions (*that, because, when, what, before, after*)
    d. articles (*the, a, an, this, those*)
    e. adverbs
        i. manner adverbs (*slowly, wistfully, courageously*)
       ii. degree adverbs (*very, extremely, rather, quite*)
      iii. locative adverbs (*here, there, everywhere*)
      iv. frequency adverbs (*often, occasionally, frequently, never*)

By and large, the answer to our question is that only the prepositions (along with some related adverbs and subordinating conjunctions) seem to be phrasal heads that play major roles in determining the external syntax of the phrases in which they occur. For example, the three-word phrase *in the house* has its external behavior determined solely by the word *in*, and the external behavior of a "clause" like *because he lost his checkbook* is determined by the word *because*. Even here, though, we must note a difference between prepositions, on the one hand, and common nouns, adjectives, and verbs on the other. With prepositions, we find no rules that allow the class of prepositions as a whole to head phrases that fulfill a certain function. What we find instead are rules that refer to phrases headed by subclasses of prepositions: *locative prepositions* (prepositions of place), *motion prepositions*, and so forth. In later discussions of relative clauses and questions, we will see rules that refers to the class of prepositions as a whole; however, they are different in kind from the rules we are considering here. Some of the other parts of speech listed above (or some of their subclasses) will also prove their usefulness by being mentioned in particular syntactic rules of English, but, as with the prepositional rule just mentioned, these rules are different from the ones discussed earlier in this chapter.

2.8 Additional Types of Phrases

We have now accumulated a list of several different phrase types, each one exhibiting a distinctive external behavior. In each of the examples studied so far, the behavior of the phrase is determined by the part-of-speech membership and (in the case of verbs) by the inflectional form of the head word. In preparation for the work of the next chapter, we will discuss three additional types of phrases, each of which can be defined on the basis of a shared external behavior. These latter three types differ in one significant respect from those already discussed: It is harder to define them by referring to some single kind of head word.

2.8.1 Noun Phrases

This class of phrases consists, roughly speaking, of those sequences that can serve as subjects of sentences and also can fulfill some other functions. Following a standard but somewhat misleading usage, we will refer to these phrases as *noun phrases* (NP for short). The following sentences give examples of a few of the most frequent types of noun phrases; the phrases serving as subjects are italicized.

(64) (These consist of *the* plus a common noun phrase.)

$$\left\{ \begin{array}{l} \text{a. } \textit{The + king of Spain} \\ \text{b. } \textit{The + chairman of the committee} \\ \text{c. } \textit{The + sheriff} \end{array} \right\} \text{ expelled the monkeys.}$$

(65) (These consist of *pronouns*.)

$$\left\{ \begin{array}{l} \text{a. } \textit{I} \\ \text{b. } \textit{She} \\ \text{c. } \textit{You} \end{array} \right\} \text{ should know the answer.}$$

(66) (These consist of *proper nouns*.)

$$\left\{ \begin{array}{l} \text{a. } \textit{John} \\ \text{b. } \textit{Shirley} \\ \text{c. } \textit{Alice} \end{array} \right\} \text{ lost the money.}$$

(67) (These consist of noun phrases in possessive form plus common noun phrases.)

$$\left\{ \begin{array}{l} \text{a. } \textit{The women's + brother} \\ \text{b. } \textit{My + donkey} \\ \text{c. } \textit{Alice's + picture of Joe} \\ \text{d. } \textit{Joe's + beer} \end{array} \right\} \text{ has disappeared.}$$

With this large class of phrases identified, we can state a more specific rule for independent sentences:

(68) A sentence can consist of a *noun phrase* and a *finite verb phrase*.

With one exception, the noun phrases that we use as subjects can also be used in other ways, several of which we will discuss in the next chapter. The

exception concerns pronouns: subject pronouns must be *nominative* (*I,*
you, he, etc.), whereas nonsubject pronouns must be *accusative* (*me, her, you,*
etc.). The general category of noun phrases exhibits a great many other
patterns, which will be discussed in more detail in chapter 5.

Exercise

1. Below are listed a variety of sequences that appear within English
sentences, with an example of each one in an actual sentence context. For
each sequence, determine whether it could possibly be a noun phrase. Do
this by constructing an experimental sentence in which the sequence is
used as the subject, and judge the acceptability of the sentence.
- a. the dog in the cage
  (Fred bought *the dog in the cage.*)
- b. the cat to the hospital
  (We sent *the cat to the hospital.*)
- c. the man drunk
  (The policeman found *the man drunk.*)
- d. the letter to Fred
  (Martha read *the letter to Fred.*)
- e. the man that Martha hired Fred
  (We informed *the man that Martha hired Fred.*)
- f. the man that Martha hired.
  (We informed *the man that Martha hired.*)

2.8.2 Locative Phrases

Phrases in this class are used to indicate stationary location, as in the
following examples:

(69) a. Joe stayed *at the cemetery.*
 b. Jane found the turtle *over there.*
 c. The keys are *right up here on the counter.*

As these examples show, phrases in this group take a variety of different
forms, and (as with noun phrases) it is sometimes hard to identify one
particular kind of word that serves as head. For the time being, we will
chiefly make use of locative phrases consisting of only a locative prepositional phrase—that is, phrases of the sort exemplified by (69a).

2.8.3 Motion Phrases

These phrases typically indicate some kind of movement in a certain
direction or toward a certain location. Here are some examples:

(70) a.   The monkey fell *into the soup.*
      b.   The chairman walked *back up here onto the stage.*
      c.   The antelope moved *toward the anteater.*
      d.   Jones took the lawnmower *around the house.*

Motion phrases are often quite similar in form (or even identical) to locative phrases, so the interpretation of a sequence of such words often depends on the context in which it is found. Example (71) contains a locative phrase and an identical motion phrase.

(71) a.   Jane kept her turtle *over there.*   (locative phrase)
      b.   Jane took her turtle *over there.*   (motion phrase)

Here is how we can tell that these classifications are correct. We need to pick out a phrase that could only be a motion phrase, and substitute it in both of these sentences. For instance, a phrase introduced by *to* is reliably a motion phrase and not a locative phrase. We then construct the following examples:

(72) a.   *Jane kept her turtle *to the party.*
      b.   Jane took her turtle *to the party.*

These examples show us clearly that *kept* calls for a locative phrase, whereas *took* calls for a motion phrase.

Exercise
1. As noted above, the phrase *over there* can be either a locative phrase or a motion phrase, depending on the context. Below are six sentences containing this phrase. For each one, decide which of these two phrase types the context requires. Do this by constructing some experiments like the one done in the text.
      a.   Joe placed the chair *over there.*
      b.   He should have brought it *over there.*
      c.   Jane left the paper *over there.*
      d.   Joe arrived *over there* at ten o'clock.
      e.   Greta is *over there.*
      f.   Jerry rolled the cart *over there.*

Chapter 3

Phrase-Internal Syntax: Heads and Their Complements

3.1 Complements, Minimal Phrases, and Modifiers

In the first section of the preceding chapter, we saw that some phrases contain key words that can be referred to as *heads,* and that certain properties of the heads (their part-of-speech classification and in some instances their inflectional form) play key roles in determining whether the phrases can be used in the formation of larger structures. In the present chapter, we will shift our attention to the way in which head words dictate the *internal* structure of their phrases. In particular, we will assume that individual head words may choose certain types of phrases as *complements,* and that the head and its complements, if there are any, join together to make a *minimal phrase.* This minimal phrase will represent a basic action, event, or state. As an example of what is meant by these terms, let us look again at the following sentence:

(1)   The king kept putting his gold under the bathtub.

Here the word *putting* is followed by two phrases: a noun phrase (*his gold*) and a locative phrase (*under the bathtub*). These two phrases go together with *putting* to form a minimal phrase. The minimality of this particular phrase is especially easy to see, since leaving out either phrase would make the phrase headed by *putting* sound incomplete, as example (2) shows.

(2)   a. *The king kept [putting his gold].
      b. *The king kept [putting under the bathtub].

Here, in addition to containing two complements to the verb *putting,* the entire bracketed phrase itself serves as a complement for the verb *kept.* Again, leaving out the complement leaves a strong sense of incompleteness:

(3)   *The king [kept].

   In some instances, we will consider phrases to be complements even when leaving them out does not lead to a sensation of incompleteness. For instance, consider the question of whether the locative phrase *in the garage* is a complement in sentence (4).

(4)   John locked it in the garage.

If we make a new sentence by leaving out the locative phrase, the results are completely acceptable:

(5)   John locked it.

Yet we can notice a clear difference in the sense of the verb *locked* as it is used in these two sentences. In (4), the word *it* refers to some object John kept inside the garage by locking the entrances, whereas in (5) the same word can only be understood as referring to one of these entrances. Thus, the locative phrase in (4) really does help to define the basic action of the larger phrase in which it is contained. For this reason, we are justified in considering *locked it in the garage* a minimal phrase, and *in the garage* a complement of the verb *locked,* just as much as *under the bathtub* was a complement of *putting* in (1). It is as if there are two different verbs *locked.* One of them has a certain meaning and takes two complements, whereas the other has a different meaning and requires only one complement.

   Besides a head and one or more complements, a phrase may also contain *modifiers.* Words or phrases used as modifiers provide a description for the minimal phrase consisting of head plus complement(s). Thus, the word *carefully* in (6a) and the phrase *at noon* in (6b) serve as modifiers.

(6)   a.   Jane [read the book *carefully*].
       b.   Fred [freed the monkeys *at noon*].

In (6a), the minimal action (reading the book) is described as having been done carefully; in (6b), the minimal action (freeing the monkeys) is described as having occurred at noon.

   Certain types of phrases have a dual use, being sometimes complements and sometimes modifiers. Consider the locative phrases in the following pair of sentences:

(7)   a.   Fritz locked Fido *in the garage.*
       b.   Fritz bathed Fido *in the garage.*

As we saw a few paragraphs earlier, *in the garage* must be considered a complement in (7a), since *lock* in this sense requires a locative phrase as complement in order to have a completely defined basic action. (In fact, *Fritz locked Fido* makes no sense by itself.) By contrast, the sequence *bathed Fido* defines a complete basic action by itself, and the locative phrase here just serves as a modifier, identifying the place where the basic action occurred.

For the remainder of this chapter, we will leave modifiers aside and concentrate exclusively on the ways in which head words combine with complements to build minimal phrases. The greater part of the discussion will be devoted to verbs and their complements; then there will be briefer discussions of complementation with adjectives and nouns.

3.2 Paradigm Sets and Complement Choice

As preparation for our discussion of verbs and their complements, it will be helpful for us to consider what properties of individual words are relevant for complement choice. Let us take as an example the word *gone*. This word can serve as the head of a phrase such as *gone to the door*. One important fact about *gone* is that it is a past participle. It is this fact that allows the phrase it heads to be joined with the word *have*.

(8)   The workmen have [*gone* to the door].

What property of the word *gone* is responsible for allowing it to join with the motion phrase *to the door*? This possibility is clearly not shared by all past participles, as the following ungrammatical sentences show:

(9)   *The workmen have $\left\{ \begin{array}{l} \text{[carried to the door].} \\ \text{[forgotten to the door].} \\ \text{[fastened to the door].} \end{array} \right\}$

On the other hand, the possibility of combining with *to the door* is shared with other forms of *go:*

(10) a.   The workmen are [*going* to the door].   (present participle)
    b.   The workmen [*went* to the door].   (past tense)
    c.   The workmen [*go* the the door].   (present plural)
    d.   The workmen will [*go* to the door].   (bare stem)

We will use the expression "GO" to refer to this set of related verb forms as a whole. (We will refer to this set and others like it as *paradigm sets*.) We can then represent in the following way the fact that the word *gone* is the past participial form from the paradigm set GO:

(11) *gone*
      [GO]
      [Past Part]

The differing contributions of the [GO] property and the [Past Part] property are shown in the following diagram:

(12) have [gone   to the door]

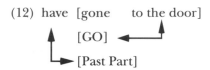

The [GO] property (i.e., the fact that *gone* is a particular form from the set {*go, went, gone, goes, going, go*}) allows the word *gone* to be joined with a motion phrase like *to the door*; the [Past Part] property allows the phrase as a whole to be accepted by the verb *have*.

What is true for *gone* is true for other verbs as well: The inflectional form of the head verb of a phrase has a great deal to do with where the phrase fits into larger constructions, but has virtually nothing to do with the complements that join together with the verb itself. This second matter is determined almost exclusively by the paradigm set to which the verb belongs.

3.3 A Way of Expressing Complement Possibilities

One part of the knowledge that English speakers have consists of a vast number of small rules concerning the complement-taking properties of individual words. We stated one such rule when we observed that the verb GO can join with a following motion phrase. Such rules concerning what complements are taken by each individual head word can be expressed as in (13), which gives the rule that is needed for GO.

(13) GO [—MotP]

We will refer to the expression on the right of rule (13) as a *complement specification,* and to the entire rule as a *complementation rule.* The blank indicates the place of the head itself, and MotP indicates that this head may join with a motion phrase. Thus, the whole rule expresses the idea that a member of the paradigm set GO can combine with a motion phrase to make a minimal phrase of its own. Paradigm sets whose members cannot occur with motion phrases will not be assigned this particular complement specification. Thus, for example, the unacceptability of (14) can be accounted for by noting that CARRY cannot join with a motion phrase by itself.

(14) *John carried to the door.

Another way to make the same point is that the rule given in (15) is not an actual rule of English:

(15) CARRY   [—MotP]

3.4 Two Functions of Noun Phrases as Complements

We are almost ready now to see how complements are chosen by individual verbs. But before we turn to this project, one last preliminary matter requires attention.

In chapter 2, we identified a group of phrases that could serve as subjects of sentences; we referred to members of this group by the standard term *noun phrases*. These phrases can also serve as complements to verbs, but with different verbs we find them serving in two fundamentally different ways. In the vast majority of cases, noun phrases serve as *arguments*: They identify the person or thing playing a certain role. In other instances, though, they serve as *predicates*, providing information about someone or something mentioned earlier in the sentence. The following two ex-amples illustrate this difference:

(16) a. Jesse kicked a doctor.
     b. Jesse became a doctor.

In (16a), the verb *kicked* requires that two roles be filled: the role of assailant and the role of victim. The noun phrase *a doctor* describes the person filling the second of these roles but indicates nothing at all about Jesse. In (16b), by contrast, *a doctor* does not identify the person filling a second role in the sentence, but instead provides a description of Jesse. In (16a), then, the noun phrase *a doctor* serves as an argument, whereas in (16b) it serves as a predicate. Clearly, some difference between *kicked* and *became* is responsible for this difference in the interpretation of the noun phrase in question. In general, the particular verb with which a noun-phrase complement occurs will dictate whether it is an argument or a predicate. Because argument noun phrases are so much the more com-mon, we will often use the term "noun phrases" to refer to them instead of the more cumbersome term "argument noun phrases."

3.5 Some Verb + Complement Combinations

We are now ready to see what complements are chosen by particular verbs. Below is a list of some of the common possibilities. We will make a traditional distinction here and divide this list of verb phrases into *intransitive* and *transitive*. The intransitive list will consist of phrases in which there is no *direct object*, that is, no argument noun phrase called for directly by the verb itself. The transitive list will be made up of phrases in which such a direct object is present.

3.5.1 Intransitive Complement Configurations

(17) Some verbs can stand in a phrase without any complements at all:
    a.   John [disappeared].
        DISAPPEAR [—]
    b.   The bottle [broke].
        BREAK [—]

(18) Some verbs can combine with a predicate noun phrase:
    a.   Jane [became   *a surgeon*].
        BECOME [—NP$_{Pred}$]
    b.   Fred [is   *a swindler*].
        BE [—NP$_{Pred}$]

(19) Some verbs can combine with an adjective phrase:
    a.   Alice [is   *intelligent*].
        BE [—AdjP]
    b.   The rule [seems   *unfair to the staff*].
        SEEM [—AdjP]
    c.   Fred [became   *fond of Ruth*].
        BECOME [—AdjP]

(20) Some verbs can combine with a locative phrase:
    a.   Martha [stayed   *at the hospital*].
        STAY [—LocP]
    b.   Fred [resides   *in Chicago*].
        RESIDE [—LocP]

(21) Some verbs can combine with a motion phrase:
    a.   Robert [went   *to the hospital*].
        GO [—MotP]
    b.   Alice [moved   *into the room*].
        MOVE [—MotP]

(22) Some verbs can combine with a present-participial phrase:
    a. Joseph [is *stealing cookies*].
       BE [—VP$_{PresPart}$]
    b. Jean [keeps *asking questions*].
       KEEP [—VP$_{PresPart}$]

(23) One verb can combine with a past-participial verb phrase:
    a. Carolyn [has *taken the money*].
       HAVE [—VP$_{PastPart}$].

(24) Some verbs (specifically, the modals) can combine with a bare-stem verb phrase:
    a. John [must *be happy*].
       MUST [—VP$_{Stem}$]
    b. Jill [may *be sick*].
       MAY [—VP$_{Stem}$]

(25) Some verbs can combine with an infinitival verb phrase:
    a. Kathy will [try *to write a letter*].
       TRY [—InfP]
    b. Jeff [hopes *to get a job*].
       HOPE [—InfP]

3.5.2 Transitive Complement Configurations

(26) Some verbs combine with a noun phrase:
    a. Joe [saw *Fred*].
       SEE [—NP]
    b. Alice [broke *the bottle*].
       BREAK [—NP]
    c. Kate [made *a birdhouse*].
       MAKE [—NP]

(27) Some verbs can combine with an noun phrase and a predicate noun phrase:
    a. Jane [considers *Bill*   *a good friend*].
       CONSIDER [—NP NP$_{Pred}$]
    b. Alex [called *his brother*   *a liar*].
       CALL [—NP NP$_{Pred}$]

(28) Some verbs can combine with a noun phrase and an adjective phrase:
    a. Joe [kept *it*   *cold*].
       KEEP [—NP AdjP]
    b. Fido [made *Alice*   *quite angry*].
       MAKE [—NP AdjP]

(29) Some verbs can combine with a noun phrase and a locative phrase:

    a.   Joe [kept   *it*   *in the garage*].
        KEEP [—NP LocP]

    b.   Martha [placed   *them*   *on the counter*].
        PLACE [—NP LocP]

(30) Some verbs can combine with a noun phrase and a motion phrase:

    a.   We [moved   *it*   *into the room*].
        MOVE [—NP MotP]

    b.   Fred [took   *Alice*   *to the hospital*].
        TAKE [—NP MotP]

(31) Some verbs can combine with a noun phrase and a present-particip-ial verb phrase:

    a.   Joe [heard   *Fred*   *asking questions*].
        HEAR [—NP $VP_{Pres\ Part}$]

    b.   The police [caught   *John*   *stealing hubcaps*].
        CATCH [—NP $VP_{Pres\ Part}$]

(32) Some verbs can combine with a noun phrase and a bare-stem verb phrase:

    a.   We [made   *George*   *be quiet*].
        MAKE [—NP VP_{Stem}]

    b.   Martha [watched   *David*   *open the letters*].
        WATCH [—NP VP_{Stem}]

(33) Some verbs can combine with a noun phrase and an infinitival phrase:

    a.   We [persuaded   *John*   *to keep the money*].
        PERSUADE [—NP InfP]

    b.   Martha [asked   *Alice*   *to open the door*].
        ASK [—NP InfP]

3.5.3 Ditransitive Complement Configurations

One more transitive complement configuration requires mention. This configuration is illustrated in (34).

(34) a.   John [sent   *Martha*   *a check*].
     b.   We [gave   *Fred*   *a wastebasket*].

In each of these sentences, the verb is followed by two noun phrases. Unlike the examples with CONSIDER and CALL, however, the last noun phrase in each of these examples serves as an argument rather than as a predicate. Instead of describing some noun phrase mentioned earlier in the sentence, it identifies the object conveyed to the person identified by the noun phrase before it. In traditional grammar, the second of these argument noun phrases is analyzed as the direct object, corresponding to the objects of the verbs that we have already seen, while the noun phrase that precedes it is called the *indirect object*. For these two verbs, we need the following rules:

(35) a. SEND [—NP NP]

    b. GIVE [—NP NP]

Exercises

1. Below are some sentences that illustrate the complement-taking properties of some intransitive verbs. For each sentence, give the complement specification that allows that verb to appear with the particular complement with which it appears in that sentence. Choose the specifications from the following list:

$[-NP_{Pred}]$ $[-VP_{PresPart}]$

$[-AdjP]$ $[-VP_{PastPart}]$

$[-LocP]$ $[-VP_{Stem}]$

$[-MotP]$ $[-InfP]$

  a. The officers [*should* release the gorilla.]

  b. Geraldine [*stood* on the platform].

  c. Fred [*started* asking Phil to free the iguanas].

  d. Alice [*became* the president of the senate].

  e. The peach [*tasted* sweet].

  f. The hyenas [*long* to be popular].

  g. Jerry's car [*rolled* into the kitchen].

  h. Robert [*has* disowned his ostrich].

2. Below are given some sentences that illustrate the complement-taking possibilities of some transitive verbs. For each sentence, give the complement specification that allows the verb to appear with the particular complements found in that sentence. Choose your answers from the following list of specifications:

$[-NP \ NP_{Pred}]$ $[-NP \ VP_{PresPart}]$

$[-NP \ AdjP]$ $[-NP \ VP_{Stem}]$

$[-NP \ LocP]$ $[-NP \ InfP]$

$[-NP \ MotP]$ $[-NP \ NP]$

The job essentially involves looking at what comes after the verb, and breaking it up into a noun phrase plus one of the other phrase types.

    a.   Joe [*let* Martha's cat eat the frog].

    b.   Sarah [*asked* me to let Harry keep the elephant].

    c.   Brenda [*allowed* the ducks to cross the road].

    d.   Louis [*heard* the chairman of the committee ask Fred to open a window].

    e.   Jane [*left* her picture of Groucho in the lounge].

    f.   Fred [*brought* his goat to the concert].

    g.   We [*saw* the leader of the group writing a note].

    h.   Joe should [*have* the children keep the rabbits in the basement].

    i.   George [*mailed* the warden his photograph of the raven].

    j.   Hard work [*made* Horatio the president of the company].

3. The following list of sentences contains a mixture of transitive and intransitive verbs. As in the two preceding exercises, for each sentence give the complement specification that allows the italicized verb to appear in the minimal verb phrase in which it appears in that example. In each case, choose your answer from the two groups of specifications given above plus the following two additional ones:

    [—]   [—NP]

A good first question to ask might be whether the verb is intransitive, transitive, or ditransitive.

    a.   Carol [*hid* the manuscript in the refrigerator].

    b.   The monkeys [*made* the leopards confess their crimes].

    c.   Joseph [*found* the mayor's keys].

    d.   Fred [*hired* Sharon to change the oil].

    e.   Martha [*found* John an overcoat].

    f.   They [*pushed* us into the truck].

    g.   Fran [*hopes* to persuade Harry to make the monkeys wash the dishes].

    h.   The lecture [*ended*].

4. There are several verbs in English that show no outward difference between past tense, past participle, and bare stem. Three such verbs are *hit*, *let*, and *cut*. The following sentences contain several italicized occurrences of these words. For each such occurrence, decide whether the verb is a past tense, a past participle, or a bare stem. Justify your answer on the basis of a previously discussed rule that requires the use of one or the other inflectional form. Some of the rules needed will be complementation rules.

    a.   Joe intends to make Bill *cut* the log.

    b.   Janet *let* George open the letter.

    c.   The monkeys must have *cut* the wire.

    d.   You may *let* the monkeys peel the banana.

    e.   The ball *hit* the ceiling.

    f.   We watched the ball *hit* the ceiling

3.5.4 *Do* + Bare Stem: A Special Tensed Construction

One more type of English verb phrase that deserves attention here is a type of finite phrase that plays a special role in English syntax. Phrases of this kind are formed when a tensed DO combines with a bare-stem verb phrase. These phrases are sufficiently different from ordinary verb phrases to merit a separate discussion.

We can get an initial look at verb phrases of this new type by examining their use in one variety of emphatic sentence. The pairs of sentences in examples (36)–(38) show the contrast between the ordinary finite verb phrases used in nonemphatic sentences and the new type of verb phrases used in their emphatic counterparts.

(36) a.   I went to the post office.

      b.   I DID go to the post office.

(37) a.   Sheila likes apples.

      b.   Sheila DOES like apples.

(38) a.   They live in Boston.

      b.   They DO live in Boston.

The difference between each (a) sentence and its corresponding (b) sentence can be described as follows: Whereas the (a) sentence contains a phrase headed by an ordinary tensed verb, the (b) sentence exhibits a corresponding phrase headed by a bare-stem form, and this phrase serves as a complement of some tensed form of DO. This contrast can be seen more clearly in (39), where the left column contains ordinary tensed verb phrases and the right column contains the special verb phrases headed by DO.

(39)

	Ordinary verb phrases	Verb phrases headed by DO	
a.	went to the post office	did	go to the post office
	(past-tense verb phrase)	(past DO +	bare-stem verb phrase)
b.	likes apples	does	like apples
	(pres sg verb phrase)	(pres sg DO +	bare-stem verb phrase)
c.	live in Boston	do	live in Boston
	(pres pl verb phrase)	(pres pl DO +	bare-stem verb phrase)

Let us refer to the verb phrases found in the (a) sentences as *general-purpose finites* and to those in the (b) sentences as *special-purpose finites.*

We can provide for verb phrases of this new type by giving a special environmental specification for the verb DO:

(40) DO: $[\text{—VP}_{\text{Stem}}]$

This specification, which DO shares with the modals, allows DO to take a bare-stem verb phrase as a complement. Thus, it allows the formation of all the special-purpose phrases given in the right column of (39).

In addition to saying how special-purpose phrases are formed, we need rules to spell out how they are used. By the end of this book, we will have accumulated a variety of such rules. Right now we are in a position to state our first rule, one that accounts for emphatic sentences:

(41) To form an emphatic affirmative sentence:
    (i)   use a special-purpose verb phrase;
    (ii) put extra stress on the finite verb.

Taken together, the rules in (40) and (41) allow us to account for a broad range of emphatic sentences. However, some further examples of this construction are not accounted for. In the each of the three sets of sentences given in (42)–(44), the (a) sentence is an unemphatic sentence, the (b) sentence is the emphatic counterpart predicted by rules (40) and (41), and the (c) sentence is the actual emphatic counterpart.

(42) a. John has gone to the library.
     b. *John DOES have gone to the library.
     c. John HAS gone to the library.

(43) a. We are trying to solve the puzzle.
     b. *We DO be trying to solve the puzzle.
     c. We ARE trying to solve the puzzle.

(44) a. Jack can play the fiddle.
     b. *Jack DOES can play the fiddle.
     c. Jack CAN play the fiddle.

Although these additional examples might appear to pose a problem for rule (41), they can actually be accounted for without complicating the rule at all. We simply need to say that for a small handful of exceptional verbs the special-purpose structures are identical to the corresponding general-purpose structures. These exceptional verbs include tensed forms of BE, tensed forms of perfect HAVE, and all the so-called modals (CAN, COULD, MAY, MIGHT, SHALL, SHOULD, WILL, WOULD, and MUST).

As we will see in later chapters, these few verbs are exceptional in exactly the same way in all the other situations in which special-purpose finite phrases are required.

Exercise

1. The rules given above yield (ii) as an emphatic counterpart for (i):

    (i)   Jason wrecked his motorcycle.

    (ii)   Jason DID wreck his motorcycle.

In addition, though, it is possible to retain the general-purpose structure and place emphatic stress on *wrecked:*

    (iii)   Jason WRECKED his motorcycle.

Think about the differences between the contexts in which (ii) would be a natural thing to say and those in which (iii) would be natural. Describe these differences as clearly as you can.

3.6 Multiple Complement Specifications

As is indicated by the examples presented above, many verbs admit more than one possible environment. Thus, for instance, BREAK occurs alone as well as with an object noun phrase. The relevant examples are repeated in (45).

(45) a.   The bottle [broke].
          BREAK [—]
      b.   Alice [broke *the bottle*].
          BREAK [—NP]

Likewise, the verb MAKE occurs in three of the configurations listed above:

(46) a.   Kate [made *a birdhouse*].
          MAKE [—NP]
      b.   Fido [made *Alice quite angry*].
          MAKE [—NP AdjP]
      c.   We [made *George be quiet*].
          MAKE [—NP VP$_{Stem}$]

Many other verbs are like these two in allowing more than a single complement configuration. In many instances, such multiple environments do not follow any general pattern. For instance, the possibilities for MAKE illustrated in (46) have to be learned as three separate facts about this verb. In other instances, though, pairs of environments for a verb are related by rather regular rules. BREAK, for example, is just one of several "change-of-state" verbs that have intransitive and transitive pairs related to each other in the same way. Consider the following examples:

(47) a.   The music [changed].   [—]
      b.   Alice [changed *the music*].   [—NP]

(48) a.   The door [closed].   [—]
      b.   Joe [closed *the door*].   [—NP]

(49) a.   The ice [melted].   [—]
      b.   The sun [melted *the ice*].   [—NP]

We see a similar relation for verbs expressing movement:

(50) a.   The house [moved].   [—]
      b.   The men [moved *the house*].   [—NP]

(51) a.   The cart [rolled *into the garage*].   [—MotP]
      b.   Josephine [rolled *the cart into the garage*]. [—NP MotP]

(52) a.   The box [slid *onto the lawn*].   [—MotP]
      b.   Joe [slid *the box onto the lawn*].   [—NP MotP]

In each of the pairs of sentences in these two groups, the relation in meaning between the intransitive and the transitive sentence can be expressed by the following rule:

(53) If a certain verb can occur as an intransitive verb expressing change of state or motion, then the same verb can be used as a transitive verb expressing the *causation* of the state of affairs expressed by the intransitive verb.

A different regular relation between intransitive and transitive uses of the same verb is shown in examples (54) and (55).

(54) a.   Joe [shaved].   [—]
      b.   Joe [shaved *Fred*].   [—NP]

(55) a.   Fred [dressed].   [—]
      b.   Fred [dressed *the baby*].   [—NP]

Here the transitive verb is more basic, and the intransitive use is understood as expressing an idea that could have been expressed by a transitive sentence with a reflexive pronoun as the object of the verb. For example, *Joe shaved* has the same meaning as *Joe shaved himself.* This possibility exists for a large class of verbs that might be called *personal-care verbs,* some of which have particles associated with them (SHAVE, DRESS, BATHE, CLEAN *up*, WASH *up*). We can state the following rough rule:

(56) If a certain verb can be used as a transitive verb denoting personal care, then the same verb can be used as an intransitive verb, with an understood reflexive pronoun as object.

3.7 Complement Specifications Mentioning Particular Words

Thus far, we have looked at many examples of verbs that call for broad, general categories—noun phrases, adjective phrases, motion phrases, and so forth. For some verbs, however, specific individual words need to be mentioned in stating complement possibilities. One such word is GIVE, as it occurs in (57).

(57) Joe [gave   *the sandwich   to the dog*].

At first glance, *to the dog* might appear to be just another motion phrase, as it would be in a sentence such as *Joe ran to the dog*. Yet when we try to construct sentences in which GIVE appears with other motion phrases, the resulting sentences—given in (58)—are unacceptable.

(58) a. *Alice [gave   *the book   into the room*].
     b. *Fred [gave   *the banana   onto the wagon*].

Thus, *to* appears to be the only preposition that goes well with GIVE. The rule that we must state for GIVE, then, is that it can be joined with a noun phrase and a "*to* phrase" (a phrase headed by the particular preposition *to*). Thus, the appearance of *to* in this particular configuration is allowed by the following rule:

(59) GIVE [—NP *To*-P]

We have a similar situation with the verb DEPEND:

(60) We can [depend   *on his cooperation*].

The preposition *on* is often used as a locative preposition, as in sentences like *Sam stayed on the porch*. Yet *on* does not seem to have a locative meaning with DEPEND. Furthermore, DEPEND does not permit other locative prepositions—see (61).

(61) *We can [depend $\left\{ \begin{array}{l} \text{in good weather].} \\ \text{at his cooperation].} \\ \text{above the truth of his testimony].} \end{array} \right\}$

Thus, we must say that the verb DEPEND accepts a phrase headed by the particular preposition *on*. This "*on* phrase" is mentioned in the following environmental rule:

(62) DEPEND [—*On*-P]

Most of the individual words that are mentioned as such in complement specifications are taken from the class of prepositions, or from the related class of words called *particles* (which will be discussed in detail in chapter 6).

Exercise
1. Each of the sentences given below contains an italicized verb phrase and is followed by two possible complement specifications, one mentioning a general class of phrases and the other mentioning phrases headed by a specific word. Decide which specification is the correct one for the verb. Justify your answer by giving additional acceptable or unacceptable sentences.

    a. John [blamed *the accident on Fido*].
      i. [—NP LocP]
      ii. [—NP *On*-P]

    b. Jane [left *the book on the table*].
      i. [—NP LocP]
      ii. [—NP *On*-P]

    c. Martha [moved *it to the kitchen*].
      i. [—NP MotP]
      ii. [—NP *To*-P]

    d. Fred [proved *it to the police*].
      i. [—NP MotP]
      ii. [—NP *To*-P]

3.8 Possible and Impossible Complement Specifications

In the complement specifications that have been given so far, two kinds of units have been mentioned. The first kind consists of general phrase types, such as NP, MotP, LocP, and AdjP. The second type consists of phrases headed by specific individual words—phrases with names like *To*-P and *On*-P. A natural question to address now is whether we also need to allow complement specifications such as [—N_{proper}] and [—Adj]—that is, specifications that refer to types of individual words rather than to types of phrases.

At first glance, it might seem that there would be nothing wrong with mentioning word types rather than phrase types. Consider again the complement specification that permits MAKE to appear in (63).

(63) Fido [made *Alice angry*].

For this occurrence of MAKE, we gave [—NP AdjP] as the complement specification. But in this situation, could we not just as well have given the specification [—N$_{proper}$ Adj]? This second possibility certainly looks reasonable as long as we are looking only at sentence (63). But a difficulty arises as soon as we look at additional examples, such as those in (64).

(64) a.   Fido [made *Alice very angry*].
     b.   Fido [made *her angry*].
     c.   Fido [made *the trainer angry*].

The original specification, which mentioned the general phrase types NP and AdjP, accounts for these new examples immediately, with no changes or additions required. By contrast, the specification for (63) in terms of the word types N$_{proper}$ and Adj does not cover the three new examples at all. Just for the three extra sentences given in (64), the following added specifications would be necessary:

(65) a.   [—N$_{proper}$ Deg Adj]   ("Deg" stands for *degree adverb*)
     b.   [—Pro Adj]
     c.   [—Det N Adj]

We thus have good reason to think that the original specification in terms of phrase types was the correct one. We find additional reason in the fact that no head words are known, in English or any other language, that call specifically for pronouns or specifically for single-word adjectives. In the remainder of this book, then, we will assume that all such complement specifications must be stated completely in terms of general phrase types or phrases headed by particular individual words.

Exercise
1. Below is a list of verb phrases. With each example, two complement specifications are given, both of which allow that particular verb phrase. The first specification in each pair obeys the restriction proposed above, whereas the second does not. For each such pair, show that the second specification is too narrow. Do this by constructing an acceptable sentence that the permitted complement specification allows but the illegal one does not.

   a. Jane [*saw* him leave the room].

       [—NP VP$_{\text{Stem}}$] (permitted)

       [—NP V$_{\text{Stem}}$ NP] (not permitted)

   b. We [*sold* the picture of Fred to Angela].

       [—NP *To*-P]

       [—Art N *Of*-P *To*-P]

   c. Fred [*considers* us eager to make the monkeys learn Latin].

       [—NP AdjP]

       [—Pro Adj InfP]

3.9 Complements of Adjectives and Nouns

In chapter 2 we saw several examples of phrases headed by adjectives and common nouns. The adjective phrases shared with one another the external property of going well with the verb SEEM; the common noun phrases could combine with the word *the* or with possessive words to make noun phrases. Let us look at these two phrase types in turn.

3.9.1 Adjectives and Their Complements

In several of the examples considered in chapter 2, and also in many other examples, the phrase that an adjective heads consists of the adjective alone:

(66) a. The monkey seems [*despondent*].

      b. The suitcases seem [*light*].

      c. Joanna seems [*intelligent*].

      d. The barometer seems [*unreliable*].

      e. The porter seems [*tired*].

      f. Alice seems [*angry*].

In other examples, we find the adjective followed by a phrase that serves as its complement:

(67) a. The monkeys seem [*eager* to leave the meeting].

      b. The chickens seem [*fond* of the farmer].

      c. The foxes seem [*compatible* with the chickens].

      d. The partridges seem [*similar* to the ptarmigans].

      e. Your friends seem [*tired* of the conversation].

      f. The inmates seem [*angry* at the warden].

These examples suggest that there are rules of English that specify the complementation possibilities for each individual adjective, just as there are rules that do the same thing for individual verbs. The examples given above provide evidence for the following complement specifications:

(68) a. DESPONDENT [—]   b. LIGHT [—]
   c. INTELLIGENT [—]   d. UNRELIABLE [—]
   e. TIRED [—]   f. ANGRY [—]
   g. EAGER [—Inf]   h. FOND [—*Of*-P]
   i. COMPATIBLE [—*With*-P]   j. SIMILAR [—*To*-P]
   k. TIRED [—*Of*P]   l. ANGRY [—*At*-P]

As might be guessed from these examples, the complementation combinations found with adjectives are much less varied than those found with verbs. The most common complement specifications for adjectives call either for no complements at all or else for single complements of various sorts. There are no adjectives that can take two complements, in the way that verbs such as PERSUADE and MAKE can.

3.9.2 Common Nouns and Their Complements

With common nouns, we find almost the same complement configurations that we found with adjectives. By far the most frequent configuration is the one in which the noun has no complements, as in (69).

(69) a. the [*plan*]   PLAN: [—]
   b. Joe's [*book*]   BOOK: [—]
   c. the [*beer*]   BEER: [—]

However, there are also a fair number of nouns that take phrases headed by particular prepositions, and also some that take infinitive phrases:

(70) a. their [*proximity* to their neighbors]   PROXIMITY: [—*To*-P]
   b. Bill's [*faith* in Fred's sister]   FAITH: [—*In*-P]
   c. the [*king* of England]   KING: [—*Of*-P]
   d. the [*bottom* of the barrel]   BOTTOM: [—*Of*-P]
   e. the [*effort* to find a vaccine]   EFFORT: [—InfP]
   f. Jack's [*desire* to become famous]   DESIRE: [—InfP]

3.10 A Method of Representing Phrase Structure

We have already discovered a large number of rules about how phrases of different types are constructed, and about how these phrases are used to build larger constructions. Moreover, we now know enough to start analyzing particular individual sentences, such as (71).

(71) The offer made Smith admire the anteaters.

The most important hint we have concerning the structure of this sentence is provided by the basic rule for sentences, given in (72).

(72) A sentence consists of a noun phrase and a finite verb phrase.

This rule leads us immediately to look for a way of dividing this sentence into a noun phrase and a finite verb phrase, where (once again) a finite verb is in the present or the past tense or else is a modal. *The offer* is a possible noun phrase, and the remainder of the sentence (*made Smith admire the anteaters*) is headed by a past-tense verb and thus qualifies as a finite verb phrase. We thus arrive at the statement in (73a), which is represented graphically in (73b).

(73) a. The sentence *The offer made Smith admire the anteaters* consists of two
        parts: a noun phrase (*the offer*) and a past-tense verb phrase (*made
        Smith admire the anteaters*).

      b.

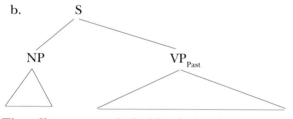

We might now want to analyze the verb phrase in more detail. The head verb is MAKE, a verb that we looked at earlier. The three complement specifications that we found for MAKE were the following:

(74) a.   [—NP]
      b.   [—NP AdjP]
      c.   [—NP VP$_{Stem}$]

The last of these is the one called for here: *Smith* is a possible noun phrase, and *admire the anteaters* qualifies as a bare-stem verb phrase. Thus, we get the following additional statement, with an associated diagram:

(75) a. The past-tense verb phrase *made Smith admire the anteaters* consists
        of three parts: the verb *made*, a noun phrase (*Smith*), and a bare-
        stem verb phrase (*admire the anteaters*).

b.

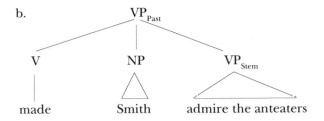

Finally, it is not hard to see how the phrase *admire the anteaters* should be analyzed:

(76) a. The bare-stem verb phrase *admire the anteaters* consists of two parts: the verb *admire* and a noun phrase (*the anteaters*).

b.

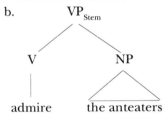

We have now made three statements about sentence (61), and we have three diagrams that express the contents of these statements in pictures. If we wanted to, we could keep these three pictures separate. On the other hand, if we want to get a comprehensive view of the organization of this sentence, we can combine the three smaller diagrams into a single large one. One way to accomplish this is to start with the smallest diagram and substitute it for its less detailed representation in the next smallest diagram. This process can be pictured as in (77).

(77)

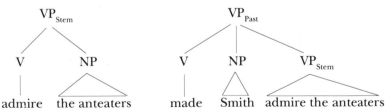

Result:

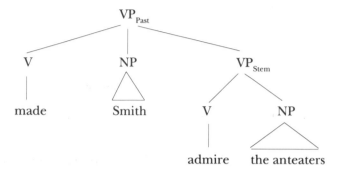

We then take this more detailed picture of the past-tense VP *made Smith admire the anteaters* and substitute it for the less detailed picture in the first diagram, ending up with the following diagram for the sentence as a whole:

(78)

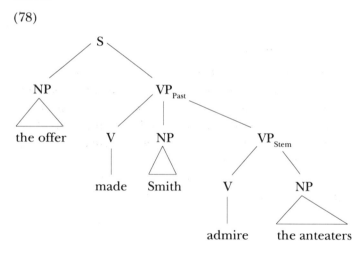

This single diagram combines all three of our original statements about the way in which this sentence is formed. Diagrams of this sort are referred to as *tree diagrams*, or just *trees*, and are now used quite widely in scholarly works and in textbooks.

The drawing of tree diagrams is in no way an end in itself. Its major justification is that it provides a quick and efficient way of representing some important properties of the organization of individual sentences. It takes much less time to draw the tree in (78) than to write out all three of the statements that the tree expresses.

There are other systems providing exactly the same kind of information about sentence structure. One is the *labeled bracketing* illustrated in (79).

(79) [$_s$[$_{NP}$ the offer] [$_{VP-Past}$ [$_V$ made] [$_{NP}$ Smith] [$_{VP-Stem}$ [$_V$ admire] [$_{NP}$ the anteaters]]]]

Our choice of the tree-diagram system over other systems rests mainly on two considerations. The first is that it is relatively easy to learn and use. The second is that it has been adopted more widely in recent years than any other system, so that familiarity with it will be helpful to those readers who go on to other works on English syntax.

Exercises

1. The following is a tree diagram for the sentence *The duke must have seen the butler let the cat drink the wine:*

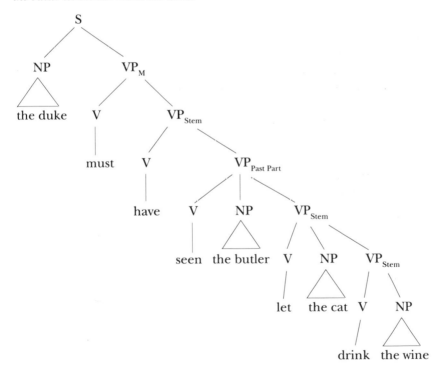

One statement expressed by this tree is the following.

> The sentence *The duke must have seen the butler let the cat drink the wine* consists of two parts: a noun phrase (*the duke*) and a modal verb phrase (*must have seen the butler let the cat drink the wine*).

Write out the remaining five statements expressed in the tree.

2. We have seen many examples of complementation rules in this chapter, each of which links a particular verb with a complement specification. One of our rules was the following:

MAKE [—NP VP$_{Stem}$]

With the device of tree diagrams, there is another way that we can express the content of this rule, together with the fact that MAKE is a verb:

MAKE

This diagram indicates that we can form a minimal phrase by combining any form of MAKE with an argument noun phrase and a bare-stem verb phrase. Below are given some of the other lexical rules presented above. For each one, give the alternate version in tree form.

    a.   HEAR [—NP VP$_{PresPart}$]
    b.   MOVE [—MotP]
    c.   KEEP [—NP AdjP]
    d.   DISAPPEAR [—]
    e.   BECOME [—NP$_{Pred}$]
    f.   BREAK [—NP]
    g.   PERSUADE [—NP InfP]
    h.   KEEP [—NP LocP]

Chapter 4

Clauses as Complements
and Subjects

In chapter 2, *noun phrases* were introduced as a special class of phrases that could serve as subjects of sentences. In chapter 3, it was noted that noun phrases could also serve as complements of verbs and as objects of prepositions.

In this chapter, we examine some structures of a different sort that can serve as complements and also as subjects. What sets these new structures apart from noun phrases is that one of their essential parts is a construction that is either identical to an ordinary sentence or else very similar to one. We will refer to these structures as *clauses*. In section 4.1 we will examine the internal structure of three basic types of clauses. In subsequent sections, we will discuss the external syntax of clauses of these types, that is, the ways in which they can be used in the formation of still larger structures.

4.1 The Internal Structure of Clauses

4.1.1 *That* Clauses
A first type of clause is illustrated in (1):

(1) a. Harry believes [that Jane's chameleon is honest].
     b. Beth warned Bill [that the cow jumped over the moon].

In each of these examples, the bracketed structure can be broken down into two main parts. The first part is just the word *that;* the second is a sequence that could qualify as a well-formed independent sentence:

(2) a. Jane's chameleon is honest.
     b. The cow jumped over the moon.

Let us refer to the bracketed structures in (1) as "*that* clauses." Then the following simple rule spells out their structure:

(3)   A *that* clause can consist of the word *that* plus a sentence.

In tree form, the same rule can be expressed in the following picture:

(4)   *That-C*

This rule assigns the following structures to the *that* clauses in (1):

(5)   *That-C*   *That-C*

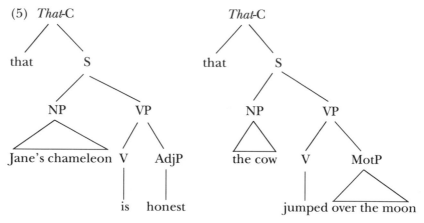

Each of the *that* clauses that we have examined so far consisted of the word *that* joined to a sequence of words that qualifies as a sentence. English also allows another variety of *that* clause, exemplified by (6).

(6)   a.   I insist [that he guard the chickens].
      b.   The rules require that [the executives be polite].

At first glance, these clauses might look just like those considered already. However, taking away the *that* from the bracketed sequences in (6) gives sequences that are unacceptable by themselves:

(7)   a. *He guard the chickens.
      b. *The executives be polite.

Despite their unacceptability, these sequences show a clear similarity to well-formed sentences. In particular, they have exactly the same subject-predicate division, and nominative pronouns like *he* are used as subjects. The only difference is that the main verb of the complements in (6) is a bare-stem instead of a finite verb. Thus, we get *guard* in (6a), where a present-tense verb would have to be *guards*, and we get *be* in (6b) instead of the present-tense *are*.

Our problem now is to find a way of describing these constructions that reveals both their similarity to ordinary *that* clauses and their one significant difference. As the first step toward a solution, we make two new assumptions:

(8) a. Sentences can have predicates headed by words other than finite verbs.

  b. Sentences as well as verb phrases can be classified according to the inflectional form of the head verb.

Thus, for example, *he guards the chickens* would be a present-tense sentence, whereas *he guard the chickens* would be a bare-stem sentence. This analysis would dictate the following tree diagrams for these sentences:

(9) a. S_{Pres} b. S_{Stem}

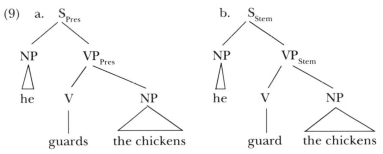

We now allow *that* clauses to be formed from either of these two types of sentences, and mark the resulting clause according to the inflectional form of the sentence that it contains:

(10) A *that* clause consists of the word *that* plus either (i) a finite sentence (present or past or modal), or (ii) a bare-stem sentence.

(11) A *that* clause is classified according to the inflectional form of the head verb of its sentence.

These rules allow us to use the sentence structures in (9) to create the *that* clauses in (12).

(12) a. *That*-C_{Pres} b. *That*-C_{Stem}

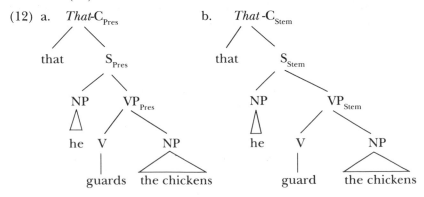

One remaining matter requires attention. In chapter 2, the following rules for the formation of sentences were given:

(13) A verb phrase is finite if it is headed by a present-tense verb, a past-tense verb, or a modal.

(14) The predicate of a sentence must be finite and must agree with its subject in person and number.

As rule (14) is stated, it is violated by the structure in (12b), which contains a sentence whose head verb is not finite. Thus, rule (14) needs to be replaced by rule (15), which singles out *independent* sentences.

(15) Independent sentences must be finite.

This rule will allow independent sentences like (16a) but will prevent those like (16b).

(16) a. Harley is at the meeting.
     b. *Harley be at the meeting.

At the same time, it will permit non-independent sentences to be based on either finite verb phrases or bare-stem verb phrases, thus allowing the two distinct types of *that* clauses that actually occur:

(17) a. that Farley is at the meeting
     b. that Farley be at the meeting

4.1.2 Infinitival Clauses

Another type of sentence-like structure is illustrated in (18).

(18) a. Fred intends [for Sam to review that book].
     b. Sally would prefer [for the children to finish the porridge].

In each of these two sentences, the italicized construction consists of the word *for*, a noun phrase, and an infinitival phrase. Intuitively, we perceive the noun phrase as having the same kind of relation to the infinitival verb phrase as the subject of an independent sentence has to its verb phrase:

(19) a. Sam reviewed the book.
     b. The children finished the porridge.

We thus have some initial reason for viewing these constructions as clauses on a par with the types considered earlier. Further justification for treating them as clauses will become apparent later in this chapter when we consider their external behavior.

In order to get a complete view of the structure of infinitival clauses, we need to get ahead of our story for a moment and consider their external syntax. The infinitival clauses that we observed in (18) occurred as complements of the verbs INTEND and PREFER. As it happens, each of these verbs also allows a complement consisting of an infinitive alone, as (20) shows.

(20) a.   Fred intends [to review that book].
     b.   Sally would prefer [to finish the porridge.]

In fact, the parallel examples in (18) and (20) illustrate a perfectly general regularity of English: In every situation in which a clause introduced by *for* can be used, it is possible to have an infinitival phrase by itself. We thus have reason to believe that the infinitival phrases in (20) are serving there as abridged versions of the longer constructions introduced by *for*. We will thus refer to the bracketed constructions in both (18) and (20) as *infinitival clauses*. The two rules given in (21) state how this type of clause can be formed.

(21) a.   An infinitival clause can consist of a *for* phrase plus an infinitival phrase.
     b.   An infinitival clause can consist of an infinitival phrase alone.

These rules can be given in tree form as follows:

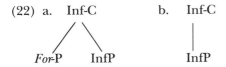

(22) a.   Inf-C   b.   Inf-C

         For-P   InfP   InfP

The structures of (18a) and (20a) will be the following:

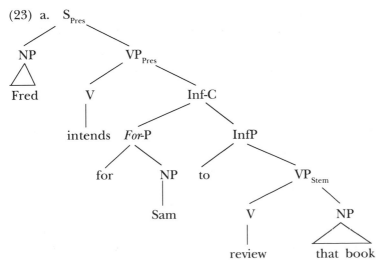

(23) a. S_{Pres}

b.

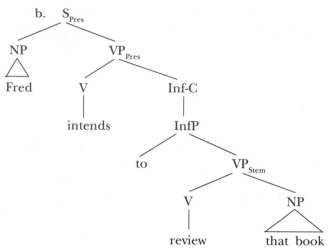

Exercise

1. For each of the following sentences, draw a phrase-structure tree.
    a. Joan says that Larry uses the code.
    b. The company requires that Larry use the code.
    c. Thomas would like for Larry to use the code.
    d. Thomas would like to use the code.
    e. We hope that Fred knows that the dog ate his parakeet.
    f. David says that he would like for you to pay the fiddler.
    g. Doris would like for Max to realize that the problems seem difficult.

4.1.3 Indirect Questions

An even more complex type of clause is illustrated in the sentences in (24).

(24) a. John knows [whose alligator the plumber located].
      b. Dr. Smith has forgotten [which goat George was shouting at].
      c. Janet told me [how many employees Karen introduced to the visitors].

The bracketed sequences in these sentences look similar to the following independent structures, to which we commonly refer as *questions*:

(25) a. Whose alligator did the plumber locate?
      b. Which goat was George shouting at?
      c. How many employees did Karen introduce to the visitors?

In what follows, we will assume that the bracketed structures in (24) deserve to be called questions too. One suggestive piece of evidence for this view is that John knows whose alligator the plumber located if and only if he knows the answer to the question "Whose alligator did the plumber locate?" In order to distinguish between these two constructions, we will refer to the questions in (24) as *indirect questions* and to those in (25) as *direct questions*. The only significant difference between them, the difference in verbal structure and word order, will be discussed in chapter 15.

The first thing we notice about the indirect questions in (24) is that they all begin with phrases containing what we can call "wh words." (This terminology is loose; the word *how* actually begins with *h* instead of *wh*). In all of these indirect questions, the initial phrases happen to be noun phrases:

(26) a. [$_{NP}$whose alligator]
     b. [$_{NP}$which goat]
     c. [$_{NP}$how many employees]

We will call such noun phrases *questioned noun phrases;* the abbreviation for such noun phrases will be NP$_Q$. We should note in passing that *who, whom,* and *what* can be single-word questioned noun phrases:

(27) a. John knows [[$_{NP}$*what*] the plumber located].
     b. Dr. Smith has forgotten [[$_{NP}$*who*] George was shouting at]. (informal)
     c. Janet told me [[$_{NP}$*whom*] Karen introduced to the visitors]. (formal)

In each of the indirect questions in (24), the second major part is a sequence that follows the questioned noun phrase. In the examples under consideration, these sequences are exactly like incomplete sentences:

(28) a. the plumber located.
     b. George was shouting at.
     c. Karen introduced to the visitors

All three of the incomplete sentences in (28) contain particular words (*located, at,* and *introduced,* respectively) that ordinarily require noun-phrase objects. Thus, what we seem to have here are sentences in which one particular noun phrase is "missing." We might get a clearer picture of these sequences if we wrote them with blanks to indicate the position of the missing noun phrase, as in (29).

(29) a. the plumber located ___
     b. George was shouting at ___
     c. Karen introduced ___ to the visitors

We will refer to such structures as "sentences with missing noun phrases," which we will abbreviate as S/NP.

We are now ready to state a tentative rule for forming indirect questions of the type illustrated in (24). This rule is given in (30), both in words and in a diagram.

(30) An indirect question (IQ) can consist of a questioned noun phrase ("NP_Q"), followed by a sentence with a missing noun phrase (S/NP).

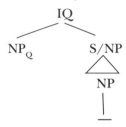

For the particular indirect questions that we have been discussing, we get the tree structures shown in (31).

(31) a.

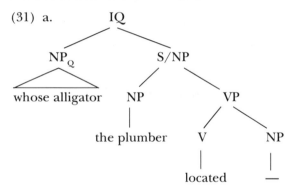

b.

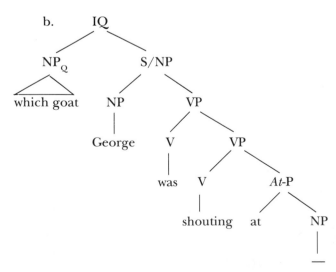

c.

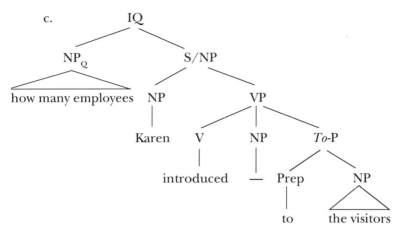

Now that we have made a start at describing the syntax of indirect questions, let us make some comments about their interpretation. The most basic matter concerns the missing noun phrase. In independent sentences, such missing noun phrases are unacceptable:

(32) a. *The plumber located ___.
      b. *George was shouting at ___.
      c. *Karen introduced ___ to the visitors.

LOCATE, AT, and INTRODUCE all must have objects provided for them in some manner. The usual way to identify an object is to put an actual noun phrase in the normal position for the object, as in the following simple sentences:

(33) a. The plumber located *Robert's alligator.*
      b. George was shouting at *that goat.*
      c. Karen introduced *ten employees* to the visitors.

However, the indirect questions that we are now examining illustrate an additional way in which objects in a phrase may be identified: They may be identified by some outside noun phrase. As we can tell intuitively, in each indirect question it is the questioned noun phrase that identifies the missing object. We can think of the questioned noun phrase as being linked to the missing noun phrase in two steps. First, the questioned noun phrase is coupled with the following sequence—that is, to the sentence with the missing noun phrase:

(34)

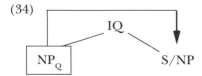

Then this identification is passed on to the missing noun phrase itself:

(35)   S/NP

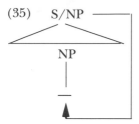

Putting these two processes together, we get the complex identification process represented in (36).

(36)

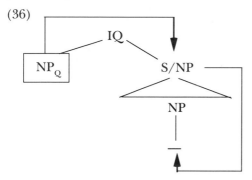

The questioned noun phrase has donated its meaning to a particular kind of incomplete sentence, and this incomplete sentence has used this donated meaning to provide an identification for its missing noun phrase.

For our original set of indirect questions, we now obtain the diagrams shown in (37), which contain information about the structures involved and about the way in which these structures are interpreted.

(37) a.

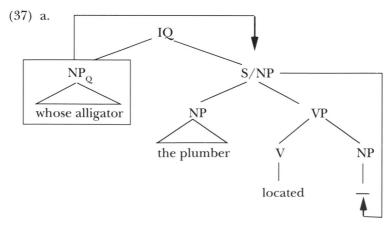

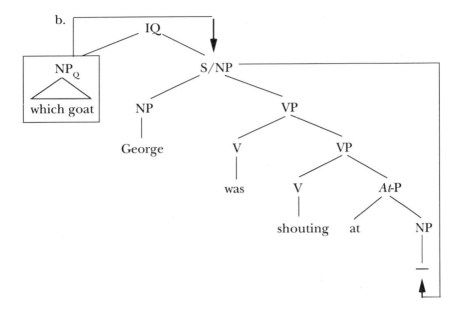

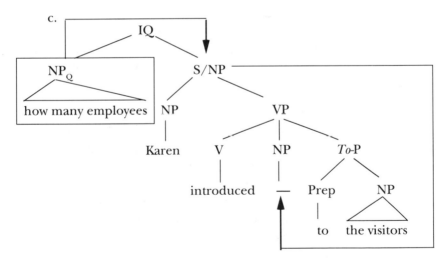

In all three of the examples considered so far, the questioned noun phrase has donated its meaning to a missing noun phrase somewhere inside the verb phrase. Not surprisingly, we also have indirect questions in which the questioned noun phrase provides an interpretation for the subject. A typical example is given in (38).

(38) Smith knows [*which clerk* opened the letter].

The analysis that we developed with the earlier three examples in mind can be extended easily to this new one. The bracketed sequence can be divided into an interrogative noun phrase (*which clerk*) followed by a sentence with a missing noun phrase (___ *opened the letter*). In this case, of course, the missing noun phrase is just the subject:

(39)

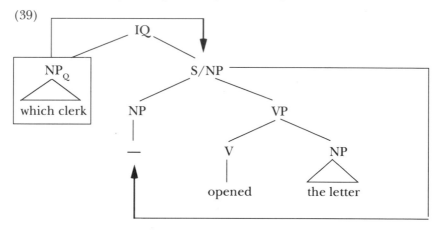

In the situation where objects of prepositions are questioned, we actually have two alternative ways of forming an indirect question. The way that we have seen already is shown in (40a), while the other way is shown in (40b):

(40) a. Dr. Smith has forgotten [*which room* George stayed *in* ___]
      b. Dr. Smith has forgotten [*in which room* George stayed ___]

In the first of these questions, the questioned noun phrase introduces the question and the preposition appears in its normal position in the verb phrase. In contrast, the second question is introduced by the entire prepositional phrase, and we find an unoccupied prepositional-phrase position in the verb phrase instead of an unoccupied noun-phrase position. Let us define a *questioned prepositional phrase* (PrepP$_Q$) as a prepositional phrase whose noun phrase is a questioned noun phrase. Then we need the following additional rule:

(41) An indirect question can consist of a questioned prepositional phrase (PrepP$_Q$), followed by a sentence with an empty prepositional phrase (S/PrepP).

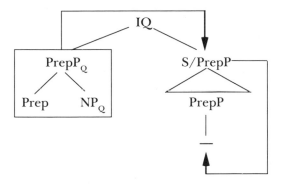

For the indirect question in (40b), the tree diagram (42) is appropriate.

(42)

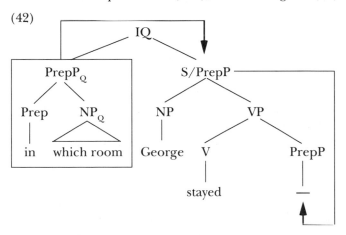

One question concerning the labeling of the phrases in (42) must be addressed. In chapter 2 we classified sequences like *in this room* and *at the theater* as locative phrases. Why, then, is the sequence *in which room* called a prepositional phrase in (42) instead of being called a locative phrase? The answer to this question is that *in which room* (like *in this room* and *at the theater*) is both a prepositional phrase and a locative phrase. We used the prepositional-phrase label in (42) because the prepositional property is the one that is important in determining the possibility of using the phrase to introduce an indirect question. As the examples in (43) show, virtually all kinds of prepositional phrases can be fronted in indirect questions.

(43)

⎧ a. into which room the patient went ___. ⎫
⎪ b. with which surgeon the patient consulted ___. ⎪
Dr. Smith has ⎨ c. on which nurse the patient depended ___. ⎬
forgotten ⎪ d. for whom the orderly made the bed ___. ⎪
⎩ e. to whom the patient sent the money ___. ⎭

What particular kind of prepositional phrase they happen to be is of no importance for their capacity to introduce indirect questions.

In addition to indirect questions that begin with questioned noun phrases and prepositional phrases, we also find indirect questions that begin with questioned phrases of other types. In each such question, there is an empty phrase of the same type in the accompanying sentence. Several examples are given in (44), each one accompanied by a normal declarative sentence that shows the usual position of a phrase of the type being questioned.

(44) a. Laura told me [*how fond of chocolates* the monkeys are]. (adjective phrase)
       (The monkeys are *very fond of chocolates.*)
    b. Matthew knows [*when* the concert will begin]. (time phrase)
       (The concert will begin *at eight o'clock.*)
    c. Caligula told us [*where* his horse is]. (locative phrase)
       (His horse is *in the library.*)

In (44a), the indirect question is introduced by an interrogative adjective phrase (*how fond of chocolates*), which is followed by a sentence with an empty adjective phrase (*the monkeys are* ___). In (44b), the initial interrogative phrase is a time phrase (*when*), which is followed by a sentence with an empty time phrase (*the concert will begin* ___). In (44c), the interrogative phrase is a locative phrase (*where*), which is followed by a sentence with an empty locative phrase (*his horse is* ___). In much-simplified tree form, these indirect questions have the following divisions into two parts apiece:

(45)

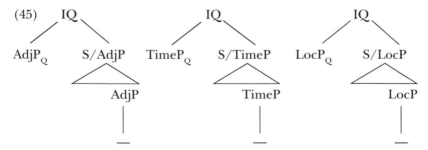

When the associations between questioned phrases and empty phrases are added to the diagrams, the following pictures result:

(46)

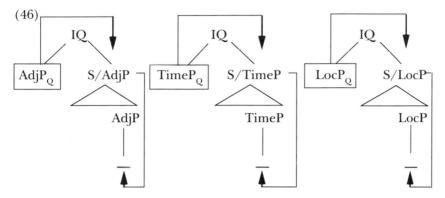

As general rules for all the indirect questions considered so far, we can give the following statements:

(47) a. An indirect question can consist of a questioned phrase of any sort (an XP_Q) plus a sentence containing an empty phrase of the same sort (an S/XP).

b. The initial questioned phrase is donated to the incomplete sentence, which then uses it to identify its missing phrase.

From (47a), we get the diagram in (48a). The addition of the interpretive information in (47b) gives the diagram in (48b).

(48) a.   b.

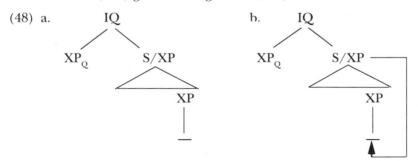

In addition to questions of the type discussed so far, there is a group of indirect questions that do not contain missing phrases. These questions are introduced by *whether* and *if;* they correspond to direct questions that call either for yes-or-no answers or for a choice of alternatives. Two examples, and the direct questions that correspond to them, follow.

(49) a.   Joseph will tell you [*whether* Martha is leaving].

b.   Joseph will tell you [*if* Martha is leaving].

b.   Is Martha leaving?

(50) a.   We want to know [*whether* John sued Karen or Karen sued John].

b.   We want to know [*if* John sued Karen or Karen sued John].

c.   Did John sue Karen or did Karen sue John?

For the yes-no questions, we can add a simple rule:

(51) An indirect question may consist of the word *whether* or *if* plus a finite
sentence.

The structure for the indirect question in (50a) is then as follows:

(52)

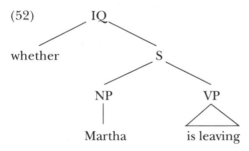

For the indirect questions that give alternatives, the rules that we need will
be discussed in chapter 16 in the course of a systematic treatment of
conjoined structures.

In all the indirect questions considered so far, what follows the initial
phrase is a finite sentence, with or without an empty phrase. English also
allows indirect questions based on infinitival phrases:

(53) a.   Fred knows [*which politician* to vote for].

b.   Karen asked [*where* to put the chairs].

These structures, like similar ones containing finite sentences, contain
empty phrases. Specifically, the preposition *for* requires a noun-phrase
object, and the verb *put* requires a locative phrase. For these structures,
then, we need the following rule:

(54) a.   An indirect question can consist of a questioned phrase (XP$_Q$)
followed by an infinitival phrase that contains an empty phrase
of the same sort (InfP/XP).

b. The initial questioned phrase is donated to the incomplete infinitival phrase, which then uses it to identify its missing phrase.

The structures that (54a) creates are shown in (55a). The identifications created by (54b) are added in (55b).

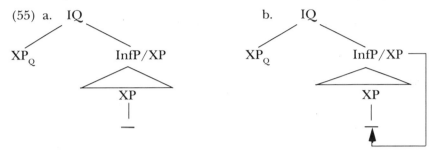

(55) a. IQ

b. IQ

For the particular indirect questions in (53), we get the following structures:

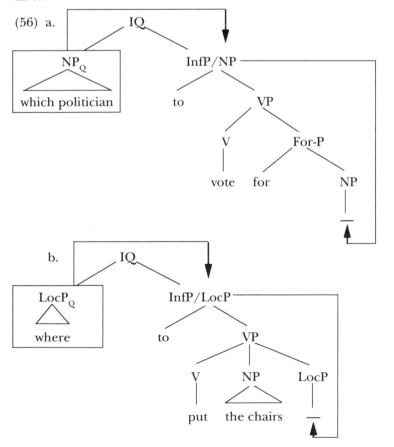

(56) a.

b.

In addition, as with questions based on finite sentences, infinitival indirect questions can be introduced by *whether*:

(57)   Marcos needs to decide [*whether* to capture Joe's queen].

In this case, once again, the infinitival phrase does not contain an empty phrase, and the rule we need is just the following:

(58) An indirect question can consist of *whether* plus an infinitival phrase.

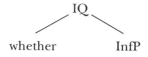

For the particular indirect question in (57), we have the following tree:

(59)

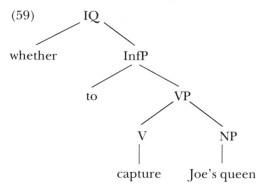

Before leaving this section, let us summarize the rules that we have developed. Indirect questions can be built up from either of two basic structures, finite sentences and infinitival phrases. One variety consists of *whether* plus a complete basic structure. The other variety consists of a questioned phrase of some sort (an XP_Q) plus a basic structure with a corresponding missing phrase.

The indirect-question construction is the first "missing-phrase" construction that we have seen so far. In later chapters, we will encounter many other such constructions. In each of them, a corresponding phrase from outside will provide an identification for this empty phrase. Thus, each of these constructions will look, in part, like (60).

(60)

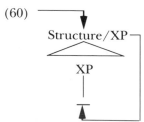

Exercises

1. Each of the sentences below contains an indirect question. Begin by dividing each such indirect question into its two basic parts: the questioned phrase and the structure containing the empty phrase. Then indicate the position of the empty phrase by putting in a dash. Finally, say what type of construction each of the two parts is. The first sentence is done as an illustration.

    a.   We have forgotten *which dog we wanted to buy.*

         ANSWER: Questioned phrase: which dog (NP$_Q$)

                  Structure containing empty phrase:

                  we wanted to buy—(S/NP)

    b.   Joseph has forgotten *how many matches he has won.*

    c.   Caroline will remember *how much money to send to the bank.*

    d.   Noah knows *where to keep the kangaroos.*

    e.   The committee knows *whose efforts to achieve peace the world should honor.*

    f.   Jack asked Nora *which policeman had given her a ticket.*

    g.   Brenda wanted to know *how dull the meeting was likely to be.*

    h.   Jasper wonders *which book he should try to persuade his students to read.*

2. Using the preliminary work that you have done in the previous exercise, draw a tree diagram for each of the indirect questions. You need not provide detailed structures for the questioned phrases themselves.

4.2 The External Syntax of Clauses

Now that the four basic types of English clauses have been described, let us study their external behavior. In other words, let us try to discover the rules that dictate the way in which these structures figure in the formation of larger constructions. We will begin by looking at their use as verb complements, and then consider their use as complements of adjectives, prepositions, and nouns. Then we will study their use as subjects, and examine a rather surprising construction in which they are understood as subjects even though they give the appearance of being complements.

4.2.1 Clauses Used as Verb Complements

All four types of clauses discussed in section 4.1 can be used as verbal complements. In particular, all of them can occur alone with a head verb, as in (61).

(61) a. Jane *knows* [that George hates olives].   (finite *that* clause)

   b. Mark *insists* [that Debby keep the change].   (bare-stem *that* clause)

   c. Nancy *would* prefer [for Freddy to stay in the nursery]. (infinitival clause)

   d. George will *know* [which dog treed White-Paws].   (indirect question)

This general configuration is represented in (62).

(62)   VP

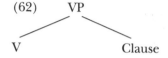

V   Clause

In addition, finite *that* clauses, as well as indirect questions, can appear with a preceding noun-phrase object, as in (63).

(63) a. Richard told Martha [that Edward stole the cookies].   (finite *that* clause)

   b. Dana taught Orville [where to find snails].   (indirect question)

This general configuration is represented in (64).

(64)   VP

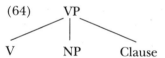

V   NP   Clause

As with all of the previous verb-phrase configurations that we have considered, there is a great deal of variation among verbs as to which of the two above configurations they allow, and also as to what particular kind(s) of clauses they are compatible with. We will look briefly at the verbs that take each of the four clause types as complement.

4.2.1.1 Verbs Taking Finite *That* Clauses   The verbs that allow finite *that* clauses make up a large class of English verbs. We begin with the examples in (65) and (66), which are divided between those in which the clause is the only complement and those in which the clause follows a noun phrase.

(65) a. We *believe* [that the war has ended].

   b. Carla *knows* [that her friends have arrived].

   c. Norman *realizes* [that your brother wants his job].

   d. Smith *claims* [that Jones wrecked Fred's truck].

   e. Jones *says* [that Smith is a liar].

    f.   Anna *guessed* [that Fred would get the job].

    g.   We *assume* [that these sentences are acceptable].

(66) a.   Joe *warned* the class [that the exam would be difficult].

      b.   We *told* Marsha [that she should consult an accountant].

      c.   Carol *convinced* me [that the argument was sound].

      d.   The teachers *taught* the children [that mathematics was tedious].

Roughly speaking, these verbs include all those that involve knowing, believing, and saying. For each one of these verbs, we need a complement specification that allows it to occur with a finite *that* clause. For instance, BELIEVE will be assigned the specification in (67a), whereas WARN will be assigned the one in (67b).

(67) a. BELIEVE: [—*That*-C$_{Fin}$]   b. WARN: [—NP *That*-C$_{Fin}$]

These two specifications can be given in tree form as in (68).

Diagram (69) is a complete tree for a sentence containing an object *that* clause.

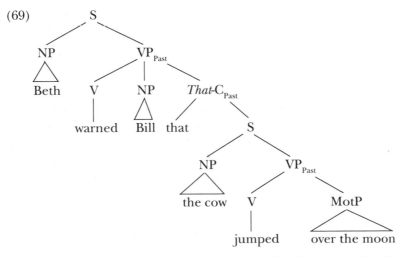

As this diagram shows, the rule for forming *that* clauses has the effect of allowing us to use a small sentence (*the cow jumped over the moon*) as a part of a larger one. Actually, this larger sentence can itself be used in a *that* clause, which can serve as the object of an even larger sentence, as in (70).

(70) a. You may know [that Beth warned Bill [that the cow jumped over the moon]].

b.

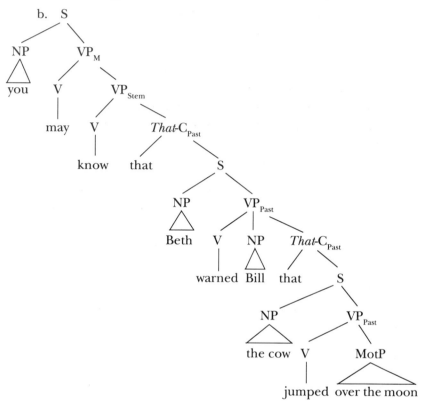

Exercises

1. For each of the verbs given below, answer two questions: Does it have the complement specification [—*That*-C$_{Fin}$]? Does it have the complement specification [— NP *That*-C$_{Fin}$]? With each Yes answer, provide an acceptable sentence; with each No answer, provide an unacceptable sentence. In testing for the [—NP *That*-C$_{Fin}$] possibility, use pronouns or proper nouns in the NP position.

a.	WANT	e.	PERSUADE
b.	HOPE	f.	MAINTAIN
c.	SAY	g.	TRY
d.	TELL	h.	REPLY

2. Draw tree diagrams for the following sentences:
   a. Fred will warn Martha that she should claim that her alligator is tame.
   b. Doris said that the king of France told the nobles that he would save them.

4.2.1.2 Verbs Taking Bare-Stem *That* Clauses Bare-stem *that* clauses, like their finite cousins, can serve as complements of verbs. As was noted earlier, this clause appears in only one verb-phrase configuration: the one in which it is the only complement. This configuration is depicted in (71).

(71)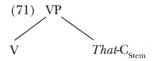

The verbs that allow this type of clause are quite limited in number. INSIST and REQUIRE are clear examples, as (72) shows.

(72) a. I *insist* [that the fox guard the chickens].
     b. The rules *require* [that the executives be polite].

For these verbs, then, the following specifications are needed:

(73) a. INSIST: [—*That*-C$_{Stem}$]   b. REQUIRE: [—*That*-C$_{Stem}$]

The same specifications are given in tree form in (74).

(74)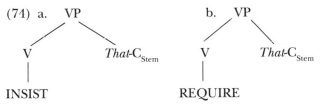

Exercises

1. Each of the following sentences contains a *that* clause. Each of these clauses contains a verb that in isolation could be either a finite verb (a present plural) or a bare stem. For each example, construct an experimental sentence that will enable you to decide whether the italicized verb calls for finite clauses or for bare-stem clauses.
   a. We *hope* [that the members of the jury understand the law].
   b. Sharon has *requested* [that the candidates stay in the hall].
   c. Joe *suspects* [that the agents open his mail].
   d. Ellen *asked* [that you read her letters].

4.2.1.3 Verbs Taking Infinitival Clauses   Verbs allowing infinitival clauses
are much less common than those taking *that* clauses. This class of verbs
includes WANT, PREFER, and LIKE, as (75) shows.

(75) a.   Karen *wants* [for Bill to get a diploma].
  b.   Charles would *prefer* [for the butler to open the bottle].
  c.   Curt *likes* [for the poodle to stay under the porch].

Each of these verbs requires the complement specification [—Inf-C]. The
same information is expressed in tree form in (76).

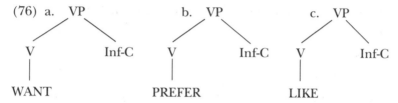

One special matter deserves attention in this section. In chapter 3, when
we talked about infinitival phrases, we assigned several verbs the complement specification [—InfP]. Yet the rule just given for infinitival *clauses*
might appear to allow us to view all infinitival phrases as just infinitival
clauses. For example, the verb INTEND would need only the complement
specification [—Inf-C]. This one specification would allow for the appearance of this verb in both of the sentences in (77).

(77) a.   Maxine intends [for Harry to buy a car].
  b.   Maxine intends [to buy a car].

It is now natural to ask: Are there any verbs that should be specified as
requiring infinitival *phrases* rather than infinitival *clauses,* or are all the
verbs we are concerned with just like INTEND, which calls for infinitival
clauses? The answer is that the specification for infinitival *phrases* appears
to be correct for several verbs—specifically, those that do not allow the *for*
construction:

(78) a.   Beth tried to ask a question.
  b. *Beth tried for Bill to ask a question.

(79) a.   George tends to avoid confrontations.
  b. *George tends for Marsha to avoid confrontations.

(80) a.   Jane persuaded Bill to finish the book.
  b. *Jane persuaded Bill for George to finish the book.

(81) a.   Joe hoped to find a solution.
     b.   *Joe hoped for Beth to find a solution.

Thus, our complement specifications for these four verbs and for others that do not allow the *for* construction will continue to mention only infinitival *phrases*. However, for verbs like INTEND, WANT, and LIKE we will use specifications that mention infinitival *clauses*, so that both *for* constructions and infinitival constructions without *for* can appear with them.

Exercises

1. The following sentences contain several italicized verbs. For each one, decide whether the verb should be given the specification [—InfC] or the specification [—InfP]. Justify your decisions by constructing experimental sentences in which the verbs are accompanied by infinitival clauses introduced by *for*.
     a.   John *decided* to keep the money.
     b.   Fred *needs* to wash the dishes.
     c.   Carol *seems* to enjoy calculus.
     d.   Marsha *attempted* to unlock the door.
     e.   Jerry *longed* to return to Iowa.

2. Draw tree diagrams for the following sentences:
     a.   Carlton would like for Marsha to play a sonata.
     b.   Ned prefers to stay in Boston.

4.2.1.4 Indirect Questions as Complements   Like *that* clauses, indirect questions occur as complements of a large number of English verbs. The examples in (82) and (83) illustrate the two basic configurations in which they occur.

(82) a.   John *knows* [whose boat sank].
     b.   Geraldine *wondered* [which goat George wanted to sell].

(83) a.   Janet *asked* me [how many forks to give to the customer].
     b.   Charles *told* us [how tall his brother's wife was].

With KNOW and WONDER, the indirect question is the only complement. Thus, these verbs call for the complement specification [—IQ]. With ASK and TELL, the indirect question is preceded by an indirect-object noun phrase. For these two, then, we need the specification [—NP IQ]. In tree form, we can express the relevant complementation rules for these verbs as follows:

(84)

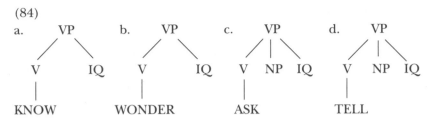

Most of the verbs that take indirect questions also take *that* clauses, WONDER and INQUIRE being the main exceptions. We might at first be tempted to think that all verbs allowing *that* clauses also allow indirect questions, but the following pairs of examples show that such a view would be false.

(85) a. Harvey *denied* [that he had been reading that article].
      b. *Harvey *denied* [which book he had been reading].

(86) a. Henrietta *thinks* [that your dog was irresponsible].
      b. *Henrietta *thinks* [whose dog was irresponsible].

(87) a. Carol *claimed* [that she had spent five thousand dollars].
      b. *Carol *claimed* [how much money she had spent].

These examples show that we cannot predict that a certain verb will allow indirect questions merely by knowing that it allows *that* clauses. Many verbs will be specified for both constructions, but many others will be specified only for *that* clauses.

Is there some other way of guessing which verbs will take indirect questions? A careful inspection shows that certain "meaning classes" of verbs seem to favor them. One small class consists of "interrogative verbs." This class includes ASK, WONDER, and INQUIRE:

(88)

John $\left\{ \begin{array}{l} \textit{asked} \\ \textit{wondered} \\ \textit{inquired} \end{array} \right\}$ [which book he should read] $\left\{ \begin{array}{l} \text{(ASK: [—IQ])} \\ \text{(WONDER: [—IQ])} \\ \text{(INQUIRE: [—IQ])} \end{array} \right\}$

Another class, a much larger one, consists of "verbs of knowledge," including verbs such as KNOW, LEARN, and FORGET, which involve an increase or decrease in knowledge:

(89)

Karen $\left\{ \begin{array}{l} \textit{knew} \\ \textit{learned} \\ \textit{forgot} \end{array} \right\}$ [which drawer contained the money] $\left\{ \begin{array}{l} \text{(KNOW: [—IQ])} \\ \text{(LEARN: [—IQ])} \\ \text{(FORGET: [—IQ])} \end{array} \right\}$

This class also includes verbs that take indirect objects, where the subject of the verb causes an increase in knowledge on the part of the indirect object:

(90)

$$
\text{Pete} \left\{ \begin{array}{c} taught \\ told \\ informed \end{array} \right\} \text{Fred [which plants were edible]} \left\{ \begin{array}{c} \text{(TEACH: [—IQ])} \\ \text{(TELL: [—IQ])} \\ \text{(INFORM: [—IQ])} \end{array} \right\}
$$

Other smaller verb classes whose members allow indirect questions include "decision verbs" and "verbs of concern."

(91) Marsha will *decide* [which book Carol should review]   (DECIDE: [—IQ])

(92) Bill never seems to *care* [how many armadillos he has overlooked]   (CARE: [—IQ])

Exercise
1. All the verbs listed below allow *that* clauses as complements. Construct experimental sentences to determine which ones also allow indirect questions and which ones do not. Warning: Constructions that start with *what*, *when*, and *where* do not give reliable results here, since they sometimes represent a construction of an entirely different type that will be discussed in chapter 7. Better results can be obtained with *why*, with *whose* plus a noun, or with *how much*.

    a. GUESS   e. MAINTAIN
    b. REPLY   f. NOTICE
    c. OBJECT   g. SPECIFY
    d. FEEL   h. CONFESS

4.2.2 Clauses Used as Complements of Adjectives, Nouns, and Prepositions

In the preceding subsection we examined the use of clauses as complements of verbs. Many of these clause types also occur as complements of certain adjectives, as the following examples show:

(93) Jerry is *confident* [that the elephants respect him].
     CONFIDENT: $[—That\text{-}C_{Fin}]$

(94) George is [insistent *that the witnesses be truthful*].
     INSISTENT: $[—That\text{-}C_{Stem}]$

(95) a. Cornelia seems [eager *for her brother to catch a cold*].
  b. Cornelia seems [eager *to catch a cold*].
  EAGER: [—Inf-C]

(96) Carol is [uncertain *which articles you read*].
  UNCERTAIN: [—IQ]

In diagram form, these specifications look like this:

(97) a. AdjP   b. AdjP

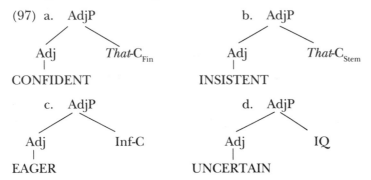

Clauses are much more restricted in their occurrence with prepositions. As a matter of fact, neither *that* clauses nor infinitival clauses may occur as objects of prepositions:

(98) *Fred is thinking [about *that the chimps refuse to learn English*].

(99) a. *We are counting [on *for Nathan to make an announcement*].
  b. *Fred is talking [about *to stay in Laredo*].

The only clauses that work well as prepositional objects are indirect questions, as in (100).

(100) a. The outcome depends [on *how many candidates participate in the election*].
   b. Fred is thinking [about *whether he should stay in Laredo*].

Clausal complements also occur with many nouns. The noun phrases in (101), for example, show that the noun EAGERNESS can take an infinitival clause as its complement:

(101) a. John's *eagerness* [for Harriet to win the election]
   b. John's *eagerness* [to win the election]
   EAGERNESS: [—Inf-C]

Here the relation in meaning between the noun EAGERNESS and the following infinitival clauses is very much the same as that between the adjective EAGER and the same clauses:

(102) a.   John is *eager* [for Harriet to win the election].
       b.   John is *eager* [to win the election].

At first glance, the noun phrases in (103) might seem to show that *that* clauses have a similar capacity to occur as complements of nouns.

(103) a.   the *allegation* [that the pigs respect the sheep]
       b.   the *belief* [that the directors were present]

The relation between noun and clause here might appear to be the same as that between verb and clause in (104).

(104) a. Bill *alleged* [that the pigs respect the sheep].
       b. We *believed* [that the directors were present].

Yet the noun phrases in (103) do not stand for acts of alleging and believing, respectively. Instead, they describe the propositions denoted by the two *that* clauses. The preceding noun in (103a) characterizes the associated *that* clause as an allegation, and the preceding noun in (103b) characterizes its *that* clause as a belief.

The noun phrases in (103) thus show interesting similarities to another group of noun phrases in English. This second group is illustrated by the examples on the left in (105).

(105) a.   the number seven   a.   seven
       b.   the verb *create*   b.   *create*
       c.   my friend Elmer   c.   Elmer

The noun phrases on the left refer to the same entities as the corresponding ones on the right. The major difference is that the left-hand noun phrases provide extra descriptions of these entities: seven is characterized as a number, *create* is characterized as a verb, and Elmer is characterized as my friend.

In view of these observations, we will analyze these examples as being divided between a definite noun phrase and either a *that* clause or a proper noun. This analysis yields tree structures like the following, where "PN" stands for "proper noun":

(106)

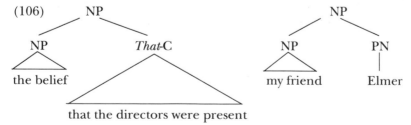

A significant number of other nouns are also appropriate for this construction. In (107) several examples of such nouns are given; (108) exhibits a number of nouns that cannot occur in this context.

(107) a.   Columbus's *conviction* [that the earth is round]
       b.   Bertram's *claim* [that the earth is flat]
       c.   the *idea* [that James can play the flute]
       d.   the *view* [that Martha knows how to bake croissants]

(108) a.   *Columbus's *attention* [that the earth is round]
       b.   *George's *article* [that the earth is flat]
       c.   *the *ignorance* [that James can play the flute]
       d.   *the *expertise* [that Martha knows how to bake croissants]

Exercise

1. Do experiments to determine which of the following nouns take *that* clauses. As your sample *that* clause, use the clause *that all cows eat grass*, or *that John stayed in Denver*. These sequences are unambiguously *that* clauses. In particular, neither one is a relative-clause structure of the sort that will be discussed in chapter 10.

a.	FEAR	e.	THOUGHT
b.	REMORSE	f.	PROPOSITION
c.	ENJOYMENT	g.	BOOK
d.	THEORY	h.	REFUSAL

4.2.3 Clauses Used as Subjects

4.2.3.1 Some Initial Examples   In the preceding subsection, we examined four different clause structures that could be used as complements of various sorts of English words. In this subsection, we will look at the possibilities for using these structures as subjects.

We begin by considering a single example:

(109) [That Jane sold the ostrich] surprised Bill.

The first five words of this sentence clearly make up a finite *that* clause. The remaining two words of the sentence (*surprised Bill*) just make up a past-tense verb phrase. Thus, the structure of the sentence as a whole is as follows:

(110)

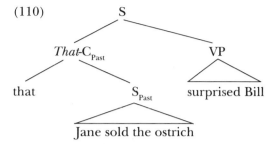

To account for this example, we need the following new rule:

(111) A sentence can consist of a *that* clause plus a verb phrase.

We also find sentences in which other kinds of clauses are used as subjects:

(112) a. *For Caligula to fire his horse* would be desirable. (infinitival clause)
      b. *That the king be present at the wedding* is mandatory. (bare-stem *that* clause)
      c. *Which otter you should adopt* is unclear. (indirect question)

For these examples, we need to revise the rule in (111) so as to allow for additional clause types as subjects. We can do this by referring to clauses in general in the following rule:

(113) A sentence can consist of a clause plus a verb phrase.

For the examples in (112) above, we have the following tree diagrams:

(114) a.

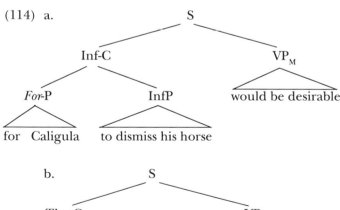

    b.

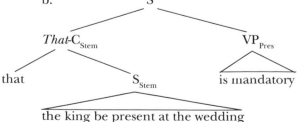

c.

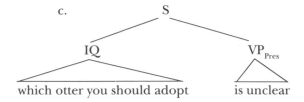

which otter you should adopt   is unclear

Exercise

1. Divide each of the following sentences into a clause plus a verb phrase, and identify the clause type. (The first is done as an example.)

a. That Cora burned her textbooks made her teachers suspicious. (Answer: The sequence *That Cora burned her textbooks* is a finite *that* clause; the sequence *made her teachers suspicious* is the verb phrase that it joins with.)

b. How many goldfish Harry swallowed seems to be unclear.

c. Which books Holmes will put on the reading list remains a mystery.

d. That George intends to let the monkey play his recorder made Susan despondent.

e. For Iris to take the parakeet to the pound would break Arthur's heart.

f. That Bill tried to discover which drawer Alice put the money in made us realize that we should have left him in Albuquerque.

g. For Bill to tell his brother that the dog had eaten the canary was inexcusable.

4.2.3.2 Restrictions on Subjects   Here, we face the same kind of problem with regard to subjects that we faced in earlier sections of this chapter with regard to objects. We saw then that verbs can differ as to whether they allow clausal objects, as in (115).

(115) a.   Jane told Bill that the story was true.
       b.   *Jane gave Bill that the story was true.

We can now construct examples that show the same kind of differences with respect to subjects:

(116) a.   *The explosion* surprised Fred.
       b.   *That the firecracker exploded* surprised Fred.

(117) a.   *The delegates* nominated Bill.
       b.   *That Fred was unpopular* nominated Bill.

These examples indicate clearly that, whereas SURPRISE allows both noun phrases and *that* clauses as subjects, NOMINATE allows only noun phrases.

Our earlier specifications for individual verbs mentioned allowable complements but did not say anything about allowable subjects. Let us now replace this old kind of specification by a new kind, one that identifies subjects as well as complements. Examples of this new type of specification are given in (118).

(118) a. SURPRISE: NP [—NP]
          SURPRISE: *That*-C$_{Fin}$ [—NP]
      b. NOMINATE: NP [—NP]

These specifications, like the complement specifications employed earlier, indicate that both SURPRISE and NOMINATE take ordinary noun phrases as complements. However, they also provide information on allowable subjects, this information being given by the items to the left of the bracketed material. The two specifications for SURPRISE indicate that it allows both ordinary noun phrases and finite *that* clauses as subjects, whereas the single specification for NOMINATE limits its possible subjects to just ordinary noun phrases.

We need to provide the same kind of additional information in the specifications for adjectives. We have already seen many examples of adjectives that take various kinds of complements. We have also seen some sentences in which clauses served as subjects of verb phrases that contained adjectives; a representative set of examples is given in (119).

(119) a. [That Dorothy missed the lecture] was regrettable.   (finite *that* clause)
       b. [For Jacob to remove the motor] is unnecessary. (infinitival clause)
       c. [That Carol sign the deed] is mandatory.   (bare-stem *that* clause)
       d. [How much money Gordon spent] is unclear.   (indirect question)

Even though the main predicates of these sentences are headed by BE, the allowable subjects are determined not by BE but instead by the four adjectives. We can convince ourselves of this fact by leaving the occurrences of BE in place and changing the adjectives. It is not hard to find new adjectives that make the sentences unacceptable:

(120) a. *[That Dorothy missed the lecture] was *enjoyable*. (finite *that* clause)
       b. *[For Jacob to remove the motor] is *undeniable*. (infinitival clause)

c. *[That Carol sign the deed] is *obvious*. (bare-stem *that* clause)

d. *[How much money Gordon spent] is *true*. (indirect question)

Thus, we have good reason to think of various adjectives as requiring this or that kind of subject, even though the subject does not join directly with the adjective phrase, but instead joins with a verb phrase. The adjectives in (119), then, require the following specifications:

(121) a.   REGRETTABLE: *That*-C$_{Fin}$ [—]

      b.   DESIRABLE: *For*-C [—]

      c.   MANDATORY: *That*-C$_{Stem}$ [—]

      d.   CLEAR: IQ [—]

Chapter 8 will provide a more general treatment of how subject requirements are satisfied. Among other things, we will see why it makes sense to let the adjectives select the subjects, even though the phrases that actually join with the subjects are headed by verbs.

Exercise

1. All of the adjectives listed below allow *that* clauses as subjects. Construct experimental sentences to determine which ones also allow indirect questions as subjects and which ones do not.

      a.   TRUE   d.   APPARENT

      b.   EVIDENT   e.   UNCERTAIN

      c.   POSSIBLE   f.   UNLIKELY

4.2.4 The Clausal Substitute *It* and Pseudocomplements

We have now seen many sentences in which clauses function as subjects. Despite being acceptable, these sentences often strike speakers of English as somewhat awkward, and not completely natural for ordinary writing and conversation. At least some of the awkwardness seems to be due to the relative "heaviness" of the clause as a left-hand element in the sentence.

Fortunately, the rules of English provide an alternative method for expressing the same thoughts, one that avoids a heavy initial structure. This alternative is illustrated in (122)–(125). The (a) examples are of the type that we have already studied; the (b) examples show the new structure.

(122) a.   [That Jane sold the ostrich] surprised Bill.

      b.   *It* surprised Bill [that Jane sold the ostrich].

(123) a.   [For Martha to keep the money] would be desirable.

      b.   *It* would be desirable [for Martha to keep the money].

(124) a.   [To postpone the project] would be inadvisable.

       b.   *It* would be inadvisable [to postpone the project].

(125) a.   [Which otter you should adopt] is unclear.

       b.   *It* is unclear [which otter you should adopt].

In the (b) sentences, the pronoun *it* replaces the clause in the position of
the subject, and the clause is shifted to the right. In particular, we will
assume that the clause becomes the rightmost part of the verb phrase with
which the word *it* is linked. This gives (126) as the structure of (122b).

(126)

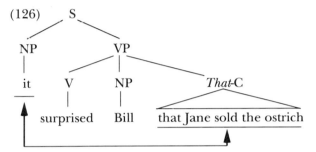

We will refer to the word *it* used in this way as a *clausal substitute*, and to the
clause in its new position as a *pseudocomplement*. By this last name we mean
that the clause is understood as the subject of the sentence but takes a
position that is appropriate for a complement.

    The fact that a *that* clause can occur as a pseudocomplement in (122b)
is clearly related to the fact that it can occur as a subject in (122a). For this
reason, it would be desirable to have the specification in (127) cover two
distinct cases.

(127) SURPRISE: *That*-C [—NP]

The first case is the one in which the *that* clause itself is found in subject
position; the second is that in which subject position is occupied by the
substitute *it*. The following principle gives the desired result:

(128) If some word can use a clause to fulfill its subject requirement, then
       the requirement can also be satisfied by the clausal substitute *it*
       linked to a pseudocomplement clause of the required type.

For example, we know from our earlier discussion that the verb SURPRISE
permits a *that* clause as subject. Now principle (128) tells us that we can
also have *it* as subject, linked to a *that*-clause pseudocomplement. Thus,
both of the structures shown in (129) will satisfy the specification in (127).

(129) a.

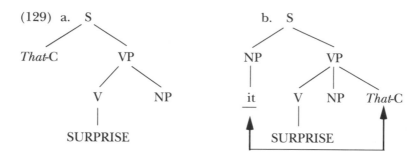

Similarly, the specification allowing *that* clauses as subjects of the adjective CLEAR would be satisfied by both of the structures shown in (130).

(130) a.

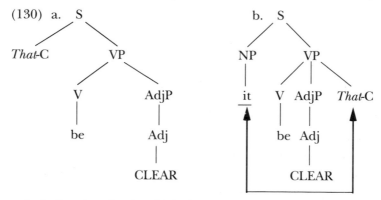

A similar situation in which the clausal substitute *it* appears arises with verbs such as MAKE and CONSIDER. As we saw in chapter 3, these verbs occur in the configuration depicted in (131).

(131)

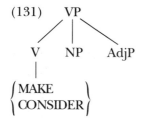

The sentences in (132) exemplify this structure, with ordinary noun phrases occupying the object position.

(132) a.   Martha made the test difficult.

    b.   Joe considered the payment insufficient.

In (132a), *the test* not only satisfies the object requirement of MAKE; it also satisfies the subject requirement of DIFFICULT, just as it does in the simple sentence *the test was difficult.* The noun phrase *the payment* fulfills the same dual role in (132b). Of interest to us in the present discussion is the fact that the substitute *it* can be used as the object of MAKE and CON-SIDER, with a *that* clause appearing as a pseudocomplement of the adjective:

(133) a. Joe made *it* clear [that the money had vanished].
      b. Dorothy considers *it* unlikely [that the problem is solvable].

In these examples, we will assume that the pseudocomplement is the rightmost part of the adjective phrase that accompanies the *it*, since the adjective phrase is the phrase most directly joined with *it*. Thus, the tree diagram (134) is appropriate for the first of these sentences.

(134)

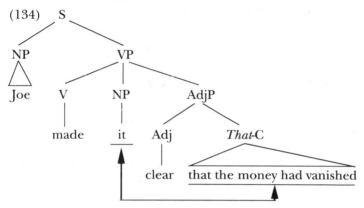

There are a few English verbs that allow *only* the configuration with *it* and a pseudocomplement, excluding sentences in which the clauses occur in ordinary subject position. Two examples are SEEM and APPEAR:

(135) a. *It* seems that John has removed the termites.
      b. *[That John has removed the termites] seems.

(136) a. *It* appears [that the gorilla has dictated a letter].
      b. *[That the gorilla has dictated a letter] appears.

Thus, for these two verbs, and also for a few other verbs and adjectives, the specification in (137a) is incorrect, since it would allow sentences in which *that* clauses occurred in normal subject position with these verbs. As a result, we must assign the specification in (137b) to these verbs directly, rather than getting the desired configuration from (137a) by using principle (128).

(137) a. *That-C* [—]
      b. *it* [—*That-C*]

Exercise

1. Draw tree diagrams for the following sentences.
    a. It amazed Pete that the ants survived the drought.
    b. It surprised Bill that it was unclear that George deserved a trophy.
    c. That it was possible that John would forget to feed the goldfish bothered Susan.

4.2.5 Impossible Positions for Clauses

We noted above that, in general, putting *it* in subject position and an associated clause in pseudocomplement position is more natural than putting the clause itself in subject position. We now need to look at several situations in which the use of the clause by itself is completely unacceptable.

As a first example, let us look again at clauses serving as first complements of MAKE and CONSIDER. In this situation, only the clausal substitute *it* can appear in the normal position of the object. When we try to put the clause itself there, the results are unacceptable:

(138) a. *Joe made *that the money had vanished* clear.
       b. *Dorothy considers *that the problem is elementary* obvious.

A clue as to how we should view the unacceptability of these sentences is provided by some additional examples in which clauses are unacceptable as subjects. To begin with, there is a sharp difference between the declarative in (139a) and the corresponding question in (139b):

(139) a. *That the money had vanished* was obvious.
       b. *Was *that the money had vanished* obvious?

With the substitute *it* used instead, both declarative and question are equally acceptable:

(140) a. *It* was obvious *that the money had vanished.*
       b. Was *it* obvious *that the money had vanished?*

In addition, there is a clear difference between a clause as a main-clause subject and the same clause used as the subject of a complement clause:

(141) a. *That the money had vanished* was obvious.
       b. *Sarah wonders whether *that the money had vanished* was obvious.

Again, these examples should be compared with the corresponding examples in which the clausal substitute is used:

(142) a. *It* was obvious *that the money had vanished.*
     b. Sarah wonders whether *it* was obvious *that the money had vanished.*

Although the actual mental rules or principles that give these results are not well understood, the observations offered above can be summarized as follows: As regards occurrence as a subject, a *that* clause is acceptable in this position only in an independent sentence, and then only when nothing occurs to its left. As for its use as a complement, a *that* clause is acceptable as a single complement , and also as a second complement. It cannot occur as the object of a verb when another complement follows. Parallel restrictions hold for other types of clauses.

4.3 The Omission of *That* and *For*

Both *that* clauses and infinitival clauses sometimes appear in a slightly abbreviated form. In addition to the (a) examples in (143) and (144), which we have already discussed, the rules of English also allow the (b) examples.

(143) a. Karen thinks *that Fred is feeding her rabbit.*
     b. Karen thinks *Fred is feeding her rabbit.*

(144) a. Barney would like *for you to hear his story.*
     b. Barney would like *you to hear his story.*

In the (b) example in each pair, the word that introduces the clause has been omitted.

The omission of the clause-introducing word is allowed only under certain restricted circumstances. It is impossible when the clause is serving as a subject:

(145) a. *That Fred is feeding her rabbit* annoys Karen.
     b. **Fred is feeding her rabbit* annoys Karen.

(146) a. *For Bill to leave the room* would be desirable.
     b. **Bill to leave the room* would be desirable.

In addition, the clause cannot be separated from the verb by an adverbial expression:

(147) a. Marshall believes very strongly *that he can train earthworms.*
     b. *Marshall believes very strongly *he can train earthworms.*

(148) a. Theresa would like very much *for you to attend the recital.*
       b. *Theresa would like very much *you to attend the recital.*

Finally, the omission is completely acceptable with some verbs and adjectives but is less acceptable with others, depending to a degree on the speaker's dialect. We have already seen sentences containing words that clearly allow the omission. In the following pairs of sentences, by contrast, the particular verbs and adjectives are less hospitable to the omission.

(149) a. Bob replied *that he needed to eat a hamburger.*
       b. ?Bob replied *he needed to eat a hamburger.*

(150) a. Nona exclaimed *that Bill's nose was frozen.*
       b. ?Nona exclaimed *Bill's nose was frozen.*

(151) a. We would prefer *for you to stay here.*
       b. ?We would prefer *you to stay here.*

Taking all these observations into consideration, we can state an optional rule for omitting *that* and *for:*

(152) Certain verbs and adjectives permit the optional omission of the clause-introducing words *that* and *for* in their clausal complements, when the clause is not separated from the verb or adjective.

The requirement that the clauses be complements prevents the rule from applying to subject clauses, thus preventing the unacceptable examples in (145b) and (146b).

For the purposes of this rule, the pseudocomplements described in the preceding section function just like real complements, as the following pair of sentences shows.

(153) a. It was clear *that something needed to be done.*
       b. It was clear *something needed to be done.*

The adjective *clear* is thus one of the words that allows the omission, and it is a pseudocomplement clause in which the omission takes place. On the other hand, just as some verbs and adjectives resist the omission in their real complements, there are some that resist it in their pseudocomplements. The word *regrettable* is one of the latter:

(154) a. It is regrettable *that Sharon failed to supervise the guinea pig.*
       b. ?It is regrettable *Sharon failed to supervise the guinea pig.*

Chapter 5

Noun Phrases

In chapter 2, we used the term *noun phrase* to refer to a large class of sequences that could serve as subject and object. Since that point, the particular noun phrases that we have used have been of just a few elementary kinds. The purpose of this chapter is to give a more detailed picture of how noun phrases are constructed.

In section 5.1 we will look at *elementary* noun phrases, a class that includes such phrases as *she, Joseph, the tadpole, your frog, one sandbag,* and *every carpenter*. In section 5.2 we will examine *partitive* noun phrases, a variety in which an *of* phrase plays a prominent role (*one of the dominoes, several of the cards, a pound of beans,* and so forth). Section 5.3 is an interpretative interlude in which the use of the definite article is discussed. Finally, in section 5.4, we will look at the *gerundive* construction, a special sentence-like noun-phrase structure.

5.1 Elementary Noun Phrases

5.1.1 Pronouns and Proper Nouns

In order to begin our inventory of noun-phrase types with the simplest ones, let us start with the pronouns. Pronouns as a group have the property of being able to make up entire noun phrases themselves. In a sentence such as *I see you,* the pronoun *I* is the entire subject noun phrase, and the pronoun *you* is the entire object noun phrase. Thus, we can give the following rule:

(1)   A noun phrase can consist of a pronoun (abbreviated "Pro").

NP
|
Pro

The major syntactic complication concerning pronouns is that they are the only English forms that retain a distinction between *nominative case* (the case of the subject) and *accusative case* (the case used for objects). Thus, for instance, we have the following contrasts:

(2)   a.   *I* love *her* and *she* loves *me*.
       b.   *Me love *she* and *her* loves *I*.

In addition to the nominative and accusative pronouns, there is also a set of corresponding *genitive* pronouns (*my, your, his, her,* etc.).

We will refer to the above-mentioned pronouns as *ordinary* pronouns, to distinguish them from the so-called *reflexive* pronouns. These pronouns, whose form we examined briefly in chapter 1, include *myself, yourself, himself, herself,* and *ourselves.* Like the accusative ordinary pronouns, these can occur as objects of verbs and prepositions. The reflexive form takes precedence over the ordinary form when the noun phrase in question refers to the same person or thing as the nearest subject or object does (if there is an object):

(3)   a.   John believes that [*we* deceived *ourselves*].
       b.   *John believes that [*we* deceived *us*].

(4)   a.   John believes that [Nora told *us* about *ourselves*].
       b.   *John believes that [Nora told *us* about *us*].

By contrast, when the nearest subject and the nearest object (if there is one) refer to someone or something else, an ordinary pronoun must be used:

(5)   a.   *We believe that [John distrusts *ourselves*].
       b.   *We* believe that [John distrusts *us*].

(6)   a.   *We believe that [John told Nora about *ourselves*].
       b.   *We* believe that [John told Nora about *us*].

The final section of chapter 8 will give a fuller treatment to the relation between reflexives and "nearest subjects," making use of the more sophisticated idea of subjecthood developed in that chapter.

One final type of English pronoun, which can occur as either an accusative or a genitive, is the *reciprocal* pronoun *each other,* whose use is illustrated in (7).

(7)   a.   *Fred and Martha* sent messages to *each other.*
       b.   *Fred and Martha* sent messages to *each other's* lawyers.

The *proper nouns* (sometimes referred to as "proper names") constitute another class of words that typically make up noun phrases all by themselves. Three such noun phrases occur in (8).

(8)   *David* introduced *Mr. Jones* to *John Smith.*

For these noun phrases, we need the following simple rule:

(9)   A noun phrase can consist of a proper noun (abbreviated "PN").

NP
|
PN

It was stated above that proper nouns "typically" appeared alone. The reason for this qualification will become apparent in subsection 5.1.7.

5.1.2 Common Noun Phrases: A Brief Review

In order to be ready for the principal work of this section, we need to review some ideas first presented in chapter 2. There we noted that a special class of words called *common nouns* could serve as heads of phrases. We called these phrases *common noun phrases.* There and in subsequent discussions, several examples of this type of phrase were presented, including those listed in (10).

(10)   a.   book   e.   king of Spain
        b.   dogs   f.   heir to the throne
        c.   beer   g.   faith in Fred's sister
        d.   leader of the army   h.   effort to find a vaccine

The common noun phrases listed as (10a)–(10c) consist of common noun heads alone; those listed as (10d)–(10h) consist of head nouns followed by complements. The complement specifications that we need for these examples are listed in (11).

(11)   a.   BOOK   [—]   e.   KING   [—*Of*P]
        b.   DOG   [—]   f.   HEIR   [—*To*P]
        c.   BEER   [—]   g.   FAITH   [—*In*P]
        d.   LEADER [—*Of*P]   h.   EFFORT [—InfP]

These specifications are represented graphically in (12).

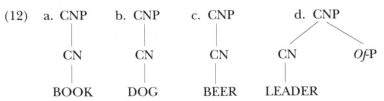

(12)   a. CNP   b. CNP   c. CNP   d. CNP
             | | | ╱   ╲
            CN   CN   CN   CN   *Of*P
             | | | |
           BOOK   DOG   BEER   LEADER

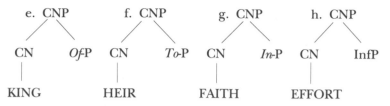

In chapter 10 we will add rules that permit common noun phrases to contain modifiers as well as complements. These rules, for example, will allow not only *book* as a common noun phrase, but also *old book, book from England,* and *book that Jill reviewed.* For our present purposes, a few simple common noun phrases will be enough for present purposes, because the remainder of this chapter is concerned with the *external* syntax of common noun phrases—that is, with the rules that regulate their appearance in larger constructions. The larger constructions in question are just various sorts of noun phrases. The relation between noun phrases and common noun phrases is represented schematically in (13).

(13)

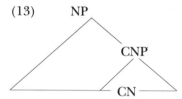

Let us recall here the comments from chapter 2 concerning this terminology. A *common noun phrase* is a phrase headed by a *common noun.* A *noun phrase* is just the conventional name for a phrase that can serve as subject, direct object, and so forth.

Before going on to the main work of this chapter, we need to note two *internal* properties of a common noun phrase that can have an important effect in determining its permitted external environments. As was noted in chapter 1, the general class of English common nouns is divided into *count nouns* and *mass nouns.* The count nouns can be divided further into *singular nouns* and *plural nouns.* In addition to applying the terms *mass, count, singular,* and *plural* to common nouns, we will find good reason to apply them to common noun *phrases* as well. This is not the first instance we have had of a word's passing certain of its properties up to the phrase that it heads. In chapter 2, we saw that verbs of various inflectional types pass their inflectional property up to the phrases that they head. For example, a present-participial marking on a verb had the effect of making the phrase that it headed a present-participial verb *phrase.* In exactly the same fashion, a mass noun will pass its mass property up to the common noun phrase that it heads, a plural count noun will pass its plural count status up to its common noun phrase, and so on. These properties of common noun phrases are represented in (14).

(14)

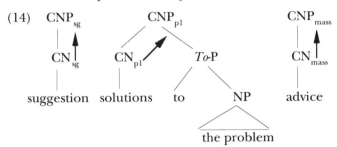

Exercise

1. Draw a tree diagram for each of the following common noun phrases:

a.	coin	e.	evidence of Fred's dishonesty
b.	maps of London	f.	road to Mandalay
c.	people	g.	edge of the cliff
d.	porridge	h.	decision to intervene

5.1.3 Elementary Noun Phrases Introduced by Determiners and Genitives

We have already seen many noun phrases in which common noun phrases were preceded by the word *the*, a word traditionally referred to as the *definite article*. We will refer to the full set of words to which *the* belongs as the class of *determiners*. In addition to *the*, this class also includes the four *demonstratives: this, that, these,* and *those.* These words combine with common noun phrases to form noun phrases:

(15) a. the [book]
      b. this [dog]
      c. that [side of the table]
      d. these [students of chemistry]
      e. those [kings of England]

For these noun phrases, we need the rule in (16), which can be expressed either in words or in tree form.

(16)   A noun phrase can consist of a determiner plus a common noun phrase.

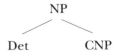

The structures to which this rule gives rise are shown in (17).

(17)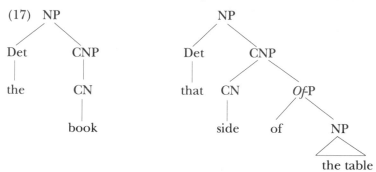

The word *the* is indifferent to the number of the following common noun phrase; it may be joined to either a singular or a plural phrase. By contrast, the demonstratives have to agree in number with the common noun phrase: *these* and *those* take plural phrases, whereas *this* and *that* take nonplural phrases:

(18) a. this [book]   c. *this [books]
      b. that [book]   d. *that [books]

(19) a. *these [book]   c. these [books]
      b. *those [book]   d. those [books]

The examples in (20) show that mass nouns as well as singular count nouns are to be taken as nonplural.

(20) a. this [advice]
      b. *these [advice]
      c. that [traffic]
      d. *those [traffic]

A final group of words included in the class of determiners consists—surprisingly—of the plural pronoun forms *we*, *us*, and *you*.

(21) a. we [leaders of the senate]
      b. us [students of chemistry]
      c. you [children]

Noun phrases introduced by determiners form part of a special semantic class; we will refer to them as *definite noun phrases*. (We will need to refer to this class later in this chapter when we discuss partitive noun phrases.) Another type of noun phrase that belongs in this class is shown in (22).

(22) a. Fred's [dog].

b. the farmer's [pig]
c. your [picture of Fred]

In each of these examples, the bracketed common noun phrase is preceded by a noun phrase in the *genitive case* (*Fred's, the farmer's, your*). *Genitive* is the traditional name for the case in English that indicates possession, among other things. For proper nouns, and also for phrases built around common nouns, the genitive case is formed by adding *'s* to a singular or an irregular plural noun, and *'* to a regular plural noun. The forms for pronouns are more irregular, and cannot be predicted from the non-genitive forms (*my* corresponds to *I/me, your* to *you, his* to *he/him,* and so on). These informal rules give us the following structures for the genitive noun phrases that occur as part of larger noun phrases in (22):

(23)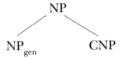

Once we have these structures, the following rule will give us the larger noun phrases in (22):

(24)   A noun phrase can consist of a noun phrase in the genitive case followed by a common noun phrase.

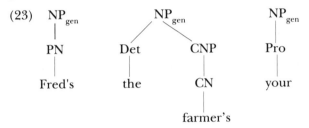

Here, then, are the complete structures for the noun phrases in (22):

(25)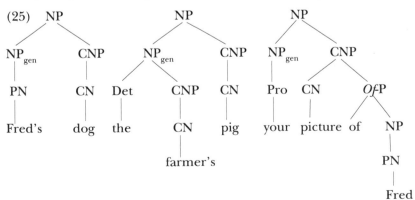

One initial reason that we can give for wanting to classify these noun phrases as definite is that they have an interpretation that is close to what we would obtain for a noun phrase introduced by *the*. For example, *Fred's dog* is much closer in meaning to *the dog that Fred owns* than it is to *a dog that Fred owns*. A second reason will become apparent in section 5.2 when we study examples like *several of those dogs* and *several of Fred's dogs*.

One other possibility for forming definite elementary noun phrases is illustrated in (26).

(26) a. the three stooges   d. the victim's four brothers
      b. these two books   e. Linda's one regret
      c. this one concert   f. Gary's many supporters

In these examples, the same elements introduce the noun phrases as in the examples considered earlier (determiners in the first three examples and genitive noun phrases in the last three). The extra element in each case is either an outright numeral, as in the first five examples, or a word that is close in meaning to a numeral, as in the last example. For noun phrases such as these, we need the following additional rule:

(27) A noun phrase may consist of either a determiner or a genitive, followed by a numeral (or a numeral-like word), followed by a common noun phrase.

Structures for two of the examples in (26) are given in (28).

(28)

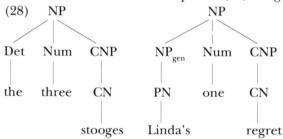

Exercises

1. Draw a detailed tree diagram for each of the following noun phrases:
      a. these distortions of Joe's views
      b. this man's assessment of the damage
      c. Joseph's idea of his rights

    d.   Ruth's father's orchard

    e.   my three sons

    f.   these two reports to the governor

2. The rules for demonstratives presented here give us a straightforward experimental way of deciding whether a certain noun in English is plural or nonplural. Construct noun phrases (some acceptable, some unacceptable) that show that *cattle* is a plural noun, whereas *traffic* is a nonplural noun.

5.1.4 Elementary Noun Phrases Introduced by Quantity Words

Another important type of elementary noun phrase consists of a *quantity word* (abbreviated "Quant") plus a common noun phrase. The class of quantity words includes *some, many, much, any, no, little, few,* and the numerals *one, two, three,* and so on. The class of quantity words includes the numerals, but also includes words such as *some, many, much, any, no, little,* and *few.* Some examples of noun phrases introduced by these words are given in (29). Each example is accompanied by an indication of the basic properties of the common noun phrase.

(29)   a. some [books] (plural)   l. few [opportunities] (plural)

        b. some [vegetation] (mass)   m. little [evidence] (mass)

        c. many [suggestions] (plural) n. one [side] (singular)

        d. several [marbles] (plural)   o. three [attempts] (plural)

        e. much [advice] (mass)   p. all [suggestions] (plural)

        f. no [bottles] (plural)   q. all [advice] (mass)

        g. no [evidence] (mass)   r. each [suggestion] (singular)

        h. no [card] (singular)   s. every [suggestion] (singular)

        i. any [bottles] (plural)   t. most [suggestions] (plural)

        j. any [evidence] (mass)   u. most [advice] (mass)

        k. any [card] (singular)

For these noun phrases, we need the following rule:

(30)   A noun phrase can consist of a quantity word followed by a common noun phrase.

Four sample noun-phrase trees that we get from this rule are given in (31).

(31)

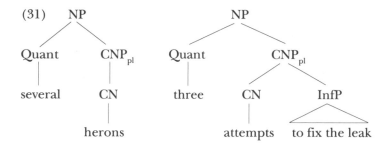

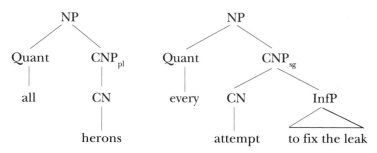

As the examples in (32) show, particular quantity words are limited as to the common noun phrases that they can take.

(32) a. *many [suggestion] (singular)   h. *one [advice] (mass)
      b. *many [advice] (mass)   i. *all [suggestion] (singular)
      c. *three [advice] (mass)   j. *each [suggestions] (plural)
      d. *three [suggestion] (singular)   k. *each [advice] (mass)
      e. *much [suggestion] (singular)   l . *every [suggestions] (plural)
      f. *much [suggestions] (plural)   m.*every [advice] (mass)
      g. *one [suggestions] (plural)   n. *most [suggestion] (singular)

Thus, each quantity word must have associated with it a specification of the one or more varieties of common noun phrases that it will accept. The specifications for several of these words are given in (33).

(33) a. MANY [— plur]   f. ANY [—plur], [—sing], [—mass]
     b. THREE [— plur]   g. ALL [— plur], [— mass]
     c. SOME [— plur], [— mass]   h. EACH [— sing]
     d. ONE [— sing]   i. EVERY [— sing]
     e. MUCH [— mass]   j. MOST [— plur], [— mass]

Two of the entries given above allow more than one type of common noun phrase: The entry for SOME allows either a plural noun or a mass noun, and the entry for ANY allows all three of the relevant types.

Exercises

1. For each of the following noun phrases, draw a detailed tree diagram.

    a. many gargoyles

    b. some people

    c. all water

    d. every picture of Fred

    e. several approaches to the problem

2. Below are listed several English nouns. With each one are two specifications. The first specification indicates whether the noun can be a count noun; the second indicates whether it can be a mass noun. Give an example to justify each of the sixteen specifications. (The justification for a "no" specification should be an *unacceptable* sentence.)

		Count noun?	Mass noun?
a.	pie	yes	yes
b.	thing	yes	no
c.	paper	yes	yes
d.	evidence	no	yes
e.	shoe	yes	no
f.	clothing	no	yes
g.	machine	yes	no
h.	equipment	no	yes

5.1.5 Bare Noun Phrases

In all the noun phrases that we have examined so far, the common noun phrase combines with some preceding word or phrase to make up a noun phrase. English also allows noun phrases in which the common noun phrase occurs without any accompanying element. Each of the sentences in (34) contains one noun phrase of this type:

(34)   a. Jock wants to buy *cookies.*

      b. Smith sells *pictures of the White House.*

      c. Horton eats *veal.*

      d. *Advice* is cheap.

The above examples are all either plural nouns or mass nouns. The sentences in (35) show that the same possibility is not available for singular nouns.

(35)   a. *Jock wants to buy *cookie.*

      b. *Smith sells *picture of the White House.*

For convenience, we will refer to noun phrases of the type in (34) as *bare noun phrases.* Their structure is given in the following rule:

(36)   A noun phrase can consist of a mass or plural common noun phrase alone.

For the italicized noun phrases in (34), this rule gives the following structures:

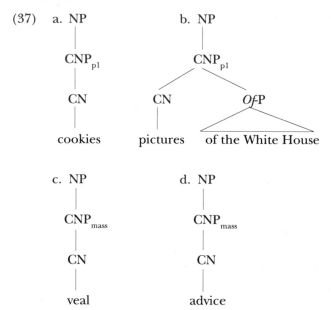

Let us turn now from the syntax of bare noun phrases to a consideration of how they are used in English. What we will find is that the simplicity of the syntactic rules for their formation is not matched by a corresponding simplicity in the set of rules for their interpretation. The next few paragraphs give a brief sketch of the possibilities.

To begin with, bare noun phrases are the most usual choice for predicate noun phrases:

(38)   a.   Your friends are *Europeans.*
        b.   This substance is *fructose.*

In addition, these noun phrases are used in so-called *generic* sentences, which convey some general truth:

(39) a. *Ostriches* are large flightless birds.
      b. *Beer* is made from barley and hops.
      c. *Pepper* makes people sneeze.

A third use is seen in sentences such as those in (40), in which habitual activities of the subjects are identified.

(40) a. John sells *shoes.*
      b. Sally brews *beer.*

A final use is seen in sentences that are neither generic nor habitual, where the use of a quantity word like unstressed *some* is also quite natural:

(41) a. Norma has *mice* in her kitchen.
      b. Norma has *some mice* in her kitchen.

(42) a. Gerald must have put *rum* in these cookies.
      b. Gerald must have put *some rum* in these cookies.

The difference in meaning between the (a) and (b) sentences in these pairs is very small, and not at all easy to describe. It seems to be primarily that the (a) sentences express something about kind but nothing about quantity. By contrast, the (b) sentences give at least a minimal indication of quantity, even if this indication only comes from *some,* the vaguest of the English quantity words.

In section 5.2, we will discover one other important use for bare noun phrases.

5.1.6 Elementary Noun Phrases Introduced by *a* or *an*
A final variety of elementary noun phrase is illustrated in (43).

(43) a. Jane found *a fossil.*
      b. Carey ate *an apple.*
      c. George met *a cousin of the king.*

These noun phrases consist of the word *a* or *an* followed by a common noun phrase.

As a preliminary matter, let us note that the choice between *a* and *an* depends completely on the first sound of the following word. If the first sound is a consonant, then *a* is used; if the first sound is a vowel, then *an* is chosen. For the operation of this rule, the actual sound is more important than the spelling. Thus, we have contrasts such as those shown in (44):

(44) a. Fred is *an only child.*
      b. We are planning *a one-year celebration.*

Despite the fact that *only* and *one* share the same first letter, the first actual sound of the word *only* is [o], whereas the first actual sound of *one* is [w].

For the purposes of syntax, then, we can think of these two words *a* and *an* as different forms of a single linguistic element. The traditional term for this element is *the indefinite article* ("Art" in tree diagrams). What we will want to consider is the question of how noun phrases introduced by this element behave in comparison with noun phrases of types that we have already studied.

In some respects, the indefinite article is similar to the numeral *one,* from which it is descended historically. Both elements are limited to common noun phrases headed by singular count nouns. This shared restriction is illustrated in (45), (46), and (47).

(45) a. Carol offered *a suggestion.* (singular count noun)
      b. Carol offered *one suggestion.*

(46) a. *Carol offered *a suggestions.* (plural count noun)
      b. *Carol offered *one suggestions.*

(47) a. *Carol offered *an advice.*   (mass noun)
      b. *Carol offered *one advice.*

Thus, at first glance, the indefinite article gives the appearance of being a special unstressed form of the numeral *one.* A careful examination, though, reveals several respects in which the article *a* or *an* differs from the numeral *one* and from other numerals. In the first place, *a* or *an* is natural in predicate noun phrases, whereas numerals are not:

(48) a. Jerry's niece is *a doctor.*
      b. ?Jerry's nieces are *seven doctors.*

In the same way, many nonpredicate noun phrases in which *a* or *an* is natural sound odd when they are introduced by *unstressed* numerals:

(49) a. Yesterday Ned succeeded in selling *a painting.*
      b. ?Yesterday Ned succeeded in selling *nine paintings.*   (with low stress on *nine*)

These examples show several contexts in which *a* or *an* is natural but numerals are not.

An observation of the opposite sort concerns certain special situations in which unstressed numerals occur naturally, as in (50).

(50) a. MY three uncles are bigger than YOUR three uncles. (low stress on *three*)

b. THESE four books are more popular than THOSE four books.
(low stress on *four*)

In such situations, we might expect that we could also use an unstressed version of *one*. But neither *one* itself nor the indefinite article is acceptable here, and the indefinite article is, if anything, worse:

(51) a ?*MY one uncle is bigger than YOUR one uncle.
  b. *MY an uncle is bigger than YOUR an uncle.

Thus, in the one situation where unstressed numerals are natural, the indefinite article is completely impossible.

If the indefinite article does not belong with the numerals, then what linguistic elements does it belong with? In a number of contexts, it appears to give rise to noun phrases that are the singular equivalents of the bare noun phrases discussed in the preceding subsection. This parallel shows up very clearly in the predicate noun phrases in (52).

(52) a. Jerry's niece is *a doctor*.   (singular predicate noun phrase)
  b. Jerry's nieces are *doctors*.   (plural predicate noun phrase)

It also shows up in the generic noun phrases in (53).

(53) a. *A hummingbird* eats constantly. (singular generic noun phrase)
  b. *Hummingbirds* eat constantly.   (plural generic noun phrase)

These examples might lead us to suppose that a noun phrase introduced by the indefinite article should just be considered a singular version of a bare noun phrase.

Other contexts exist, though, in which the indefinite article shows a closer kinship to the vague unstressed quantity word *some*. In the context of (54), for instance, a bare noun phrase is much less natural than one introduced by *some*.

(54) a. ?Yesterday Ted finally succeeded in selling *paintings*.
  b. Yesterday Ted finally succeeded in selling *some paintings*.

Even though the bare noun phrase is unnatural here, a noun phrase introduced by the indefinite article is perfectly normal-sounding:

(55)   Yesterday Ted finally succeeded in selling *a painting*.

Thus, in this instance, a singular noun phrase introduced by the indefinite article is closer to a plural introduced by *some* than it is to a bare plural.

The import of all of these observations is that the indefinite article has two distinct uses in English. In its first use, it creates singular noun phrases that correspond to the bare noun phrases of subsection 5.1.5. In its second use, it is interpreted as a singular quantity word corresponding to the unstressed *some* that occurs with plurals and mass nouns.

5.1.7 A Special Possibility for Proper Nouns

In subsection 5.1.1, proper nouns were described as "typically" appearing by themselves in noun phrases. In their most common, basic use, this is exactly what they do. The rules of English, however, also allow them to be used as if they were common nouns. This use is illustrated by (56).

(56) a. *No John Smiths* attended the meeting.
      b. *This John Smith* lives in Brookline.
      c. Greta knows *thirteen John Smiths.*
      d. I have never met *a John Smith.*

All the italicized noun phrases here have something inside them in addition to the proper noun. These examples might tempt us to believe that there is really no difference between proper nouns and common nouns. But let us see what the consequences would be if we were to drop this distinction. A first consequence is that if *John Smith* were a common noun, it would have to be a singular count noun, as its occurrence with the indefinite article in (56d) shows. But it would then go against the rule that only plural common nouns and mass common nouns can stand by themselves:

(57) a. *John Smith* issued a plea.
      b. **Minister* issued a plea. (Compare: *The minister* issued a plea.)

A second consequence is that if *John Smith* were a common noun, it should be able to occur with the definite article. The fact is that it cannot:

(58) **The John Smith* issued a plea.

The best thing to say, then, seems to be the following: Although *John Smith* may be used *as if* it were a common noun, it is in essence a member of the quite distinct class of proper nouns.

5.1.8 Some Special Combined Forms

Before leaving the topic of elementary noun phrases, we need to note the existence of some special English words that are interpreted as a combination of a quantity word and a noun. These forms are illustrated in (59).

(59) a. *Someone* did *something.*
      b. *Nobody* said *anything* to *anybody.*
      c. *Everyone* looked *everywhere.*

The four English quantity words that can serve as the first element in these combinations are *some, any, no,* and *every.* The four noun-like stems to which they can be attached are *-one, -body, -thing,* and *-where.* The first two of these (*-one* and *-body*) denote human entities; *-thing* denotes a nonhuman entity; *-where* denotes a place and is used to form locative and motion phrases.

We will refer to all these forms by the rather bulky term *quantifier-plus-noun combination,* which will be abbreviated Quant + N. Now let us add the following rule:

(60)   A noun phrase can consist of a quantifier-plus-noun combination.

This gives the following structure for the noun phrase *something:*

(61)   NP
       |
       Quant + N
       |
       something

5.2 Partitive Noun Phrases

In every noun phrase we have studied so far, the noun phrase has consisted of some syntactic element (a word or a phrase) followed directly by a common noun phrase. In this section we will examine *partitive noun phrases*—special noun-phrase constructions in which an *of* phrase figures prominently.

5.2.1 Partitive Noun Phrases Introduced by Quantity Words
For our first illustrations, let us consider a situation in which we wish to refer to a part of some plural or mass entity that we can identify by a noun phrase. In the following sets of noun phrases, the (a) phrase is just a noun phrase and the remaining examples provide illustrations of larger noun phrases denoting parts of these entities.

(62)   a.   [those suggestions]
       b.   *some* of [those suggestions]
       c.   *many* of [those suggestions]
       d.   *three* of [those suggestions]
       e.   *all* of [those suggestions]

(63) a. [George's advice]
      b. *some* of [George's advice]
      c. *much* of [George's advice]
      d. *all* of [George's advice]

For these noun phrases, we need the following rule:

(64) A noun phrase can be formed by combining a quantity word with
      an *of* phrase.

The trees in (65) show complete structures for one example each from
(62) and (63).

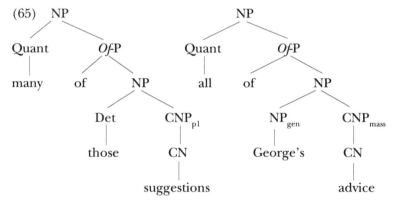

It is necessary to impose restrictions on the use of quantity words when
they occur in partitive structures, just as it was when they occurred in elementary noun phrases. For instance, we saw earlier that *many* may not
combine with a common noun phrase headed by a mass noun to make an
elementary noun phrase (*many advice*). Likewise, *many* cannot be used
in a partitive structure with a noun phrase built around a mass noun (e.g.,
many of the advice).

In one respect, however, the restrictions that hold for nonpartitive noun
phrases are different from those that hold for partitive noun phrases. The
difference is illustrated by examples involving words like *one* and *each*:

(66) a. one suggestion   c. *one of the suggestion
      b. *one suggestions   d. one of the suggestions

(67) a. each suggestion   c. *each of the suggestion
      b. *each suggestions   d. each of the suggestions

These examples show that words like *one* and *each,* which require a singular count noun in nonpartitive noun phrases, require a plural count noun when they occur with a partitive *of* phrase. Thus, as far as the partitive construction is concerned, the major division in the total class of quantity words is between those that can go with a plural noun phrase (*many, several, one, three, each*) and those that can go with a mass noun phrase (*much, less*). Several words, of course, belong to both subclasses (*some, any, none, enough*).

Exercises
1. Draw detailed tree diagrams of the following noun phrases:
    a. Much of this cheese
    b. Many of George's colleagues
    c. Few of Martha's portraits of Bill
    d. Two of Alice's sister's articles

2. All the partitive structures presented in the text have been built up from noun phrases containing either mass nouns or plural count nouns. These are by far the most commonly used nouns in partitive structures. However, it is also possible to find partitive structures built around singular count nouns, as the following sentences show:
    a. [Most of John's *boat*] has been repainted.
    b. [Some of the *record*] contained evidence of wrongdoing.
    c. [None of the *story*] has appeared in your newspaper.
Not all quantity words are acceptable with singular-count-noun partitives:
    d. *[Each of John's *boat*] has been repainted.
    e. *[Many of the *record*] contained evidence of wrongdoing.
    f. *[One of the *story*] has appeared in your newspaper.
Try to devise a general rule that dictates which quantity words allow partitives built on singular count nouns. The rule might take the following form: "If a certain quantity word ..., then it allows partitive structures based on singular count nouns." The problem is to say what "..." should be replaced by.

5.2.2 Partitive Noun Phrases Built around Measure Nouns
In the preceding subsections, we have seen several examples of English words that indicate quantity (*many, several, three,* etc.). In addition to these words, there are a large number of quantity-indicating words that are much more noun-like in their behavior, in that they themselves can be preceded by quantity words and the indefinite article. These words include common terms for weight, length, and volume (for instance,

pound, ounce, yard, inch, quart, and *pint*) and words that have an alternative use as names of containers (*bottle, can, carton,* and *bag*). We can use these words to form partitive constructions based on definite noun phrases, just as we could with *several, much,* and *three:*

(68)   a.   one *pound* of [those beans]
       b.   three *feet* of [that wire]
       c.   a *quart* of [Bob's cider]
       d.   two *cartons* of [the yogurt]
       e.   several *boxes* of [those strawberries]

The structures that we propose for these examples will be different from those proposed for quantity words. Each of these measure nouns will be treated structurally in the same way as other common nouns. In particular, each will head a common noun phrase and take an *of* phrase as a complement. An illustrative tree diagram is given in (69).

(69)

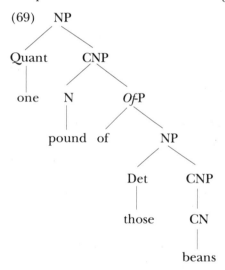

In addition to permitting *of* phrases containing definite noun phrases, measure nouns also allow *of* phrases that contain bare noun phrases:

(70)   a. one pound of [beans]
       b. three feet of [wire]
       c. a quart of [cider]
       d. two cartons of [yogurt]
       e. several boxes of [strawberries]

Here measure nouns part company with quantity words, as the unacceptable examples in (71) show.

(71) a. *many of [beans]
      b. *some of [wire]
      c. *much of [cider]
      d. *none of [yogurt]
      e. *one of [strawberries]

One possible explanation for the unacceptability of these examples is that another structure already exists for these words that does the same work—namely, the elementary structure discussed in subsection 5.1.4. In effect, the partitive noun phrases in (71) above are "crowded out" by the elementary noun phrases in (72).

(72) a. many beans
      b. some wire
      c. much cider
      d. no yogurt
      e. one strawberry

For measure nouns, the situation is different. As the examples in (73) show, they cannot occur in elementary structures (if we leave aside the special abbreviated syntax of recipes).

(73) a. *one pound beans
      b. *three feet wire
      c. *a quart cider
      d. *two cartons yogurt
      e. *several boxes strawberries

Since these measure nouns do not occur in elementary structures, there is no elementary-noun-phrase competitor for the partitive construction with a bare noun phrase. As a result, such partitive constructions are possible with measure nouns, so that *one pound of beans* and *three feet of wire* are perfectly acceptable.

Exercise
1. Draw a detailed tree diagram for each of the following noun phrases:
      a. several truckloads of furniture
      b. three bushels of those peaches
      c. two boxes of John's letters to Marsha

5.2.3 Some Defective Measure Nouns

In the last two subsections we have seen reasons for distinguishing between quantity words and measure nouns. We can summarize the differences as follows:

(74) a. Quantity words may occur in elementary noun phrases (*one book, many apples*), whereas measure nouns may not (**one pound beans, *three feet wire*).

   b. Quantity words may not occur with null-quantifier partitive structures (**one of books, *many of apples*), whereas measure nouns may (*one pound of beans, three feet of wire*).

   c. Quantity words may not be preceded by numerals (**one many of the books, *several much of the beer*), whereas measure nouns may be preceded by numerals (*one pound of the beans, three feet of the wire.*)

In this subsection, we will consider several English words whose behavior places them halfway between these two clear classes.

The first word that deserves special mention is *few*. In the use that we have already considered (*few books, few of your friends*), *few* is just an ordinary quantity word. However, it also occurs in combination with the word *a*, which gives it a somewhat noun-like appearance:

(75)   a few of your friends

Despite its article-plus-noun appearance, though, *a few* acts much more like a quantity word than like an article followed by a measure noun. In the first place, it occurs in elementary structures rather than in bare-noun-phrase partitive structures; in the second place, it cannot be preceded by other numerals and quantity words. In (76), the sequence *a few* is compared with a typical quantity word and a typical measure noun.

(76)

A few	**Quantity word**	**Measure noun**
a. a few suggestions	several suggestions	*a can tomatoes
b. *a few of suggestions	*several of suggestions	a can of tomatoes
c. *one few suggestions	*one several suggestions	one can of tomatoes

These contrasts suggest that the two-word sequence *a few* should be treated as a compound quantity word. The tree diagrams in (77) illustrate the structures that arise in this analysis.

(77)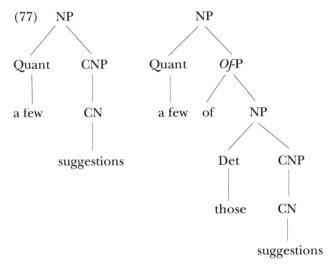

Another intermediate word is *lot*, which occurs either with the indefinite article (*a lot*) or all by itself in the plural (*lots*). Unlike *a few*, both *a lot* and *lots* occur in partitive structures rather than in elementary structures:

(78)   a.   a lot of suggestions, lots of suggestions
        b.   *a lot suggestions, *lots suggestions

However, unlike measure nouns, *lot* and *lots* may not be counted, if we ignore the special technical meaning that the word has in commercial affairs (*John bought several lots of old books*):

(79)   a.   *one lot of suggestions
        b.   *several lots of suggestions

We see a similar pattern for the word *deal* as it is used in the combinations *a good deal* and *a great deal:*

(80)   a.   a good deal of money, a great deal of money
        b.   *a good deal money, *a great deal money
        c.   *several good deals of money, *several great deals of money

In view of their similarity to measure nouns in every characteristic except the last, we will treat *lot* and *deal* as "defective" measure nouns. We will assign them structures just like those of other measure nouns:

(81)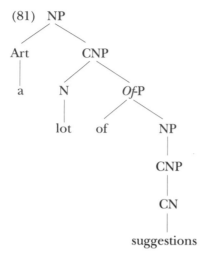

suggestions

The major difference between *lot* and the ordinary measure nouns is that *lot* has no independent meaning as a noun; it must combine with *a* or with the plural marker to make a fixed idiom. Because of its lack of an independent meaning, any attempt to preface it with other quantity words results in a combination that has no meaning attached to it.

Another class of words whose behavior leaves them somewhere between quantity words and measure nouns consists of number words such as *dozen*, *hundred*, and *thousand*. These words are like measure nouns in their capacity to be preceded by numerals and quantity words:

(82)   a. one dozen of your eggs
       b. one hundred of his books

Yet even here, they are peculiar in requiring a singular form even when the word before them would ordinarily require a plural noun:

(83)   a.   three hundred of your friends
       b. *three hundreds of your friends

(84)   a.   several thousand of Karen's supporters
       b. *several thousands of Karen's supporters

In addition, they are like quantity words and unlike measure nouns in that they occur in elementary noun phrases rather than in bare-noun-phrase partitives:

(85)   a. one dozen roses   *one dozen of roses
       b. three hundred friends   *three hundred of friends
       c. several thousand supporters *several thousand of supporters

Even here, though, there is a complication. These words may all be used in plural form when not preceded by a quantity word (*dozens, hundreds, thousands,* etc.). When occurring in the plural, they require partitive structures rather than elementary structures:

(86) a. dozens of roses   *dozens roses
      b. hundreds of friends   *hundreds friends
      c. thousands of supporters *thousands supporters

Exercise

1. *Number* and *bunch* are two more examples of English words that allow partitive structures:

      a. A number of letters were sent.

      b. A bunch of Joe's friends attended his funeral.

Construct some experimental sentences that will provide evidence indicating how *a number* and *a bunch* behave. In particular, do they resemble *a few, a lot,* or *a(n)* plus a measure noun?

5.2.4 A Special Compound Structure: *All* + Numeral

The quantity word *all* can combine with a following numeral to form a two-word sequence which itself has the force of a quantity word. The partitive noun phrases italicized in (87) provide examples.

(87) a. *All four of your sons* are geniuses.
      b. Gordon ate *all thirteen of the pancakes.*

These special forms are subject to the following rule:

(88) A special compound quantity structure can be formed by combining *all* with a numeral.

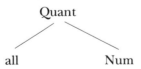

The tree diagram in (89) shows the structure of the noun phrase in (87a) that contains a compound quantity structure.

(89)

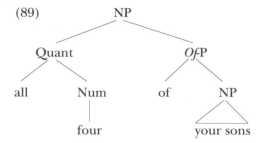

Besides being special in its own right, this combination of *all* and a numeral enters into a special larger structure, illustrated in (90).

(90) a. *All four lions* eat meat.
      b. George replied to *all three letters.*

An obvious structure for these noun phrases is one in which they are treated as elementary noun phrases:

(91) a.   b.

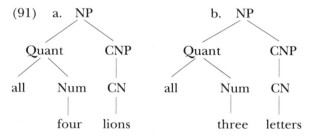

Although these seem to be perfectly ordinary structures, their interpretation is not ordinary at all. Unlike the partitive examples discussed in the preceding subsection, the omission of the numeral from the sentences in (90) changes their interpretations quite drastically:

(92) a. *All lions* eat meat.
      b. George replied to *all letters.*

In order to get close paraphrases of the sentences in (90), we need to resort to partitive noun phrases:

(93) a. *All four of the lions* eat meat.
      b. George replied to *all three of the letters.*

Thus, noun phrases such as *all four lions* have the odd property of being elementary in form, but partitive in interpretation.

5.2.5 Special Noun Phrases Introduced by *All* and *Both*

As was noted in subsection 5.2.1, *all* is like other quantity words in its capacity to occur in partitive noun phrases:

(94)   a.   Karen met *all of the senators.*
       b.   Joseph insulted *all of Fred's cousins.*

As a special extra possibility, *all* can occur with the same following definite noun phrases, but without any intervening *of:*

(95)   a.   Karen met *all the senators.*
       b.   Joseph insulted *all Fred's cousins.*

Here again we clearly have noun phrases with a partitive interpretation. These examples appear to call for the following rule:

(96)   A noun phrase can consist of the quantity word *all* followed by a noun phrase.

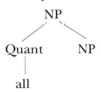

This rule gives rise to the following structures for the italicized noun phrases in (95):

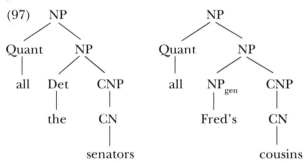

The last special structure to be dealt with involves the word *both.* In addition to the regular partitive structure illustrated in (98a), *both* appears in the structure illustrated in (98b).

(98)   a.   Karen fed *both of the alligators.*
       b.   Karen fed *both alligators.*

Just as was the case with *all four lions,* we have a structure that is elementary in form, but partitive in interpretation. The structure for *both alligators* is diagrammed in (99).

(99)   NP

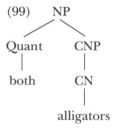

Quant   CNP
  | |
 both   CN
           |
        alligators

5.3 The Use of the Definite Article

Now that we have examined the structures of a variety of types of noun phrases, including structures introduced by the determiner *the,* let us look briefly at the conditions under which this particular word must be used in English. The word *the* is one of the most common words in the English language. In even a short conversation, a fluent speaker in effect decides many times whether or not to use it. Decades of linguistic research have shown that the unconscious rules responsible for the use of this word require complex calculations on the part of speakers and hearers. Besides being a source of challenging puzzles for linguists, these complexities have been a source of grief for many adult learners of English. The following paragraphs will give a brief summary of the most central of the rules involved.

Before going to particular cases, let us consider an abstract characterization of the situation in which a decision concerning the definite article must be made. Typically, the speaker has in mind an *intended set* of one or more persons or objects—the individual(s) that the speaker wishes to refer to. The speaker also has in mind a *description*—in the form of a common noun phrase—that is satisfied by the members of this intended set. The speaker's decision concerning the definite article depends on the relation between the intended set and some *established set* connected with the same description. More will be said about how an established set is determined; right now, we will simply note that the definite article can and must be used when the intended set and the established set are identical. Such a situation is depicted in (100).

(100) established set: ▮▮▮▮▮▮▮▮▮▮   intended set: ▭▭▭▭▭▭
       intended set equals established set
       definite article required

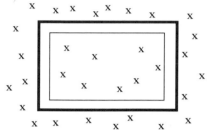

On the other hand, the definite article cannot be used if no established set exists, or if the intended set includes only some of the members of the established set. The diagrams in (101) depict these two situations.

(101) a. no established set;   b. intended set smaller;
          definite acticle disallowed   definite article disallowed

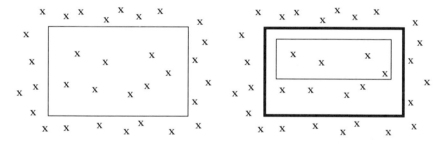

The use of the definite article is complicated by the task of determining what can count as an established set in various conversational contexts.

Let us begin our examination of particular cases by imagining a situation of the simplest type: one in which there is no previous conversational context. The intended set that the speaker is thinking of consists of one hundred persons, all of them current U.S. senators; the description he or she has in mind is just *current U.S. senators*. The rule that determines an established set in this situation is a simple one:

(102) In the absence of any previous context, the set consisting of all of the individuals that satisfy the description can count as an established set.

In the example under discussion, the set of all the current U.S. senators can count as an established set. The relation between this established set and the intended set is depicted in (103).

(103)

```
┌─────────────────────────┐
│ ┌───────────────────┐   │
│ │ XXXXXXXXXXXXXXXXX  │   │
│ │ XXXXXXXXXXXXXXXXX  │   │
│ │ XXXXXXXXXXXXXXXXX  │   │
│ │ XXXXXXXXXXXXXXXXX  │   │
│ │ XXXXXXXXXXXXXXXXX  │   │
│ └───────────────────┘   │
└─────────────────────────┘
```

Because the two sets coincide exactly, the speaker can and must use the definite article in a sentence like (104).

(104) I know the names of [$_{NP}$ *the* current U.S. senators].

Knowing the rule that the speaker must have used here, the hearer can infer that the speaker's intended set contains all the current U.S. senators.

Suppose now that there is again no significant previous conversational context, but that this time the intended set consists of only sixty of the current U.S. senators:

(105)

```
┌─────────────────────────┐
│ ┌───────────────────┐   │
│ │ XXXXXXXXXXXXXXXXX  │   │
│ │ XXXXXXXXXXXXXXXXX  │   │
│ │ XXXXXXXXXXXXXXXXX  │   │
│ └───────────────────┘   │
│   XXXXXXXXXXXXXXXXX      │
│   XXXXXXXXXXXXXXXXX      │
└─────────────────────────┘
```

With this new intended set, the definite article would be unacceptable, since some individuals that are members of the established set lie outside the intended set. Instead, the description *current U.S. senators* would have to be preceded by some quantity word as in (106).

(106) a. I know the names of [$_{NP}$ *several* current U.S. senators].
       b. I know the names of [$_{NP}$ *sixty* current U.S. senators].

When the previous conversational context is nonexistent and the definite article is used with a singular count noun, the same sort of calculation yields a clear implication that the individual in the set is the only one that satisfies the description. We see the effects of this implication in the contrast between (107a), where the implication is warranted, and (107b), where it is not.

(107) a. [$_{NP}$The Chief Justice of the Supreme Court] is related to George.
       b. ??[$_{NP}$The Supreme Court Justice] is related to George.

The basis for this difference in acceptability is shown in (108).

(108) a.

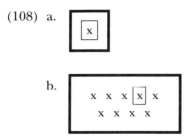

b.

In (108a), no individuals satisfying the description lie outside the intended set, whereas in (108b) this condition is not satisfied. Hence (107a) is acceptable in this situation, and (107b) is not.

Our discussion so far has been limited to situations in which there is no previous conversational context. As was noted above, in such situations the set of all individuals that satisfy the description in question can constitute an established set. The discourse in (109) provides an initial example of a definite article that is interpreted with regard to a different kind of established set.

(109)   Sarah gave a geography questionnaire to *twenty senators* and twenty representatives. Not a single one of *the senators* was able to name the capital of Wyoming.

In this discourse, the noun phrase *the senators* is most plausibly taken to refer not to the set of all one hundred U.S. senators, but instead to a different set: one consisting of the twenty senators referred to in the preceding sentence. Thus, the noun phrase *twenty senators* in the first sentence serves to create a special established set, one that takes precedence over the set of all one hundred senators. The following definite article is then interpreted with regard to this less inclusive, conversationally derived established set. This situation is depicted in (110).

(110)

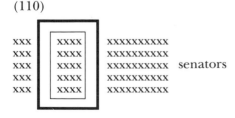

Many other small discourses can be constructed in which noun phrases serve to establish sets, which may later serve as established sets for the interpretation of definite articles. Here are several more examples:

(111) a. George found *several bananas* on the counter and *two apples* in the
           refrigerator. *The bananas* were green, but *the apples* were ripe.
       b. Gordon ate *some vegetables* and drank some beer. He blamed the
           resulting stomach ache on *the vegetables*.

The interpretation of the definite article before *apples* in (111a) is diagrammed in (112).

(112)

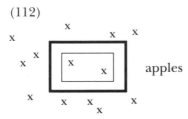

apples

In the extreme case, the noun phrase that creates the established set is
singular and thus separates out just one individual:

(113) a. On the way to market, Smith met *a cat* and a dog. *The cat* was
           playing a fiddle.
       b. Yesterday *one of Jones's dogs* picked a fight with Fred's cat. Only
           the intervention of the milkman kept *the dog* from getting killed.

The diagram in (114) indicates the basis for the use of the definite article
before *cat* in (113a).

(114)

cat

The following discourse shows another way in which a conversational
context may establish a set that requires the use of a definite article:

(115) We just received *five old Studebakers* today. I told Jonah to check *the
       carburetors* before he did anything else.

Here, at first glance, it would appear that the only set established in the first
sentence is a set consisting of the five old Studebakers. With the establishment of that set, however, a number of other sets are established implicitly,
in a kind of parasitic operation on the set of cars. For a normal set of five
old Studebakers, these implicit sets include the following, among many
others:

(116) a. a set of five carburetors
       b. a set of five cigarette lighters
       c. a set of ten headlights
       d. a set of twenty wheels

Each of these implicitly established sets can require a definite article in the same manner that the set of old Studebakers did. Just as with the established sets mentioned above, the speaker's intended set must be identical to the established set. Thus, for instance, the noun phrase *the carburetors* in (115) must be taken to refer to the set consisting of the carburetors in all five of the cars, not just those in two or three of them:

(117)

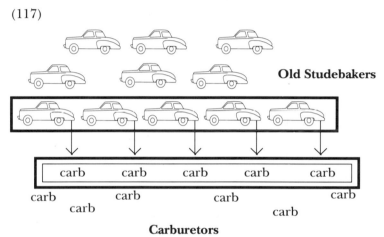

One final type of established set is illustrated by the examples in (118), each of which we can imagine hearing without any preceding discourse to establish a set.

(118) a. Do you know what *the mayor* did yesterday?
       b. Did Mabel feed *the parakeet?*
       c. *The children* are younger than Phil's cousin.

Such examples are natural when an obvious set satisfying the description is provided by the external setting in which the discourse takes place. For instance, *the mayor* might naturally refer to the mayor of the town in which the speaker lived or was located, whereas *the parakeet* might naturally refer to a family pet. Likewise, *the children* could be used to refer to the children in the speaker's family, or just to the children in the speaker's immediate environment. Just as with established sets of the other types, the intended sets here must coincide exactly with these externally established sets.

Thus, if there are four children in the externally established set in (118c), all four of them must be younger than the Phil's cousin in order for the definite article to be used. Among the established sets of this last type are those that have some kind of special, permanent place in the human environment. The noun phrases *the sun, the moon, the sky,* and *the stars* are just a few of the many examples of this type.

The discussion in this section has been limited to an outline of the most important use of the definite article. Other, more special uses exist, some of which are illustrated by the following exercises.

Exercises

1. In Austin, Texas, a city with several major hospitals, the following discourse would be perfectly natural:

Speaker A: Did you hear the news? John is in the hospital.

Speaker B: Which hospital?

Speaker A: He's at Saint David's.

Explain why the definite article with the noun *hospital* is unexpected, in view of what was said in the discussion above. What would the discussion have led you to expect? What special rule could be given for this case? (This use of the definite article is characteristic only of American English; the British equivalent would be *John is in hospital.*)

2. The following examples illustrate some special situations in which the definite article is required and some special situations in which it is forbidden:

a. the Mississippi River	*Mississippi River
b. the Wabash River	*Wabash River
c. the James River	*James River
c. *the Clear Lake	Clear Lake
d. *the Walden Pond	Walden Pond
e. *the Waller Creek	Waller Creek
f. the Great Smoky Mountains	*Great Smoky Mountains
g. the Adirondacks	*Adirondacks
h. *the Lookout Mountain	Lookout Mountain
i. *the Nob Hill	Nob Hill

Try to state some informal general rules that give correct results for these cases.

5.4 The Gerundive Construction

We turn, finally, to an English construction whose external behavior identifies it as a noun phrase but whose internal organization resembles that of a sentence. Structures of this sort, which will be referred to as *gerundives,* are illustrated in (119).

(119) a. We regret *your having called the police.*
b. *Martha's getting a splinter in her toe* annoyed Sally.
c. *The mayor's admitting the theft* was inconvenient for Stuart.

In each of these examples, the italicized phrase consists of two parts. The first part is a noun phrase in the genitive form; the second is a present-participial verb phrase. The two parts for the gerundives given in (119) are listed in (120).

(120) **Genitive Noun Phrase**   **Present-Participial Verb Phrase**
a. your   having called the police
b. Martha's   getting a splinter in her toe
c. the mayor's   admitting the theft

Gerundives may also appear without the genitive noun phrase, as the examples in (121) show.

(121) a. We regret *having called the police.*
c. *Getting a splinter in her toe* annoyed Sally.
d. *Admitting the theft* was inconvenient for Stuart.

We can thus state the following rule:

(122) A *gerundive phrase* can consist either of a genitive noun phrase plus a present participial verb phrase, or of a present-participial verb phrase alone.

Translating the two possibilities in this rule into tree diagrams, we get the two structures diagrammed in (123).

(123) a. Gerundive   b. Gerundive

The external behavior of gerundive phrases is different in several major respects from the external behavior of the clauses that we studied in chapter 4. In the first place, gerundives do not appear as pseudocomplements linked to the substitute subject *it.* For example, of the two examples in (125), each of which corresponds to one of the unpostponed examples in (124), only the first is completely natural.

(124) a. *That John went to town* surprised us.
     b. *John's going to town* surprised us.

(125) a. *It* surprised us *that John went to town.*
     b. ?*It* surprised us *John's going to town.*

To the extent that (125b) is acceptable at all, it is because of the possibility (which exists even for ordinary noun phrases) of using a pronoun as subject and then, as an afterthought, identifying it by a full noun phrase set off by a special intonation at the end of the sentence:

(126) a. *It* bit me on the ankle, *the raccoon that Fred gave me for my birthday.*
     b. *They* were very helpful, *the people who operate the sawmill.*

This afterthought interpretation and intonation, which is essential for this construction, is necessary to make (125b) acceptable. Thus, an acceptable version of (125b) should be written with a comma, as in (127), just as commas were used in the sentences in (126).

(127) *It* surprised us, *John's going to town.*

No such special interpretation or intonation is involved in sentences like (125a).

   A second external property of gerundives that they share with ordinary noun phrases but not with clauses has to do with their appearance as complements of adjectives. Certain adjectives that can directly take clauses as complements can take noun phrases only indirectly, with the help of the preposition *of:*

(128) a. Sandra is uncertain *that Fred is competent.*
     b. Sandra is uncertain *how competent Fred is.*

(129) a. *Sandra is uncertain Fred's competence.
     b. Sandra is uncertain of Fred's competence.

Here the gerundives pattern with the ordinary noun phrases rather than with the clauses:

(130) a. *Sandra is uncertain Fred's being competent.
     b. Sandra is uncertain of Fred's being competent.

   A final property that gerundives share with ordinary noun phrases is the ability to appear in various sentence-internal positions in which clauses are unacceptable. The unacceptable examples in (131) are taken from subsection 4.2.5; corresponding examples with gerundives are given in (132).

(131) a. *Dorothy considers *that the problem is elementary* obvious.
       b. *Was *that the money had vanished* obvious?
       c. *Sarah wonders whether *that the money had vanished* was obvious.

(132) a. Dorothy considers *Bill's keeping his fish in the bathtub* quite
            unimportant.
       b. Was *Bill's keeping his fish in the bathtub* really important?
       c. Sarah wonders whether *Bill's keeping his fish in the bathtub* was
            really important.

Because of these respects in which the external behavior of gerundives is like that of ordinary noun phrases, we will classify gerundives as noun phrases. Thus, the following tree diagrams will be adopted for sentences containing this construction.

(133) a.

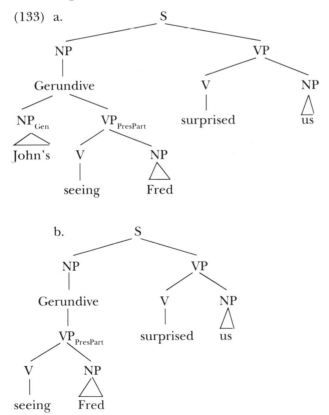

Exercises

1. Draw tree diagrams for the following sentences:
    a. Karen's catching the error prevented the destruction of the corporation.
    b. Joe believed that Bernice's feeding the llamas would make the donkeys jealous.
    c. Joe maintains that cleaning chimneys keeps him young.

2. Some of the present-participial verb phrases that occur without genitive noun phrases clearly deserve to be classified as gerundives. For instance, we would call the italicized phrase in (i) below a gerundive, since the longer phrase italicized in (ii) is possible in the same environment:

    (i) *Riding in the Derby* disturbed Martha.
    (ii) *John's riding in the Derby* disturbed Martha.

However, in other environments, only the verb phrase by itself is acceptable:

    (iii) Janet kept *asking for a doctor.*
    (iv) *Janet kept *Bill's asking for a doctor.*

These two examples would lead us to say that the verb KEEP takes present-participial verb phrases rather than that it takes gerundives. For each of the following verbs, construct a sentence that shows that the verb can be followed by a present-participial verb phrase. Then construct a sentence that shows whether it should be viewed as taking gerundives or only as taking present-participial verb phrases.

    a. CONTINUE   c. BEGIN
    b. REPORT   d. REGRET

Chapter 6

Locative Phrases, Motion Phrases, and Particles

Chapter 3 included some brief remarks about what were referred to as *locative phrases* and *motion phrases*. The purpose at that point was to say just enough to make it possible to talk about verbal environments. For instance, we needed to be able to say that *go* went together with a motion phrase to make a verb phrase, whereas *put* made a verb phrase by combining with a noun phrase and a locative phrase. We noted a few examples of each type of phrase, without looking at the rules for forming them.

6.1 Basic Structures of Locative and Motion Phrases

Perhaps the best way to get an initial idea of the richness of English constructions of these types is to look at a particular collection of examples. The examples in (1) happen to be locative phrases. With a different verb (*took*, for example), an exactly parallel collection of motion phrases could be listed.

(1) Joe put the jar

a. right	back	out	here	in the yard.
b. ——	back	in	there	in the house.
c. right	——	up	here	on the shelf.
d. ——	——	out	there	in the pasture.
e. right	——	——	here	in the refrigerator.
f. ——	——	——	here	in the yard.
g. right	back	——	there	under the cottonwood.
h. ——	back	——	here	in the kitchen.
i. right	back	up	——	in the attic.
j. ——	back	down	——	in the cellar.

k. —— back —— —— in the yard.

l. right back in here ——.

m.right back —— here ——.

n. right —— —— here ——.

All fourteen of the phrases in this list are constructed by combining five elements:

- the word *right*
- the particle *back*, indicating return to a location occupied earlier, or else movement toward or position in the rear of some entity
- particles such as *in, out, up,* and *down,* which suggest an implicit contrast relative to some other location
- *here* or *there,* which indicate relative proximity to the speaker
- a prepositional phrase that specifies an absolute location of some kind.

All five of these elements are optional, except that at least one of the last four has to be present.

With these phrases—in contrast with many of the other phrasal constructions that we have studied—it is difficult to single out one element that is more essential to the phrase than any other, and that can thus be identified as the head. In the absence of any clear evidence for a more detailed picture of the structure of these phrases, we will assume that these phrases can be divided into two basic parts. The first part is an optional occurrence of the word *right*; the second is a sequence constructed from the remaining four elements.

(2)   A locative phrase or a motion phrase can consist of a locative sequence (LocSeq) or a motion sequence (MotSeq), optionally preceded by the word *right.*

(3)   A locative or motion sequence can consist of one or more of the following parts, in the order given:
        the particle *back*
        a directional particle
        here or *there*
        a prepositional phrase headed by a preposition of location or motion.

These two rules give structures of the sort diagrammed in (4):

(4)   a. LocP

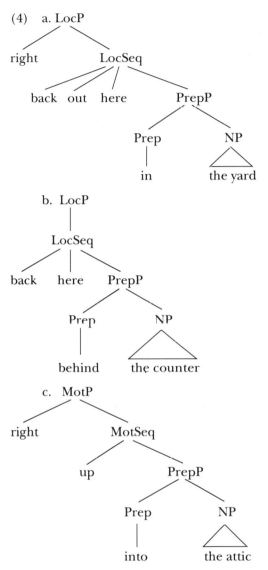

At this point, an alternative analysis in which a sentence like (5) is analyzed as containing four separate motion phrases instead of just one might appear attractive.

(5)   John came   *back*   *out*   *here*   *into the yard.*

On this alternative analysis, the structure of the verb phrase in this sentence would look like (6).

(6)

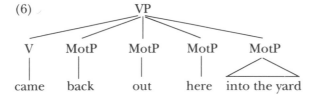

The chief attraction of this view is that each of the parts can appear alone as a motion phrase in its own right:

(7) a. John came *back.*
     b. John came *out.*
     c. John came *here.*
     d. John came *into the yard.*

Despite the initial plausibility of this analysis, there are at least two important reasons for viewing *back out here into the yard* as a single phrase in (5). The first is that if each element were really a separate locative phrase in its own right, we would expect a high degree of freedom in the order in which the various elements appeared. In fact we do not find this, as (8) shows.

(8) a. John came   *here*   out   back   *into the yard.*
     b. John came   *into the yard*   out   here   back.

The second reason for viewing *back out here into the yard* as a single motion phrase is that we can then account for the fact that the whole sequence can move to the front of sentences containing motion verbs such as *come* and *go*, whereas smaller parts cannot move. The sentences in (9) show this.

(9) a. *Back out here into the yard* came John.
     b. **Here into the yard* came John *back out.*
     c. **Into the yard* came John *back out here.*

6.2 A Special Ordering Rule for Particles

One syntactic property of certain locative and motion phrases requires special attention. When the locative or motion phrase occurs with the object of a transitive verb, the rules given so far would position it after the object. In some instances, however, we find a different order. In (10) and (11), each (a) example shows the normal order and each (b) example shows what we will call the "shifted order."

(10) a. Joe took the garbage *out.*
      b. Joe took *out* the garbage.

(11) a.   We carried the money *back*.
  b.   We carried *back* the money.

The tree diagrams in (12) show the contrast between the normal order and the shifted order.

(12) a.   Normal Order   b.   Shifted Order

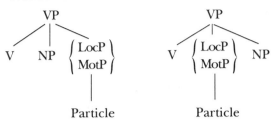

Use of the shifted order is subject to a severe restriction: This order is possible only when the locative or motion phrase consists solely of a particle. The results of violating this restriction are shown in the unacceptable (b) sentences in (13)–(15).

(13) a.   Joe took the garbage *back out*.
  b.   *Joe took *back out* the garbage.

(14) a.   We carried the money *right back*.
  b.   *We carried *right back* the money.

(15) a.   Fred brought some apples *over here*.
  b.   *Fred brought *over here* some apples.

A second condition limiting the shifted word order concerns the object: The particle can be put next to the verb only when the object is not a pronoun. The sentences in (16) and (17) show the contrast between full noun phrases and pronouns as direct objects with shifted particles.

(16) a.   Joe brought *Marsha* in.
  b.   Joe brought in *Marsha*.
  c.   Joe brought *her* in.
  d.   *Joe brought in *her*.

(17) a.   We put *the refrigerator* back.
  b.   We put back *the refrigerator*.
  c.   We put *it* back.
  d.   *We put back *it*.

The sentences in (18) show that it is only *unstressed* pronouns that prevent the shift of the particle.

(18) a. Janice called HIM up.
      b. Janice called up HIM.

This restriction may be a special case of a more general English regularity, to the effect that unstressed pronoun objects cannot be separated from their verbs by anything. Another contrast of this kind is evident in (19).

(19) a.   Jane gave the book to Freddy.
      b.   Jane gave Freddy the book.
      c.   Jane gave it to Freddy.
      d. *Jane gave Freddy it.

Here the noun phrase *the book* can come directly after the verb, as in (19a), or else can be separated from the verb by the indirect object *Freddy*, as in (19b). By contrast, the pronoun *it* has the first option, as in (19c), but does not have the second, as in (19d).

Exercise
1. Draw a tree diagram for each of the following sentences:
      a.   Joanna took the packages out.
      b.   Jasper brought in the wine.
      c.   The sheriff followed us in.

6.3 Verb+Particle Idioms

In all the sentences in which we have seen particles, they have been serving as elements of either locative phrases or motion phrases. Particles used in this way contribute a regular and predictable element of meaning to the sentences in which they occur. In addition, though, we find in English many instances in which particles combine with verbs to give *idiomatic expressions*—expressions whose meanings are not easily deduced from the meanings of the parts. Some intransitive combinations are given in (20), some transitive examples in (21).

(20) a.   Donna *sounded off*. ('Donna stated her opinions forcefully.')
      b.   Frank *threw up*. ('Frank vomited.')
      c.   James *flunked out*. ('James was expelled from school for an excessive number of low grades.')

(21) a.   Ruth *sounded* her brother *out*. ('Ruth elicited her brother's opinions.')
      b.   Sidney *called* his boss *up*. ('Sidney called his boss on the telephone.')

    c. Joe *called* the meeting *off.* ('Joe canceled the meeting.')

    d. Kevin *knocked* Gregory *out.* ('Kevin rendered Gregory unconscious.')

Syntactically, these particles are almost exactly like those that serve as locative or motion phrases. In particular, in a transitive verb phrase they can be shifted to a position immediately after the verb when the object is not a pronoun:

(22) a. Ruth *sounded out* her brother.

      b. Sidney *called up* his boss.

      c. Joe *called off* the meeting.

      d. Kevin *knocked out* Gregory.

Verbs that participate in idioms such as these require environmental specifications that mention individual particles:

(23) a. SOUND: [—*off*]

      b. THROW: [—*up*]

      c. FLUNK: [—*out*]

(24) a. SOUND: [—NP *out*]

      b. CALL: [—NP *up*]

      c. CALL: [—NP *off*]

      d. KNOCK: [—NP *out*]

In addition to these special complement specifications, these idioms require special semantic statements about the unpredictable meanings of the verb phrases in which they appear.

Exercise

1. For each of the following sentences, decide whether (i) the particle that it contains is a locative or motion phrase, or (ii) it is part of an idiomatic verb+particle combination. (For some of the examples, the answer may be that it could be either one.) Give a brief justification for each of your answers.

    a. The airplane took off.

    b. George took his jacket off.

    c. Nancy carried it in.

    d. Sherman carried out Grant's orders.

    e. Jeremy blended in the raisins.

    f. Jerry rubbed out his competitors.

    g. Sandra strolled out.

    h. Terry struck out.

    i.   Florence put it down.

    j.   George kept it up.

6.4 Distinguishing Shifted Particles from Prepositions

Because of the possibility of putting particles between transitive verbs and their objects, two different structures can arise which yield similar sequences of words:

(25) a. Shifted particle structure   b. Intransitive prepositional structure

The sentences in (26) illustrate the kind of practical problem that can arise.

(26) a. Nina brought in the armchair.

      b. Nina sat in the armchair.

For each of these two sentences, two questions arise:

- Can it have the shifted particle structure?
- Can it have the intransitive prepositional structure?

As with many of the practical problems that we have studied previously, attempting to answer these questions about the particular sentences in (26) forces us to ask the corresponding questions about the relevant verbs:

- Does such-and-such a verb allow a shifted particle structure?
- Does such-and-such a verb allow an intransitive prepositional structure?

Let us begin by asking the first question about each of these sentences in turn. The key experiment depends on something that we already know about particles: If a word is truly a left-shifted particle, then putting it back on the right side of the object should yield an acceptable sentence. The results we obtain when we try this experiment with the original sentences are given in (27).

(27) a. Nina brought the armchair in.

      b. *Nina sat the armchair in.

From these results we can conclude that BRING can occur in the shifted particle configuration in (25a), whereas SIT cannot. This, of course, gives an immediate answer to the corresponding question about the two individual sentences in (26): We can have the particle construction in (26a), but we cannot have it in (26b). As it happens, the affirmative answer to the particle question in the case of (26a) follows from two simple facts of a more general sort:

- BRING has the specification [—NP MotP].
- A motion phrase can consist of the particle *in*.

Let us now ask our second question: Can the sequence of words *in the armchair* be analyzed as a prepositional phrase in our two sentences? One of the rules that we discussed above can help us to answer this question. As we noted, a particle cannot come between a verb and a pronoun object. Thus, whenever *in*+pronoun appears and the sentence is acceptable, we know that the sequence can only be a prepositional phrase. To see whether BRING and SIT occur in the prepositional structure shown in (25b), we can just change the noun phrase in each original example into a pronoun:

(28) a. *Nina brought in it.
      b. Nina sat in it.

From these results we can conclude that SIT can appear in the intransitive prepositional structure, whereas BRING cannot. This conclusion clearly implies that only the second of the sentences in (26) can have the intransitive prepositional structure.

For some speakers of English, this last test is difficult to apply, since it rests on a rather subtle judgment. Another test can be used to determine whether a certain verb allows a prepositional structure. This test relies on properties of a construction that we will be talking about in chapter 10, the *bound-relative-clause* construction. The main fact of interest for us right now is that a prepositional structure allows the formation of a relative clause in which the preposition stands at the beginning of the relative clause, whereas a particle can never introduce this construction. We see this in (29) and (30), where (a) is a sentence and (b) is a noun phrase modified by a relative clause.

(29) a. Nina brought in the chair.
      b. *the chair [in which Nina brought]

(30) a. Nina sat in the chair.
      b. the chair [in which Nina sat]

The unacceptability of (29b) shows that *in* cannot be a preposition in (29a), whereas the acceptability of (30b) shows that *in* can be a preposition in (30a). The results of this second test yield exactly the same conclusion as the results of the first test: *in the chair* can be a prepositional phrase after SIT but not after BRING.

Before leaving this topic, let us ask the same two questions about one additional example:

(31) Conrad looked over the newspaper.

To see whether *over* could be a shifted particle here, we construct a sentence in which the order of particle and noun phrase is reversed:

(32) Conrad looked the newspaper over.

The acceptability of (32) shows that (31) can have the shifted particle structure. Going on to the question of whether *over* could be a preposition in this sentence, we try replacing *the newspaper* by a pronoun:

(33) Conrad looked over it.

The acceptability of (33) shows that (31) can also have the intransitive prepositional structure. If we had any doubt about our judgment of this sentence, we could apply the other prepositional test:

(34) the newspaper [over which Conrad looked]

Here again, the acceptability of the result indicates that the intransitive prepositional structure is one in which LOOK can appear. Thus, we are led to conclude that (31) can have either of two structures. This structural ambiguity is associated with a corresponding semantic ambiguity: Conrad can be examining the newspaper (the interpretation that goes with the shifted particle structure) or he can be looking over the top of the newspaper (the interpretation that goes with the intransitive prepositional structure).

The point of this particular example, then, is that some sentences can have both the shifted particle structure and the intransitive prepositional structure. One practical consequence is that a Yes answer to either of our two questions does not necessarily imply that the answer to the other is No. Thus, for instance, we cannot use an affirmative result on the particle test to justify a negative answer to the prepositional question. Likewise, we cannot conclude from an affirmative result on one of the two preposition tests that the sentence cannot have the particle structure. This possibility of ambiguity, then, provides the reason why we always need to ask the two questions separately.

Exercise

1. In each of the following sentences, answer two questions:

- Can the sentence be analyzed as having the shifted particle structure?
- Can it be analyzed as having the intransitive prepositional structure?

Indicate how you decided on each answer.

a. Jonah stayed on the platform.
b. Holmes called in the inspector.
c. Freddy ate up the cookies.
d. Horace carried out the orders.
e. The manager spoke over the intercom.
f. Pete rolled over the barrel.
g. Over which barrel did Pete roll?
h. James pulled on it.

Chapter 7
Free Relative Clauses

In this chapter, we turn our attention to two major constructions that help to fill out various phrase types in English. These phrase types include noun phrases very prominently, but they also include adjective phrases, locative and motion phrases, time phrases, and a variety of other types. The two constructions will be grouped under the single term *free relative clause*. The first will be referred to as *definite*, the second as *indefinite*.

7.1 Definite Free Relative Clauses

The first of the free relative constructions is illustrated in (1).

(1) a. Karen ate [what Fred offered to her].
    b. [What Harry fixed for Sally] went into the trash.

A close look at the bracketed sequences reveals that each consists of two parts. The first part is just the single word *what*. The second part is a sequence that sounds like an incomplete independent sentence:

(2) a. *Fred offered to her.
    b. *Harry fixed for Sally.

Each of these sentences is incomplete by virtue of needing one more noun phrase than it actually has. When the word *something* is inserted after *offered* and after *fixed*, the sentences become perfectly acceptable:

(3) a. Fred offered *something* to her.
    b. Harry fixed *something* for Sally.

Thus, a better representation for the sequences that come after *what* in (1) would include blanks to indicate the position of missing noun phrases:

(4) a. Fred offered ___ to her.
    b. Harry fixed ___ for Sally.

These representations show clearly that this is a construction based on a sentence with a missing noun phrase. Thus, the structure of these examples might be represented as in (5).

(5)

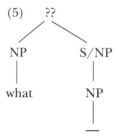

We have seen sequences like this before; they look exactly like the indirect questions discussed in chapter 4.

7.1.1 Definite Free Relative Clauses Contrasted with Indirect Questions

Given this striking resemblance between the bracketed sequences in (1) and the indirect questions studied earlier, we might be tempted to wonder whether the present sequences really represent a new construction. What reasons are there to believe that they are not indirect questions?

If we look just at the two sequences in isolation, we find no grounds for viewing them as anything other than indirect questions:

(6) a. [what Fred offered to her]
    b. [what Harry fixed for Sally]

The rules that we developed in chapter 4 for indirect questions definitely allow the creation of these sequences. Thus, we will not be able to call the bracketed sequences in (1) something other than indirect questions on the basis of their internal structure.

When we we turn our attention to the external behavior of these sequences, one striking fact becomes immediately apparent: These sequences are found in positions that do not allow a broad range of indirect questions. This fact becomes clear when we try to substitute other indirect questions in place of the bracketed sequences:

(7) a. *Karen ate $\left\{\begin{array}{l}\text{which dish Norton served her.}\\ \text{whose turnips Bill had bought.}\\ \text{how much pasta Fred offered her}\end{array}\right\}$

    b. $\left\{\begin{array}{l}\text{*Which dish Norton served her}\\ \text{*Whose turnips Bill had bought}\\ \text{*How much pasta Fred offered her}\end{array}\right\}$ went into the trash.

These sets of examples contrast sharply with the corresponding sets in which *knew* is used instead of *ate*, and *was unclear* is used instead of *went into the garbage*:

(8) a. *Karen knew $\left\{\begin{array}{l}\text{which dish Norton served her.}\\ \text{whose turnips Bill had bought.}\\ \text{how much pasta Fred offered her.}\end{array}\right\}$

b. $\left\{\begin{array}{l}\text{Which dish Norton served her}\\ \text{Whose turnips Bill had bought}\\ \text{How much pasta Fred offered her}\end{array}\right\}$ went into the trash.

The simplest account of these substantial differences in acceptability can be summarized informally as in (9).

(9) a. KNOW allows indirect questions as complements, whereas EAT does not.
   b. UNCLEAR allows indirect questions as subjects, whereas GO does not.

If these statements are correct, then we have an initial argument that the original bracketed sequences, repeated in (10), are not indirect questions.

(10) a. Karen ate [what Fred offered to her].
      b. [What Harry fixed for Sally] went into the trash.

Our earlier discussion of indirect questions also provides a second justification for viewing the bracketed sequences as representing a different type of construction. The argument applies specifically to occurrences of this construction in subject position, as in (10b). We observed in chapter 4 that whenever an indirect question could be used as a subject, it could also appear as a pseudocomplement linked to the substitute subject *it*. This dual possibility is illustrated by the sentences in (11), each of which contains the predicate UNCLEAR.

(11) a. [What Fred offered to her] was unclear.
      b. *It* was unclear [what Fred offered to her].

The same possibility does not exist for the bracketed sequence when the predicate is changed to *went into the trash*:

(12) a. [What Fred offered to her] went into the trash.
      b. ?**It* went into the trash [what Fred offered to her].

This last sentence is possible only with an "afterthought" interpretation, which requires a distinctive intonation in spoken English and a special comma punctuation in written English:

(13)   *It* went into the trash, [what Fred offered to her].

In sum, *what Fred offered to her* can be used as a pseudocomplement when the predicate is one like UNCLEAR—that is, one that allows the full range of indirect questions. However, this same sequence cannot be so used with a predicate that does not allow indirect questions in general. The argument that results from these considerations is given in (14).

(14)   a.   Sentences that have indirect questions as subjects are matched by corresponding sentences in which the indirect questions are pseudocomplements.
        b.   Sentence (12a) is not matched by a corresponding acceptable sentence in which *what Fred offered to her* is a pseudo-complement.
        c.   Therefore, *what Fred offered to her* is not an indirect question in (12a).

A comparison of the interpretation of an indirect question with that of our new type of sequences reveals another respect in which the two constructions are markedly different despite their superficial similarity. As was pointed out in chapter 4, the interpretation of a sentence with KNOW plus an indirect question involves knowing an answer. Sentence (15a), for example, has an interpretation that can be paraphrased as in (15b).

(15)   a John knows [what Martha ate].
        b. John knows the answer to the question "What did Martha eat?"

With the new construction, the interpretation is quite different. We can see this by considering the interpretation of (16):

(16)   John cooked what Martha ate.

Here it makes no sense to give an interpretation parallel to the one in (15b):

(17)   *??John cooked the answer to the question "What did Martha eat?"

Instead, sentence (16) is best understood as involving the following two propositions:

(18)   a.   Martha ate something X.
        b.   John cooked X.

7.1.2 Structure of Definite Free Relative Clauses
We now have three arguments to support the view that sequences such as *what Fred offered to her* can be something other than indirect questions. We will refer to this construction in general as the *free relative clause*, abbreviated F-Rel. In anticipation of the introduction of the second variety of free relative clauses, we will refer to the ones under study now as *definite free*

relative clauses. Let us now try to develop some rules for this new construction.

As has been noted, our initial examples of this construction had two basic ingredients: the word *what* and a sentence with a missing noun phrase. These examples, then, conform to the general pattern illustrated by (19).

(19)   F-Rel

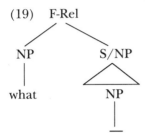

Just as with indirect questions, we can think of the noun phrase *what* as being "donated" to the incomplete sentence, which then uses this donated noun phrase to identify its missing noun phrase:

(20)

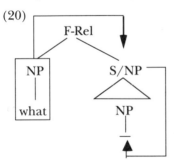

For the particular free relative clause with which we started this discussion, we have the structure shown in (21).

(21)

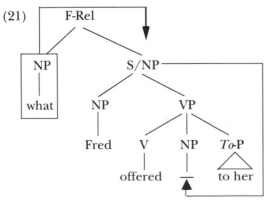

All the free relative clauses that we have seen so far have been introduced by the noun phrase *what*. A natural question to ask now is what other kinds · of phrases can serve this function. Since *what* can also serve as a questioned phrase, we might look at other questioned phrases. When we do this, we find that the list is extremely small. The examples in (22) show that none of the other kinds of interrogative noun phrases can introduce free relative clauses.

(22)   a. *Fred wants to meet [*who* Sally hired].
       b. *Norton wrote [*how many letters* George wrote].
       c. *George bought [*which car* Sheila wanted to sell to him].

All three of these sentences are easy to interpret, but none of them is acceptable. The conclusion is that *what* is the only noun phrase that can be used to introduce definite free relative clauses.

When we expand our view to include other types of phrases as well as noun phrases, we find two additional words that can introduce them:

(23)   a.   Nathan put the money [*where* Billy told him to put it ___].
       b.   The admiral goes [*where* he wants to go ___].
       c.   The concert started [*when* the bell rang ___].

The word *where* is joined to a sentence with either a missing locative phrase or a missing motion phrase, whereas *when* is joined to a sentence with a missing time phrase. Other questioned phrases, however, cannot serve in this extra role of introducing free relative clauses, as the examples in (24) demonstrate.

(24)   a. *You solved the puzzle [how Marsha solved it ___].
            (Compare: You solved the puzzle the same way that Marsha solved it.)
       b. *George worked [*how long* Billy worked ___].
            (Compare: George worked the same amount of time as Billy worked.)
       c. *Carol walked out of the meeting [why Arthur walked out ___].
            (Compare: Carol walked out of the meeting for the same reason that Arthur walked out.)

Thus, our entire list of introducing phrases for definite free relative clauses consists of the three items *what*, *where*, and *when*, and the entire set of acceptable structures consists of those illustrated in (25).

(25) a.

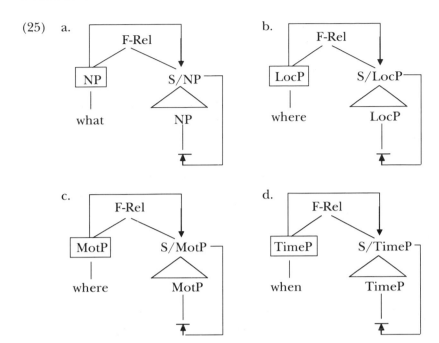

Now let us consider for a moment the other key ingredient of these constructions, and ask whether any further sorts of structures can be joined to the introducing phrases. In the case of indirect questions, we found that the structure containing the missing phrase could be either a finite sentence or an infinitival phrase:

(26)   a. Jacob always knows [what he should wear ___].
       b. Jacob always knows [what to wear ___].

(27)   a. Fido rarely knows [when he should bark ___].
       b. Fido rarely knows [when to bark ___].

The examples in (28) and (29) show that only the former option is available for free relative clauses.

(28)   a. Jacob always wears [what he should wear ___].
       b. *Jacob always wears [what to wear ___].

(29)   a. Fido rarely barks [when he should bark ___].
       b. *Fido rarely barks [when to bark ___].

Exercise
1. Draw a tree diagram for each of the following free relative structures:
    a. [what Bruce tried to make]
    b. [what Helen asked Christine to bring to the office]
    c. [where Washington wanted to stay]

    d. [where Rex took the dominoes]
    e. [when the package arrived in Evansville]

7.2 Indefinite Free Relative Clauses

Indefinite free relative clauses are quite distinctive in appearance. These constructions always begin with a phrase that looks like a questioned phrase except for having the suffix -*ever* attached to the interrogative word itself:

(30)   a.   Fred will say [*whatever* you tell him to say ___].
       b.   Keith will read [*whichever book* you leave ___ for him].
       c.   Ronnie may keep [*whichever of the toys* he likes ___].
       d.   Rhoda dances with [*whoever* ___ asks her to dance].
       e.   [*Who(m)ever* you elect ___ to the presidency] will face many problems.
       f.   Dorothy can eat [*however many cookies* Clarence bakes ___ for her].

The only questioned noun phrases that fail to have corresponding -*ever* phrases are those introduced by *whose*. Thus, we have a questioned phrase *whose dog*, but no free relative phrases like **whosever dog* or **whoever's dog*. The second of these phrases may not seem drastically unacceptable in isolation, but it creates problems in actual free relative clauses. In (31), for example, it is unclear whether it is the dog or the dog's owner that has to make a trip to the pound.

(31)   ?[Whoever's dog bit your mailman] will have to make a trip to the pound.

   Indefinite relative clauses can also be introduced by a variety of phrases other than noun phrases, and can take on a corresponding variety of roles in the larger sentences in which they appear. This variety is illustrated by the examples in (32).

(32)   a.   John will sit [*wherever* he wants to sit ___]. (locative phrase)
       b.   You should call me [*whenever* you have a question ___]. (time phrase)
       c.   George will make the cake [*however big* you want it to be ___]. (adjective phrase)
       d.   Candace will call the mayor [*however often* she needs to call him ___]. (frequency adverb)

   Just as with definite relative clauses, indefinite relative clauses can only be based on finite sentences. The effects of violating this restriction are evident in sentences (33b) and (34b).

(33)   a.   Jacob always wears [whatever he should wear ___].
        b. *Jacob always wears [whatever to wear ___].

(34)   a.   Florence always adopts [whichever dog she should adopt ___].
        b. *Florence always adopts [whichever dog to adopt ___].

Exercise
1. Draw a tree diagram for each of the following indefinite free relative
clauses. Decide which kind of phrase is introducing each one, but do not
bother drawing the internal structure of the introducing phrase.
        a. [whatever Fred ate].
        b. [wherever he put the bananas]
        c. [who(m)ever he found lurking in the pantry]
        d. [whichever book you think that you want to read]
        e. [however much money you asked him to pay]
        f. [however silly his remark might have seemed]

7.3 External Behavior of Free Relative Clauses

In the preceding discussion, we have seen many examples of free relative
clauses in the larger context provided by the sentences in which they
appear. While our primary focus has been on free relative clauses that
serve as noun phrases, we have also seen several that serve other functions.
Here are two sets of examples, divided between those in which the free
relative as a whole serves as a noun phrase and those in which the free
relative serves as a phrase of some other type:

(35)   a. Karen ate [*what* Fred offered ___ to her].   (NP)
        b. [*What* Harry fixed ___ for Sally] went into the trash.   (NP)
        c. Fred will say [*whatever* you tell him to say ___].   (NP)
        d. Ronnie may keep [*whichever of the toys* he likes ___].   (NP)
        e. Rhoda dances with [*whoever* ___ asks her to dance].   (NP)
        f. Dorothy can eat [*however many cookies* Clarence bakes __ for her].
           (NP)

(36)   a. Nathan put the money [*where* Billy told him to put it ___].
           (LocP)
        b. The concert started [*when* the bell rang ___].   (TimeP)
        c. John will sit [*wherever* he wants to sit ___].   (LocP)
        d. George will make the cake [*however big* you want it to be ___].
           (AdjP)

In all these examples, we see a close connection between the phrase type
of the free relative clause as a whole and the phrase type of the smaller
phrase that introduces it. In particular, the free relative clauses in (35) are
all occupying NP positions, and in each sentence the italicized phrase that

introduces the free relative is itself an NP. In similar fashion, each of the
free relative clauses in (36) serves a role that is exactly identical to that of
the introducing phrase. These individual situations can be pictured
as in (37).

(37)

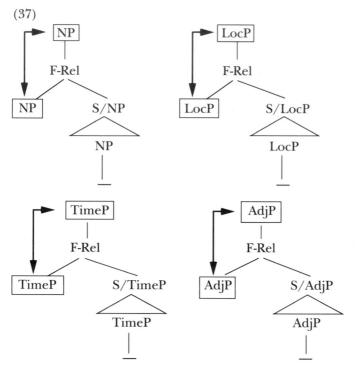

We can summarize this state of affairs in the following rule, and we can
represent it in the following diagram.

(38)   A free relative clause that is introduced by a certain type of phrase
        can serve as a phrase of the same type in the sentence of which it is
        a part.

(39)

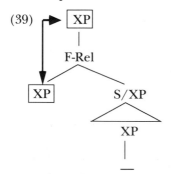

One note of caution is in order here: Although the rule stated in (38) *allows* a free relative clause to serve as a phrase of the same type as its introducing phrase, it does not *require* it to do so. As we will see in chapter 11, indefinite free relative clauses have another entirely distinct use in English.

7.4 Interpretation of Definite and Indefinite Relative Clauses

At first glance, it may seem that definite and indefinite free relative clauses are understood in much the same way. However, an examination of the use of these two varieties reveals a clear difference. This difference is best illustrated by comparing a *what* relative with a *whatever* relative:

(40)   a. Terry must have read [what Leah wrote].
        b. Terry must have read [whatever Leah wrote].

A speaker can use (40a) even if he or she has a very clear idea of what Leah wrote and can add a comment identifying it more precisely, as in (41).

(41)   Terry must have read [what Leah wrote], namely an article on penguins.

The same option is not possible for (40b), as (42) shows.

(42)   *Terry must have read [whatever Leah wrote], namely an article on penguins.

It was in anticipation of this difference that the terms *definite* and *indefinite* were introduced early in this section.

7.5 Identifying Free Relative Clauses and Indirect Questions

At the beginning of section 7.4 it was argued that, despite their superficial similarities, a definite free relative clause and an indirect question are two entirely different constructions. We noted differences in the rules for forming them and in the rules for their use in larger structures. Our goal in this section will be to summarize these differences in a way that will help us to make correct identifications in particular cases.

7.5.1 Internal Requirements
We need to recall at the outset that both a definite free relative clause and an indirect question must have a missing phrase of some sort (leaving aside indirect questions introduced by *whether*). Thus, the presence of a missing phrase will not help us decide between the two constructions. However, there are other internal characteristics that will help us decide in particular cases.

First, let us consider what structures are allowed as indirect questions. Here there are almost no special restrictions. Indirect questions can be introduced by phrases built up around the full range of *wh* words. In addition, the structure containing the missing phrase can be either a finite sentence or an infinitival phrase.

For definite free relative clauses, the requirements are much more restrictive. In the first place, the relative structure must be finite; this immediately means that no infinitival construction can possibly be a free relative. In the second place, the only *wh* words that can introduce a definite free relative are *what, where,* and *when.*

Let us see what these conditions imply for several sets of specific examples. The first set is given in (43):

(43)   a. [whose dog Fred fed]
        b. [how much money Julie earned]
        c. [which picture Smith sold]

Naturally, these sequences could qualify as possible indirect questions. However, they fail to satisfy the internal requirements for definite free relative clauses, since each of them is introduced by some phrase other than *what, where,* or *when.*

Now let us look at a second set of examples:

(44)   a. [what to say to Martha]
        b. [where to hide the money]
        c. [when to start the roast]

Here again, all the sequences clearly qualify as possible indirect questions. In addition, each of the three initial phrases is one that is permitted to introduce free relative clauses. However, the structures to which these introducing phrases are joined are all infinitival phrases, and that disqualifies the sequences as possible free relative clauses.

Finally, let us consider a third set of examples:

(45)   a. [what Carla put in the ice chest]
        b. [where Hans is keeping the chairs]
        c. [when we came to Austin]

Once again, these sequences clearly qualify as possible indirect questions. In addition, they are introduced by *what, where,* and *when,* and the following structures are finite sentences. Thus, at last, we have sequences that satisfy the internal requirements for definite free relative clauses as well as those for indirect questions.

Exercise

1. For each of the sequences listed below, answer two questions:

   •Does it satisfy the internal requirements for indirect questions?
   •Does it satisfy the internal requirements for definite free relative clauses?

Explain each negative answer briefly but clearly. (With some of these sequences, you may want to answer both questions affirmatively.)

    a. [what to say]
    b. [where Francis wanted to stay]
    c. [how John managed to find the manuscript]
    d. [whose car we should ride in]
    e. [which book to read]
    f. [when the dance began]
    g. [what Karen wants us to do]

7.5.2 External Requirements

Let us begin our comparison of the external requirements for indirect questions and definite free relative clauses by reviewing what was said in chapter 4 about indirect questions. In that discussion, we saw that every indirect question that occurs as a subject or a complement in a sentence must be "licensed" by some particular predicate that specifically permits indirect questions. The sentences in (46) contain some examples of such predicates.

(46)   a. John *wondered* [how far the travelers would go].
       b. Marsha *knows* [how much money we collected].
       c. Jones *told* Smith [why Williams canceled the program].
       d. Robert is not *sure* [how much his opponents know].
       e. [Which candidate will spend the most money] is *clear*.
       f. [Which telephone you use] does not *matter*.
       g. [How much money Bruce made] *depended* on [how many encyclopedias he sold].

Thus, when we want to decide whether a certain sequence satisfies the external requirements for being an indirect question, we need to determine whether it occurs as the subject or complement of one of the permitting words.

In some cases, we may remember that a certain predicate permits indirect questions as complements. Suppose, for instance, that we are given sentence (47).

(47)   Brenda knows [what her dog swallowed].

We would be likely to remember, from several earlier examples, that KNOW is a verb that allows indirect questions. We would then conclude immediately that the sequence in question satisfied the external requirements for being an indirect question.

Suppose, however, that we are given the sentences in (48), neither of which contains a predicate about which we have any previous information.

(48)   a. Joe *guessed* [what Marsha gave Bill].
       b. Joe *borrowed* [what Marsha gave Bill].

Here we clearly need to find out whether GUESS allows indirect questions, and then to answer the same question for BORROW. The sentences in (48) do not give us an answer to this question, since the bracketed sequences satisfy the internal requirements for free relative clauses as well as those for indirect questions.

A natural strategy here is to construct some additional sentences containing these two predicates. What we need to do, specifically, is provide complements for these sentences that could only be indirect questions. One possibility is to use a sequence introduced by something other than *what, where*, or *when*; two good choices might be *why* and *how much money*. When we take this step, the resulting judgments are clear:

(49)   a. Joe *guessed* [why the receipts were unavailable].
       b. Joe *guessed* [how much money Arthur earned].

(50)   a. *Joe *borrowed* [why the receipts were unavailable].
       b. *Joe *borrowed* [how much money Arthur earned].

These judgments give us the information that we need: GUESS allows indirect questions as complements, whereas BORROW does not. It is now easy to answer the question posed about our original examples:

(51)   a. Joe *guessed* [what Marsha gave Bill].
       b. Joe *borrowed* [what Marsha gave Bill].

The bracketed sequence in (51a) satisfies the external requirements for indirect questions, whereas that in (51b) does not.

Let us turn our attention now to the external requirements for free relative clauses. These requirements are quite different from those for indirect questions. During our discussion of free relative clauses, we never identified any verbs or adjectives that specifically called for free relative clauses as subjects or complements. Instead, we developed a general rule that determined the phrase type of the construction as a whole on the basis of the type of the introducing phrase. The particular cases of this rule that apply to definite free relative clauses are summarized in (52).

(52)   a.   Definite free relative clauses introduced by *what* can be used wherever nonhuman noun phrases are permitted.

        b.   Definite free relative clauses introduced by *where* can be used wherever locative or motion phrases are permitted.

        c.   Definite free relative clauses introduced by *when* can be used wherever time phrases are permitted.

Thus, in a situation where a *what* sequence can be a free relative clause, other inanimate noun phrases (e.g., *something* or *it*) should also be possible. Likewise, in a situation in which a *where* sequence can be a free relative clause, other locative or motion phrases (e.g., *there*) should also be possible in the same position. Finally, in a situation where a *when* sequence can a free relative clause, it should be possible to substitute other time phrases.

Let us look now at some concrete examples. Our first set involves *what* sequences:

(53)   a.   Fred liked [what he saw].

        b.   [What John cooked] made Martha sick.

The positions of both of the bracketed sequences also allow simple nonhuman noun phrases:

(54)   a.   Fred liked *something*.

        b.   *Something* made Martha sick.

Thus, the bracketed sequences in (53) satisfy the external conditions for being free relative clauses.

Now let us consider the *where* sequences given in (55).

(55)   a.   Karen stayed [where Cora had wanted to stay].

        b.   Karen discovered [where Cora had wanted to stay].

Substitution of the simple locative phrase *there* in these two sentences gives markedly different results:

(56)   a.   Karen stayed *there*.

        b. *Karen discovered *there*.

Sentence (56a) shows that locative phrases can occur immediately after STAY, whereas (56b) shows that they cannot occur immediately after DISCOVER. Thus, the bracketed sequence in (55a) satisfies the external requirements for being a free relative clause, whereas that in (55b) does not.

A similar line of reasoning applies to *when* sequences, as the following pair of examples shows:

(57)   a.   Jacob left [when Martha stopped playing the piano].
        b.   [When Martha stopped playing the piano] was unclear.

Substitution of *then* for the two bracketed sequences yields the following results:

(58)   a.   Jacob left *then*.
        b.   **Then* was unclear.

Our conclusion is that only (57a) satisfies the external conditions for being a free relative clause.

Exercise
1. For each of the bracketed sequences in the sentences below, answer two questions:

    •Does it satisfy the external requirements for indirect questions?
    •Does it satisfy the external requirements for relative clauses?

For each negative answer, say what requirement is not satisfied.
        a.   Bill said [what John told him].
        b.   [What Shakespeare wrote] is clear.
        c.   John put the money [where the children would not find it].
        d.   [When Shakespeare lived] is clear.
        e.   George discovered [where Shakespeare lived].
        f.   George wanted to put up a monument [where Shakespeare lived].
        g.   [What Shakespeare wrote] is difficult.

7.5.3 A Compatibility Requirement for Free Relative Clauses
Besides satisfying ordinary internal and external conditions, free relative clauses must satisfy a compatibility condition—a condition that arises as a result of their interpretation. Let us begin by looking again at a free relative clause introduced by *what* and at its interpretation:

(59)   a.   John cooked [what Martha ate ___].
        b.   Martha ate something X.
              John cooked X.

In general, if a free relative clause is to be interpreted coherently, then the kinds of entities that could serve in place of X in the first part of the interpretation must include some that could also serve in place of X in the second part. This condition clearly holds for the pair of statements in

(59b); we can think of many kinds of entities (spaghetti, boiled potatoes, etc.) that would make sense in place of *X* in both statements.

In other sentences containing *what* sequences, the compatibility condition fails. Example (60) provides a clear illustration.

(60)   John realized [what Martha ate].

By the rule discussed above, the interpretation that this would have if the bracketed sequence were a free relative clause would be expressible in the following two sentences:

(61)   Martha ate something *X*.
         John realized *X*.

The problem here is that EAT and REALIZE take different kinds of entities as objects. The objects of EAT must be physical objects (preferably foods), whereas the objects of REALIZE must be true propositions. Thus, the two occurrences of *X* are incompatible. As a result, it is impossible to view the bracketed sequence in (60) as a free relative clause. The only coherent interpretation for this sentence is one in which the the complement is taken to be an indirect question.

The compatibility requirement has a special consequence for sentences containing *when* sequences. Such sentences receive the same kind of interpretation as those containing *what* sequences. An example is given in (62).

(62)   a. Nora saw the smoke [when the bomb exploded].
        b. Nora saw the smoke at some time *X*.
           The bomb exploded at time *X*.

Here there is nothing to prevent the two times from being the same. Thus, the compatibility requirement is satisfied, and the bracketed sequence can be a free relative clause.

Now let us consider (63a) with the interpretation given in (63b).

(63)   a. Nora will tell us [when the bomb exploded].
        b. Nora will tell us at time *X*.
           The bomb exploded at time *X*.

The times mentioned in the two statements here are not compatible. The word *will* in the first statement indicates a time for the event of telling that is later than the present, and the past-tense form *exploded* puts the time of that event earlier than the time of telling. It is thus impossible for the two times to be the same. As a result, the *when* sequence in (63a) cannot be a free relative clause. Only an indirect-question interpretation is possible.

Exercise

1. Each of the following sentences contains a *wh* sequence. For each one, say whether it satisfies the compatibility requirement for free relative clauses.

    a.   Bill saw [what John constructed].

    b.   Kay knows [what her sister knew].

    c.   Harley lives [where Washington bought his horses].

    d.   [What John said] is untrue.

    e.   Harley knows [when Washington bought his horses].

7.5.4 Residual Ambiguities

After studying all the differing requirements that indirect questions and free relative clauses must meet, one might think it likely that every instance of one of these constructions could always be identified unambiguously when it appeared in a sentence. As it happens, however, ambiguous sentences do exist. One example is given in (64).

(64)   Martha knows [what John knows].

The bracketed sequence in isolation would clearly be allowed by the rules for forming indirect questions. In addition, it occurs here as the object of the verb KNOW, one of the verbs that accept indirect questions as objects. Thus, our rules allow this sequence to be analyzed here as an indirect question.

By checking one requirement at a time, we find that a free-relative structure is just as legitimate. The construction is introduced by *what*, one of the permitted phrases. The structure that follows is a finite sentence. Thus, the internal requirements are satisfied. As for the external requirements, the verb KNOW is one that accepts nonhuman noun phrases:

(65)   Martha knows *something*.

Finally, the free-relative interpretation would give us the two statements in (66).

(66)   John knows something X.
        Martha knows X.

Clearly, the same entities that are objects of John's knowing can also be objects of Martha's knowing. Therefore, this sentence can have a structure in which the bracketed sequence is a free relative clause.

A very definite ambiguity in meaning goes along with this structural ambiguity. It is not at all difficult to imagine situations in which either of the two interpretations would be true and the other false. On the one hand, Martha might be able to give a correct answer to the question "What does John know?" without having the same knowledge herself. For instance, she might know that John knows the names of the Seven Dwarfs, even though she does not know their names. In this situation, the sentence would be true on the indirect-question interpretation but false on the free-relative-clause intepretation. On the other hand, Martha might not know anything at all about John. In particular, she might have no knowledge of what he knows or doesn't know. But suppose that Martha and John each separately know the names of the Seven Dwarfs. Then the sentence would be true on the free-relative-clause interpretation but false on the indirect-question interpretation.

Exercise

1. For each of the sentences listed below, answer two questions:

  • Can it be a free relative?
  • Can it be an indirect question?

Be sure to check both internal and external requirements in making your determination, and also check the compatibility requirement for free relative clauses. (Be on the alert for sentences that are ambiguous between the two structures.)

  a.   [What Bill said to Sharon] made her laugh.
  b.   [What Shakespeare wrote] is unclear.
  c.   Jack will tell us [when to leave the room].
  d.   John didn't stay [where Bill told him to stay].
  e.   John didn't say [where Bill told him to stay].
  f.   Bill didn't remember [how Sheila remembered the solution].
  g.   Martha told me [what to tell Bill].
  h.   Billy knows [what Einstein knew].
  i.   Sarah remembers [why she confessed to Bill].
  j.   George believed [what we told him].

Chapter 8

Subjects of Phrases

In chapter 4 it was suggested that verbs and adjectives could impose restrictions on subjects of sentences as well as on complements. In particular, we noted that some words allowed only ordinary noun phrases as subjects, whereas others allowed clauses of certain types as well. Thus, for instance, we made a distinction between SURPRISE and NOMINATE:

(1) a. SURPRISE: NP [—NP]
         SURPRISE: *That*-C [—NP]
     b. NOMINATE: NP [—NP]

Although both SURPRISE and NOMINATE take ordinary noun phrases as subjects, only SURPRISE takes *that* clauses as well. These specifications were adequate to account for the sentences in (2) and (3).

(2) a. *The explosion* [surprised Fred].
     b. *That the firecracker exploded* [surprised Fred].

(3) a. *The delegates* [nominated Bill].
     b. **That Fred was unpopular* [nominated Bill].

Something more needs to be said as soon as we look at some slightly more complicated examples, such as those in (4) and (5).

(4) a. *The explosion* may have [surprised Bill].
     b. *That the firecracker exploded* may have [surprised Bill].

(5) a. *The delegates* may have [nominated Bill].
     b. **That Fred was unpopular* may have [nominated Bill].

According to the way we are now interpreting the environmental specification in (1a), SURPRISE calls for either a noun phrase or a *that* clause as subject. But in neither of the examples in (4) is the verb phrase headed by *surprised* a sentence predicate. As a result, neither verb phrase appears with a "subject" (that is, a structure that joins with it to make a sentence). In each of these two sentences, the only phrase that does have a subject in this sense of the word is the phrase headed by *may*. In order to solve this problem, we need to expand our idea of what a subject is. After we have taken this step, we will find that subject specifications like those in (1) work just as well with complicated sentences as with simple ones.

8.1 An Expanded Idea of "Subjects"

What would it mean to speak of "the subject of a phrase"? A convenient way to begin is to think about what we have been calling "the subject of a sentence," and to see what it does for the verb phrase that accompanies it. Consider, for instance, a simple sentence such as the one diagrammed in (6), the subject of which is *James.*

(6)
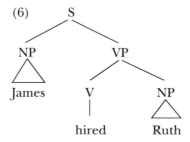

Suppose that we are asked whether the verb phrase *hired Ruth* expresses a complete proposition. Our intuitions would tell us that it does not. What is felt to be lacking is an identification for one of the participants in the event of hiring. In effect, the phrase by itself could be thought of as □ *hired Ruth.* In order to arrive at a complete interpretation for this phrase, we use something that lies outside the verb phrase to identify this absent element. In this case, the noun phrase *James* makes the necessary identification.

This phrase is typical of a general pattern: Most phrases have some specific part of their interpretation that is not expressed by anything inside the phrase but has to be provided by something outside the phrase. When we talk about the *subject of a phrase,* we will be talking about the outside noun phrase or clause that provides this missing part of the interpretation.

This idea can easily be put in graphic form. Every phrase that serves as a predicate will have with it an empty box, standing for the element in its interpretation that needs to be attached to something outside the phrase. The subject of the phrase—that is, the outside entity that fulfills this role— will be linked to this box by an arrow. Thus, the tree for the simple sentence considered above would be redrawn in (7).

(7)

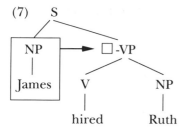

We can express the kind of subject identification found in this situation by the following rule:

(8)   If a verb phrase is the predicate of a sentence, then the structure that joins with the verb phrase serves as its subject.

In the above sentence, the subject of the verb phrase is an ordinary noun phrase; in other examples, of types that we have already seen, a clause of one sort or another serves as the subject.

In other constructions the rules for identifying subjects are slightly different. In a full infinitival clause, the subject of the verb phrase inside the infinitive phrase is just the object of *for*; this is diagrammed in (9).

(9)

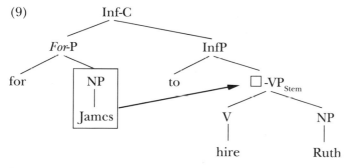

Similarly, in the gerundive construction, it is the genitive noun phrase that serves as the subject of the present participial verb phrase; see (10).

(10)

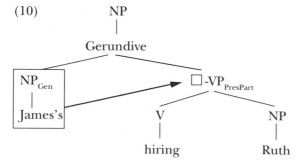

We see yet another situation when we try to identify the subject of the bare-stem phrase *hire Ruth* in sentence (11).

(11)   Katy persuaded James to *hire Ruth.*

Just as in (7), (9), and (10), the subject of this verb phrase will be the person who did the hiring. By consulting our intuitions as speakers of English, we can tell that *James* is the noun phrase that fulfills this role here. In this instance, then, the object of the larger verb phrase serves also as the subject of the complement verb phrase. We can picture this situation as in (12).

(12)

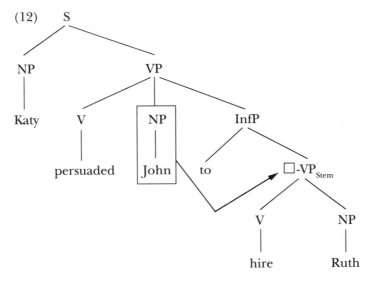

The following simple rule delivers the right results:

(13)   If a certain verb phrase occurs as the complement of a transitive verb, then the object of the transitive verb serves as the subject of the complement verb phrase.

In all the above situations, the subject of a phrase is identified in an extremely simple and direct way. A situation in which a subject is identified less directly is given in (14).

(14)   John tried to hire Ruth.

What we are concerned with here is identifying the subject of *hire Ruth.* We have a clear intuition here that *John* is to be understood as the agent in the act of hiring. Thus, we are led to conclude that the subject of *hire Ruth* is just the subject of the larger verb phrase that contains it. This two-step identification is diagrammed in (15).

(15)

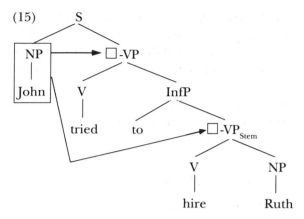

The use of the subject of the larger verb phrase in (15) as the subject of the smaller one is typical of what happens with complements of intransitive verbs. Thus, we have the following general rule:

(16)   If a certain verb phrase occurs as the complement of an intransitive verb, then the subject of the higher verb phrase also serves as the subject of the lower one.

This rule provides subjects not only for infinitival constructions but also for gerundives that lack preceding genitive noun phrases:

(17)   Cora regrets [living in Toledo].

The way in which the subjects are determined in this sentence is diagrammed in (18).

(18)

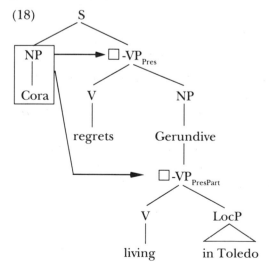

The first identification here is direct: The subject noun phrase *Cora* serves as the subject of the main verb phrase. The second is indirect and falls under the rule in (16): When we want to find the subject of the complement, we first need to determine the subject of the larger phrase in which it occurs.

In a more complicated sentence, a number of indirect identifications may be required. This successive identification of ever lower subjects is illustrated by the manner in which the subject of *finish the book* is determined to be *Nelda* in (19).

(19)   Nelda intends to try to finish the book.

The successive identifications are diagrammed in (20).

(20)

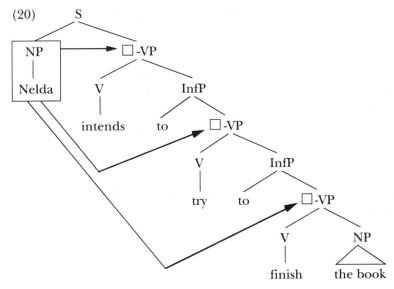

Again, the first identification is direct: The noun phrase *Nelda* serves as the subject of the largest verb phrase. Now, because it is the subject of this top verb phrase and because the top verb phrase does not have an object, *Nelda* is also picked by rule (16) to serve as the subject of the next verb phrase down, the verb phrase headed by *try*. Finally, by virtue of serving as the subject of this intermediate verb phrase, it is picked as the subject of the lowest verb phrase by another application of rule (16).

Exercise

1. In each of the following sentences, a verb phrase is italicized. In each such instance, say which noun phrase or clause in the sentence serves as

the subject of this phrase, and draw a tree diagram in which the successive identifications are indicated by arrows. (In many instances, a chain of two or more identifications will be required.)

    a.   Alma asked George to try to remember to *feed the cats.*
    b.   Gib may have promised to *let Mae mow the lawn.*
    c.   Mark must be refusing to let Debbie *poison the goldfish.*
    d.   Kate's wanting to keep *giving parties* bothers Steve.
    e.   Pat's taking Lawrence to the veterinarian *relieved Warren.*
    f.   Mrs. Bolton would like for the judge to agree to *drown his cats.*
    g.   It *surprised Kathy* that Gaylord agreed to plant a magnolia.

8.2 Specification of Subjects

We are now in a position to end the digression and look again at the question that prompted it. That question concerned the way in which an environmental specification like that in (21a) could be satisfied by a sentence like (21b), where the *that* clause and the relevant verb phrase are separated by two other verbs.

(21)   a.   *That-C* [—NP]
         b.   *That the puffins held a meeting* may have [surprised George].

The answer is clear as soon as we draw a tree diagram for this sentence and identify subjects by the rules that have been suggested:

(22)

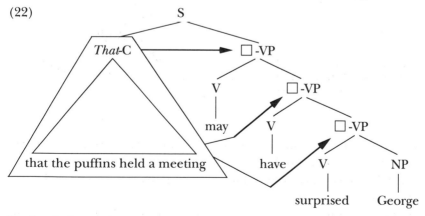

By the chain of separate identifications that our rules establish, the *that* clause that serves as the subject of the largest verb phrase eventually comes to serve also as the subject of the verb phrase *surprised Bill.* Thus, we really want an environmental specification like (21a) to be satisfied whenever the object is an ordinary noun phrase and the subject is identified—either directly or indirectly—as a *that* clause.

8.3 Subjects of Adjective Phrases

So far in this chapter, we have confined our attention to identifying subjects of verb phrases of various sorts. Exactly the same approach works well with adjective phrases. A first example is provided by sentence (23).

(23)   *That Joe steals hubcaps* is [clear].

In chapter 4, one of the environmental specifications that we assigned to CLEAR was the following:

(24)   CLEAR: *That*-C [—]

In interpreting this specification, we had to ignore temporarily the problem of how the *that* clause could be understood as the subject of CLEAR when it was actually joined with a phrase headed by *is*. But if we now treat CLEAR just as we treated SURPRISE, we find that the *that* clause that serves as the subject of the sentence as a whole comes to be identified as the subject of the adjective phrase. This is illustrated by (25).

(25)

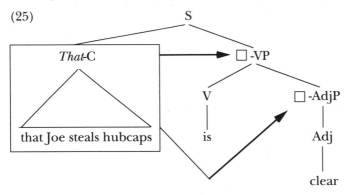

Thus, *clear* in this example satisfies the environmental specification in (24) so long as we understand that specification as requiring that the subject of CLEAR be a *that* clause, without insisting that this *that* clause be adjacent to the adjective phrase.

In the same way, an adjective phrase that serves as the complement of a transitive verb commonly looks to the object of the transitive verb for its subject. We see this in (26a), which is diagrammed in (26b).

(26)   a.   Joe made Fido glum.

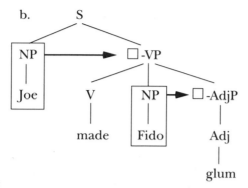

Thus, the requirement that the subject of *glum* be an ordinary noun phrase is satisfied in this example.

A slightly more complex example illustrating the same point is provided by (27).

(27)   Joe made it clear that he would resign.

Here the word *it* serves as a clausal substitute, standing in place of a postponed *that* clause. We have said that CLEAR allows a *that* clause as subject. As in chapter 4, we will assume that this subject specification is just as well satisfied by the word *it* linked to a *that* clause as it is by a *that* clause itself. A complete picture of the various relations among parts of this sentence is given in (28).

(28)

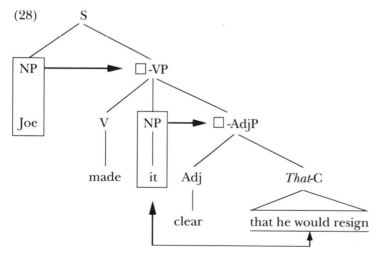

Just as in the simpler example in (26), the object of MAKE serves as the subject of the adjective phrase. In this example, the object is the clausal substitute *it*, which here is linked to a *that* clause. This *that* clause is thus understood as fulfilling any functions of the object. One of these functions is to serve as the subject of the adjective phrase that serves as the complement of MAKE. Thus, by an indirect route, the structure in (28) satisfies the following specification:

(29)   CLEAR: *That*-C [—]

So far in this section, we have seen that adjective phrases deserve to be thought of as having subjects, and have their subjects identified by much the same rules as do verb phrases. We might also note that adjective phrases are like verb phrases in their ability to assign their own subject the additional role of serving as the subject of a complement. Example (30) shows this process at work.

(30)   Freddy seems eager to *buy the house.*

The rules that we have developed so far will have the effect of making *Freddy* the subject of the adjective phrase headed by *eager.*

(31)

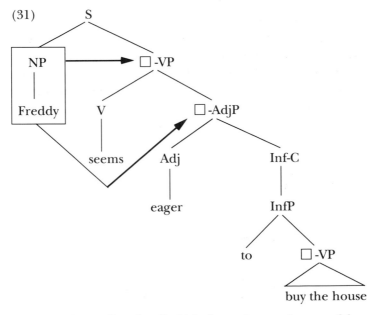

Our intuitions tell us that *Freddy* is the understood agent of the verb phrase *buy the house.* We can achieve this result if we let the adjective *eager* behave just like an intransitive verb, assigning its own subject the added role of being the subject of its complement. This last step completes the indirect link that we want between *Freddy* and the subject of the lowest verb phrase:

(32)

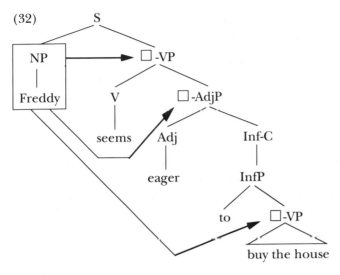

Exercise

1. In each of the following sentences, an adjective phrase is italicized. In each such instance, say which noun phrase or clause in the sentence serves as the subject of this phrase, and draw a tree diagram in which the successive identifications are indicated by arrows.

    a.   George appears to have wanted to be *loyal to the company.*

    b.   Fred's receiving a ticket made his sister *angry at the sheriff.*

    c.   Carla wants Bill to try to remain *calm.*

    d.   Jones would like for it to be *clear to Fred* that the goldfish have succumbed.

8.4 Exceptional Verbs

In the preceding sections, we have assumed a general rule to the effect that in a structure with an object noun phrase it is the object that serves as the subject of a following complement. For most English verbs that take both an object and a predicate complement, this rule holds true. There is a small handful of verbs, however, that are exceptional. Even though these verbs take objects followed by predicate complements, it is the subject rather than the object that plays the role of subject of the complement.

One verb that is exceptional in this way is *promise.* In three of the complement configurations that *promise* allows, nothing out of the ordinary occurs:

(33)   a. John promised that he would leave the room.

    b. John promised Nancy that he would leave the room.

    c. John promised to leave the room.

In (33a) and (33b), the complement subject is just *he*, the subject of the finite sentence within the *that* clause; in (33c), it is the higher subject, as expected. The exceptional case arises with an additional complement configuration allowed by many speakers of English:

(34)   John promised Nancy to leave the room.

Here our general rule would lead us to expect that the object noun phrase *Nancy* would serve as the subject of the complement, but instead it is the subject noun phrase *John* that performs this function. This sentence can be contrasted with (35), where the object serves the role of complement subject.

(35)   John persuaded Nancy to leave the room.

The contrasting patterns of subject determination in these two sentences are shown in (36) and (37), with the normal pattern given first.

(36)   **Normal pattern**

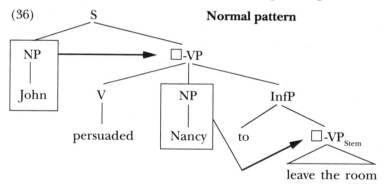

(37)   **Exceptional pattern**

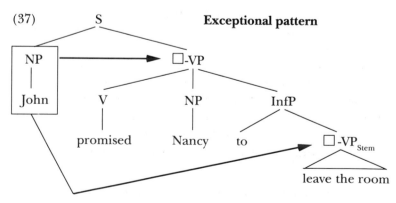

There is another pair of verbs that shows exceptional behavior with regard to predicate complements. In this instance, the complements are of a type that we have not yet studied. Before looking at the exceptional cases, we will look at this new type of complement as it is used with normal verbs. The complement is italicized in the sentences in (38).

(38) a. Fred [regards John *as capricious*].
      b. Susan [regards Bill *as being eager to succeed*].
      c. Smith [regards Jones *as a threat to the company*].

Each of the italicized complements consists of the word *as* plus another phrase. In (38a) the following phrase is an adjective phrase, in (38b) it is a present-participial verb phrase, and in (38c) it is a noun phrase. Each of these phrases needs to have a subject, and in every case above it is the direct object of REGARD that fills this role. Similar examples can be constructed which show that the verb VIEW has exactly the same behavior.

Now let us turn to STRIKE, an exceptional verb taking the same kinds of *as* phrases as REGARD and VIEW:

(39) a. Fred [strikes John *as capricious*].
      b. Susan [strikes Bill *as being eager to succeed*].
      c. Smith [strikes Jones *as being a threat to the company*].

Here the choice of the complement subject is entirely different: In each case, it is the subject of STRIKE rather than the object that fills this role. The diagrams in (40) contrast the complement-subject choice dictated by REGARD and that dictated by STRIKE.

(40) a.

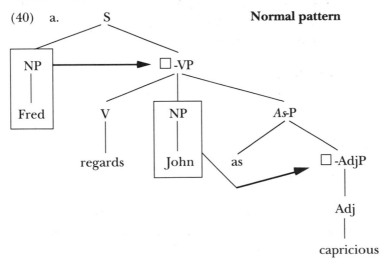

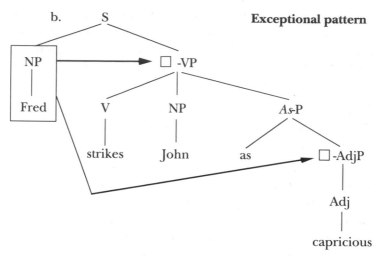

As these diagrams indicate, REGARD is normal in much the same way as PERSUADE, whereas STRIKE is exceptional in much the same way as PROMISE.

To summarize, most of the transitive verbs in English that also take predicate complements follow the general rule of having the object serve as the subject of the predicate complement. A few verbs, however, are exceptions to this rule, and would need to be so marked in any complete grammar of English.

Exercise

1. Using your intuitions as a guide, say what the understood subject of the infinitive phrase is in each of the following examples:
   a.   Karen asked Nellie to wash the car.
   b.   Terry told Kevin to feed the dog.
   c.   Karen asked Nellie how often to wash the car.
   d.   Terry told Kevin how often to feed the dog.
Do the general rules given in the preceding sections cover all four of these examples, or is it necessary to give one or more special rules? If you think that a special rule is needed, say what it is.

8.5 Subjects of Subject Constructions

We have now developed some simple rules that identify subjects of phrases in several different situations. So far, though, our rules say nothing about what happens when infinitives and gerundives occur as subjects themselves, as in (41).

(41) a. *To move to Vienna now* would be difficult for Jane.
     b. *Reading unfavorable stories* must have bothered Fred.

We will now look briefly at how subjects are identified in this situation.

The two examples in (41) illustrate one common situation. In these examples, an English speaker's intuitions will be that *Jane* is the subject of *move to Vienna* and that *Fred* is the subject of *reading unfavorable stories*. The rules that we developed in the preceding sections dictate that the infinitival clause in (41a) must serve as the subject of the phrase *difficult for Jane*. In similar fashion, the gerundive in (41b) must be the subject of the phrase *bothered Fred*. In picture form, the subjects of these adjective phrases are determined as follows:

(42)

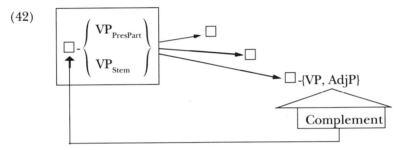

Using these observations, we can propose the following rule:

(43) If a gerundive or an infinitive is the subject of some other phrase, and this other phrase contains a complement, then this complement can go back and serve as the subject of the gerundive or infinitive.

Let us now see how this rule works with the particular example given in (44).

(44) To move to Vienna would be difficult for Jane.

The tree diagram of this sentence, given in (45), illustrates the effects of the identification rules discussed earlier in this chapter. These rules tell us that the infinitival construction as a whole serves as the subject of the verb phrase headed by *would*, and that it indirectly identifies the subject of each of the phrases nested below it. Let us now look for a way to apply our new rule. If one of these phrases contains an appropriate complement, we can use it to identify the subject of the infinitive. The lowest of these phrases, the one headed by *difficult*, does indeed contain a complement: a prepositional phrase whose object is *Jane*. This object is now used as the subject of the infinitival construction itself, as (46) shows.

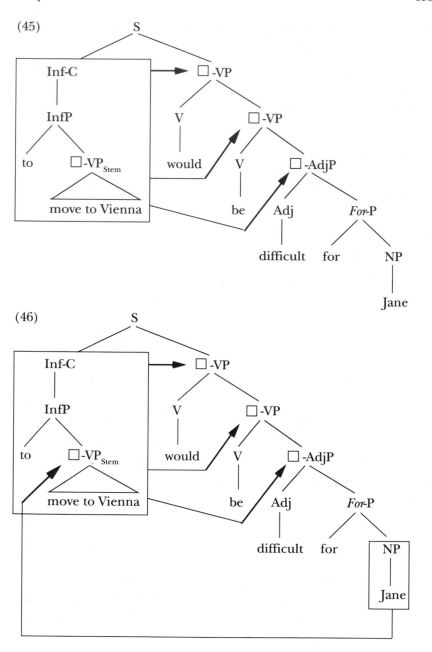

The infinitival subject of the sentence as a whole serves as the subject of *difficult for Jane*, and in turn the complement of this adjective phrase serves as the subject of the verb phrase inside the infinitival.

Now let us look at a sentence that is similar to (44) in every respect except one:

(47)   To move to Vienna would be difficult.

This sentence is just like the one that we have been discussing, except that the adjective *difficult* has no complement associated with it. Thus, the rule given in (43) does not appear to be applicable to this sentence.

In order to see how the subject of this infinitival clause is identified, it will be helpful to put the sentence as a whole in several different conversational contexts, as in (48)–(50).

(48)   I would like to leave Italy and go to Austria, but I haven't saved much
       money. Thus, *to move to Vienna* would be difficult.

(49)   The price of rental housing is very high, and you do not have much
       money saved. Thus, *to move to Vienna* would be difficult.

(50)   The price of rental housing is very high, and George is not being
       offered much money. Thus, *to move to Vienna* would be difficult.

In (48), it is natural to interpret the subject of the italicized infinitive as being identical to the speaker. In (49), by contrast, the context predisposes us to understand the subject as *you*, the person to whom the speaker is talking. Similarly, in (50) we tend to interpret the missing subject as *George*. These conversations help us identify the person for whom something would be difficult. We can say that they help us to determine an "understood complement" of the adjective *difficult,* answering the question "difficult for whom?" This understood complement can do just as well as an expressed complement in identifying the subject of an infinitive or a gerundive in subject position.

One more situation deserves attention here. Suppose that we are given the sentence (51) in isolation.

(51)   Riding tigers is difficult.

Even in this situation, speakers of English have a clear idea concerning the subject of the gerundive: The understood subject here is something like "people in general." This identification of the subject is made with the help of two distinct rules. One is the rule that we have already seen, which takes the complement of DIFFICULT and uses it as the subject of the gerund. The other rule actually provides an understood complement for DIFFI-CULT in situations like this. It identifies "people in general" as the complement when no other understood complement can be retrieved from the context. As a matter of fact, the same rule operates in a sentence in which no subject gerundive construction is present, such as (52).

(52)   Chemistry problems are difficult.

Just as in the previous example, the understood complement here is taken to be "people in general" (in the absence of a context that picks out someone else).

We can indicate the effect of the understood complement in (51) by including a parenthesized complement in the tree diagram:

(53)

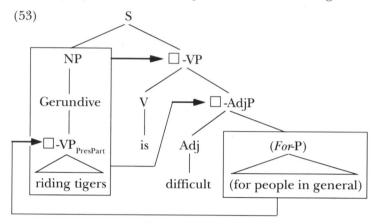

The subject of *riding tigers* is thus identified in the same manner as it would have been if it had occurred in a sentence in which *difficult* had an expressed complement.

Exercise

1. In each of the following sentences, a phrase is italicized. In each such instance, say which noun phrase or clause in the sentence provides the ultimate identification for the subject of this phrase, and list the steps by which this identification is established. Alternately, draw a tree diagram in which the successive identifications are indicated by arrows. If you encounter a case where "for people in general" is an understood complement, write it into the tree with parentheses around it to indicate that it is implied but not expressed.

    a.   Being able to *understand French* appears to have been important to Jane.

    b.   Wanting to be *clever* seems to be natural.

    c.   Fred believes that it is easy to avoid *making enemies.*

    d.   Carol thinks that being unable to *keep the farm* bothers Henry's mother.

8.6 Subjects and Reflexive Pronouns

So far, our chief reason for giving rules identifying subjects has been to account for the ability of a fluent speaker to look at a sentence and some predicate inside it and pick out the particular noun phrase described by that predicate. The view of subjects that has been developed with this goal in mind receives strong independent support from the behavior of reflexive pronouns.

We looked at reflexive pronouns briefly near the beginning of chapter 5. It was stated there that such pronouns were used just in the case where the nearest subject or object (if there was an object) referred to the same person or thing. The key examples from the earlier discussion are repeated here:

(54)   a.   John believes that [we deceived ourselves].
       b.   *John believes that [we deceived us].

(55)   a.   John believes that [Nora told us about ourselves].
       b.   *John believes that [Nora told us about us].

(56)   a.   *We believe that [John distrusts ourselves].
       b.   We believe that [John distrusts us].

(57)   a.   *We believe that [John told Nora about ourselves].
       b.   We believe that [John told Nora about us].

The pairs of examples in (54) and (55) illustrate situations in which a reflexive pronoun is required; in (56) and (57), only an ordinary pronoun is allowed.

Although the sentences in (54)–(57) support this treatment, other sentences can be found that appear to pose problems. One such pair of sentences is the following:

(58)   a.   *We made John proud of ourselves.
       b.   We made John proud of us.

According to the idea of subject that we assumed prior to this chapter, the noun phrase *we* would count as the subject nearest to the final pronoun, as in (59). As a consequence, we would expect the reflexive pronoun to be acceptable and the ordinary pronoun to be unacceptable—just the reverse of what is actually the case.

Here the new idea of subjects yields a better result. The treatment that we have developed in this chapter dictates (60) as the structure for these sentences.

(59)

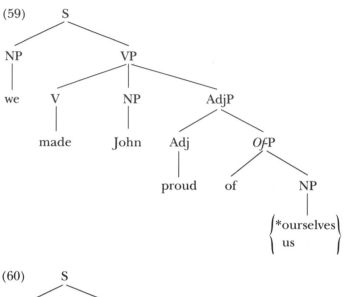

(60)

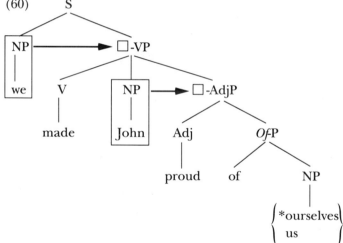

In this structure, the nearest subject is not the subject of the sentence as a whole; instead, it is the subject of the adjective phrase, which is identified by the noun phrase *John*. Thus, the noun phrase that serves as the object of *of* does not refer to the same person or thing as the nearest subject does. As a result, we correctly predict that the reflexive will be unacceptable here.

This new treatment also sheds light on the kind of contrast illustrated by the pairs of sentences in (61) and (62).

(61)   a.   Kevin told Anne to be loyal to herself.
       b.   *Kevin told Anne to be loyal to her.

(62)   a. *Kevin promised Anne to be loyal to herself.
       b. Kevin promised Anne to be loyal to her.

Prior to this chapter, we would have said that in all four of these sentences
the nearest subject was *Kevin* and the nearest object was *Anne*. We would
thus have been left without any reason to expect the contrast that we
actually find between (61) and (62). However, with the new ideas about
subjects, we find that the nearest subject in (61) and the nearest subject in
(62) are not the same:

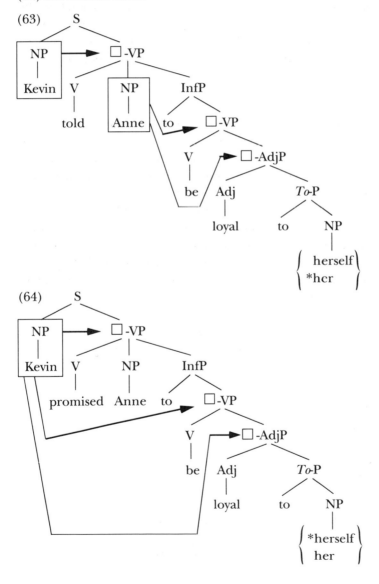

The verb TELL and the verb PROMISE identify the subjects of their complement infinitive phrases in distinct ways. This difference in the subjects of the two infinitive phrases yields a corresponding difference in the subjects of the adjective phrases. Thus, the nearest subject in (61) is *Anne*, whereas the nearest subject in (62) is *Kevin*.

8.7 A Revised View of Missing Subjects

In the preceding sections, we succeeded in developing rules that have the effect of picking out one of several noun phrases in a sentence as the "understood subject" of a phrase that does not have an expressed subject of its own. Suppose, for instance, that we are asked to determine the subject of the italicized verb phrase in (65).

(65)   Alice told Frank that Martha hopes to *receive a promotion.*

Even though three different noun phrases appear in this sentence, our rules dictate that *Martha* is the only one that can serve as the understood subject of *receive a promotion*. This result is in agreement with our actual intuition about this sentence: We understand the *that* clause to mean that Martha hopes that she, Martha, will receive a promotion.

However, consideration of some slightly more complex examples suggests that this idea about the understood subjects of such verb phrases is not quite correct. Though there is no doubt that the person named Martha is hoping for a promotion, we will see some reasons to think that the noun phrase *Martha* is not the understood subject of *receive a promotion*, and we will see evidence that the understood subject is actually more like a pronoun.

Let us begin by considering some additional examples involving the verb HOPE. The first example is just the sentence contained in the *that* clause of sentence (66).

(66)   a. Jane hopes to receive a promotion.

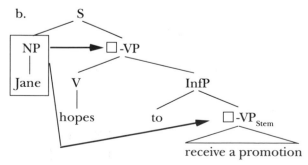

Because HOPE also allows *that* clauses, it is possible to form a sentence with an identical meaning in which the infinitival construction is replaced by a *that* clause. When we do this, the most natural subject for the *that* clause is the pronoun *she*:

(67)   *Jane* hopes that *she* will receive a promotion.

In particular, the pronoun is more natural here than a repeated use of the name *Jane*:

(68)   ?*Jane* hopes that *Jane* will receive a promotion.

These examples thus give us an initial reason to think that the subject of the infinitival might be very much like a pronoun, rather than a copy of the higher subject.

The case for this view becomes stronger when we look at sentences in which the subject of the sentence as a whole contains a word such as *each* or *every*. The following example illustrates what happens:

(69)   *Each woman* hopes to receive a promotion.

Let us once again look for a synonymous sentence in which the complement of HOPE is a *that* clause. Using a pronoun inside the *that* clause gives us (70), which means exactly the same thing as (69).

(70)   *Each woman* hopes that *she* will receive a promotion.

By contrast, if we simply repeat the subject of the sentence as a whole, the result means something entirely different from (69):

(71)   *Each woman* hopes that *each woman* will receive a promotion.

We can imagine a situation in which each woman wants a promotion for herself but not for every other woman. In such a situation, (71) would be false, whereas both (69) and (70) would be true. The interpretation of the sentence with an infinitival complement is thus the same as the interpretation of the sentence with a *that* clause having a pronoun as subject. Thus, we get the correct interpretation for (69) if we say that the unexpressed subject of the lower verb phrase is understood as if it were a pronoun. On the other hand, we get the wrong interpretation if we maintain that the unexpressed subject of the lower verb phrase is understood as if it were an actual copy of the subject of the main clause.

There are many other verbs (and also many adjectives) for which the description given above holds true. Consider this sentence, where the main-clause verb phrase is headed by PERSUADE:

(72)   Martha persuaded one of the boys to feed the dog.

Now let us compare the following two revised versions of this sentence, in both of which the infinitival phrase is replaced by a *that* clause:

(73) a. Martha persuaded *one of the boys* that *he* should feed the dog.
      b. Martha persuaded *one of the boys* that *one of the boys* should feed the dog.

Clearly (73a) is nearer than (73b) to the meaning of sentence (72).

We find evidence for exactly the same view of understood subjects when we look more closely at infinitival and gerundive constructions in subject position. The following sentence provides a clear illustration:

(74) Receiving a ticket annoyed *one of the boys*.

Here again, we happen to have the possibility of expressing the same idea with a *that* clause instead of a gerundive. Moreover, we can compare two possible choices for the subject of the *that* clause. In (75a) we use a pronoun as the subject of the sentence; in (75b) we use a repeated occurrence of *one of the boys*.

(75) a. That *one of the boys* received a ticket annoyed *one of the boys*.
      b. That *he* received a ticket annoyed *one of the boys*.

Sentence (75b) is clearly more accurate than (75a) as a paraphrase for (74). In particular, both (74) and (75b) give the impression that the boy receiving the ticket and the boy who was annoyed are one and the same. In (75a), they could very well be different. This finding exactly parallels the result that we obtained with HOPE: The subject of the gerundive is interpreted more like a pronoun than like a full noun phrase. In these two cases, then, the rules as developed in preceding sections should not be thought of as picking out the actual subjects. Instead, the real subjects of these phrases are "understood pronouns," and the rules pick out their "antecedents" (the noun phrases we use to determine their reference).

Not all missing subjects are understood in the way just described. For a significant class of verbs in English, it makes sense to say that the understood subject of their complement is *identical* to the subject of the larger phrase, rather than that the understood subject is a pronoun. It is as if the subject that we actually express with these verbs is not understood with them at all, but instead is simply passed down to a complement phrase.

A careful examination of the behavior of the verb SEEM reveals that it has this property. Let us begin by looking at the following sentence:

(76) a. Freddy seems to dislike the principal.

b.

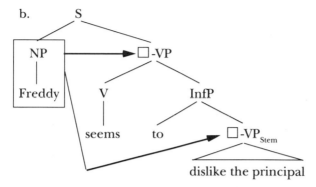

dislike the principal

The verb SEEM is like the verb HOPE in allowing *that* clauses as well as infinitivals. In the case of HOPE, the subject of the infinitival phrase was a pronoun that was coreferential with the subject of the main sentence. With SEEM, by contrast, the subject in the infinitival phrase is referred to only once in the *that*-clause sentence:

(77)   a.   It seems that Freddy dislikes the principal.
       b.   *Freddy seems that he dislikes the principal.

This single role that Freddy plays in (77a) is that of the subject of the lower sentence. Thus, we have reason to suspect that sentence (76a), our original SEEM example, is interpreted as if the subject of the lower verb phrase is actually *Freddy* rather than a pronoun having *Freddy* as its antecedent.

As in the HOPE case, we can get additional evidence by looking at a sentence whose subject contains something other than just a simple name:

(78)   One of the boys seems to dislike the principal.

On one interpretation, this sentence means exactly the same thing as (79).

(79)   It seems that one of the boys dislikes the principal.

We could use either sentence in a situation in which the principal's door has been nailed shut by an unknown hand. In such a situation, it would not be right to make the following claim:

(80)   Boy A seems to dislike the principal or Boy B seems to dislike the principal or Boy C seems to dislike the principal.

This sentence would imply that some specific boy gave the impression of disliking the principal. We would only be justified in making a claim like the following:

(81)   It seems that [Boy A dislikes the principal or Boy B dislikes the principal or Boy C dislikes the principal].

This is the interpretation that we would get for sentence (78)—the sentence with an infinitival complement—if we interpreted *one of the boys* as the actual subject of the lower verb phrase, rather than viewing the subject of the lower verb phrase as a pronoun.

Verbs such as APPEAR and HAPPEN and adjectives such as LIKELY and CERTAIN exhibit the same behavior. Listed below are several pairs of sentences involving these words. The first sentence in each pair contains an infinitival complement, whereas the second contains a corresponding *that* clause. In each instance, the two sentences are synonymous, and the noun phrase that serves as the subject of the sentence as a whole in the (a) examples serves as the lower subject in the (b) examples.

(82) a. *Several coins* appear to have disappeared.
      b. It appears that *several coins* have disappeared.

(83) a. *A policeman* happened to be near the corner.
      b. It happened that *a policeman* was near the corner.

(84) a. *One of the children* is likely to find the egg.
      b. It is likely that *one of the children* will find the egg.

(85) a. *Some of the records* are certain to be faulty.
      b. It is certain that *some of the records* are faulty.

What distinguishes words like HOPE from words like SEEM? The central difference seems to reside in a difference in what the two verbs require in order to be interpreted. The verb HOPE has a role associated with it (the role of the "hoper") that needs to be filled in any sentence in which the verb appears, and the job of identifying the occupant of this role falls to the subject of HOPE. By contrast, the verb SEEM does not have any such use of its own for its subject. The only thing that it does with its subject is hold it for use as the understood subject of its complement.

From this point on we will refer to SEEM and other such verbs as *transparent*, because of the way in which they let their subjects pass down to their complements. In chapter 13, in the course of studying two special English constructions, we will discover some simple strategies for identifying transparent verbs and adjectives.

Chapter 9

Passives and the *Easy* Construction

In the preceding chapter, we discussed subjects of phrases and considered some rules governing the way in which subjects are identified. We noted that the primary use for subjects was to identify the first role required by the head verb or adjective, and that a secondary use was to serve as the subject of a complement verb phrase or adjective phrase. In this chapter, we will examine two constructions in which the subject of a phrase is used quite differently.

9.1 The Passive Construction

Traditional English grammar books distinguish between "active voice" and "passive voice," and sometimes also between "active sentences" and "passive sentences." The contrast is often described as a difference in what the subject contributes to the interpretation of the sentence. The following pairs of examples exhibit this contrast:

(1)   a.   Alice has taken John to the library.   (active)
      b.   John has been taken to the library.   (passive)

(2)   a.   We chose Phil for the position.   (active)
      b.   Phil was chosen for the position.   (passive)

The subjects of the active sentences identify the "agents" or "actors," whereas the subjects of the corresponding passive sentences identify the persons toward whom the actions are directed—the persons who "undergo" the action.

9.1.1 Internal Structure of the Passive Construction

In order to understand how passive voice is conveyed in English, it will be useful to isolate the following sequences taken from the sentences in (1b) and (2b):

(3)   a.   taken to the library
       b.   chosen for the position

As we will see later in this chapter, the rules of English allow sequences such as these to be used in a variety of circumstances. We will refer to such sequences as *passive phrases.*

The two examples in (3) illustrate two important characteristics of the passive construction. The first is that the head verbs, *taken* and *chosen,* are past participles. As the examples in (4) show, this is the only form that is allowed here.

(4)   *John has been $\begin{Bmatrix} \text{take} \\ \text{took} \\ \text{taking} \end{Bmatrix}$ to the library.

The second characteristic is that both TAKE and CHOOSE normally require objects, yet no objects are visible in the sequences in (3). We can see that objects are normally required with these verbs by trying to use these sequences with perfect *have,* as in (5).

(5)   a.   *John has [taken to the library].
       b.   *Phil has [chosen for the position].

We can also see that the noun phrase must be missing from the passive sequences; if we try to use expressed objects in sentences (1b) and (2b), the results are completely unacceptable:

(6)   a.   *John has been [taken Bill to the library].
       b.   *Phil was [chosen Martha for the position].

We can indicate the missing objects in the phrases in (3) by rewriting them in the way that we have done with the missing-phrase constructions studied earlier:

(7)   a.   taken ___ to the library.
       b.   chosen ___ for the position.

By doing this, we express two facts about these phrases: that these verbs normally require objects, and that the objects must be "understood" in this construction rather than expressed.

Only the noun phrase nearest to the verb is eligible to be the missing noun phrase of a passive construction. Thus, we can form passive structures in which an object noun phrase is missing (as in the above examples), or structures in which the object of a preposition is missing, when this preposition comes immediately after the verb:

(8)   a.   This matter has been [looked into ___].
        b.   The baby is being [cared for ___].

On the other hand, it is not possible to form a passive with some other noun phrase missing:

(9)   a. *George was [given a book to ___].
                (Someone gave a book to George.)
        b. *Sally was [received a gift from ___].
                (Someone received a gift from Sally.)

To summarize, a passive structure must be headed by a past participle. It must also contain a missing noun phrase, and this noun phrase must be the first one after the verb. If we just had to express a missing-noun-phrase requirement, we could do it with the symbol $VP_{PastPart}/NP$, meaning a past-participial verb phrase with a missing noun phrase. In order to express the first-noun-phrase requirement as well, we incorporate this additional information into the symbol: $VP_{PastPart}/1stNP$. As formidable as this symbol looks, all it stands for is a past-participial verb phrase with a missing first noun phrase.

The following pairs of tree diagrams give a picture of the difference between active past-participial verb phrases and the corresponding passive structures.

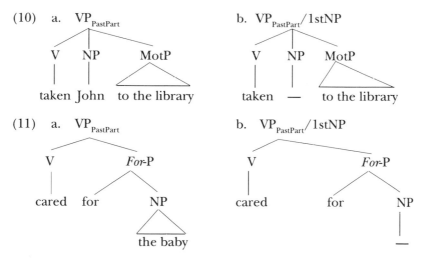

Passive phrases in English have one more important property, one that distinguishes them from passive constructions in many other languages. This is that they allow an optional *by* phrase to identify the agent of the action expressed by the head verb. For instance, in addition to (12a), which is a structure of the type we have seen already, we also have the possibility of adding a *by* phrase:

(12) a. John was [taken ___ to the library].
      b. John was [taken ___ to the library *by Alice*].

A tree diagram for the passive phrase in (12b) is given in (13).

(13)   VP$_{PastPart}$/1stNP

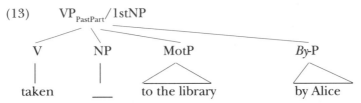

V	NP	MotP	*By*-P
taken	___	to the library	by Alice

A *by* phrase that identifies the agent of an action is possible only in passive phrases. Trying to use it in active phrases produces unacceptable results:

(14) *Fred has [taken John to the library by Alice].

The only types of *by* phrases that are acceptable in active structures are those that indicate proximity, as in (15a), or those that identify a method of doing something, as in (15b).

(15) a. Fred is standing *by the river.*
      b. Yasir blunted Nigel's attack *by forcing an exchange of queens.*

Exercise
1. For each of the following passive phrases, draw a tree diagram. Be sure to indicate the position of the missing noun phrase.
      a. put on the table
      b. eaten by a tiger
      c. considered intelligent
      d. told that the monkeys had revolted
      e. carried into the room by the butler
      f. asked to open the letter

9.1.2 Passive Phrases as Complements

In subsection 9.1.1 we saw how passive phrases are formed; in the present subsection we will see how they can be used as complements to certain English verbs. In the interest of simplifying the appearance of rules and trees, we will use PassP as an abbreviation for the somewhat cumbersome VP$_{Past\ Part}$/1stNP.

We have already seen one example of a verb that allows passive phrases as complements, namely, BE:

(16)   a.   John has [been *taken to the library*].
       b.   Phil will [be *chosen for the position*].

Thus, for the verb BE, we want to add the following complement specification:

(17)   BE: [—PassP]

This rule can be expressed in tree form as in (18).

(18)

```
        VP
       /  \
      V    PassP
      |
     BE
```

There are also several other verbs that allow passive phrases, including the ones listed in (19).

(19)   a.   Fred [got *kicked by the mule*].
            GET: [—PassP]
       b.   Fred [got Bill *elected to the committee*].
            GET: [—NP PassP]
       c.   Sharon [had the carpet *cleaned*].
            HAVE: [—NP PassP]
       d.   Smith [wants the picture *removed from the office*].
            WANT: [—NP PassP]
       e.   George [saw his brother *beaten by the soldiers*].
            SEE: [—NP PassP]

In later chapters, we will see that passive phrases have several other uses in addition to their use as complements.

Exercises

1. Below are listed several verbs, each accompanied by a subcategorization specification that mentions passive phrases. For each such listing, construct an experimental sentence that indicates whether that verb allows that complement configuration. The first is done as an example.
       a. KEEP: [—PassP]
       ANSWER: No. * John kept taken to the library by Alice.
       b. MAKE: [—NP PassP]
       c. HEAR: [—NP PassP]

    d. SEEM: [—PassP]
    e. NEED: [—NP PassP]
    f. CAUSE: [—NP PassP]

2. Draw a complete tree diagram for each of the following sentences. Feel free to use the symbol PassP instead of VP$_{PastPart}$/1stNP. Be sure to indicate the position of the missing noun phrase in any passive phrase that you find.

    a. Peter has been asked to resign.
    b. Frances has had the drapes cleaned.
    c. Shirley seems to have gotten Fred promoted.
    d. Molly must have asked to be taken to the station.

9.1.3 Interpretation of the Passive Construction

As the preceding subsections made clear, the passive construction differs from ordinary verb phrases in both its internal structure and its external surroundings. As was noted at the beginning of the chapter, it is also markedly different from ordinary verb phrases in the manner in which it uses its subject. It is this difference that accounts for the way in which sentence (20) is interpreted.

(20)   John was taken to the library.

In particular, it accounts for the fact that the subject of the sentence as a whole is used to identify the understood object of the verb *taken*.

    Let us look in detail at the interpretation of sentence (20). The tree diagram is given in (21), where once again the longer symbol VP$_{PastPart}$/1stNP is used to stand for the passive phrase.

(21)

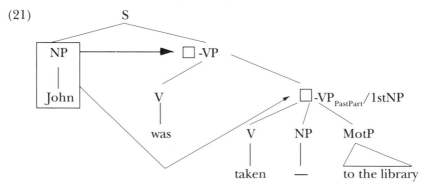

The choice of *John* as the subject of the main verb phrase comes about as a result of the first rule of chapter 8. Since *was* is an intransitive verb, the subject of the phrase that it heads also serves as the subject of its complement, again by one of the rules of chapter 8. Thus, we now have identified *John* as the subject of the passive phrase. If we were to use this subject in the usual way within this lower phrase, we would use it to identify the agent of the verb *taken*. But we know that *John* is not the the understood agent of *taken*. What happens instead is that inside the passive phrase, the subject is used to identify the missing noun phrase in object position. Thus, the subject is "deflected" from making its usual identification, and instead identifies a missing noun phrase associated with the construction. This entire situation is diagrammed in (22).

(22)

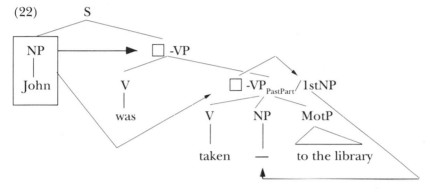

We see the same kind of deflection in a transitive verb phrase in which a passive phrase serves as the second complement. Such a structure is diagrammed in (23).

(23)

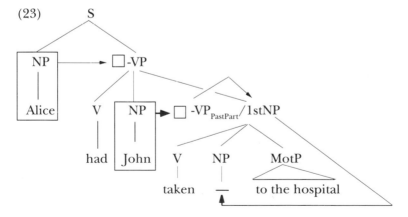

Here the rules of chapter 8 dictate that the direct-object noun phrase should serve as the subject of the complement that follows it. Thus, *John* is the subject of the passive phrase. But the subject of the passive phrase is now used in the same way as in the previous example. Instead of being used to identify the agent of *taken*, it is used to identify the missing noun phrase associated with the construction.

As was noted earlier in this chapter, English makes a special provision for identifying agents within passive phrases by means of the *by* phrase, exemplified in (24).

(24)   John was taken to the hospital *by the doctor.*

But what about a sentence like (25), where there is no noun phrase that identifies the agent?

(25)   John was taken to the hospital.

In such cases, our intuitive interpretation is that some unspecified person is the agent.

Even in situations like this one, in which no agent is expressed, the passive construction requires us to understand one as having played a role. This property of passives stands out quite clearly in the behavior of certain verbs of motion that can occur both in intransitive verb phrases and in passive phrases. *Roll* is one such verb:

(26)   a. The barrel [rolled down the hill].   (intransitive verb phrase)
        b. The barrel was [rolled down the hill].   (passive phrase)

In (26a) we have a strong sense of the barrel's having moved of its own accord, whereas in (26b) we have an equally strong sense that some agent must have been involved in making it roll. This latter interpretation is felt just as strongly here as in the active sentence (27), in which the agent is identified in the normal way by the subject.

(27)   Someone rolled the barrel down the hill.

To summarize, what makes the interpretation of the passive phrase unusual is that its subject is given the role of identifying a missing object of a verb or a preposition, rather than the more usual role of identifying an agent. In addition, the agent is either identified by a *by* phrase or left unidentified.

Exercise

1. Each of the following sentences contains an italicized passive phrase. For each sentence, draw a tree diagram in which you indicate all the subject identifications that contribute to the interpretation of the passive phrase. (If the ultimate identifier for the passive object is several phrases away, there will of course be several relevant links.)

     a. Karen was *introduced to Gordon.*

     b. We had John's phone *disconnected.*

     c. Jacob will regret having been *brought to the meeting.*

     d. Trying to be *examined by a specialist* is impossible for Bill.

9.1.4 Distinguishing Passive Phrases from Other Verb Phrases

Let us shift our attention now to the more practical matter of determining in specific examples whether we have a passive phrase or a nonpassive phrase. Even though this discussion will be practical in nature, we will rely heavily on particular rules discussed in this chapter and in earlier chapters. A construction in a certain situation will qualify as a passive phrase only if it satisfies two sets of requirements. The first set will consist of *internal requirements*, rules regulating the way in which the structure itself is built. The second set will consist of *external requirements*, rules stating the larger contexts in which the structure can be used. We will see that both kinds of requirements provide useful clues in the correct identification of phrase types in individual sentences.

9.1.4.1 Internal Requirements of Passive Phrases

Let us begin with the internal requirements of passive phrases. The first rule about passive phrases given in this chapter was that they must be headed by past participles. Thus, the first question to ask about an example phrase is whether its head verb in isolation could be analyzed as a past participle. Suppose, for instance, that we were asked about phrases that were headed as follows:

(28)   a. [taken...]

       b. [returned...]

       c. [put...]

       d. [forgot...]

       e. [remove...]

       f. [carrying...]

We know that *taken* is a past participle and nothing else; we also know that *returned* and *put* can be past participles, among other things. By contrast, none of the remaining three verbs can possibly be analyzed as a past participle, since the past participles for FORGET, REMOVE, and CARRY are *forgotten, removed,* and *carried.* Our temporary conclusion, then, would be that the first three phrases *might* be passive phrases, whereas the last three could not possibly be.

The other major requirement about the internal structure of passive phrases is that they have a missing first noun phrase, as compared with corresponding active verb phrases. Thus, when we want to know whether a certain phrase could possibly qualify as a passive phrase, our second question should be whether there is an acceptable active verb phrase in which a noun phrase is present after the same verb. In answering this question, we are relying on what we already know, unconsciously or consciously, about complement specifications for individual verbs. Some examples are given in (29).

(29)   a.   [taken to the office]
       b.   [killed]
       c.   [rolled down the hill]
       d.   [gone to the office]
       e.   [died]
       f.   [fallen down the hill]

The verbs in these examples are divided equally between those that allow a direct object in active structures and those that do not. Either we know this already or we can remind ourselves of it by doing experiments as in (30).

(30)   a.   John [took *Ted* to the office].   TAKE: [—NP MotP]
       b.   Shirley [killed *the crabgrass*].   KILL: [—NP]
       c.   Sam [rolled *the barrel* down the hill].   ROLL: [—NP MotP]
       d.   *John [went *Ted* to the office].   * GO: [—NP Mot]
       e.   *Shirley [died *the crabgrass*].   * DIE [—NP]
       f.   *Sam [fell *the barrel* down the hill].   * FALL: [—NP MotP]

These considerations lead us to conclude that the first three phrases in (28) might ultimately qualify as passive phrases, whereas the last three cannot possibly qualify.

In many situations, looking at internal requirements permits a definite decision as to whether a certain phrase is a passive phrase or an active phrase. Yet in one large class of examples, internal requirements by themselves are not sufficient. The problem examples are those whose head verb can occur in active phrases either with an object or without one. *Eat, shave,* and *roll* all have these dual possibilities:

(31) a. The canary [ate].   EAT: [—]
      b. The canary [ate *its lunch*].   EAT: [—NP]

(32) a. Bill [shaved].   SHAVE: [—]
      b. Bill [shaved *Fred*].   SHAVE: [—NP]

(33) a. The barrel [rolled down the hill].   ROLL: [—MotP]
      b. John [rolled *the barrel* down the hill]. ROLL: [—NP MotP]

Suppose we are given the phrase *eaten* in isolation and asked whether it is a passive phrase or an active phrase. *Eaten* is a past participle, so it could head a passive phrase. Also, the verb EAT allows following objects, so we could analyze this phrase as taking the form [*eaten* ____]. But the past participle *eaten* could also head an active verb phrase, of the sort that we found occurring with the verb HAVE. And EAT can be used in active sentences without an object, as we saw in (30a). Thus, this sequence can be analyzed simply as [*eaten*]. The result of these considerations is that we cannot really identify this phrase one way or another in isolation from a larger context.

We get an even more indeterminate result when we try to identify the phrases *shaved* and *rolled down the hill* in isolation. Both of these sequences can be analyzed as either past-participial active verb phrases or passive phrases. In addition, both qualify as past-tense active phrases, since *shaved* and *rolled* serve as past-tense forms as well as past participles.

In view of the existence of such examples, it is necessary to study the external requirements of passive phrases, paying particular attention to the ways in which they differ from the external requirements of past-participial and past-tense active phrases. Except for a few recalcitrant ambiguities (see exercise 2 of subsection 14.1.4), this attention to external requirements will allow us to make clear determinations in situations where internal requirements are not sufficient.

Exercise

1. Determine whether each of the following phrases could possibly be a passive phrase. When the answer is Yes, construct an example in which the phrase is used as a complement to BE. When the answer is No, say what requirement is not satisfied.

      a. handed to the mayor
      b. roll down the hill
      c. watched Bill open the safe
      d. told to leave the room
      e. traveled to Tehran
      f. moving into the kitchen

g.   closed
h.   flown across the border

9.1.4.2 External Requirements of Passive Phrases   Let us review briefly what we have learned about the positions in which passive phrases, past-participial active phrases, and past-tense active phrases can be used. We will be particularly interested in the question of whether the three possibilities overlap at all.

We have established that passive phrases can be used as complements to particular verbs, including BE, GET (both intransitive and transitive), HAVE (transitive), and WANT (transitive). In the following examples, we use the phrase *examined by the specialist*, whose internal structure dictates that it can only be a passive phrase.

(34)   a.   Fido [was *examined by the specialist*].   BE: [—PassP]
       b.   Fido [got *examined by the specialist*].   GET: [—PassP]
       c.   Alice [got Fido *examined by the specialist*].   GET: [—NP PassP]
       d.   Alice [had Fido *examined by the specialist*]. HAVE: [—NP PassP]

As for past-participial active phrases, we noted in chapter 3 that they can occur as complements of (intransitive) HAVE. Example (35) contains a phrase that has a direct object and thus can only be active.

(35)   Fido [has *examined the specialist*].   HAVE: [—VP$_{PastPart}$]

Finally, past-tense active phrases have been used in three situations so far. In chapter 2 we saw them used as predicates of simple sentences, and in chapter 4 we saw them used as predicates inside *that* complements and indirect questions:

(36)   a.   Fido [*ate* the biscuit].
       b.   Fred claims [that Fido [*ate* the biscuit]].
       c.   Fred wonders [whether Fido [*ate* the biscuit]].

Each of the environments mentioned above is the exclusive domain of just one of the three constructions. We already know from chapter 3 that past-tense active phrases and past-participial active phrases occupy completely different niches. In addition, if we try to use a past-tense or past-participial active phrase in one of the situations where passive phrases are allowed, the results are completely unacceptable:

(37)   a.   *Fido [was *examined the specialist*].   *BE: [–VP$_{PastPart}$]
       b.   *Fido [got *examined the specialist*].   *GET: [–VP$_{PastPart}$]
       c.   *Alice [got Fido *examined the specialist*].   *GET: [–NP VP$_{PastPart}$]
       d.   *Alice [had Fido *examined the specialist*]. *HAVE: [–NP VP$_{PastPart}$]

We get similar results if we try to use a passive phrase as the complement of intransitive HAVE, or as the predicate of an independent sentence or a sentence within a *that* clause or an indirect question:

(38)   *Fido [has *examined by the specialist*].   *HAVE: [–PassP]

(39)   a. *Fido *examined by the specialist.*
       b. *Fred claims that Fido *examined by the specialist.*
       c. *Fred wonders whether Fido *examined by the specialist.*

This discussion has a pleasant conclusion: In each of the contexts that we have studied so far, only one of the three phrase types under consideration is possible. We can see the full force of this conclusion by putting the phrase *rolled down the hill* in several different contexts. (As we saw in the preceding subsection, this phrase in isolation can be either a passive phrase, a past-participial active phrase, or a past-tense active phrase.) Suppose that we are asked to determine how this sequence should be analyzed in each of the following examples.

(40)   a.   The barrel has *rolled down the hill.*
       b.   The barrel was *rolled down the hill.*
       c.   Joe had the barrel *rolled down the hill.*
       d.   The barrel *rolled down the hill.*
       e.   Joe wanted the barrel *rolled down the hill.*
       f.   Jane says that the barrel *rolled down the hill.*
       g.   Jane says that the barrel has been *rolled down the hill.*

Here are the answers that we can give, along with the reasons:

(41)   a.   past-participial active phrase—complement of intransitive HAVE
       b.   passive phrase—complement of BE
       c.   passive phrase—complement of transitive HAVE
       d.   past-tense active phrase—finite predicate of independent sentence
       e.   passive phrase—complement of transitive WANT
       f.   past-tense active phrase—finite predicate of sentence in *that* clause
       g.   passive phrase—complement of BE.

This demonstration suggests the surprising possibility that we can distinguish passive phrases from past-tense and past-participial active phrases solely by paying attention to the contexts in which the phrases are used, without having to give any attention to their internal structure beyond making sure that the head verb is a possible past participle. This has a significant import for a fluent user of English, whose unconscious syntactic rules we are trying to mirror in our written rules. Suppose that this user is listening to an incoming sentence whose first four words are *The barrel got rolled....* Without hearing the remainder of the sentence, he or she knows already that *rolled* heads a passive phrase. From this the user can deduce that it will be followed by an understood object, and that the subject of this passive phrase is to be used to identify this object. On the other hand, suppose that the first four words of the incoming sentence are *The barrel has rolled....* In this sentence, the intransitive *has* tells the hearer to expect a past-participial active phrase, whose subject should be used in the way appropriate in active intransitive sentences.

Our discussion so far has dealt with situations in which we already know whether a certain verb allows a passive phrase. What can we do, though, in a situation in which we need to determine whether a new verb takes a passive complement or an active complement? For example, suppose that we are asked whether the italicized phrase in (42) is passive, active, or both.

(42)   John needs his car *moved to the back yard.*

This particular sequence happens to satisfy the internal requirements of both passive and active constructions, because *move* can be either intransitive or transitive. The phrase under study appears to be serving as a second complement of the verb *needs*, which we have not discussed in this chapter. Thus, what we want to find out is which of the following two complement specifications is correct for NEED:

(43)   a.   NEED: [—NP PassP]
       b.   NEED: [—NP VP$_{PastPart}$]

In order to test the first possibility, we need a phrase that can only be a passive phrase. The simplest possibility here is a phrase that contains an agent *by* phrase, such as *repaired by an expert.*

(44)   John needs his car *repaired by an expert.*

We can test the second possibility by substituting a phrase whose head verb can only be intransitive. STAY is a good example of such a verb, so *stayed in the back yard* should tell us what we want to know:

(45)   *John needs his car *stayed in the back yard.*

These two experimental sentences show us that (43a) is a correct specification for NEED, whereas (43b) is not. In other words, NEED allows passive phrases as second complements, but not past-participial active phrases.

In future chapters, we will discuss several additional contexts in which phrases headed by past participles can appear. Two such contexts are presented in (46).

(46)   a.   The barrel *rolled down the hill* belonged to Fred.
        b.   When *moved to a new position,* Harrison tries to adapt to his new surroundings.

Without taking up the question of exactly what the rules are that govern these constructions, let us see if we can determine whether the rules in question call for passive phrases or past-participial phrases. In such a situation, one in which we do not yet know consciously what the rules are, it is once again appropriate to devise experiments that will tell us whether our unconscious rules allow passives, actives, or both. We need to do the same thing that we did with NEED above. That is, we must find phrases that satisfy the internal requirements for only one of the two constructions, and substitute these phrases in the sentences in (46). To get phrases that can only be passive, we can include *by* phrases expressing agents:

(47)   a.   The barrel *rolled down the hill by Alice* belonged to Fred.
        b.   When *moved to a new position by his superiors,* Harrison tries to adapt to his new surroundings.

From the fact that these two experimental sentences are acceptable, we can conclude that passive phrases are allowed by the rules for the larger constructions.

Now let us see whether past-participial active phrases are also allowed. To test for this possibility, we need to substitute phrases that could only be active. The clearest examples are phrases headed by verbs that are always intransitive and phrases with transitive verbs and expressed objects. Example (48a) is of the former type; example (48b) is of the latter.

(48)   a.   *The barrel *vanished from the yard* belonged to Alice.
        b.   *When *received a new job,* Harrison tries to adapt to his new surroundings.

The unacceptability of these sentences shows that the rules for the larger constructions do not allow past-participial active phrases.

Exercises
1. Each of the following sentences contains the sequence *moved into the kitchen.* This sequence satisfies the internal requirements for being either a passive phrase, a past-participial active phrase, or a past-tense active

phrase. However, in each of the sentences there is only one correct analysis for the phrase. Using what was said above about the differing external behavior of these phrase types, identify the correct choice for each sentence and give your reason.

    a. The table has been *moved into the kitchen.*
    b. You should have it *moved into the kitchen.*
    c. The smoke *moved into the kitchen.*
    d. The fact that the table was *moved into the kitchen* is irrelevant.
    e. The dog has been *moved into the kitchen.*
    f. The dog has *moved into the kitchen.*
    g. Sally said that the dog has *moved into the kitchen.*

2. List all the passive phrases in the following paragraph. In making your list, try to decide exactly where the passive phrase starts and where it ends. It will be helpful to remember that it is identical to a past-participial verb phrase with a missing noun phrase and a possible extra *by* phrase.

> If Patricia was told that the books had been returned, then she should have decided to have the bills revised. The customers were persuaded to let their money be returned. The dealer was informed that strong words were uttered.

9.2 The *Easy* Construction

We now turn to a second construction in which the subject of a phrase makes an unusual contribution to the interpretation of the phrase. The construction of interest is a certain type of adjective phrase that can be headed by *easy*, *difficult*, and certain other adjectives. We are already familiar with one of the situations in which these adjectives occur:

(49)   a.   *It* was easy for Charlie *to solve the problem.*
       b.   *It* is difficult *to reason with this banker.*

In each of these sentences, the clausal substitute *it* is linked to a postponed infinitival phrase. The situation is entirely different in the construction to which we now turn.

9.2.1 Syntactic Properties of the *Easy* Construction
Two examples of the new construction are given in (50).

(50)   a.   The problem was [easy for Charlie *to solve*].
       b.   This banker is [difficult *to reason with*].

At first glance, this construction does not look too much different from the old one. A close inspection, however, reveals two major differences. The first is that the subject of this construction is an ordinary noun phrase rather than the clausal substitute *it*. The second is that there is something peculiar about the infinitival phrases that follow the adjectives: Each sequence lacks a noun phrase in a position where one would normally be required. Both the verb SOLVE and the preposition WITH must have objects, as we can see by trying to do without them in the simple sentences of (51).

(51) a. *Charlie solved.
      b. *Someone reasoned with.

To see the same point in another way, observe that infinitival sequences such as the ones in (50) are impossible with our earlier examples of adjectives that allowed ordinary infinitival complements, adjectives such as *eager* and *unlikely*:

(52) a. Charlie is eager to solve *it*.
      b. Fred is unlikely to reason with *him*.

(53) a. *Charlie is eager to solve.
      b. *Fred is unlikely to reason with.

Missing noun phrases are absolutely required in the new construction. The same complete infinitival phrases that gave good results with *eager* and *likely* give bad results in this new environment:

(54) a. *The problem was easy for Charlie to solve it.
      b. *This banker is difficult to reason with him.

   Because of the missing noun phrases required in this infinitival construction, it has often been treated as a variant of the passive construction that we studied in the section 9.1. But in fact the two constructions differ in a significant way. Whereas the missing noun phrase in the passive construction had to be the first noun phrase after the verb, the missing noun phrase in the infinitival after EASY can be farther away from the verb. We see this contrast in examples (55) and (56).

(55) a. *This drawer was [kept the files in ___].   (passive)
             (Compare: Someone tried to keep the files *in this drawer*.)
      b. This drawer was hard [to keep the files in ___].
             (*easy* construction)

(56)   a. *Jane was [tried to persuade ___].   (passive)
          (Compare: Someone tried to persuade *Jane*.)
       b.   Jane was hard for us [to try to persuade ___].
          (*easy* construction)

   For this construction, then, all that we need to require is that there be
a missing noun phrase. We do not have to add the requirement that it be
the first one after the verb. What follows the adjective in these examples,
then, is just an infinitival phrase with a missing noun phrase, which we will
denote with the symbol InfP/NP. With this symbol in hand, we can provide
complement specifications for the adjectives that take this construction.
The specifications for EASY and DIFFICULT are given in (57).

(57)   a.   EASY: [— *For*-P InfP/NP]; [—InfP/NP]
       b.   DIFFICULT: [— *For*-P InfP/NP]; [—InfP/NP]

Translated into trees, the specifications for EASY look as in (58).

Thus, the tree diagrams appropriate for our original sentences are as
given in (59).

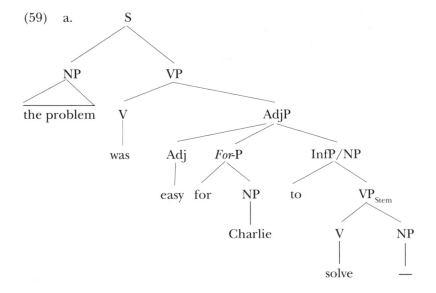

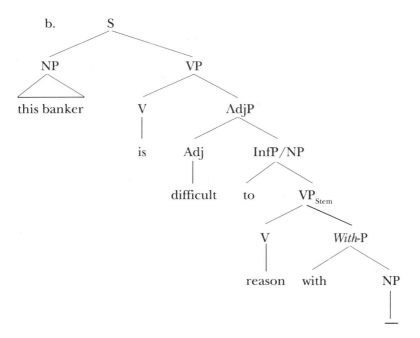

Exercises

1. In the sentences given below, insert a blank in the position of the missing noun phrase called for by the *easy* construction.

     a. Jack was easy to take to Boston.

     b. This fiddle is difficult to play sonatas on.

     c. This horse is hard to keep happy.

     d. John is easy to talk about baseball with, but he is hard to persuade to play.

2. Draw the tree that goes with each of the following sentences. Be sure to indicate the position of any missing noun phrase.

     a. I consider this sentence hard to diagram.

     b. This question seems easy to answer.

     c. The outline may help to make the material easy for Alice to explain.

     d. That Bill will be easy to talk to is hard for me to believe.

9.2.2 Interpretation of the *Easy* Construction

Let us examine the interpretation of the two central examples from the discussion just concluded:

(60)   a.   The problem was easy for Charlie to solve.

        b.   This banker is difficult to reason with.

If asked to identify the "understood object" of the verb *solve* in (60a), a fluent English speaker would immediately pick out *the problem*, the subject of the sentence as a whole. Similarly, the same speaker would have no trouble in identifying *this banker* as the "understood object" of the preposition *with* in (60b). In this subsection we will consider how this identification takes place—how the link is formed between the subject of the sentence as a whole and the missing noun phrase down inside the infinitive phrase.

Let us begin with (60a), and apply one at a time the subject-identification rules developed in chapter 5. First, the noun phrase *the problem* serves as the subject of the verb phrase headed by *was*. Then, by the rule about complements of intransitive verbs, this subject identifies the subject of the adjective phrase headed by *easy*. The object of *for* identifies the subject of the infinitive phrase, just as it identifies an infinitival subject when the infinitive phrase itself is the subject of EASY. The three links established so far are shown in (61).

(61)

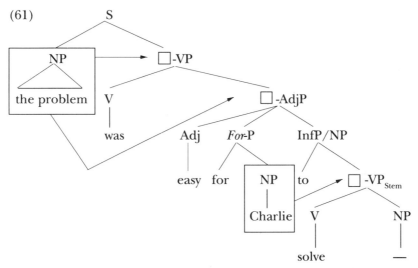

Two other connections must be made. In the first place, the subject of EASY must be deflected, so that it identifies the missing noun phrase associated with the infinitival construction rather than identifying the subject of any lower phrase. In the second place, the empty noun phrase after *solve* needs to be picked out as the missing noun phrase required by the larger constructions. These connections are evident in (62), which is a revised version of (61).

(62)

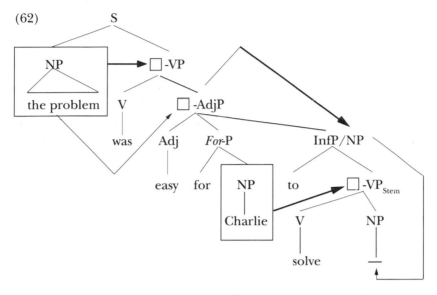

We now have an unbroken chain of links between the subject of the sentence as a whole and the missing noun phrase down inside the infinitival clause.

The linking of the subject of the sentence with a missing noun phrase proceeds in much the same way when the adjective lacks a *for* phrase. The diagram in (63) shows the links that would be established for (60b).

(63)

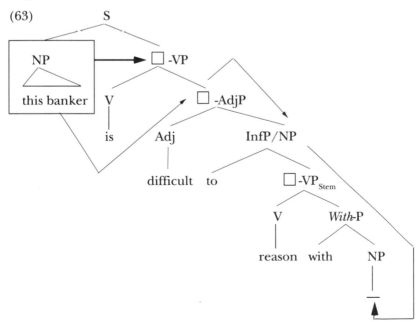

According to the rules that we have used so far, the only subject that is not provided with identification from the outside is the subject of the bare-stem verb phrase inside the infinitival clause. And this result seems to be consistent with our intuitions as speakers of English: The "understood subject" of this verb phrase is something like the impersonal "people in general," just as it was for some of the subject infinitival constructions examined in chapter 8. Here again, we can describe the results by referring to an understood *for* phrase that goes along with adjectives like EASY and DIFFICULT.

Exercise

1. In exercise 2 at the end of the preceding section, you were asked to diagram the following sentences:

    a. I consider this sentence hard to diagram.

    b. This question seems easy to answer.

    c. The outline may help to make the material easy for Alice to explain.

    d. That Bill will be easy to talk to is quite hard for me to believe.

Add to each tree diagram the links that are relevant to the identification of the missing noun phrase in the *easy* construction.

III
The Syntax of Phrases: Modification

Chapter 10

Modification of Nouns and Noun Phrases

In this chapter we will discuss the constructions that are employed in English to provide *modification* for nouns and noun phrases. For the purposes of this chapter, we will use the term *modifier* to mean a word or a construction that tells more about the thing modified. We can make a further division between *restrictive modification*, which applies to common noun phrases, and *nonrestrictive modification*, which applies to noun phrases and other larger syntactic units. Section 10.1 gives a brief sketch of the semantic effect of restrictive modification. In section 10.2 we will discuss restrictive relative clauses, and in section 10.3 we will examine a variety of nonclausal modifying constructions. In section 10.4, we will look at nonrestrictive relative clauses and note some of the ways in which they differ syntactically and semantically from restrictive clauses.

10.1 Restrictive Modification

The general concept of restrictive modification is illustrated by the pairs of related examples in (1)–(3). In each pair, the (a) sentence contains a noun phrase whose head noun is unmodified; the (b) sentence contains a corresponding noun phrase in which the same head noun is restricted.

(1) a. Gregory knows [a pianist].
     b. Gregory knows [a pianist *who lives in Boston*].
(2) a. Janet met [a student].
     b. Janet met [a student *from Sweden*].
(3) a. We spoke with [an artist].
     b. We spoke with [a *young* artist].

We can picture the sets of individuals that are denoted by *pianist, student,* and *artist* as circles:

(4)

When these nouns stand alone, they denote the entire sets. By contrast, when the same nouns are modified, the sets of individuals denoted by the whole expression are those that belong both to the original set and at the same time to a second set, as (5) shows.

(5)

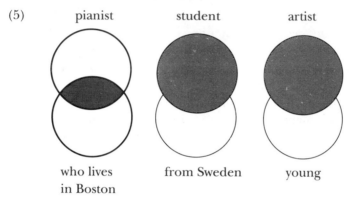

Thus, when these modifiers are combined with their nouns, the set of persons denoted is "more restricted" than the set which the noun by itself denotes. In what follows, we will refer to the construction *who lives in Boston* as a *bound relative clause*, thus distinguishing it from the free relative clauses studied in chapter 7. The phrases *from Sweden* and *young* will be referred to as *nonclausal modifiers*, the former *postnominal* and the latter *prenominal*.

10.2 Restrictive Bound Relative Clauses

10.2.1 The Structure of Restrictive Bound Relative Clauses
Let us begin our examination of bound relative clauses by looking at some actual examples, grouped according to their internal structure.

(6) a. The senators [who(m) Fred voted for] have resigned.
     b. The report [which Karen submitted] implicated several of her friends.
     c. The guy [whose dog you fed] has left town.
     d. The journalists [who exposed the fraud] are being sued.

(7)   a.   We read the article [that Smith recommended].

        b.   The safe [that Henry keeps his money in] has been stolen.

        c.   The people [that voted for Bill] dislike his policies.

(8)   a.   The accident [Jason caused] will be investigated.

        b.   The problem [you told us about] has been resolved.

As with two constructions studied earlier (indirect questions and free relative clauses), it makes sense with the first two of these groups of relative clauses to divide them up into an introducing element of some sort, followed by a finite structure:

(9)   a.   who(m)   Fred voted for

        b.   which   Karen submitted

        c.   whose dog   you fed

        d.   who   exposed the fraud

(10)   a.   that   Smith recommended

        b.   that   Henry keeps his money in

        c.   that   voted for Bill

In the third group, the relative clauses consist of finite structures alone, without any introducing element preceding them:

(11)   a.   ——   Jason caused

        b.   ——   you told us about

(For convenience, we will refer to this last type as "bare relative clauses.") To summarize, the types of relative clauses illustrated above can be introduced in the following ways:

- by a noun phrase that either consists of one of the three "relative pronouns" *who, whom,* and *which* or else contains the genitive relative pronoun *whose*
- by the word *that*
- by nothing.

Let us now look at the right-hand structures in these relative clauses. Besides being finite, they have one other important property: Each of them is understood as containing a missing noun phrase.

(12)   a.   Fred voted for ____   (Compare: Fred voted for *them.*)

        b.   Karen submitted ____   (Compare: Karen submitted *it.*)

        c.   you fed ____   (Compare: You fed *his dog.*)

        d.   ____ exposed the fraud   (Compare: *They* exposed the fraud.)

(13) a. Smith recommended ____   (Compare: Smith
                                                                         recommended *it.*)

       b. Henry keeps his money in ____   (Compare: Henry keeps
                                                                         his money in *it.*)

       c. ___ voted for Bill   (Compare: *They* voted
                                                                         for Bill.)

(14) a. Jason caused ____   (Compare: Jason caused *it.*)

       b. you told us about ____   (Compare: You told us about *it.*)

In all three of these groups, the missing phrase is clearly a noun phrase.

   With these observations in hand, we are ready to state rules for forming bound relatives of the kind shown so far. We begin by defining *relative noun phrase* as in (15).

(15)   A *relative noun phrase* consists of one of the following:

   •   the word *who*, the word *whom*, or the word *which*
   •   the word *whose* plus a common noun phrase.

We can then state the following rule:

(16)   A restrictive bound relative clause can consist of one of the following combinations:

   •   a relative noun phrase followed by a finite sentence
       with a missing noun phrase
   •   the word *that*, followed by a finite sentence
       with a missing noun phrase
   •   a finite sentence with a missing noun phrase.

These possibilities are presented in diagram form in (17).

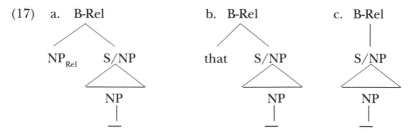

(17) a. B-Rel   b. B-Rel   c. B-Rel

A special restriction must be stated for bare relative clauses, as the examples in (18) indicate.

(18)   a. *The journalists [___ exposed the fraud] are being sued.

       b. *The people [___ voted for Bill] dislike his policies.

When the missing noun phrase is the subject of the sentence, the bare-relative-clause structure cannot be used. Instead, some introducing phrase must be present—either a relative noun phrase or the word *that*:

(19) a. The journalists [*who* ___ exposed the fraud] are being sued.
      b. The people [*who* ___ voted for Bill] dislike his policies.

(20) a. The journalists [*that* ___ exposed the fraud] are being sued.
      b. The people [*that* ___ voted for Bill] dislike his policies.

(21) a. *The journalists [___ exposed the fraud] are being sued.
      b. *The people [___ voted for Bill] dislike his policies.

Relative clauses are also possible in which the missing phrase is something other than a noun phrase. A first group is exemplified in (22).

(22) a. The official [*to whom* Smith loaned the money] has been indicted.
      b. Martha's sister is the person [*on whom* Fred depends].
      c. The man [*on whose lap* the puppet is sitting] is a ventriloquist.

In these relative clauses, the introducing phrase is clearly a prepositional phrase:

(23) a. to whom   Smith loaned the money
      b. on whom   Fred depends
      c. on whose lap   the puppet is sitting

This introductory prepositional phrase consists itself of a preposition followed by a relative noun phrase. The finite structure that follows this introducing phrase correspondingly contains a missing prepositional phrase of the same kind:

(24) a. Smith loaned the money   (Compare: Smith loaned the money *to him*.)
      b. Fred depends   (Compare: Fred depends *on her*.)
      c. the puppet is sitting   (Compare: The puppet is sitting *on his lap*.)

Two rules give the structure of these relative clauses. The first rule defines *relative prepositional phrases* in terms of the already defined relative noun phrases:

(25) A *relative prepositional phrase* is a prepositional phrase the object of which is a relative noun phrase.

The next rule specifies this kind of relative structure as a whole:

(26) A relative clause can consist of a relative prepositional phrase, followed by a finite sentence with a missing prepositional phrase of the same kind.

Rules (25) and (26) together create structures of the form diagrammed in (27).

(27)

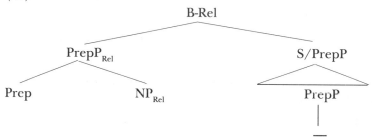

A second group of relative clauses that contain missing phrases other than noun phrases are illustrated in (28).

(28) a. The hotel [where Gloria stays] is being remodeled.
      b. The room [where Joe is taking his tools] is in Byron's basement.
      c. The day [when Jim got fired] was a great day for Christianity.

These relative clauses can be divided as in (29).

(29) a. where   Gloria stays
      b. where   Joe is taking his tools
      c. when   Jim got fired

The sequences on the right can be understood as containing a locative phrase, a motion phrase, and a time phrase, respectively:

(30) a. Gloria stays   (Compare: Gloria stays *there.*)
      b. Joe is taking his tools (Compare: Joe is taking his tools *there.*)
      c. Jim got fired   (Compare: Jim got fired *then.*)

These relative clauses, then, can be described by the following rule:

(31) A relative clause can consist of

      • the word *where*, followed by a sentences with a missing locative phrase
      • the word *where*, followed by a sentences with a missing motion phrase
      • the word *when*, followed by a sentences with a missing time phrase.

In pictures, these rules take the following form:

(32)   a.   B-Rel   b.   B-Rel

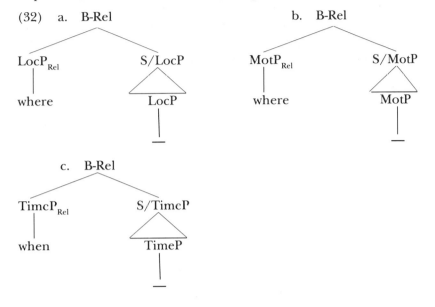

Exercise

1. Draw a tree diagram for each of the following relative clauses:

     a.   [that Harry would object to]
     b.   [which Patricia wanted to see]
     c.   [that struck Norman]
     d.   [Fred ate]
     e.   [whose father Joseph cured]
     f.   [in which Katy kept the records]
     g.   [in which the records were kept]
     h.   [where Gloria intends to put the sofa]

10.2.2 An Additional Structure: Infinitival Relative Clauses

Bound relatives of still another sort are based on infinitival structures rather than finite structures. Two of these types are illustrated in (33) and (34).

(33)   a.   a book [for you to give to Alice]
      b.   a bench [for you to sit on]

(34)   a.   a book [to give to Alice]
      b.   a bench [to sit on]

The relatives in (33) are based on full infinitival clauses; those in (34) are built on infinitival clauses that lack a *for* phrase.

Like all our previous kinds of relative clauses, these constructions involve missing phrases. We see this when we try to make finite sentences that correspond to the infinitival clauses in (33) and (34):

(35)   a. *You gave to Alice.
        b. *You sat on.

Thus, (36) and (37) represent these relative clauses in more revealing fashion.

(36)   a. [for you to give ___ to Alice]
        b. [for you to sit on ___]

(37)   a. [to give ___ to Alice]
        b. [to sit on ___]

The rule that we can give for them is very simple:

(38)   A bound relative clause can consist of an infinitival clause with a missing noun phrase.

This rule gives one of the two structures illustrated in (39), depending on whether or not the infinitival clause has a *for* phrase.

(39)   a.   b.

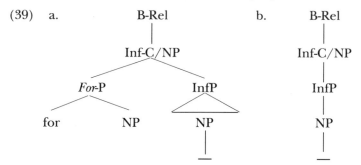

Another infinitival relative structure is also possible:

(40)   a. a bench [on which to sit ___]
        b. a refrigerator [in which to put the beer ___]

This construction is introduced by a relative prepositional phrase, and has a missing prepositional phrase inside it. In contrast with the previous construction, a full infinitival clause is impossible here:

(41)   a. *a bench [on which for Jerry to sit ___]
        b. *a refrigerator [in which for you to put the beer ___]

We might think that we should also be able to introduce an infinitival relative clause with just a relative noun phrase instead of a relative prepositional phrase. However, this option is not allowed, as the examples in (42) show.

(42)   a. *a book [which to give ___ to Alice]
       b. *a bench [which to sit on ___]

For the examples in (39), then, we need a rule that limits the introducing phrases to *prepositional* phrases and also requires the following structure to be an infinitival *phrase*. Such a rule is given as (43).

(43)   A bound relative clause can consist of a relative prepositional phrase followed by an infinitival phrase with a missing prepositional phrase of the same kind.

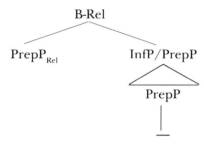

Exercise
1. Draw a tree diagram for each of the following infinitival relatives:
       a.   [for Bill to examine]
       b.   [to take to Harry's party]
       c.   [on whom to rely]
       d.   [in which to hide the bottles]

10.2.3 How Bound Relative Clauses Fit into Noun Phrases
In subsection 10.2.2 we described the structure of several different varieties of English relative clauses. It is time now to consider the question of how they fit into noun phrases.

The first fact to be observed is that these relative clauses as a group go particularly well with common noun phrases—much better than with proper nouns or pronouns. This is particularly clear with relatives introduced by *that*:

(44)   a.   the *man* [that grows peaches]
       b.   the *king of England* [that grows peaches]
       c.   *John Smith* [that grows peaches]
       d.   *?him* [that grows peaches]

In view of these differences, we do not want to say that a noun phrase joins with a relative clause to make a bigger noun phrase:

(45)   NP

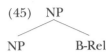

NP   B-Rel

If we adopted such a structure for the noun phrases in (44a) and (44b), our rules would also allow the construction of the unacceptable noun phrases in (44c) and (44d). This is because *John Smith* and *him* count as noun phrases just as much as *the man* and *the king of England*.

(46)   **NP**   **Rel**
    a.   the man   that grows peaches
    b.   the king of England   that grows peaches
    c. *John Smith   that grows peaches
    d. *?him   that grows peaches

Combinations of the type shown in (46d) were possible in English at an earlier time:

(47)   a.   *He who laughs last* laughs best.
      b.   *He who is without sin among you*, let him first cast a stone at her.

However, they are definitely perceived by modern speakers as archaic.

The analysis that we will adopt instead will rest on a rule that links these relative clauses specifically with *common noun phrases*. A partial version of this rule is stated in (48).

(48)   A common noun phrase can be joined with a relative clause. (The phrase so formed is of a type yet to be determined.)

Such a rule would give the following kind of structure for the noun phrase in (44a):

(49)   NP

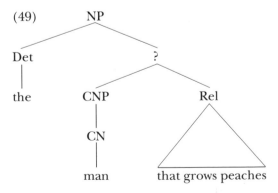

In diagram (49), the undetermined phrase type is indicated by a question mark. Some helpful evidence on what this phrase type might be is provided by the fact that another relative clause can be joined to the phrase *man who grows peaches*:

(50)   the man [who grows peaches] [who lives near your cousin]

Out of all the men who grow peaches, this second relative clause picks out the one who lives near your cousin. A reasonable structure for this larger noun phrase is given in (51).

(51)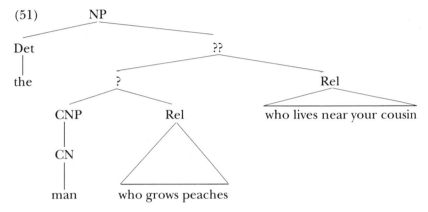

The relative clause *who grows peaches* was brought into the noun phrase by being attached to the common noun phrase *man*. If we wish to have the second relative clause attached by the same rule, then *man who grows peaches* must itself be analyzed as a common noun phrase. That is, we wan to have the following structure for *man who grows peaches*:

(52)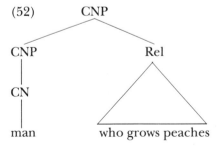

Exactly this structure will allow it to be the "smaller" common noun phrase to which a second relative clause can be joined.

We can now complete the rule stated in partial form above:

(53)   A common noun phrase joins with a following relative clause to make a (larger) common noun phrase.

With this finished rule in hand, we are in a position to replace the incomplete diagram in (51) with the complete picture in (54).

(54)

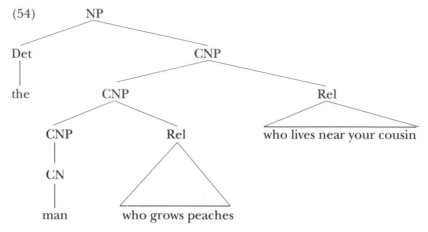

Although relative clauses are most commonly found next to the common noun phrase that they modify, they may optionally be moved to the end of a sentence. The pairs of sentences in (55) illustrate this possibility. The first sentence in each pair has the relative clause in its usual place; the second sentence has it at the end.

(55) a. *A man [who likes George's music]* has been found.
      b. *A man* ___ has been found [*who likes George's music*].
(56) a. George borrowed *the book [that he had been wanting to read]* from Sally.
      b. George borrowed *the book* ___ from Sally [*that he had been wanting to read*].

Exercises

1. Draw a tree diagram for each of the noun phrases listed below. Some of the noun phrases contain more than one common noun phrase, and you will want to decide which one has the relative clause attached to it.

      a. the play that Brenda wrote
      b. several people who knew your brother
      c. a list of the movies that were shown at the festival
      d. a list of the movies that was posted on the bulletin board
      e. a list of the movies that were shown at the festival that was posted on the bulletin board
      f. the pictures of Chicago that John sent to Marsha
      g. the book that Bill wrote that Frank edited

2. The following noun phrase has two possible structures:

the picture of the desk that is kept in Joe's basement

Draw a tree diagram for each structure.

3. Draw a tree diagram for each of the following sentences. Be sure to give a detailed structure for noun phrases containing relative clauses.

    a. The person who hired Biil has been reprimanded.
    b. Bernice will put the magazines that she has read in Julia's attic.
    c. The keys were kept in the cupboard in which the files were kept.
    d. Velma saw the book that Karen wrote that Mike edited.

10.2.4 Interpretation of Relative Clauses

We have so far described the structures that can be employed in bound relative clauses and also the rules governing their use in larger constructions. One additional topic that deserves special attention is the way in which these constructions are interpreted.

Though there are several different ways of describing the interpretation of relative clauses, the one that will be presented here will have the twin advantages of being simple and being well suited for a practical discussion that will come later in the chapter. The interpretive rules that we will develop will have the effect of associating with a noun phrase like (57a) the somewhat awkward-sounding paraphrase in (57b).

(57)   a. the wagon [that Herman wrecked ___]
        b. the wagon such that [Herman wrecked *that wagon*]

Essentially, what the rules will do is bring something into the relative clause from outside. In (57), the relative clause was augmented by the insertion of the noun phrase *that wagon* in the position of the missing noun phrase.

As a first step in building these interpretations, let us assume that every relative clause modifying a common noun phrase has a special understood noun phrase fabricated for it. This noun phrase consists of either *that* or *those*, together with the smaller common noun phrase with which the relative clause is joined. The examples of large noun phrases in (58) illustrate how this understood noun phrase is obtained.

(58)   a. the woman [that Gordon greeted]
            common noun phrase to which relative clause is joined: *woman*
            donated noun phrase: *that woman*
        b. the king [whose daughter Arnold married]
            common noun phrase to which relative clause is joined: *king*
            donated noun phrase: *that king*

We can include these donated noun phrases in the relevant tree diagrams as shown in (59).

(59)   a.

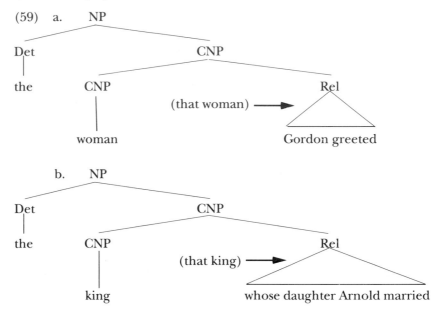

b.

Let us now see how these donated noun phrases are used. When the relative clause is introduced by *that* or by nothing, the donated noun phrase is passed directly to the sentence with the missing noun phrase, which then uses it to identify the missing phrase as in (60).

(60)

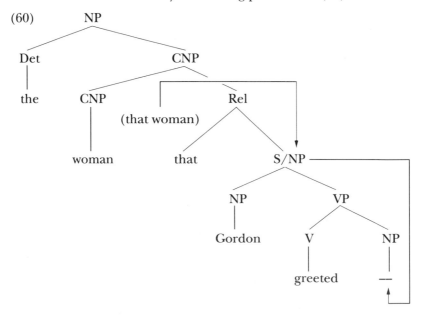

When we carry out the indicated substitution, we get the representation in (61).

(61)   the woman such that [Gordon greeted *that woman*]

The situation is more complex in one significant respect when the relative clause starts with a relative noun phrase or prepositional phrase, that is, a phrase containing *who, whom, whose,* or *which.* In this situation, the interpretation has to be accomplished in two steps instead of one. First, the relative clause uses the donated noun phrase to identify the *wh* word. Then the introducing phrase as a whole is handed over to the structure containing the missing phrase, which uses it in the usual way. How this complex process works for the example in (58b) is shown in (62).

(62)

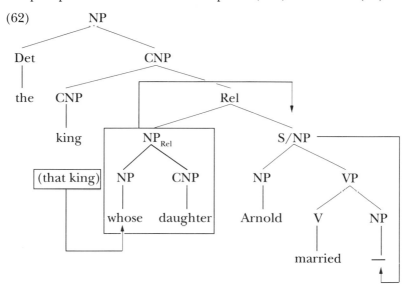

The first step is to substitute the donated noun phrase *that king* for the *who* in *whose.* We then substitute the result as the object of *married.* The result is the following representation in (63), which expresses exactly the meaning of the entire noun phrase.

(63)   the king such that [Arnold married *that king's daughter*]

Exercises

1. For each of the following noun phrases, give an interpretation of the kind discussed above.

      a.   the wagon that Martha painted

      b.   the steak we ate

    c.   the picture of George that we hung in our attic
    d.   the cupboard in which the prints were kept
    e.   the person whose dog the postman detests
    f.   the woman in whose attic George found a masterpiece
    g.   the movie that Shirley enjoyed that bored Alfred

2. As was noted in exercise 2 of subsection 10.2.3, the following noun phrase can have two different structures:

    the picture of the desk [that is kept in Joe's basement]

Give the two distinct interpretations that result from these different structures.

10.2.5 The Proper Identification of *That* Sequences

The relative-clause structure introduced by *that* is the second kind of subordinate sentence structure we have seen that starts with the word *that*. In chapter 4, we discussed *that* clauses—constructions of the sort illustrated in (64).

(64)   a.   Martha knows [that John was elected].
        b.   [That John was elected] surprised Frank.
        c.   It surprised Frank [that John was elected].
        d.   The fact [that John was elected] surprised Frank.
        e.   Martha told Bill [that John was elected]

An attempt will be made here to give some hints about how the two constructions can be distinguished when they occur in sentences. As in earlier cases of the same sort, the strategies will rest on ideas about particular syntactic rules. As usual, two groups of rules will be important: those that dictate where these constructions may occur (their *external syntax*) and those that dictate how they are built (their *internal syntax*).

10.2.5.1 External Requirements for *That* Clauses

First, let us review the external syntax of *that* clauses. The most important general point here is that this structure always appears with the permission of some particular word. Sometimes this word is a verb or adjective that takes the clause as a complement, as in (65).

(65)   a.   We *know* [that...].
        b.   We are *certain* [that...].

Sometimes it is a verb that takes a *that* clause as a second object, after an ordinary noun phrase, as in (66).

(66)   a.   We *told* Bill [that...].
        b.   We *warned* Bill [that...].

Sometimes it is one of a limited class of nouns, as in (67).

(67) a. The *fact* [that...] surprised us.
      b. Joe argued against the *view* [that...].

Finally, certain verbs and adjectives allow *that* clauses as subjects, either postponed or unpostponed, as in (68).

(68) a. [That...] *surprised us*.
      b. It *surprised* us [that...].
      c. [That...] is *certain*.
      d. It is *certain* [that...].

Let us look at a practical problem now. Suppose that we are asked to decide whether the *that* sequences in (69) satisfy the external requirements for *that* clauses.

(69) a. The opinion [that...] surprised us.
      b. The number [that...] surprised us.

This problem reduces to finding out whether the noun *opinion* allows a *that* clause and then answering the same question for the noun *number*. Here we can construct experiments of the kind that we have already seen several times earlier in this book. We proceed by putting something after these nouns that could only be a *that* clause. As we will be reminded below when we review the internal syntax of relative clauses, the sequence *that all cows eat grass* cannot be a relative clause under any circumstances. So now let us judge the noun phrases in (70).

(70) a. the opinion that all cows eat grass
      b. *the number that all cows eat grass

These two experimental examples show us immediately that the noun *opinion* does allow *that* clauses, whereas the noun *number* does not. These observations about the behavior of the two nouns enables us to answer our original question concerning the examples in (69). The *that* sequence in (69a) could be a *that* clause, at least as far as its external syntax is concerned, whereas the corresponding sequence in (69b) could not possibly be a *that* clause.

We can deal with (71) in the same way.

(71) a. Joe persuaded the man [that...].
      b. Joe kicked the man [that...].

Here again, the question whether the bracketed sequences satisfy the external requirements for *that* clauses reduces to a question about the verbs *persuade* and *kick*: Which of these words (if either) allows a *that* clause as a second object? As before, the sequence *that all cows eat grass* cannot be anything but a *that* clause. Thus, we can substitute it for the *that* sequences in (71) and see how the resulting sentences sound:

(72) a. Joe persuaded the man that all cows eat grass.
      b. *Joe kicked the man that all cows eat grass.

The results are clear: *Persuade* allows a *that* clause as a second object, whereas *kick* does not. Thus, the *that* sequence in (71a) satisfies the external conditions for being a *that* clause, whereas the one in (71b) does not.

Exercise
1. For each of the bracketed sequences below, say whether or not it satisfies the external requirements for *that* clauses.
      a. John wants to be sure [that Joe hid in the attic].
      b. We want to remove the papers [that Joe hid in the attic].
      c. We want to tell the reporters [that Joe hid in the attic].
      d. The lamp [that Joe hid in the attic] was useful to the police.
      e. The information [that Joe hid in the attic] was useful to the police.
      f. It surprised the man [that Joe hid in the attic].

10.2.5.2 External Requirements for Relative Clauses   For relative clauses introduced by *that*, we find an external requirement of a completely different kind. The basic requirement for these relative clauses is simply that they be associated with common noun phrases. The simplest kind of common noun phrase consists of a common noun by itself, as in (73).

(73) a. the *dog* [that...]
      b. several *people* [that...]

Other common noun phrases may consist of a common noun plus a complement:

(74) a. the *king of England* [that...]
      b. the *student of physics* [that...]

Still others may consist of a smaller common noun phrase joined with a relative clause:

(75) a. the *person that John interviewed* [that...]
      b. the *fellow we hired* [that...]

In most cases, the relative clause will be directly preceded by the common noun phrase, but in some sentences we may find the relative clause shifted to the right.

As was noted earlier, neither proper nouns used in the usual way nor pronouns give rise to common noun phrases, and therefore they cannot be modified by relative clauses introduced by *that*. Thus, neither of the *that* sequences in (76) satisfies the external condition for being a relative clause.

(76)   a.   We told *John* [that...].
       b.   We told *him* [that...].

Exercise

1. Say whether each of the bracketed sequences in the following sentences satisfies the external conditions for being a relative clause. (The bracketed sequence used throughout is one that satisfies the internal requirements for both *that* clauses and relative clauses.)

       a.   John wants to be sure [that Joe hid in the attic].
       b.   We want to remove the papers [that Joe hid in the attic].
       c.   We want to tell the reporters [that Joe hid in the attic].
       d.   The lamp [that Joe hid in the attic] was useful to the police.
       e.   The information [that Joe hid in the attic] was useful to the police.
       f.   It surprised the man [that Joe hid in the attic].
       g.   It surprised Bill [that Joe hid in the attic].
       h.   The man was taken into custody [that Joe hid in the attic].

10.2.5.3 The Internal Requirements of the Two Constructions   Let us turn now to the internal requirements of these two constructions. The essential internal requirement for a *that* clause is that it consist of *that* plus S, whereas the corresponding requirement for a relative clause is that it consist of *that* plus a sentence with a missing noun phrase. The difference is illustrated in (77).

(77)   a.   *That*-C   b.   B-Rel

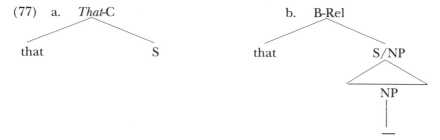

The two tree diagrams in (77) look quite different, which might lead to the expectation that the choice between them for particular examples would always be clear. In some instances the choice actually is easy; in others it is impossible to tell just by looking at the sequence which of the two structures it represents.

The clear cases are those—such as (78)—in which the sequence after *that* has no room for an extra noun phrase.

(78)   a.   [that *all cows eat grass*]
       b.   [that *Joe disappeared*]
       c.   [that *we will speak with John*]
       d.   [that *I believe Martha will stay at the university*]

These particular examples do not have any room for another noun phrase, and thus could only be *that* clauses. The same verdict also holds for the examples in (79).

(79)   a.   [that *Beth will be easy for us to work with*]
       b.   [that *Alice was elected to the committee*]
       c.   [that *Sarah ate the pie that George baked*]

These examples actually do contain missing noun phrases, as is shown in (80).

(80)   a.   [that Beth will be easy for us to work with ___]
       b.   [that Alice was elected ___ to the committee]
       c.   [that Sarah ate the pie that George baked ___]

However, each of these missing noun phrases is associated with some smaller construction within the sequence, and thus is not available for use as the missing noun phrase associated with the structure as a whole. In (80a) the missing noun phrase is associated with the *easy* construction. In (80b) it is called for by the passive phrase. In (80c) it is required by the small relative clause modifying *pie*. As a consequence, none of the three sequences after *that* has a missing-noun-phrase position that is available to be used by the entire larger construction. Hence, none of the three larger sequences can possibly be relative clauses.

The considerations of the preceding paragraph provide us with an opportunity to make a general point about "missing phrase" constructions of all kinds. When we referred to the sequence *to work with* in (79a) as "an infinitival phrase with a missing noun phrase," what we really meant would have required a few more words: "an infinitival phrase with a missing noun phrase *associated with it.*" In general, each "missing phrase" structure must not only contain a missing phrase of the right kind. In addition, that missing phrase must be specifically tied to that structure and to no other.

In what follows, it will be important to distinguish between a structure that calls for a missing phrase of its own and one that merely contains a missing phrase that is associated with some other structure.

Let us return now to the problem at hand, that of distinguishing on internal grounds between *that* clauses and relative clauses. We have just examined the clear cases, those in which the sequence after *that* cannot possibly be analyzed as a sentence that has a missing noun phrase associated with it. The tricky cases, to which we now turn, are those in which the sequence after *that* can be interpreted as containing a missing noun phrase that is not associated with any smaller construction.

The following set of examples represents one group where a definite choice is impossible:

(81)   a.   [that we hid in the attic]
       b.   [that Joe reported to the governor]
       c.   [that it is easy for us to work with]

Each of the sequences after *that* here can stand as a complete sentence by itself, or else can have another noun phrase added to it, as in (82).

(82)   a.   We hid in the attic.   We hid *it* in the attic.
       b.   Joe reported to the governor. Joe reported *the theft* to the
                                           governor.
       c.   It is easy for us to work with. It is easy for us to work
                                            with *Beth.*

In such cases, we have to look outside the sequence itself to decide whether it is really a sentence or whether it is a sentence with a missing noun phrase.

Another set of sentences for which a definite choice is impossible is shown in (83).

(83)   a.   [that Joe replaced]
       b.   [that they intend to speak with]

At first glance, it might appear that these could not possibly be *that* clauses, since the sequences after *that* cannot stand as independent sentences:

(84)   a. *Joe replaced.
       b. *They intend to speak with.

In many instances the sequences after *that* clearly are relative clauses, as in (85).

(85)   a.   The motor [that Joe replaced ___] cost thirty dollars.
       b.   The person [that they intended to speak with ___] agreed to
            reimburse us.

In other situations, however, the same *that* sequences count as *that* clauses. The examples in (86) illustrate these special situations.

(86) a. The motor that Martha thinks [that Joe replaced ＿] cost thirty dollars.

b. The person that you said [that they intended to speak with ＿] agreed to reimburse us.

The first thing to be noted is that each of the sentences contains a larger, more inclusive *that* construction. Suppose that we set off both of these larger constructions with brackets, and ask about their status:

(87) a. The motor [that Marsha thinks that Joe replaced ＿] cost thirty. dollars.

b. The person [that you said that they intended to speak with ＿] agreed to reimburse us.

We can tell by looking at the environments of these sequences that they must be relative clauses. Each sequence occurs with a common noun, and neither noun is one of those that allows *that* clauses. From the fact that they are relative clauses, we can make a further deduction: Each one must consist of *that* plus a sentence that has a missing noun phrase associated with it. Thus, both the object of *replaced* in (87a) and the object of *with* in (87b) must be associated with the S/NP's that form the essential parts of these large relative clauses. We can picture the structures for these large bracketed sequences as in (88).

(88) a. B-Rel

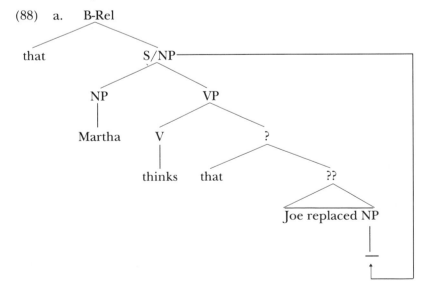

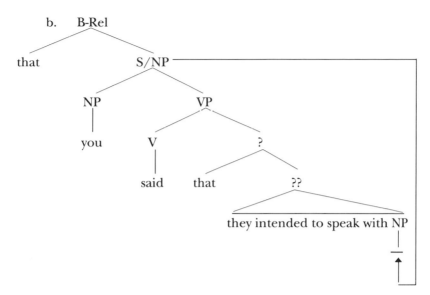

Now we can answer whether the constituents marked with double question marks are S/NP or S. They cannot be S/NP, since the only missing noun phrases that they contain are already occupied in satisfying the missing-noun-phrase requirement of a larger structure. In other words, in neither tree is there another empty noun phrase with which the smaller structures could be associated. Thus, finally, we are forced to conclude that the smaller structures must be S rather than S/NP. Consequently, the smaller *that* sequences of which they form a part must be *that* clauses rather than relative clauses.

Exercises

1. Say whether each of the following *that* sequences could possibly be interpreted as containing a missing noun phrase not associated with any smaller construction. For each positive answer, show where the missing noun phrase is. Do this by showing how a pronoun can be inserted in the sequence after *that* to give an acceptable independent sentence.

Example: that Joseph sent to Cairo

Answer: Yes, it can be interpreted as containing a missing noun phrase as follows:

      that Joseph sent ___ to Cairo

      (Acceptable independent sentence: Joseph sent *it* to Cairo.)

a.   [that Jane would remain]

b.   [that Jane would require]

c.   [that it is hard for us to understand]

d.   [that the problem is hard for us to understand]

e.   [that the person whose brother you talked with has hidden in
     the attic]

f.   [that the person whose brother you talked with has stayed in
     the attic]

g.   [that Bill said that Harry slept in the cellar]

h.   [that Bill said that Harry hid in the cellar]

i.   [that Bill said that Harry found in the cellar]

j.   [that Bill should have spoken to]

k.   [that Bill should be spoken to]

2. Each of the following sentences contains a bracketed *that* sequence. Each of the bracketed sequences contains a missing noun phrase that is not associated with any smaller structure. Using clues provided by the larger structures in which the bracketed sequence occurs, determine whether it should be considered a *that* clause or a relative clause.

a.   We know the man [that Bill hired ___].

b.   Alice knows whose assistant Pete thinks [that Bill hired ___].

c.   Alice told Fred that Pete informed the man [that Bill hired __].

d.   We want to determine who told the man [that Bill hired ___].

e.   David interviewed the man that Fred claims [that Bill hired].

3. The following two sentences are ambiguous. For each sentence, draw two tree structures to indicate what the two interpretations are.

a.   The fact that Stanley reported to the governor surprised many
     reporters.

b.   Georgia told the men that we think Sam had hidden in the
     attic.

c.   Joe is aware of the fact that Shirley will discover when Bill visits
     her sister.

Note: On one interpretation of the third sentence, *when Bill visits her sister* is interpreted as an indirect question, whereas on the other interpretation it is interpreted as a free relative clause. When interpreted as a free relative clause, it has an adverbial function. In the next chapter, the basic phrase structure proposed for verb phrases containing phrase-final adverbial modifiers will be as follows:

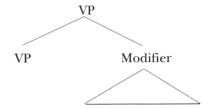

For the particular sequence that we are dealing with in this exercise, the diagram corresponding to one of the interpretations will contain a structure of the following form:

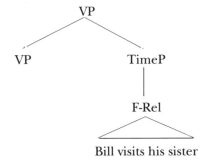

Bill visits his sister

10.2.5.4 The Compatibility Requirement for Bound Relatives Introduced by *That*   There is one more requirement that a structure must satisfy if it is to qualify as a bound relative clause: a requirement of compatibility that is similar to the one for free relative clauses discussed in chapter 7. The effects of this requirement are illustrated by the bracketed sequence in (89).

(89)   The fact [that Joe ate at noon] is completely irrelevant.

The bracketed sequence clearly satisfies both the external and the internal requirements for *that* clauses. In the first place, it goes with the word *fact*, one of the small group of nouns that allows *that* clauses. In addition, the sequence *Joe ate at noon* is completely acceptable as an independent sentence. It also seems that the sequence satisfies both the external and the internal requirements for relative clauses. The sequence is preceded by a common noun, and there is a place for a missing noun phrase, as the sentence in (90) shows.

(90)   Joe ate *it* at noon.

Yet, in reading sentence (89), we have a strong intuition that the bracketed sequence can only be interpreted as a *that* clause.

The property of sentence (89) that accounts for our intuition that it is not a relative clause is the lack of compatibility between being a fact and being eaten by Joe at noon. No imaginable entity of any kind can be both at once. We can see the situation in a particularly dramatic light by applying the interpretive procedure of subsection 10.2.4 to the key noun phrase. This procedure will insert *that fact* in the position where a missing noun phrase is possible, with the following result:

(91) a. the fact that [Joe ate __??__ at noon]
      b. the fact such that [Joe ate *that fact* at noon]

This bracketed sequence is clearly nonsensical. As a result, the only natural way to interpret the bracketed sequence in (89) is as a *that* clause. In cases such as this one, our intuitions are based not on grammatical rules as such but rather on judgments concerning the plausibility or implausibility of the interpretation that the rules yield.

Exercise

1.   For each of the following sentences, decide whether the bracketed sequence *in the given context* satisfies the compatibility condition for bound relative clauses. Specifically, decide whether it could join with the preceding common noun phrase to give a coherent interpretation. In each case, give the representation that results from the interpretive procedure of subsection 10.2.4.

   a. The book [that Sally wanted Martha to give to the church] cost thirty dollars.
   b. The fact [that Sally wanted Martha to give to the church] amazed Bruce.
   c. The fact [that Sally wanted Martha to hide from the police] has come to our attention.
   d. John told the officer [that Bill reported to the governor].

10.2.6 The Proper Identification of *Wh* Sequences

Bound relative clauses introduced by *who, which, whose, where,* and *when* constitute a third construction on our list of constructions introduced by *wh* words. The indirect-question construction of chapter 4 was the first one, and the definite free relative clause of chapter 7 was the second. Chapter 7 also included a practical discussion of how to distinguish indirect questions from definite free relative clauses. This subsection will add some comments on how to distinguish bound relatives from the other two constructions.

Let us recall at the outset that all three of these constructions have to be based on a structure that contains a missing phrase of some sort. Thus, the presence of a missing phrase will not be of any help in deciding which of these construction types is present in a particular example. However, other characteristics can be found which help to distinguish bound relatives from the other two constructions. We will concentrate here on the kinds of considerations that will help us to answer the question: Can such-and-such a *wh* sequence be a bound relative?

10.2.6.1 Internal Requirements for Bound Relatives   A bound *wh* relative can be either finite or infinitival. If it is finite, it must be introduced by one of the following limited types of phrases:

- a bound-relative noun phrase (*who, whom, whose* plus common noun phrase, *which*)
- a bound-relative locative or motion phrase (*where*)
- a bound-relative time phrase (*when*)
- a prepositional phrase having one of the above as its object.

If the bound relative is infinitival, there is only one allowable type of introducing phrase, namely a prepositional phrase with one of the *wh* phrases as its object.

Exercise
1. Decide whether each of the following sequences could ever be a bound relative in an appropriate context. Give an explanation for each of your negative answers.
    a.   [when Bill returned]
    b.   [what Gloria remembered]
    c.   [who(m) to send to the office]
    d.   [how many books your father wrote]
    e.   [where to put the marbles]
    f.   [to whom the president was speaking]
    g.   [with whom to attend the concert]
    h.   [which car he prefers]

10.2.6.2 External Requirements for Bound Relatives   The main external requirement for a bound relative introduced by a *wh* phrase is the same as for a relative introduced by *that*: It has to be associated with a common noun phrase. In the standard case, the relative will be directly adjacent to the common noun phrase that it modifies. However, it is possible for a bound relative to modify the common noun phrase at a distance in a case where the relative clause has been postponed to the end of the sentence as a whole.

Exercises

1. Each of the following sentences contains a *wh* sequence whose internal structure would allow it to be either a bound relative or an indirect question. For each such sequence, decide from its external surroundings whether it could possibly be a bound relative. For each positive answer, identify the common noun phrase that the sequence could modify.

     a.   Katy told me [who was present at the lecture].

     b.   [Whose dog Fred assaulted] was not clear to the onlookers.

     c.   A lady teaches German here [who likes to show slides of Bavaria].

     d.   Most of the prisoners [who questioned the authorities] were banished.

     e.   Ralph told the officer [who(m) he had hired].

     f.   The witness mentioned the time [when everyone heard the bell ring].

2. Decide whether each of the above *wh* sequences satisfies the external requirements for indirect questions.

10.2.6.3 The Compatibility Requirement for *Wh* Bound Relatives   Bound relatives introduced by *wh* phrases must satisfy a compatibility condition similar to the one for bound relatives introduced by *that*. As before, a convenient way to check that this condition is satisfied is to carry out the interpretive procedure of subsection 10.2.4.

    Let us start by looking at a sentence in which this condition is satisfied:

(92)   Smith hired the man [whose report you have copied].

The noun phrase that is donated to the relative clause in this example is *that man*. This noun phrase is used to replace the *who* of *whose*, and then the entire introducing phrase is put back in the position of the missing noun phrase:

(93)   the man such that [you have copied *that man's* report]

The sentence in brackets here makes perfect sense, and thus the compatibility requirement is satisfied.

    Let us look now at another example:

(94)   We told the woman [whose widow Jones wants to marry].

We are interested in the possibility that the following subsequence is a noun phrase within the larger sentence:

(95)   the woman [whose widow Jones wants to marry]

The noun phrase donated to the relative clause would be *that woman.*
Replacing *whose* and positioning the introducing phrase in the position of
the missing noun phrase gives (96).

(96)   ??the woman such that [Jones wants to marry *that woman's* widow]

Given that only a man can have a widow, the bracketed sequence fails to
make sense. For sentence (92), then, a relative clause interpretation is
excluded. The only possible analysis is one in which *the woman* is the first
object of the verb *told* and the *wh* sequence is an indirect question serving
as the second object.

Exercise
1. Each of the following sentences contains a bracketed *wh* sequence.
Each of these sequences satisfies the internal and external requirements
for both relative clauses and indirect questions. Determine whether each
sentence satisfies the compatibility requirement for relative clauses.

   a.   Martha told the man [who wrote the letter].
   b.   We told the woman [whose wife wrote the letter].
   c.   We told the woman [whose daughter wrote the letter].
   d.   John told the woman [who perjured himself].
   e.   John told the woman [who believed that John perjured
        himself].

10.3 Nonclausal Noun Modifiers

In the first part of this chapter, we examined the variety of restrictive
bound relative constructions that English allows. In the present section we
will study several important varieties of nonclausal modifiers of nouns—
that is, modifying constructions based on phrases and words rather than
on sentence-like structures. The discussion will be divided between *postnominal modifiers* (those that come after the common noun phrase that they
modify) and *prenominal modifiers* (those that come before the modified
phrase).

10.3.1 Postnominal Modifiers
We begin with several varieties of postnominal modifying phrases that we
have encountered in other uses. In particular, all the postnominal modifiers in these first groups of examples can also be employed as complements of the verb BE.

(97)   a.   The boy [in the doorway] waved to his father.
            (The boy is [in the doorway].)
       b.   The baby [out there in the kitchen] is Jerry's niece.
            (The baby is [out there in the kitchen].)

(98)   a.   The man [holding the bottle] disappeared.
            (The man is [holding the bottle].)
       b.   The boy [waving to his father] lives in Tulsa.
            (The boy is [waving to his father].)

(99)   a.   The papers [removed from the safe by the robbers] have not
            been found.
            (The papers were [removed from the safe by the robbers].
       b.   The men [brought before the judge] remained silent.
            (The men were [brought before the judge].)

The types of phrases being used as modifiers in these examples are not
hard to identify. The modifiers in (97) are locative phrases, those in (98)
are present-participial verb phrases, and those in (99) are passive phrases.

As with relative clauses, these modifiers go better with common nouns
than with either proper nouns or pronouns:

(100) a.   The boy in the doorway waved to his father.
       b.   *John in the doorway waved to his father.
       c.   *?He in the doorway waved to his father.

Thus, just as with relative clauses, we will assume that these new modifiers
join with common noun phrases and that the resulting phrases are
themselves common noun phrases. The rules we want are these:

(101) a. CNP   b.   CNP   c.   CNP

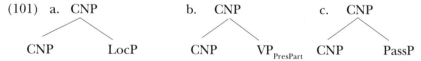

       CNP   LocP   CNP   VP$_{PresPart}$ CNP   PassP

Adjective phrases are one final group of phrases that appear both as
complements of BE and as postnominal modifiers. As the examples in
(102) show, they are rather marginal as modifiers.

(102) a.   ?The woman [eager to start the meeting] is John's sister.
            (Compare: The woman [who is eager to start the meeting] is
            John's sister.)
       b.   ?A speaker [hard to understand] should come to the stage.
            (Compare: A speaker [who is hard to understand] should
            come to the stage.)

Even less acceptable as postnominal modifiers are adjective phrases without following complements, as in (103).

(103) a. *A baby [healthy] was born to Margaret Smith.
       b. *A soldier [very young] just walked into the room.

Anticipating the discussion of the next subsection, we will note that English does provide an alternative means of using adjectives without complements to modify nouns. This alternative is simply to put the adjective before the noun instead of after it:

(104) a. A [healthy] baby was born to Margaret Smith.
       b. A [very young] soldier just walked into the room.

There are two important varieties of nonclausal modifiers that do not serve as complements of BE. The first variety, which is related to simple sentences with HAVE rather than simple sentences with BE, is shown in (105)–(108).

(105) a. The players [with the best records] will meet in the championship match.
       b. *The players are [with the best records].
       c. The players [have the best records].

(106) a. The fellow [with a fly on his nose] owns this establishment.
       b. *The fellow is [with a fly on his nose].
       c. The fellow [has a fly on his nose].

(107) a. The student [with a monkey sitting on his lap] deserves a C+.
       b. *The student is [with a monkey sitting on his lap].
       c. The student [has a monkey sitting on his lap].

(108) a. The woman [with a string tied to her finger] knocked at the door.
       b. *The woman is [with a string tied to her finger].
       c. The woman [has a string tied to her finger].

The modifying phrases in the (a) examples consist of the word *with* followed by a noun phrase and, in (106)–(108), another phrase. This last phrase can be either a locative phrase (*on his nose*), a present-participial verb phrase (*sitting on his lap*), or a passive phrase (*tied to his finger*). Thus, a modifier headed by *with* must have one of the structures in (109).

(109)   a. *With*-P   b.   *With*-P

        with   NP   with   NP   LocP

The second kind of postnominal modifier that does not occur as a complement of BE is shown in the following examples, where brackets mark the noun phrase as a whole and italics indicate the postnominal modifier itself:

(110) We are using [an idea *of Carol's*].

This construction, which we will refer to as the *postnominal genitive*, can be accounted for by the following rule:

(111) A postnominal genitive can be formed by combining the preposition *of* with a genitive noun phrase.

This structure can appear with a common noun phrase in a variety of situations:

(112) a. I can't get [this car *of Bob's*] to start.
      b. [The book *of Jane's* that we want you to read] is on the coffee table.
      c. [Any other possessions *of Carol's*] should be sent to her as soon as possible.
      d. ?[These portraits of Napoleon *of Jerry's*] will fetch a high price in London.

The one situation in which the construction is unacceptable is shown in (113).

(113)   *I can't get [the car *of Bob's*] to start.

In this example, the noun phrase as a whole is of the form *the* + common noun phrase + postnominal genitive. Perhaps it is not a coincidence that this noun phrase would have exactly the same interpretation as another noun phrase that is made available by rules that we discussed in chapter 5:

(114) I can't get [*Bob's* car] to start.

Thus, one possible explanation for the unacceptability of (113) is that the alternative structure in (114) in effect crowds it out.

In the above examples, the genitive noun phrase *Bob's* was used in both the prenominal and the postnominal constructions. This identity of form holds for every kind of genitive noun phrase except one. The single exceptional class in this regard is the class of pronouns. As can be seen in the following pairs of examples, the genitive pronouns differ in every instance except the third-person singular masculine *his*.

(115) a.   *my* friend   a friend of *mine*
       b.   *our* friend   a friend of *ours*
       c.   *your* friend   a friend of *yours*
       d.   *his* friend   a friend of *his*
       e.   *her* friend   a friend of *hers*
       f.   *their* friend   a friend of *theirs*

Let us refer to the genitive pronouns in the left column of (115) as *weak genitives* and to the genitive pronouns in the right column as *strong genitives*. We can then give the following revised rule for the formation of postnominal genitives:

(116)   A postnominal genitive can be formed by combining the preposition *of* with a following genitive noun phrase. If the genitive is a pronoun, the strong form of the genitive must be used.

We will see an additional use for the strong genitives in chapter 16.

As with the other postnominal modifiers that we have seen in this section, we will assume that these last two kinds of modifiers combine with the preceding common noun phrase to make a larger common noun phrase. These relations are diagrammed in (117).

(117)   a.   CNP   b.   CNP

       CNP   With-P   CNP   Postnom-Gen

Exercise
1.   Draw a tree diagram for each of the following noun phrases:
     a.   several people staying at the hotel
     b.   the rugs in the attic
     c.   the bricks taken from Smith's driveway
     d.   the rugs in the attic that were bought from your aunt
     e.   the woman with the dog
     f.   the necktie with a spot on it.
     g.   this bicycle of Fred's
     h.   the book of yours that Nora wants to read

10.3.2 Modifier or Complement?

In this subsection we take up a practical question similar to several that we have encountered in earlier discussions. When we are presented with a sentence containing a phrase that occurs sometimes as a postnominal modifier and sometimes as a verb complement, how do we determine whether it can be the first or the second or both? This is a question that might well be raised about the examples in (118), which at first glance look as if they differ only in the choice of verb.

(118) a.   Jocko put the car in the garage.
       b.   Jocko owns the car in the garage.
       c.   Jocko kept the car in the garage.

For each of these sentences, we want to answer two questions: whether the sequence *the car in the garage* can be analyzed as two phrases (a noun phrase followed by a locative phrase) and whether the same sequence can be analyzed as one phrase (a noun phrase). The two relevant verb phrase configurations are diagrammed in (119).

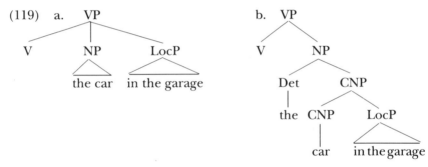

(119)   a.   VP   b.   VP

In order to answer these questions, we need to find out what kind of complement configurations these three verbs allow. We can do this by constructing simple experimental examples in which there is less ambiguity than in the present sentences. In order to determine whether a given verb is allowed in the first configuration, we will use a pronoun as the object, since a pronoun cannot be modified by a locative phrase. We can likewise use a pronoun object without a following locative phrase to test each verb for its comfort in the second configuration. The results are given in (120)–(122).

(120) a.   Jack put it in the garage.
       b.   *Jack put it.

(121) a.   *Jack owns it in the garage.
       b.   Jack owns it.

(122)   a.   Jack kept it in the garage.
        b.   Jack kept it.

These examples give us the following information:

- PUT goes only in the [— NP LocP] configuration.
- OWN goes only in the [— NP] configuration.
- KEEP goes in both configurations.

Thus, in (118a) the sequence *the car in the garage* must be two separate phrases, in (118b) it must be a single phrase, and in (118c) it can have either of the two structures. From these conclusions, it follows finally that *in the garage* is a verb complement in (118a), a postnominal modifier in (118b), and either of these in (118c). Exactly the same kind of strategy can be used in examples in which the potential modifiers are something other than locative phrases.

Exercise
1. For each of the following sentences, answer two questions:

- Could the italicized phrase be a verb complement in this context?
- Could it be a postnominal modifier in this context?

In most cases, some experiments will be useful. In a few examples, however, the answers should be immediate. Explain your answers briefly but clearly.

        a.   Joe kept the baby *in his arms.*
        b.   We saw the woman *adjusting the telescope.*
        c.   We will have three books *removed from the collection.*
        d.   The man *in the gray suit* seems to like the play.
        e.   The police caught Joe *crawling through a window.*
        f.   We talked to the man *holding the weapon.*
        g.   John oiled the machine *from the store.*
        h.   John removed the machine *from the store.*
        i.   Fred locked it *in the garage.*

10.3.3 Prenominal Modifiers

As was mentioned above, English does not generally allow adjectives without complements as postnominal modifiers:

(123)   a.   *A baby [healthy] was born to Margaret Smith.
        b.   *A soldier [very young] just walked into the room.

The alternative construction is one in which the adjectives come before the noun:

(124) a.   A [healthy] baby was born to Margaret Smith.
       b.   A [very young] soldier just walked into the room

Just as adjectives without complements are excluded as postnominal adjective phrases, adjective phrases that include complements are excluded in prenominal position:

(125) a. *a [fond of chocolates] gentleman
       b. *an [eager to succeed] corporal
       c. *a [reluctant to leave the party] teenager

Despite the unacceptability of these last examples, we will analyze these prenominal modifiers as adjective phrases rather than simply viewing them as single-word adjectives. One reason for the phrasal analysis rests in the fact that the adjective can be preceded by a degree modifier like *very*, as in (124b). Such an analysis gives rise to the following structure for (124b):

(126)

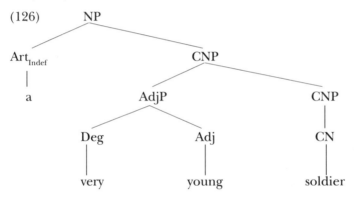

The following rule would give this structure:

(127) A common noun phrase can be joined with a preceding adjective phrase to form a larger common noun phrase.

With a rule like this, we would expect to be able to form a sequence of two adjectives before a noun by taking the common noun phrase *young soldier* and joining it with a preceding adjective. As a matter of fact, such two-adjective sequences are indeed possible, as (128) shows.

(128) a.   A tall young soldier entered the room.
       b.   A healthy little baby was born to Margaret Smith.

The structure of the subject noun phrase in (128a) is illustrated in (129).

(129)

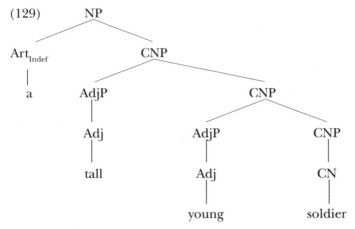

This rule allows the creation of a wide variety of noun phrases with prenominal modifiers. Although it has the attractiveness of being quite simple and general, we should take note of several restrictions in the behavior of prenominal modifiers that it does not really account for.

One problem with the rule stated in (127) is that it imposes no restrictions on the order in which different kinds of adjectives appear in the noun phrase. As examples (130)–(132) show, however, differences in order often carry with them striking differences in acceptability.

(130) a.   a little old wooden house
       b.   *a wooden old little house
       c.   ??a old little wooden house

(131) a.   a nice young soldier
       b.   *a young nice soldier

(132) a.   an old European custom
       b.   *a European old custom

What we seem to find is that adjectives tend to be ordered by general meaning classes. Adjectives having to do with nationality, material, etc. have to come as close as possible to the head noun. Adjectives having to do with age and size are next on the left, and adjectives denoting various personality characteristics come next. Before them we also have a small class of adjectives that can only occur prenominally. This class includes words like *main*, *key*, and so on:

(133) a.   the main objection
          (*This objection is main.)

b.   the key fact
     (*This fact is key.)

In addition to the restrictions on prenominal adjective order, there are a number of other restrictions that are not well understood. For example, degree modification by *very* is fully acceptable only with the leftmost adjective. Thus, both (134a) and (134b) are acceptable, and so is (134c). By contrast, (134d) and (134e) are both markedly less natural, unless an intonation break is inserted as indicated by the comma in the examples on the right.

(134) a.   a very tall soldier
       b.   a very young soldier
       c.   a very tall young soldier
       d.   ?a young very tall soldier   (a young, very tall soldier)
       e.   ?a very young very tall soldier   (a very young, very tall soldier)

We will see still more complexities in the behavior of prenominal modifiers in chapter 12 when we look further into the ways in which degree modification can be expressed.

Exercises

1. Draw tree diagrams for the following noun phrases:
       a.   several young chickens
       b.   this very handsome table
       c.   the old red rooster
       d.   that incompetent king of France

2. In English, the word *one* is often used as a substitute for a repeated common noun phrase:
       (i)   the first *picture* and the second *one*
       (ii) the *picture of King George* that you own and the *one* that I own
       (iii) this *funny story* and that *one*.
By the rules given for common noun phrases, the following sequence can have two possible structures:
       (iv) the old woman from France.
First, give the structure that this sequence must have to permit the interpretation of *one* given in (v).
       (v) the *old woman* from France and the *one* from Spain.
Then give the structure that it must have to allow the interpretation shown in (vi).
       (vi) the old *woman from France* and the young *one*.

10.4 Nonrestrictive Relative Clauses

So far in this chapter, we have confined our discussion to modifiers that are used to "restrict" a common noun phrase—that is, to create a narrower set of entities than that denoted by the common noun phrase alone. In this section we will examine a relative-clause construction that is not used restrictively.

The easiest way to see the difference between restrictive and nonrestrictive relative clauses is to compare two sentences that differ only in the status of the relative clause that they contain, such as the sentences in (135).

(135) a. The books which were written by foreign authors were burned.
      b. The books, which were written by foreign authors, were burned.

These two sentences are natural only in situations in which some set of books is understood ahead of time to be relevant to the conversation—perhaps all the books in a certain library or a certain collection. In (135a) a particular subset of these books is picked out (those written by foreign authors), and it is asserted that all the books in this subset were burned. In (135b), by contrast, we are told that all the books were burned, and then we are provided with the added assertion that they were all written by foreign authors. The relative clause in (135b) is referred to as nonrestrictive precisely because it does not ask us to form a smaller subset of the set denoted by *books*.

Because these relatives do not restrict, we can use them in situations in which restrictive relatives are unacceptable. Neither the noun phrase *Ronald Reagan* nor the noun phrase *the current president of the company* is capable of being modified by a restrictive clause, as we see in (136).

(136) a. *Ronald Reagan who began his life as a radio announcer came to hold the nation's highest office.
      b. *The current president of the company who lives in Buffalo could not attend the ceremony.

In neither of these cases can the relative clause pick out a set that is smaller than the set already picked out by the noun phrases *Ronald Reagan* and *the current president of the company*. In both of these situations, nonrestrictive relative clauses are perfectly acceptable, simply because they are not interpreted as forming smaller sets:

(137) a. Ronald Reagan, who began his life as a radio announcer, came to hold the nation's highest office.

   b.   The current president of the company, who lives in Buffalo,
        could not attend the ceremony.

Instead, these relative clauses add independent assertions about the
individual or individuals in question:

(138) a.   Ronald Reagan began his career as a radio announcer.
      b.   The current president of the company lives in Buffalo.

   Going along with this difference in function are a few small differences
in form. In the first place, a nonrestrictive relative inside a larger sentence
is set off in speaking by a special "interruption" intonation:

(139) John Wilkes Booth, who made his living as an actor, became famous
      for shooting a president.

At the end of a sentence, a nonrestrictive relative is also set off intonation-
ally, this time by a falling "end" intonation on the material preceding it:

(140) Cora wrote a letter to Smith's parents, who were pleased to hear
       from her.

In writing, the spoken intonation breaks are represented by commas, as is
other special material that represents an interruption or an independent
addition to a sentence.

   Another difference between the two types of relative clauses is that
nonrestrictive clauses can only be introduced by *wh* phrases. In (141),
(142), and (143), restrictives and corresponding nonrestrictives are
compared in this regard.

(141) a.   The man who(m) the Republicans nominated in 1980 now
           lives in California.
      b.   Reagan, who(m) the Republicans nominated in 1980, now
           lives in California.

(142) a.   The man that the Republicans nominated in 1980 now lives in
           California.
      b.   *Reagan, that the Republicans nominated in 1980, now lives in
           California.

(143) a.   The man the Republicans nominated in 1980 now lives in
           California.
      b.   *Reagan, the Republicans nominated in 1980, now lives in
           California.

How to decide on the punctuation appropriate for particular relative clauses is a traditional problem within the prescriptive grammatical tradition. This problem clearly reduces to deciding whether a relative clause that one wants to write is being used restrictively or nonrestrictively. With definite noun phrases, it is generally quite easy to decide. If the intention is to pick out a subset of the larger set denoted by the noun alone, then the clause is restrictive and no commas are called for. If the intention is to make an independent assertion about a noun phrase already clearly identified without the help of the relative clause, then the clause is nonrestrictive, and commas are required. With indefinite noun phrases, the choice is typically not so clear. What is the difference between (144a) and (144b)?

(144) a.   Yesterday John saw an animal which resembled his great uncle Fred.
b.   (?) Yesterday John saw an animal, which resembled his great uncle Fred.

The situations that these sentences could truthfully describe seem to be indistinguishable. Yet there is a significant difference, and it affords an explanation for the slight oddness of (144b). Simply put, (144a) expresses one single assertion, whereas (144b) expresses two separate ones. The reason that (144b) is slightly odd is that John's seeing an animal would not really be newsworthy in most situations that we can imagine. Thus, what might be called the "news content" of seeing an animal is too slim in its own right to warrant a separate assertion. The same line of reasoning explains why the restrictive clause is the right choice for (145a) and the nonrestrictive clause is more appropriate for (145b).

(145) a.   Last night, John was introduced to *a man who had once courted his aunt.*
b.   Last night, John was introduced to *a Martian, who had once courted his aunt.*

Being introduced to a man would almost certainly not be news in its own right, whereas being introduced to a Martian might well be news. Thus, the news content of (145a) is enough for only one interesting assertion, whereas the news content of (145b) warrants two.

In all the examples discussed so far, the nonrestrictive clause is connected to a noun phrase. For these examples, we can analyze the entire sequence of noun phrase plus following nonrestrictive as making up a larger noun phrase, as diagrammed in (146).

(146)

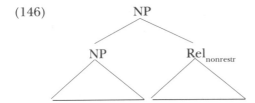

Other types of "antecedent" phrases are also possible. For instance, nonrestrictive clauses can also be linked to adjective phrases, forming larger adjective phrases as a result:

(147)

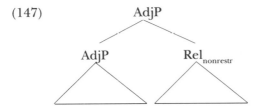

Such a use is evident in (148).

(148) At least Robert is [considerate, *which none of his friends seem to be*].

Here the nearest paraphrase is something like (149).

(149) At least Robert is considerate, and none of his friends seem to be

$$\left\{ \begin{array}{l} \text{considerate} \\ \text{?that} \\ \text{?so} \end{array} \right\}.$$

One more construction to which a nonrestrictive clause can be attached is exemplified in (150).

(150) No one showed up on time, *which Alex didn't like very much.*

Here the nonrestrictive clause is not connected with any phrase within the first clause, but instead adds an independent assertion about the fact reported by the clause as a whole. Thus, the structure that we want for (150) is one in which the nonrestrictive relative attaches to the entire clause that precedes it:

(151)

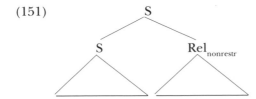

Such sentences can often be paraphrased by using *and* to join the two clauses together, and using a *that* in the position of the missing noun phrase instead of a *which* at the beginning of the sentence. This process yields the following paraphrase for (150):

(152) No one was there on time, *and* Alex didn't like *that* very much.

Exercise

1. Draw tree diagrams for the following sentences:
    a. The woman standing on the porch, who(m) you introduced to Phillip, reads fifteen languages.
    b. Jane gave the car to Martha, who gave it to Florence.
    c. Your friends say that Peter is eloquent, which he seems to want to be.
    d. The waiter found three flies in your soup, which Maxine considered inexcusable.

Chapter 11

Modification of Verb Phrases and Sentences

In the preceding chapter, we examined some of the ways in which English nominal constructions can be modified. Here we will take up the modification of verb phrases and sentences. The modifiers for these structures have an even larger range of semantic effects than was the case for nominal structures. In the present chapter, we will give primary attention to the syntax of these modifiers, sketching their meanings only briefly as a preliminary matter.

In section 11.1 a number of traditional meaning classes of modifiers will be listed. In section 11.2 the basic structural classes of modifiers will be summarized. In section 11.3 the basic positions in which modifiers appear will be discussed. In the rules that will be developed there, reference will be made both to the meaning classes in which modifiers fall and to their structural classes. Some of the syntactic peculiarities of certain clausal modifiers will be considered in section 11.4.

11.1 Meaning Classes of Verbal Modifiers

In the following discussion of the most important meaning classes of modifiers, each general statement is followed by a list of particular examples.

11.1.1 Locative Modifiers

Locative modifiers show exactly the same internal structure as the locative complements with which we are already familiar. Here are some examples of these phrases used as modifiers:

(1)   a.   Frank lost three plastic worms *there.*
        b.   *Here* you will be safe.
        c.   *Down there in Brownsville,* Joe worked as a carpenter.

  d. Frances read some of Molière's plays *in Paris.*

  e. You can grow carrots *wherever you find sandy soil.*

  f. Johnny sells souvenirs *where the two armies once clashed.*

11.1.2 Time Modifiers

These modifiers indicate the time at which some event occurred or some state obtained.

(2) a. We would *then* have called a specialist.

  b. Jones is feeling better *now.*

  c. *Today* our guests will be taken to a bull fight.

  d. *On Thursday*, the Guadalupe River left its banks.

  e. Jane wants to see you *next week.*

  f. *After the match was over*, the teams exchanged shirts.

  g. *When the first bell rings*, everybody will stop working.

  h. Joe locked the door *before he went to lunch.*

11.1.3 Aspectual Modifiers

These modifiers give information about whether some event or state of affairs is completed, is still going on, etc.

(3) a. Carolyn has seen this chapter *already.*

  b. I wonder whether Bruce has seen it *yet.*

  c. Wanda *still* would like to talk about the music festival.

  d. I doubt that Bob thinks about it *any more.*

11.1.4 Duration Modifiers

Modifiers from this class fulfill the role of indicating how long something lasted. They can perform this function by telling the length of time a certain state or activity lasted (*for three hours*), or by giving its termination point (*until she fell asleep*).

(4) a. *For three hours*, the minister talked about the eye of the needle.

  b. Joanne studied Greek *until she fell asleep.*

  c. The choir sang *(for) a long time.*

11.1.5 Frequency Modifiers

Modifiers from this class indicate the frequency of a certain type of event. Included in this class are modifiers indicating the two opposite extremes (*always* and *never*). Some of these modifiers indicate an absolute frequency (*two times, twice, many times*); others indicate a frequency per time period (*two times a month, twice a week, many times a year*).

(5) a. One *always* hears rumors.

     b. Jimmy *never* has been seen in Washington.

     c. The general would *always* have thought that he could have been a singer.

     d. *Sometimes* an answer is hard to find.

     e. Martha has seen that movie *twice*.

     f. Joe has traveled to Egypt *many times*.

     g. *On several occasions*, the police have found him asleep in his truck.

     h. Gaylord visits his wife and children *several times a year*.

11.1.6 Manner Modifiers

This class includes a wide variety of expressions that describe the manner or way in which a certain action is performed.

(6) a. John walked onto the stage *slowly*.

     b. *Quickly* Diego chipped the ball into the penalty area.

     c. Doris feeds her guppies *this way*.

     d. Ollie opens jars *like this*.

     e. Johnny introduced his guests *in a relaxed manner*.

     f. Cornelius *sadly* walked out into the pasture.

     g. Velma must have *accidentally* pulled the plug.

     h. Dr. Jekyll has been *carefully* cleaning the wound.

11.1.7 Epistemic Modifiers

Modifiers from this class serve the function of letting the hearer know something about the "security" of the proposition conveyed in the sentence—whether it is guaranteed to be true, probably true, rumored to be true, and so on down the line.

(7) a. Olivia has *probably* solved the problem.

     b. James has *allegedly* made millions of dollars from illegal enterprises.

     c. Adverbs *undoubtedly* make up a confusing class of words.

     d. *Possibly* some way will be found to save the school.

     e. George would *certainly* be cooperating with Shirley.

     f. *In the teacher's opinion*, use of a form of BE constitutes bad writing.

     g. *According to unidentified sources*, more unconfirmed rumors are expected soon.

11.1.8 Attitudinal Modifiers
These modifiers indicate the speaker's emotional attitude toward the state of affairs that he or she is reporting.

(8) a. *Unfortunately,* the state treasury cannot honor your paycheck.
 b. *Regrettably,* people exist who want to put the welfare of the human race ahead of their country's flag.
 c. *Luckily,* such people have very little influence.

11.1.9 Conditional Modifiers
These modifiers serve to put a condition of some sort on the truth of the rest of the sentence.

(9) a. You can succeed *if you try very hard.*
 b. *Unless this colonel is given lots of money,* his lawyer will never become rich.
 c. *Barring a miracle,* the Redskins will have to settle for second place.

A few special types actually assert that a certain kind of condition is irrelevant:

(10) a. *Whatever kind of work he decides to do,* Edward will find it difficult to make ends meet.
 b. *Whether or not the Celtics win tonight,* the sun will still come up tomorrow.
 c. *No matter how many funny hats she wears,* Julia will never be a star.

11.1.10 Purpose Modifiers
These modifiers indicate the purpose for which some action was performed.

(11) a. Joe sang a lullaby *to quiet the baby.*
 b. *In order to get good seats,* Tim got to the theatre at six in the morning.
 c. Carol writes poems *for money.*
 d. I bought this shredder *for you to put documents into.*

11.1.11 Causal Modifiers
These modifiers serve to identify the cause of whatever event or state is conveyed by the rest of the sentence.

(12) a. *Because Mabel has lost her license,* Fred is driving her to work.
 b. The program failed *because of a minor typing error.*
 c. *On account of a shortage of clean dishes,* Ollie is eating out tonight.

11.1.12 Universal Modifiers

These are just the three words *each*, *both*, and *all*. As we saw in chapter 5, they can all be used as quantity words in noun phrases. This additional use in verb phrases is clearly derived from their primary use in noun phrases.

(13) a. The students have *each* given a pint of blood.
      b. The twins will *both* be running in the first race.
      c. Your friends should *all* have received invitations.

11.1.13 Focusing Modifiers

This class consists of the four words *even*, *only*, *also*, and *too*. They have the common property of being associated with some special "focused" portion of the sentence in an utterance in which they occur.

(14) a. John *even* speaks ARAMAIC. (more surprising that speaking Hebrew or Arabic)
     b. John *even* SPEAKS Aramaic. (more surprising than merely reading it)
     c. John *only* speaks SPANISH. (He doesn't speak English or Basque in addition.)
     d. John *only* SPEAKS Spanish. (He doesn't read it or write it.)
     e. Kathy *also* wanted to interview BORIS. (in addition to interviewing Ivan)
     f. Kathy *also* wanted to INTERVIEW Boris. (in addition to photographing him)
     g. Dorothy swims in the POND, *too*. (in addition to swimming in the city pool)
     h. Dorothy SWIMS in the pond, *too*. (in addition to fishing in it)

Also and *too* have the effect of making explicit the parallel between the sentence in which they appear and some earlier sentence in the discourse.

11.2 Structural Classes of Modifiers

Let us now turn to the classes into which various modifiers fall by virtue of their structure. We have seen a broad range of examples above, and all of the basic structural types have been exemplified there. We can distinguish the following basic classes:

- adverbs: *usually, often, then, carefully, already, probably, each, even, easily*
- noun phrases serving as modifiers: *many times, this way, this week, last year*

- prepositional phrases: *in Austin, on Thursday, after the meeting, until ten o'clock, on several occasions, in a relaxed manner, in my opinion*
- clausal modifiers: *where the two armies once clashed, when the first bell rings, before he went to lunch, until she fell asleep, if you try very hard, for you to put documents into.*

11.3 Rules Governing Modifier Positions

11.3.1 Initial Remarks

If we were to go through the above sentences one at a time, to find out where the modifiers had appeared, we might distinguish the five positions listed below.

(15)   at the beginning of the sentence:
  a.   *Today* our guests will be taken to a bullfight.
  b.   *Possibly* some way will be found to save the school.

(16)   at the beginning of the finite verb phrase:
  a.   Wanda *still* would like to talk about the music festival.
  b.   Jimmy *never* has been seen in Washington.

(17)   after the finite verb, but before other verbs:
  a.   The general would *always* have thought that he could have been a singer.
  b.   George would *certainly* be cooperating with Shirley.

(18)   before the action or state verb:
  a.   Velma must have *accidentally* pulled the plug.
  b.   Dr. Jekyll has been *carefully* cleaning the wound.

(19)   at the end of the verb phrase:
  a.   I wonder whether Bruce has seen it *yet*.
  b.   Martha has seen that movie *twice*.

Two pairs of the above-named positions are sometimes indistinguishable in a single example. In the first place, "before the finite verb" and "before the action or state verb" determine the same position when it is the action or state verb itself that serves as the finite verb, as in (20).

(20)   a.   John *often* kissed his wife.
  b.   John *tenderly* kissed his wife.

The same kind of overlap arises with the third and fourth positions named above: "after the finite verb but before other verbs" and "before the action or state verb" may also determine one and the same location, as in (21).

(21)   a.   The queen has *definitely* ordered the servant to leave the room.

          b.   The queen has *rudely* ordered the servant to leave the room.

This occasional overlap will not create a serious problem for us, though. When we want to construct rules about where various adverbs go, it will always be possible to find examples in which the positions we are interested in are clearly distinguished. In fact, the examples in (15)–(19) all had the useful property of clearly distinguishing the position being illustrated from any of the other positions. In both of the "before the finite verb" examples the finite verbs were different from the action or state verbs, and in both of the "after the finite verb" examples the adverb was followed by a verb different from the action or state verb.

11.3.2 Preliminary Observations on Modifier Position

Let us now try to make some systematic statements concerning the positions that are possible for the various kinds of modifiers we have identified above. The first thing we can do is dispense with the clausal modifiers, the prepositional phrases, and the noun phrases. Sequences of these types are most comfortable at the beginning of the sentence or at the end of the verb phrase. Many examples of these kinds of modifiers in these two positions were given above. By contrast, they are less acceptable in sentence-internal positions, unless accompanied by a very definite "interruption" intonation or punctuation:

(22)   a.   *John *before he went to lunch* locked the door.

          b.   *You can *wherever you find sandy soil* grow carrots.

(23)   a.   John, *before he went to lunch*, locked the door.

          b.   You can, *wherever you find sandy soil*, grow carrots.

(24)   a.   *Josephine *in Austin* worked as a carpenter's helper.

          b.   *Josephine has *in Austin* been working as a carpenter's helper.

(25)   a.   ? You *many times* have asked for loans.

          b.   ? You have *many times* asked for loans.

In view of these observations, the remainder of this discussion will focus on the position of adverbs in particular.

By means of an extensive series of experiments, we can get an idea of where various adverbs are acceptable. In some cases we can give rules that refer to entire classes; in other cases it is necessary to single out individual words for special treatment. We will start by looking at a handful of experimental sentences just for the purposes of illustration.

(26) a. *Now* we have been sitting here for three hours.
          (sentence-initial)
      b. We *now* have been sitting here for three hours.
          (before finite verb)
      c. We have *now* been sitting here for three hours.
          (after finite verb)
      d. *We have been *now* sitting here for three hours.
          (before action verb)
      e. We have been sitting here for three hours *now*.
          (end of verb phrase)

(27) a. *Already* George has been making plans.
          (sentence-initial)
      b. George *already* has been making plans.
          (before finite verb)
      c. George has *already* been making plans.
          (after finite verb)
      d. *George has been *already* making plans.
          (before action verb)
      e. George has been making plans *already*.
          (end of verb phrase)

(28) a. *Cheerfully* Vivian ate the tacos.
          (sentence-initial)
      b. *Vivian *cheerfully* has eaten the tacos.
          (before finite verb)
      c. *Vivian must *cheerfully* have eaten the tacos.
          (after finite verb)
      d. Vivian must have *cheerfully* eaten the tacos.
          (before action verb)
      e. Vivian must have eaten the tacos *cheerfully*.
          (end of verb phrase)

(29) a. *Probably* Sally has been listening to Oliver.   (sentence-initial)
      b. Sally *probably* has been listening to Oliver.   (before finite verb)
      c. Sally has *probably* been listening to Oliver.   (after finite verb)
      d. *Sally has been *probably* listening to Oliver.   (before action verb)
      e. *Sally has been listening to Oliver *probably*.   (end of verb phrase)

These observations are summarized in (30).

(30)

	S-Initial	Before finite V	After finiteV	Before action V	End of VP
a. now	yes	yes	yes	no	yes
b. already	yes	yes	yes	no	yes
c. cheerfully	yes	no	no	yes	yes
d. probably	yes	yes	yes	no	no

The same kinds of experiments with a much wider range of adverbs give the results summarized in (31). Some of the entries in this table refer to individual adverbs; others refer to classes of adverbs.

(31)

		S-Initial	Before finite V	After finite V	Before action V	End of VP
a.	now	yes	yes	yes	no	yes
b.	then	yes	yes	yes	no	yes
c.	already	yes	yes	yes	no	yes
d.	still	yes	yes	yes	no	yes
e.	yet	no	no	no	no	yes
f.	any more	no	no	no	no	yes
g.	often	yes	yes	yes	no	yes
h.	sometimes	yes	yes	yes	no	yes
i.	always	no	yes	yes	no	yes?
j.	never	yes	yes	yes	no	no
k.	Epistemic	yes	yes	yes	no	no
l.	Attitudinal	yes	yes	yes	no	no
m.	Universal	no	yes	yes	no	no
n.	also	no	yes	yes	no	yes
o.	too	no	no	no	no	yes
p.	even	yes	yes	yes	no	yes?
q.	only	yes	yes	yes	no	no

Although individual speakers might disagree with some of the yes and no answers listed here, this chart gives us a reasonable overall view of how the five adverbial positions are used.

Before setting out to develop some rules, let us make a note for future reference of one odd coincidence in the way that the chart in (31) turned out. For the most part, when we compare two columns, we find that the pattern of answers is different. For instance, while the first column and the second column have a broad range of shared answers, there are definite points at which they differ. However, there is one exceptional pair here: The second and third columns contain identical answers for every entry in the chart. We will return to this matter in subsection 11.3.4.

Exercises

1. In (31), three general categories of adverbs are mentioned: epistemic, attitudinal, and universal. Explain why there is no general listing for frequency adverbs.

2. The following sentence is ambiguous, depending on whether the time modifier *today* is understood with the top verb phrase or with the bottom one:

(i)   John promised to mow the lawn today.

The ambiguity disappears when the modifier occurs at the beginning of the sentence:

(ii)   Today John promised to mow the lawn.

Explain in your own words the two meanings of sentence (i), and say which of these meanings is shared with sentence (ii). Then see if you can think of a principle that would predict the absence of ambiguity in (ii).

3. In some cases, a manner adverb (an adverb that modifies a phrase headed by an action verb) can be put at the beginning of a sentence:

(i)   Diego chipped the ball into the penalty area quickly .

(ii)   Quickly Diego chipped the ball into the penalty area.

In other cases, the same positioning gives poor results:

(iii)   Diego must have chipped the ball into the penalty area quickly.

(iv) *?Quickly Diego must have chipped the ball into the penalty area.

See if you can think of an explanation for the difference in acceptability between (ii) and (iv). Your answer to exercise 2 might prove useful.

11.3.3 Basic Rules for Modifier Position

In the discussion of modification in noun phrases in chapter 11, it was proposed that modifiers could be joined with common noun phrases to make larger common noun phrases. If we use Mod as an abbreviation for the various types of modifiers that can attach to common noun phrases, the two types of modifying configurations are just those shown in (32).

(32)   a.   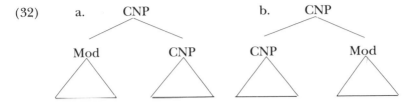   b.

Diagram (32a) represents prenominal modifying configurations; (32b) represents postnominal modifying configurations.

Let us now consider the possibility of using corresponding structures for the modifiers that we are studying in this chapter. For verb phrases, we would expect the following rule:

(33)   A verb phrase can consist of a modifier followed by a (smaller) verb phrase, or a (smaller) verb phrase followed by a modifier.

This rule would yield the two separate configurations shown in (34).

(34)   a.   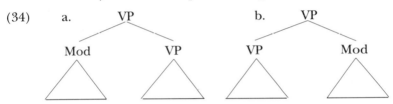   b.

The first of these trees provides immediately for two of the five positions that we have identified. Sentence (35a) has an adverb preceding the finite verb, whereas (35b) has an adverb before the action verb.

(35)   a.   George *already* has been making plans.
       b.   Vivian must have *cheerfully* eaten the tacos.

An adverb like *already* can get a position before the finite verb by attaching to the left of the finite verb phrase, as in (36).

(36)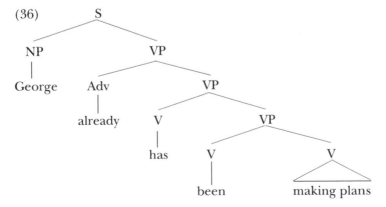

Similarly, an adverb like *cheerfully* can get a position before the action verb by attaching to the left of the phrase that this verb heads, as in (37).

(37)

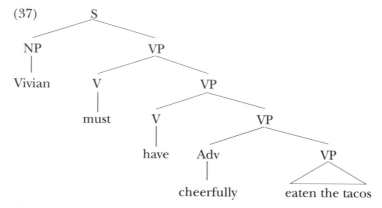

The differing positions of the adverbs in these sentences result from this difference in attachment. Because the verbs come first in the minimal verb phrases that they head, the effect is to put the adverb immediately to the left of the finite verb in the one case and immediately to the left of the action verb in the other case.

Now let us consider the two corresponding examples in which the adverbs come at the end of the verb phrase:

(38) a. George has been making plans already.
      b. Vivian must have eaten the tacos cheerfully.

These examples can be analyzed as having the structure illustrated in (34b)—the one with the modifier attached on the right side of the verb phrase. On the assumption that the adverbs will be attached to the same verb phrases to which they were attached when they preceded the verb phrase, we get the following tree diagrams for these two sentences:

(39) a.

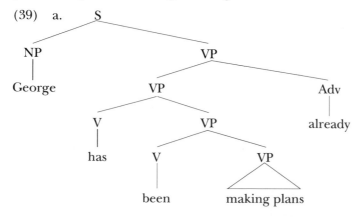

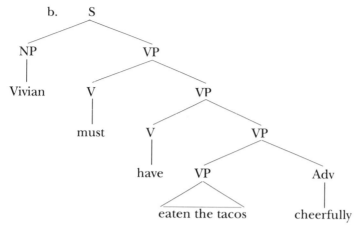

As the diagrams in (39) suggest, what appeared to be just one position is really two: to the right of the finite-verb phrase and to the right of the action-verb phrase. The reason that attachments to the left yield distinct left-to-right positions but attachments to the right do not is that a higher verb phrase and a lower verb phrase typically start at different points in the sentence but end at the same point, as illustrated in (40).

(40)

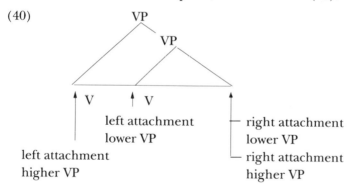

To what can we attribute the difference in the attachment behaviors of an adverb like *already*, which attaches to the finite-verb phrase, and an adverb like *cheerfully*, which attaches to the action-verb phrase? Here we might speculate that the difference in attachment behaviors is related to the differing contributions of the head verbs to the meanings of the sentences in which they occur. The finite verb, either by virtue of its tense marking or else in its own right, may indicate something about the time of the reported event, the habituality of the event, or the probable truth of the statement. Thus, with a finite-verb phrase we get adverbs like *now*, *already*, *usually*, and *probably*, which convey information of these kinds. On the other hand, a verb like EAT denotes the central action of the sentence. Since manner adverbs like *cheerfully* describe actions, they occur naturally in combination with phrases headed by verbs of this type.

We are left now with two basic adverbial positions to account for: the sentence-initial position and the position after the finite verb. For the first of these positions, we can adopt the same idea that we adopted for verb phrases, and we can give the following rule:

(41)   A sentence can consist of a modifier combined with a smaller sentence.

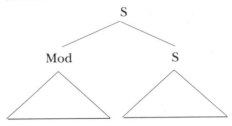

For a sentence such as (42a), this rule yields the structure given in (42b).

(42)   a.   Now we know the answer.

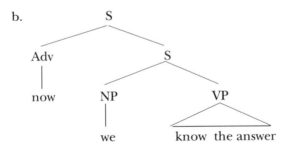

For adverbs that appear after the finite verb, however, the kinds of verb-phrase attachments that we have considered here do not yield a natural account. This is the second respect in which this particular adverbial position poses a special problem.

It is possible to construct sentences in which there is more than a single adverb in a certain position. This possibility is frequently seen with those adverbs that appear before the finite verb, as in (43).

(43)   George probably always will be singing that song.

This sentence poses no problem for the rule we have developed. We just need the same kind of "stacking" that we used for nominal modifiers:

(43)

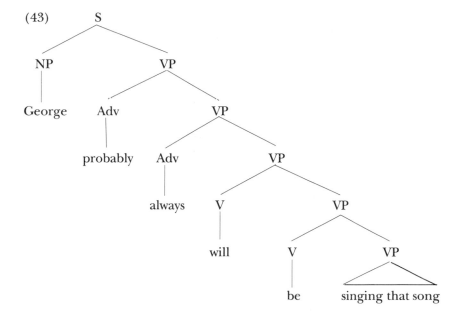

11.3.4 "Before Finite" and "After Finite" as a Single Adverbial Position

In the two preceding subsections, we discussed the various positions in which adverbs can appear, and we tried to develop rules that would account for their appearance in these positions. In the course of our discussions, we noticed two respects in which the position after the finite verb was odd. In the first place, the adverbs that can occur in this position are exactly the same as those that can occur in the position before the finite verb. In the second place, this position was the only one out of the five positions in our list that could not be readily accounted for by a rule attaching an adverb to one side or the other of a verb phrase.

When we look further, we find another mysterious fact about the position after the finite verb: The finite verbs that can be followed by adverbs such as *never*, *probably*, and *all* are actually quite limited in number, as the examples in (44) demonstrate.

(44)

a. The students *will* $\begin{Bmatrix} \text{never} \\ \text{probably} \\ \text{all} \end{Bmatrix}$ read the assignment.

b. The dogs *have* $\begin{Bmatrix} \text{never} \\ \text{probably} \\ \text{all} \end{Bmatrix}$ been groomed.

c. The children *are* $\left\{\begin{array}{l}\text{never}\\\text{probably}\\\text{all}\end{array}\right\}$ eager to go to bed.

d. *Joe's friends *send* $\left\{\begin{array}{l}\text{never}\\\text{probably}\\\text{all}\end{array}\right\}$ letters to him.

e. *The three friends *became* $\left\{\begin{array}{l}\text{never}\\\text{probably}\\\text{all}\end{array}\right\}$ accountants.

With the verbs *send* and *became*, only the position before the verb is available:

(45)

a. Joe's friends $\left\{\begin{array}{l}\text{never}\\\text{probably}\\\text{all}\end{array}\right\}$ *send* letters to him.

b. The three friends $\left\{\begin{array}{l}\text{never}\\\text{probably}\\\text{all}\end{array}\right\}$ *became* accountants.

The only verbs that allow these adverbs to follow them are the modals, the finite forms of BE, and the finite forms of perfect HAVE. Thus, all finite verbs allow these adverbs to precede them, but only a few allow the same adverbs to follow them. This observation might lead us to suspect that the position before the finite verb, which is available with all verbs, is more basic than the position after the verb, which is available with only a few.

An additional surprise is that there are two situations in which the preverbal position is much more natural even with the modals, BE, and HAVE. The first situation is illustrated in (46)–(48).

(46) a. Pete has often visited Grandmother, but Bill *never* has.
      b. *Pete has often visited Grandmother, but Bill has *never*.

(47) a. Only a few of the teachers have checked out books, but the students *all* have.
      b. *Only a few of the teachers have checked out books, but the students have *all*.

(48) a. John has definitely finished the exercise, and Martha *probably* has, too.
      b. *John has definitely finished the exercise, and Martha has *probably*, too.

These examples seem to indicate that when something is understood after these verbs, the adverb can only appear before the verb.

The second situation in which the adverb is more natural before the verb than after it is illustrated in (49) and (50), where upper-case letters indicate emphatic stress.

(49) a. Bill never WAS much of an electrician.
      b. *Bill WAS never much of an electrician.

(50) a. Doris probably COULD play that sonata.
      b. *Doris COULD probably play that sonata.

These examples seem to indicate that when one of these finite verbs is emphasized, the position after the verb is not available to these adverbs. We might now ask whether there is any property that is common to the two special situations just mentioned. We need to look for a property that would distinguish them from the situation in which these adverbs are acceptable after the verb:

(51) a. Bill has *never* visited Grandmother.
      b. The students have *all* checked out books.
      c. Martha has *probably* finished the exercise, too.
      d. Bill was *never* much of an electrician.
      e. Doris could *probably* play that sonata.

The distinguishing property is rather simple. In the examples in (51) the finite verb is stressless, whereas in the examples in (46)–(50) it is stressed. The stressed nature of the verbs in (49) and (50) is obvious, since they receive emphatic stress in these examples. Althought the (a) examples in (46)–(48) do not receive this kind of stress, they do receive what we can refer to as *normal stress*. Careful attention to their pronunciation reveals that these verbs are sharply different in pronunciation from those in (51). We can see this most easily by comparing the pronunciations of the verb *has* in the two examples in (52).

(52) a. Bill never has.   (normal stress on *has*)
      b. Bill has never visited Grandmother.   (no stress on *has*)

The pronunciation of the *has* in (52a) is [hæz], with a full vowel [æ]. By contrast, the pronunciation of the same word in (52b) is [hƏz], with the reduced vowel [Ə] that appears in English in completely unstressed syllables.

All our observations to this point are summarized in the following statements:

(53)   a.   When the finite verb is stressed, adverbs like *never, probably*, and
             all go before it.
       b.   When the finite verb is unstressed, the same adverbs are
             allowed to follow it.

The first of these two statements automatically covers ordinary finite verbs
such as *send* and *became*, since they never lose their stress. It also applies to
emphasized verbs and to verbs that have retained their stress because of
"understood" material after them.

   Even these statements can be simplified. We start by saying that the basic
position of adverbs like *never, probably*, and *all* is the position before the
finite verb. In order to account for sentences in which they appear after the
finite verb, we need only adopt the following rule:

(54)   Unstressed finite verbs may be moved to the left of any preceding
       adverbs.

This rule has the effect of converting the basic word order in (55a) into the
special word order of (55b).

(55)   a.   Bill never will read that book.   (no stress on *will*)

       b.   Bill will never read that book.

However, the rule will not apply in either of the situations shown below:

(56)   a.   Bill never WILL read that book.   (emphatic stress on *will*)

       b.   *Bill WILL never read that book.

(57)   a.   Bill never will___.   (normal stress on *will*)

       b.   *Bill will never ___.

In these last two cases, the stress on the verb keeps the leftward shift of the
verb from taking place.

   In the analysis developed here, what makes the modals, BE, and perfect
HAVE special is that they are exactly the English verbs that can have their
stress reduced. Under ordinary circumstances, this reduction is auto-
matic:

(58)   a.   Sue can [kən] apply for travel money.
       b.   Tony has [həz] papered the walls.
       c.   Harvey was [wəz] planning to play tennis.

The reduction fails to take place only if the verb is emphasized or if the verb
is followed by "understood" material.

The structure of a sentence with a shifted finite verb is represented as in (59).

(59)

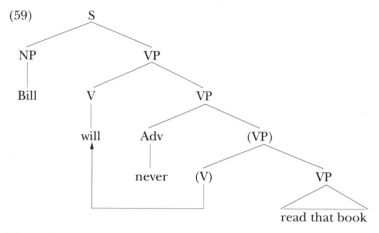

The verb *will* has been shifted to the left, joining with what follows it to make a larger verb phrase. The parenthesized V and VP show the basic position of the verb and the verb phrase that it heads, the position in which the verb would have occurred had the shift not taken place.

What grounds do we have for maintaining that it is the verb that has moved? Could we not just as well say that the adverb moves to the right of the verb? This alternative idea would give us the following tree diagram for sentence (55b), instead of the diagram given in (59).

(60)

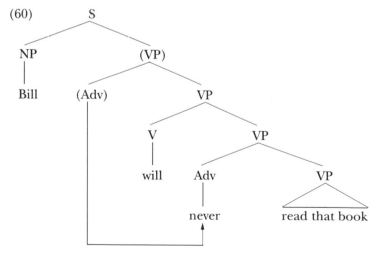

The main reason for preferring the verb-movement idea to the adverb-movement idea is that the former gives a simpler picture for sentences in which additional adverbs are involved. One such sentence is (61).

(61)   They are *probably always* playing golf.

The competing structures that the two analyses would yield for this sentence are given in (62).

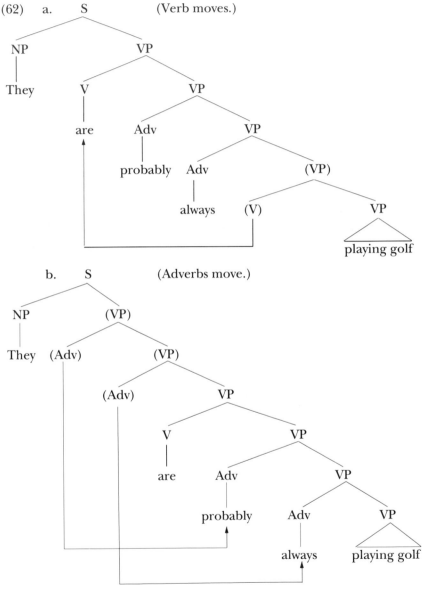

Diagram (62a) is clearly simpler than diagram (62b). Correspondingly, a rule that says "shift the head verb" yields simpler structures than one that says "shift any number of adverbs." This is the justification for claiming that it is the stressless verb that shifts rather than the adverb.

We have finally succeeded in reducing the number of basic adverbial positions from five to four, by eliminating the position after the finite verb as a separate basic position. So we are now left with the following four positions:

> sentence-initial
> before the finite verb
> before the action or state verb
> sentence-final.

11.3.5 The Syntax of *Not*

There is one special adverb whose behavior is not accounted for completely by the general word-order system developed above: the negative adverb *not*.

By way of preparation, we need to note that, in many contexts, *not* behaves in very much the same way as *never*. This is particularly clear with certain kinds of nonfinite verbal constructions. The basic position of *never* with gerundives, infinitival phrases, and bare-stem verb phrases is shown by the examples in (63).

(63) a. Jane regrets [*never* having seen the movie].
    b. We asked him [*never* to try to call us again].
    c. The rules require that you [*never* miss the monthly meeting].

As the additional examples in (64) show, the position of *not* is exactly identical.

(64) a. Jane regrets [*not* having seen the movie].
    b. We asked him [*not* to try to call us again].
    c. The rules require that you [*not* miss the monthly meeting].

These examples give us a strong initial reason to believe that *not* is like *never* in the positions that it prefers.

It is with finite verb phrases that *not* and *never* part company. Unlike *never*, *not* requires two special adjustments:

(65) a. Phillip *never* sold Martha's ring.
    b. *Phillip *not* sold Martha's ring.
    c. Phillip did *not* sell Martha's ring.

(66) a. Rhonda *never* reports errors.
    b. *Rhonda *not* reports errors.
    c. Rhonda does *not* report errors.

(67) a. The students *never* ask questions.
      b. *The students *not* ask questions.
      c. The students do *not* ask questions.

In order to see exactly what the first adjustment is, let us leave out *never* and *not* momentarily and display the verb phrases in the (a) and (c) sentences above:

(68)		**Ordinary verb phrases**	**Verb phrases headed by DO**
	a.	sold Martha's ring	did sell Martha's ring
		(past-tense verb phrase)	(past DO + bare-stem verbphrase)
	b.	reports errors	does report errors
		(pres sg verb phrase)	(pres sg DO + bare-stem verb phrase)
	c.	ask questions	do ask questions
		(pres pl verb phrase)	(pres pl DO + bare-stem verb phrase)

We see here exactly the same kind of contrast that we saw in chapter 3 between nonemphatic and emphatic sentences. Thus, we conclude that *not*, unlike *never*, requires the use the special-purpose finite phrase headed by DO.

When we put *not* back in, we note the second adjustment: The head verb must occur to the left of *not* rather than to its right:

(69) a. *Phillip *not* did sell Martha's ring.
      b. Phillip did *not* sell Martha's ring.

(70) a. *Rhonda *not* does report errors.
      b. Rhonda does *not* report errors.

(71) a. *The students *not* do ask questions.
      b. The students do *not* ask questions.

In sum, the following special rule is required for verb phrases to which *not* is attached:

(72) When *not* is attached to a finite verb phrase:
      (i) use a special-purpose finite phrase;
      (ii) shift the head verb to the left of *not*.

Both the similarities between *never* and *not* and their differences are illustrated in (73).

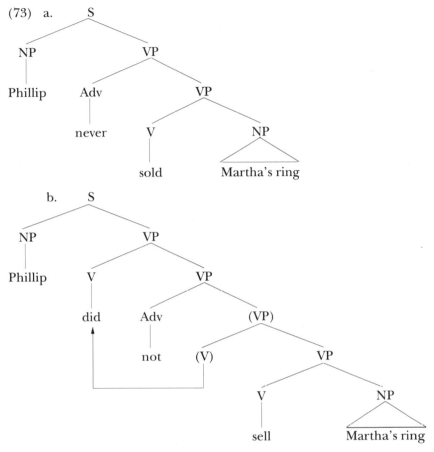

These diagrams are alike in that the adverbs occupy similar positions with respect to the verb phrase that follows them. However, (73b) differs from (73a) in two significant respects: Its verb phrase is the more complicated special-purpose finite, and its head verb has had to be shifted to the left of *not*.

We find that BE, perfect HAVE, and the modals exhibit the same kind of exceptional behavior in negative sentences as in emphatic sentences. In each set of sentences in (74)–(76), the (a) sentence is a normal affirmative, the (b) sentence is the incorrect negative that would be expected if these verbs were not exceptional, and the (c) sentence is the correct negative sentence.

(74)   a.   Max has vanished.
       b.   *Max does not have vanished.
       c.   Max has not vanished.

(75)   a.   Smith is a genius.
       b. *Smith does not be a genius.
       c.   Smith is not a genius.

(76)   a.   Sarah will open the package.
       b. *Sarah does not will open the package.
       c.   Sarah will not open the package.

The behavior of *not* with these verbs follows immediately from the statement made about them in chapter 3, where we noted that their special-
purpose structures are exactly the same as their general-purpose
structures. Using this earlier statement in conjunction with rule (72), we
automatically account for these new examples. The structures for the
acceptable negative sentences in (74)–(76) are presented in (77).

(77) a.   b.   c.

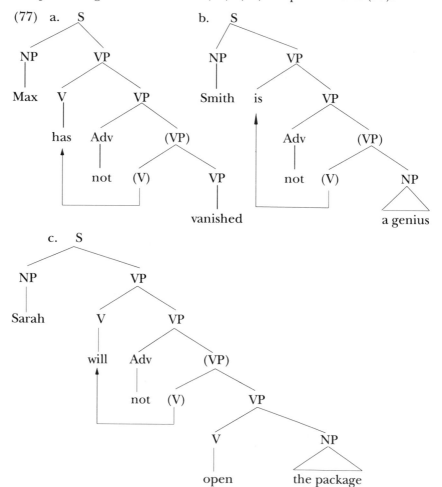

In each of these examples, a verb and *not* occur in a peculiar position relative to one another. Although the analysis just given involves moving the verb, we might ask what grounds there are for believing that the verb has moved to the left of *not* rather than that *not* has moved to the right of the verb. This alternative analysis would give us the following tree diagram for sentence (69b), instead of the one given in (73b).

(78)

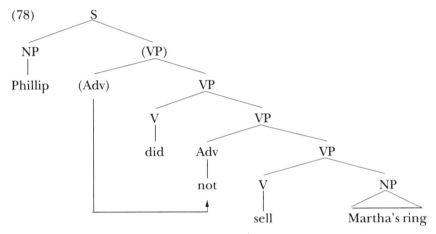

Here the critical kind of evidence is the same as that we saw in the preceding subsection when we were deciding whether stressless verbs shifted across adverbs or vice versa. In particular, it is not difficult to construct sentences in which *not* is accompanied by another adverb. One such sentence is (79).

(79)   Fido is not always barking.

Here are the competing structures that these two analyses would yield for this sentence:

(80)   a.   S   (Verb moves.)

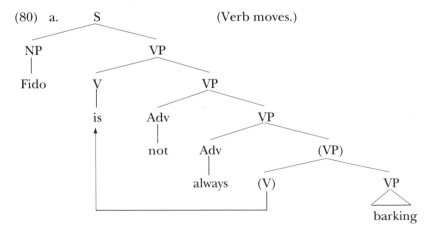

(80) b.   S   (Adverbs move.)

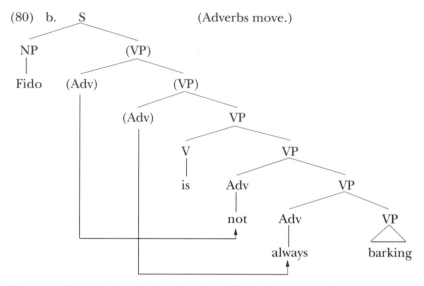

Diagram (80b) is clearly simpler than (80a). Correspondingly, a rule that says "shift the head verb" is simpler than one that says "shift the word *not*, and also any following adverb." This is the justification for claiming that it is the verb that shifts in this construction rather than the adverb *not*.

Exercise

1. For each of the following sentences, draw a tree diagram:
    a.   George did not know the answer.
    b.   Mabel is not eager to leave the meeting.
    c.   Janet does not always type her papers.
    d.   The mail will not ever be delivered.

11.3.6 Special-Purpose Head Verbs with Contracted *Not*

Corresponding to the three forms of special-purpose DO and also to most of the exceptional verbs discussed above, English has combined forms that end in -*n't*, a contracted form of *not*. Here are some examples:

(81) a.   I *did not* go to the post office.
      b.   I *didn't* go to the post office.

(82) a.   Henry *is not* here.
      b.   Henry *isn't* here.

(83) a.   The Smiths *could not* see the mountains.
      b.   The Smiths *couldn't* see the mountains.

Many of these forms are just constructed by adding -*n't* to the positive form (for example, *isn't* from *is*, *doesn't* from *does*, and *haven't* from *have*). In a few cases, though, the relation between the positive and the negative word is irregular. The most obvious example is *won't*, versus the expected **willn't*. In the case of *don't* and *mustn't*, the spellings hide irregularities; the vowel sound in *don't* is different from the sound in *do*, and the final *t* in *must* is not pronounced in *mustn't*. In addition, there is at least one positive form that does not have any contracted negative form at all: There is *am*, but no **amn't*. Finally, the forms *mayn't*, *mightn't*, and *shan't*, which still exist in at least some varieties of British English, are no longer used in American English.

The easiest way to account for these forms is to hypothesize an optional process that applies to the uncontracted negative forms after they have been arranged by the rules set forth in the preceding subsection. Let us look, for instance, at how sentence (84) would be described.

(84)   Jones hasn't ever seen the light.

We can think of the sentence as being derived in several steps, as in (85).

(85)   a.   Jones not ever has seen the light.   (*not* and *ever* before special-purpose verb phrase)
       b.   Jones has not ever seen the light.   (head verb shifted to left of *not*)
       c.   Jones hasn't ever seen the light.   (optional contraction of *not* with *has*)

The structure resulting from this derivation can be pictured in (86), where the plus sign indicates that the two elements are joined together into a single word.

(86)

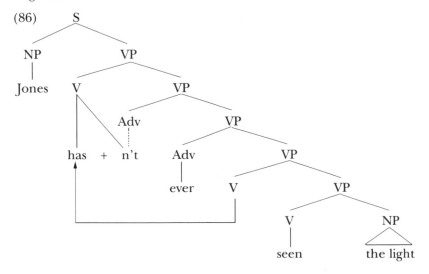

The solid line from V to *n't* indicates that this element has been incorporated into the verb. For the purposes of at least one further rule (which will be presented in chapter 14), *hasn't* and other contracted forms like it will behave as single units.

Exercise

1. For each of the following sentences, draw a tree diagram.
   a.   Holmes doesn't know the answer.
   b.   Watson couldn't diagram this sentence.
   c.   Wanda hasn't ever really decided to sell the house.
   d.   Morton couldn't always waltz.

11.3.7 A Note on "Verb-Phrase-Final" Position

In subsection 11.3.2, we saw many modifiers that were acceptable in verb-phrase-final position. A representative sample is given in (87).

(87)   a.   Rhonda loaned some money to her employees *on Thursday.*
       b.   We went to a bull fight *today.*
       c.   Carol has consulted with her attorney *already.*
       d.   Charles walked out the door *quickly.*
       e.   George stayed in his hotel room *for three nights.*
       f.   Tanya has traveled to Egypt *many times.*
       g.   Cornelius walked out the door *slowly.*

In these particular examples, these modifiers are also acceptable in some position nearer to the verb; see (88).

(88)   a.   Rhonda loaned some money *on Thursday* to her employees.
       b.   We went *today* to a bull fight.
       c.   Carol has consulted *already* with her attorney.
       d.   Charles walked *quickly* out the door.
       e.   George stayed *for three nights* in his hotel room.
       f.   Tanya has traveled *many times* to Egypt.
       g.   Cornelius walked *slowly* out the door.

In this capacity to move nearer to the verb, these relatively short modifiers contrast with clausal modifiers:

(89)   a.   *Rhonda loaned some money *when she got back to town* to her employees.
       b.   *We went *after the reception was over* to a bullfight.
       c.   *George stayed *while the legislature was in session* in his hotel room.
       d.   *Tanya has traveled *to increase her knowledge of Arabic culture* to Egypt.

Thus, the rule that we will adopt to account for the alternative word order in (88) must mention specific structural types of modifiers:

(90)   If a certain verbal modifier can appear at the end of a verb phrase, and is an adverb, a noun phrase, or a prepositional phrase, then it can also optionally be moved closer to the verb.

One firm restriction on this rule is illustrated in (91) and (92).

(91)   a.   George saw a play *on Monday*.
        b.   *George saw *on Monday* a play.

(92)   a.   The baby drank its milk *slowly*.
        b.   *The baby drank *slowly* its milk.

The restriction is that these adverbial modifiers are not allowed to come between a verb and its object. This is a special case of what is perhaps the most basic fact in English concerning the order of phrases and words after the verb: that nothing is allowed to come between a verb and its direct object. The two exceptions to this rule are the particles studied in chapter 6 and indirect objects. Also, the restriction does not apply to clausal direct objects, as we see in (93).

(93)   a.   The governor said *on Monday* that he would sign the budget bill.
        b.   I would like to ask *at this time* that all of you find seats.

In sum, the rule given originally in (90) can be stated more precisely as follows:

(94)   If a certain verbal modifier can appear at the end of a verb phrase, and is an adverb, a noun phrase, or a prepositional phrase, then it can also optionally be moved closer to the verb, provided that it does not separate the verb from a nonclausal noun phrase serving as the direct object.

Exercise

1. Two tests for distinguishing between a shifted-particle structure and an intransitive prepositional structure were proposed in chapter 6. The former structure is illustrated in (i) below, the latter in (ii):

        (i)   Paul took out the garbage.
        (ii) Paul looked out the window.

In (i), *the garbage* is the direct object of the verb *took*; in (ii), *the window* is the object of the preposition *out*. Using the observations just made about the impossibility of having adverbs between verbs and their objects, formulate a third test for determining whether a given verb phrase can have the intransitive prepositional structure. When applied to sentence (i) above, the test should give a negative result. It should give a positive result when applied to sentence (ii).

11.4 Syntactically Peculiar Clausal Modifiers

Most of the clausal modifiers that can be attached to verb phrases and sentences are relatively straightforward in structure. The majority of them consist of some "clause-taking preposition" (in traditional terms a "subordinating conjunction") plus a finite sentence. We see several examples of this kind of structure in (95).

(95)   a.   Barbara will ask for more money *because we need supplies.*
       b.   Kevin left *before the reporters could find him.*
       c.   *If it rains tomorrow,* the ceremony will be held next Thursday.

In a few other cases, the structures are familiar from previous discussions. Two clear examples are the locative modifier in (96a) and the time modifier in (96b), both of which are definite free relative clauses.

(96)   a.   My friends are playing poker *where their grandfathers played before them.*
       b.   Marsha called Connie's mother *when the hurricane was over.*

But there are other clausal modifying constructions that either involve familiar structures in an unfamiliar way, or else are structurally different from what we have seen. We will take a quick look at several of these constructions in this section.

11.4.1 Indefinite Free Relative Clauses as Conditional Modifiers
The first of the familiar structures in an unfamiliar use has already been illustrated in (10a). It is repeated here.

(97)   *Whatever kind of work he decides to do,* Edward will find it difficult to make ends meet.

When we studied free relative clauses in chapter 7, we noted that if a free relative clause was introduced by a phrase of a certain sort, then it could function as a phrase of that sort in a larger sentence. We also noted, however, that an indefinite free relative clause could serve another function. The sentence in (97) illustrates this other function. Even though *whatever kind of work* is clearly a noun phrase, the position in which the clause as a whole occurs in this sentence is definitely not a noun-phrase position. Instead, it is the same kind of adjoined position that a clause introduced by *if* can occupy. Moreover, when we think about the meaning of the sentence as a whole, we can paraphrase it as a conjunction of sentences of the following form:

(98) If he decides to do x kind of work, Edward will find it difficult to make ends meet.
      If he decides to do y kind of work, Edward will find it difficult to make ends meet.
      If he decides to do z kind of work, Edward will find it difficult to make ends meet.

A rather surprising ambiguity affords an interesting demonstration of this contrast between the use of these structures as ordinary phrases and their use as purely conditional clauses. Such an ambiguity is present in the following:

(99) Bob's sister will be happy *wherever he decides to settle.*

On one interpretation, this clause serves as a locative phrase modifier in the main sentence, indicating where Bob's sister will be happy:

(100) If Bob decides to settle at place x, his sister will be happy *there.*
       If Bob decides to settle at place y, his sister will be happy *there.*
       etc.

On the other interpretation, the purely conditional one, this clause indicates nothing about where Bob's sister will be happy:

(101) If Bob decides to settle at place x, his sister will be happy.
       If Bob decides to settle at place y, his sister will be happy.
       etc.

One additional variety of modifier that is closely related to these is illustrated in (102).

(102) a. *Whether or not Martha painted that picture,* it is worth a thousand dollars.
       b. *Whether John is suing Karen or Karen is suing John,* they ought to settle out of court.

Each of these sentences can be broken down into the conjunction of exactly two conditionals:

(103) If Martha painted that picture, it is worth a thousand dollars.
       If Martha did not paint that picture, it is worth a thousand dollars.

(104) If John is suing Karen, they ought to settle out of court.
       If Karen is suing John, they ought to settle out of court.

In older stages of English, there was actually a word *whetherever*, which corresponded more directly to the other *-ever* words and would have been used instead of *whether* in sentences like those in (102).

11.4.2 *No Matter*

A construction that has almost the same effect as the one just examined is shown in (105).

(105) a. *No matter whether John is suing Karen or Karen is suing John,* they ought to settle out of court.

b. *No matter whose car is taken to the rodeo,* someone needs to pay the parking fee.

c. *No matter what he decides to do,* Billy will need to inform his parole officer.

d. *No matter how many people come to the reception,* we will have enough forks.

Each of these modifiers consists of the fixed expression *no matter* followed by an indirect question. The interpretation of each sentence is once again the conjunction of a set of conditionals. In the first example, there are exactly two conditionals implied; in the three others, the set of conditionals is indefinitely large:

(106) If John is suing Karen, they ought to settle out of court.
       If Karen is suing John, they ought to settle out of court.

(107) If x's car is taken to the rodeo, someone needs to pay the parking fee.
       If y's car is taken to the rodeo, someone needs to pay the parking fee.
       If z's car is taken to the rodeo, someone needs to pay the parking fee.

11.4.3 Two Varieties of Purpose Clauses

As was noted in subsection 11.1.10, English provides several ways to indicate the purpose of some action. One important way of doing this is to adjoin an infinitival structure to the verb phrase. In some cases, as in (108), this infinitival structure is just a simple infinitival phrase.

(108) a. Bob went home early *to take a swim.*

b. Karen dipped her dog *to reduce the number of fleas in the house.*

In the two examples in (109), a more interesting structure is involved. (Pronoun objects are used to make it clear that we are not dealing with infinitival relative clauses.)

(109) a. Bob bought it *to clean his engine with.*
     b. Marie put it up *for Bill to keep his trophies on.*

Here, once again, we are evidently looking at another missing-noun-phrase construction, as we can see when we try to make these verb phrases finite and put them in simple sentences:

(110) a. *Bob cleaned his engine with.
     b. *Bill kept his trophies on.

These examples provide evidence for the following rule:

(111) A purpose clause can consist of an infinitival clause with a missing noun phrase.

As we can tell by the way in which we understand these sentences, the identification of the missing noun phrase is provided by the direct object of the verb phrase. Indeed, when no direct object exists, the constructions are uninterpretable:

(112) a. *Bob went home early *to clean his engine with.*
     b. *Martha worked upstairs *for Bill to put his trophies on.*

The only nontransitive situation in which the construction is acceptable is that shown in (113).

(113) a. This gadget is *to clean the engine with.*
     b. This shelf is *for Bill to put his trophies on.*

Here it is the subject that provides the identification for the missing noun phrase.

11.4.4 Reduced Clausal Modifiers
Many of the words that introduce finite clauses can also be followed by subjectless phrases of various sorts. *When,* for instance, takes several types of phrases:

(114) a. *When waiting for a bus,* one should always try to find the correct change.
     b. *When questioned by the prosecutor,* you should try to keep a straight face.
     c. *When angry,* a polar bear is a dangerous creature.
     d. *When in Rome,* do as the Romans do.

We have a present-participial verb phrase in (114a), a passive phrase in (114b), an adjective phrase in (114c), and a locative phrase in (114d). We also find passive phrases with *if* and present-participial verb phrases with *while.*

(115) a. *If opened carelessly,* this package will disintegrate.
b. *While reading this magazine,* Brenda saw an advertisement for your book.

All the predicate phrases that we see in these constructions are of kinds that can come after BE. Furthermore, their interpretation is very much the same as it would be in corresponding finite constructions in which BE actually appeared:

(116) a. *When one is waiting for a bus,* one should always try to find the correct change.
b. *When you are questioned by the prosecutor,* you should try to keep a straight face.
c. *When it is angry,* a polar bear is a dangerous creature.
d. *When you are in Rome,* do as the Romans do.
e. *If it is opened carelessly,* this package will disintegrate.
f. *While she was reading this magazine,* Brenda saw an advertisement for your book.

A construction that looks the same as (115b) at first glance is illustrated in (117).

(117) a. *After reading your letter,* John lost his temper.
b. *Before buying the house,* Julia had it checked for termites.

In these surroundings, though, the present-participial verb phrases are not interpreted as they would be as complements of BE. Instead of understanding these sentences as synonymous with (118), we are more likely to equate them with (119).

(118) a. *?After he was reading your letter,* John lost his temper.
b. *?Before she was buying the house,* Julia had it checked for termites.

(119) a. *After he read your letter,* John lost his temper.
b. *Before she bought the house,* Julia had it checked for termites.

Thus, their interpretation is more like that of the verb phrases in the gerundive construction. The gerundive in (120a), for instance, is closer in meaning to the full clause in (120c) than to that in (120b):

(120) a. John regretted reading your letter.
b. ?John regretted that he was reading your letter.
c. John regretted that he read your letter.

These constructions provide excellent opportunities for the kind of stylistic pratfall known as the "dangling participle." Some examples are given in (121).

(121) a.   While buying a newspaper, a runaway police horse knocked
            John over.
       b.   When in the right mood, Sheila's poems really amuse John.

What this sin actually amounts to is trying to use a noun phrase other than
the subject of the sentence as a whole to identify the understood subject
of one of these subjectless constructions.

Chapter 12

Degree Modification

In this chapter we look at a particularly rich area of English syntax: *degree modification*. This kind of modification applies to concepts that have *scales* associated with them. These include, for example, adjectival concepts such as *tall* and *intelligent*, adverbial concepts such as *often* and *quickly*, quantity concepts such as *much* and *many*, and even some noun concepts (*genius, idiot, jerk*, etc.) that can be thought of as being graded along a scale. English makes available a variety of syntactic devices for indicating position on these scales. In section 12.1 we will look at the methods for doing this with scales defined by adjectives and adverbs. In section 12.2 we will extend the analysis to include degree modification of the quantity words *much* and *many*. In section 12.3 we will focus on some special methods for indicating the amount of separation between two degrees on a scale. In sections 12.4 and 12.5 we will look at nonquantitative degree modification in noun phrases, and also at degree modification of verbs. Section 12.6 will be devoted to the various types of clauses that can be associated with degree words. Finally, in section 12.7, we will take a brief look at superlatives.

12.1 Simple Degree Expressions with Adjectives and Adverbs

12.1.1 Some Degree Words and Their Interpretations

Let us begin by looking at several separate groups of individual degree words in English. Each group will be shown in the context *Martha is intelligent*. What we will want to see is the exact way in which degree words from each group place the degree of Martha's intelligence on the general scale of intelligence. The reason for discussing the interpretive properties of these words so early in the chapter is that they will have an important role to play a few pages later in determining whether various degree words can themselves be modified.

The first group, illustrated in (1), consists of words that define a vague general region of the scale and place Martha's intelligence somewhere in that region.

(1)   Martha is { a. [*very* intelligent].
                     b. [*extremely* intelligent].
                     c. [*unusually* intelligent]. }

This kind of degree meaning is represented in the following diagram, which displays the meaning of the first of the three sentences in (1).

(2)   very intelligent

Here the shaded area indicates the vague range covered by the degree word *very*, and the pointer above the scale indicates where Martha's intelligence falls.

A second group of degree words consists of the two words *this* and *that*:

(3)   Martha is { a. [*this* intelligent].
                     b. [*that* intelligent]. }

These two words locate Martha's intelligence on the scale by equating it with some contextually determined degree of intelligence, as in (4).

(4)   this intelligent

The contextual determination might be made on the basis of, say, an A+ on an exam, and a person who knows of this performance might make the following comment:

(5)   Jerry doesn't know that Martha is [*this* intelligent].

The third group of degree words are comparative: they indicate Martha's degree of intelligence in relation to some other degree of intelligence used as a relative standard. (This relative standard, of course, is often defined in an *as* construction or a *than* construction.)

(6)   Martha is $\left\{\begin{array}{l}\text{a. } [as \text{ intelligent}].\\ \text{b. } [more \text{ intelligent}].\\ \text{c. } [less \text{ intelligent}].\end{array}\right\}$

The diagrams for the sentences with *as* and *more* are given in (7).

(7)   a.   as intelligent

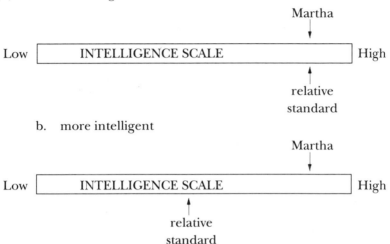

       b.   more intelligent

Next come three words that place a certain degree in relation to some region on a scale. Often (but not always), this region is defined as one where a certain result would follow from degrees that fall within the region. Since using a result to define the regions makes for clearer illustrations, some associated result clauses are included in the following examples:

(8)   a.   Martha is [*too* intelligent] to miss the problem.
       b.   Martha is [*so* intelligent] that she got an A+.
       c.   Martha is [intelligent *enough*] to get at least a B.

Diagrams for these sentences are given in (9).

(9)   a.   too intelligent to miss the problem

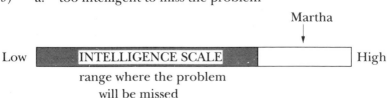

range where the problem
will be missed

b.   so intelligent she got an A+

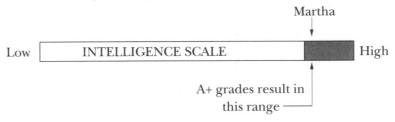

c.   intelligent enough to get at least a B

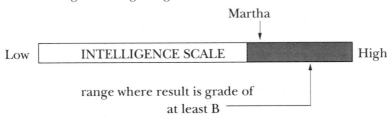

The word *too* puts Martha's intelligence above the range that produces a certain result, whereas *so* and *enough* put her intelligence inside some ranges that produce specified results.

One final degree word is *how*:

(10)   [*How* intelligent] is Martha?

How is just like other question words in leaving a blank for the hearer to fill in. Here the blank is to be filled in by some indication of Martha's intelligence. If we had to give a diagram of this meaning, it might be something like (11).

(11)   how intelligent

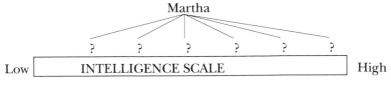

As was noted at the outset of the present section, a major motivation for going into this much detail with regard to the interpretation of the degree words is that these meaning differences will provide an explanation for why certain degree words can themselves be modified.

12.1.2 Rules for Creating Degree-Modified Structures

For all but one of these degree-plus-adjective sequences, we will assume that the degree word and the adjective are brought together by the following rule:

(12)   A degree expression and an adjective phrase can combine to create a larger adjective phrase.

The one exception, of course, is the sequence *intelligent enough*. We might at first think that *enough* comes at the end of adjective phrases. However, with adjective phrases of more than a single word, *enough* follows immediately after the head adjective, as in (13).

(13)   a.   Joe is fond *enough* of algebra.
        b.   *Joe is fond of algebra *enough*.

To account for this odd behavior, let us assume that *enough* is like other degree words in fitting in structures of the type shown in (12). We will then account for the peculiar word order that it induces by adopting a rule that is closely parallel to the special rule adopted in chapter 11 in connection with *not*. Here is the rule:

(14)   When a phrase is modified by the degree word *enough*, the head of the phrase must be shifted to the left of *enough*.

The two tree diagrams in (15) show the contrast between the ordinary structures associated with most degree words and the special structure induced by *enough*.

(15)   a.   b.

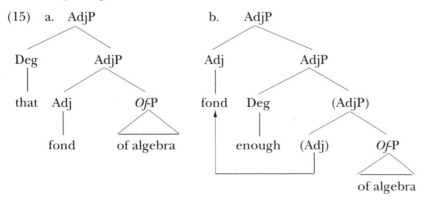

Exactly the same kinds of combinations are possible between degree expressions and adverbs:

(16)   Florence finished the work
a. [*very* quickly].
b. [*extremely* quickly].
c. [*unusually* quickly].

(17)   Florence finished the work
a. [*this* quickly].
b. [*that* quickly].

(18)   Florence finished the work
a. [*as* quickly].
b. [*more* quickly].
c. [*less* quickly].

(19)   Florence finished the work
a. [*too* quickly] to do a careful job.
b. [*so* quickly] that she was given a raise.
c. [quickly *enough* to leave at six o'clock].

(20)   [*How* quickly] did Florence finish the work?

These examples demonstrate that the rules given in (12) and (14) for the modification of adjectives really apply to both adjective and adverbial constructions rather than just to adjectival constructions alone.

12.1.3 Adjectives and Adverbs That Compare without *More*

In every example discussed so far that has involved a compared adjective, the adjective has been preceded by the degree word *more*. Although this is the most common way of forming a compared-adjective phrase, another method is used with some adjectives. This method involves adding the suffix -*er* to the adjective itself. In (21) we test various adjectives regarding the results of comparing them by these two different methods.

(21)   a.   smarter than...   *more smart than...
       b.   shorter than...   *more short than...
       c.   higher than...   *more high than...
       d.   lovelier than...   more lovely than...
       e.   narrower than...   more narrow than...
       f.   subtler than...   more subtle than...
       g. *obeser than...   more obese than...
       h. *decenter than...   more decent than...

> i. *deviouser than...   more devious than...
> j. *intelligenter than...   more intelligent than...

These adjectives conform to the following traditional rules:

(22) a. The suffix *-er* is allowed by one-syllable adjectives, and also by
          two-syllable adjectives ending in a vowel or an *-l* sound.
      b. The word *more* is allowed by adjectives of two or more syllables.

For adverbs, the allowed *-er* forms are more limited:

(23) a. faster than...   *more fast than...
      b. sooner than...   *more soon than...
      c. *quicklier than...   more quickly than...
      d. *franklier than...   more frankly than...

As these examples show, *-er* is allowed only with adverbs having no more
than one syllable.

What structure should we propose for adjective phrases compared with
the *-er* suffix? Again, as with *enough*, we need to note that the suffix comes
after the head of the phrase, and not after the phrase as a whole:

(24) a. George is [fond-*er* of Susan] now.
      b. *George is [fond of Susan]-*er* now.

We can treat the *-er* suffix in the same manner in which we treated *enough*.
In particular, we can view both of them as degree elements that induce the
head of the following phrase to shift to the left. The suffix has the
additional property of attaching to the adjective to make a single word,
much as the contracted negative suffix *n't* attached to a following verb.
This analysis gives the following structure for the adjective phrase in (24a):

(25)

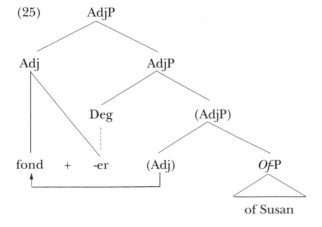

There are a few adjectives and adverbs that have completely irregular comparative forms. The uncompared adjective or adverb, the incorrect regular form, and the correct irregular form are listed in (26).

(26) a. good   *gooder   better
      b. well (adverb)   *weller   better
      c. bad   *badder   worse
      d. far   *farer   farther
      e. little (quantity word)   *littler   less

12.2 Degree Modification of *Much* and *Many*

In addition to modifying adjectives or adverbs, degree words can also modify the quantity words *much* and *many*:

(27)

Martha ate

$\begin{cases}
\text{a.} & [\textit{very} \text{ much] pie and } [\textit{very} \text{ many] apples.} \\
\text{b.} & [\textit{unusually} \text{ much] pie and } [\textit{unusually} \text{ many] apples.} \\
\text{c.} & [\textit{this} \text{ much] pie and } [\textit{this} \text{ many] apples.} \\
\text{d.} & [\textit{that} \text{ much] pie and } [\textit{that} \text{ many] apples.} \\
\text{e.} & [\textit{as} \text{ much] pie and } [\textit{as} \text{ many] apples.} \\
\text{f.} & [\textit{too} \text{ much] pie and } [\textit{too} \text{ many] apples.} \\
\text{g.} & [\textit{so} \text{ much] pie and } [\textit{so} \text{ many] apples.}
\end{cases}$

(28) [*How* much] pie and [how many] apples did Martha eat?

In order to account for the examples in (27), we will speak of quantity *phrases* instead of just quantity words. The structure of these phrases is given by the following rule:

(29) A quantity phrase can consist of a degree expression plus one of the two quantity words *much* or *many*.

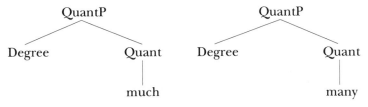

In addition, we will revise the basic rules of chapter 5 so as to allow noun-phrase structures that are introduced by these quantity phrases:

(30) a. A noun phrase can consist of a quantity phrase followed by a common noun phrase.   (elementary noun phrase)

   b.   A noun phrase can consist of a quantity phrase followed by an
        of phrase.   (partitive noun phrase)

These rules give us the two varieties of noun-phrase structure shown
in (31).

(31) a.   NP   b.   NP

     QuantP   CNP   QuantP   *Of*-P

Two specific noun-phrase structures that these rules yield are shown
in (32).

(32) a.   NP   b.   NP

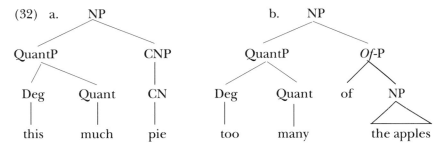

QuantP   CNP   QuantP   *Of*-P

Deg   Quant   CN   Deg   Quant   of   NP

this   much   pie   too   many   the apples

   Although these general rules give good results for most degree words,
there are three degree words—given in (33)—that cannot modify *much*
and *many* in the same way that they modify adjectives and adverbs.

(33)   Martha ate { a. * [*more* much] pie and [*more* many] apples.
                     b. * [*less* much] pie and [*less* many] apples.
                     c. * [much *enough*] pie and [much *enough*] apples. }

What account can we give now of the impossibility of using *more*, *less*, and
enough with *much* and *many*? One fact to observe is that for each of the
starred sentences, there is a corresponding acceptable sentence in which
the illegitimate combinations are replaced by something else:

(34)   a. *Martha ate [*more* much] pie and [*more* many] apples.
       b.   Martha ate [*more*] pie and [*more*] apples.

(35)   a. *Martha ate [*less* much] pie and [*less* many] apples.
       b.   Martha ate [*less*] pie and [*fewer*] apples.

(36)   a. *Martha ate [much *enough*] pie and [many *enough*] apples.
       b.   Martha ate [*enough*] pie and [*enough*] apples.

Concerning the unacceptability of *less many*, we can just say that *fewer* is a
specific replacement form for *less many*. For the other problem examples,

we can say that *much* is suppressed when it is joined to *more, less,* and *enough,* and that *many* is suppressed with it is joined to *more* and *enough.* This suppression can be indicated in a tree diagram with parentheses. Then the following structures would be assigned to the acceptable noun phrases in (34b) and (36b):

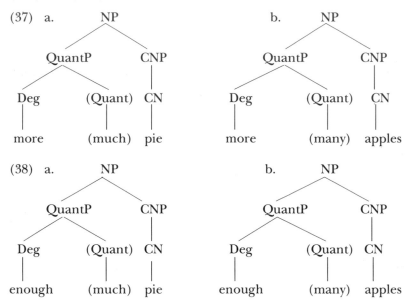

An advantage of this treatment is that it offers an explanation for why *enough* should come after adjectives and adverbs but before nouns. The explanation is that *enough* is not really modifying the noun directly, but instead is part of a quantity phrase. This quantity phrase is just in its normal position in front of the common noun phrase.

Exercise

1. Draw tree diagrams for the following sequences:
   a. so fond of Martha
   b. certain enough of her abilities
   c. this many pictures of Alexandria
   d. how much traffic
   e. too eager to win
   f. as much of your money
   g. too many of the books
   h. more of the dominoes
   i. enough of the soup

12.3 Separation Expressions

From most of the degree-modified phrases that we have examined, no larger phrases can be built. But phrases introduced by three degree words (*more*, *less*, and *too*) allow preceding quantity expressions:

(39) a.   Martha is [*much* more intelligent].
      b.   Martha is [*much* less intelligent].
      c.   Martha is [*much* too intelligent].

In having this property, these degree words contrast with the others:

(40) a. *Martha is [*much* very intelligent].
      b. *Martha is [*much* so intelligent].
      c. *Martha is [*much* this intelligent].

To see why there should be such a difference between the degree words in (39) and those in (40), we need to review what was said earlier about their meaning. As a look at our earlier diagrams will indicate, every word that does not allow a preceding *much* has either the property of determining a point that is equal to some other point or the property of setting a point within a certain region of the scale. In particular, *very* and *so* both set the degree within a certain region, whereas *this* sets the degree equal to some contextually determined degree. By contrast, the words *more*, *less*, and *too* all define the degree of Martha's intelligence as being *separated* from some point or region. With both *more* and *less*, the separation is from whatever is serving as the relative standard. With *too*, the separation is from an entire region somewhere below Martha's intelligence. Now it is simple to see what *much* does when it comes before *more*, *less*, or *too*: It simply indicates the size of this separation.

Other expressions besides *much* can indicate the size of the separation:

(41) a.   Joe is *far* more honest that Fred.
      b.   Karen is *far* too sophisticated to believe your story.

(42) a.   Susan is *way* more independent than Tanya.
      b.   Gretchen is *way* too studious to make a C.

(43) a.   We caught *several* more fish than Harry and David did.
      b.   They caught *three* too many snappers.

(44) a.   Martha is *a little bit* more careful than Fred.
      b.   Tony is *a little bit* too talkative to be able to keep that secret.

(45)   a.   George is *ten pounds* heavier than James.
       b.   George is *ten pounds* too heavy to be allowed in the welterweight
            division.

We will refer to these expressions as *separation expressions*, in recognition of
their use in these examples. Then the first of the following rules defines
them, and the second spells out the way in which they can combine with
certain degree-modified expressions:

(46)   A *separation expression* (abbreviated "Sep") can consist of the single
       words *way* or *far*, or a quantity phrase (*much, several*), or a measure
       noun phrase (*a little bit, three inches, several pounds, five feet*).

(47)   A separation expression can be combined with a degree-modified
       phrase that expresses a separation of degree, to form a larger
       phrase of the same type.

These rules together give structures of the following sorts:

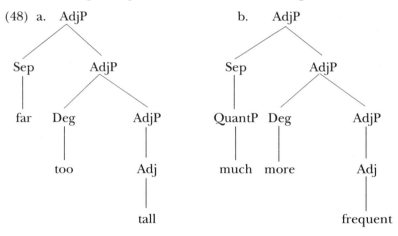

The rules that we have just given allow an even more complex structure.
We noted above that *much* and *many* could both be modified by degree
expressions themselves; this was in fact the main reason for wanting to talk
about quantity phrases instead of just quantity words. Thus, in addition to
using the single word *much* as a separation expression, we can also use *much*
preceded by a degree word, as in (49).

(49)   a.   Jonah is [*so much* more polite].
       b.   I didn't know that Fred had baked [*that much* more bread].

The following tree diagrams give the structures of the bracketed phrases:

(50) a.

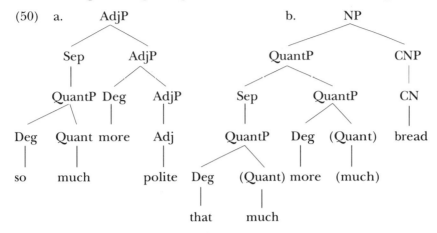

Exercise

1. Draw tree diagrams for the following phrases:
    a.   this much more frequent
    b.   so many more mistakes
    c.   as much less of his prestige
    d.   far too much more of your attention
    e.   enough more intelligent

12.4 Degree Modification in Noun-Phrase Structures

In the section just finished, we saw several examples in which quantities inside noun phrases were modified by degree expressions. Except for the absence of forms in which *much* and *many* combined with *more* and *enough*, these expressions followed the same rules as did the degree expressions that modified adjectives and adverbs. There also exists another kind of degree modification involving noun phrases, which occupies one of the more bizarre and complicated corners of English syntax. This kind of degree modification arises when we want to indicate a position on a scale defined by some adjective-noun concept (for instance, *tall man* or *good pancake*) or a scale defined by a noun alone (for instance, *genius* or *jerk*).

Let us look first at the cases involving an adjective in addition to a noun. Here there are at least a few degree words that behave as we might expect them to, coming directly before the adjective (or, in the case of *enough*, directly after it):

(51)   a.   Thomas is [a *very tall* man].
       b.   Jill is [a *more intelligent* woman].
       c.   Karen is [a *good enough* painter].

The the basic rule given in chapter 10 for prenominal modifiers, together
with the rules developed in the present chapter, assign the following
structures to these examples:

(52)   a.   b.

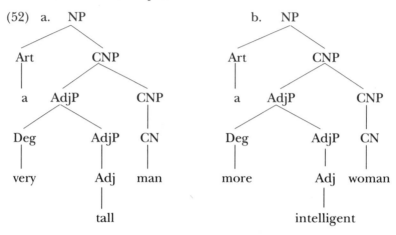

c.

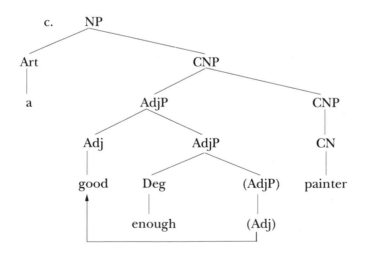

Other degree words, such as *extremely* and *unusually*, behave like *very* in this
regard, and *less* behaves just like *more*.

   The complications begin with the degree words *as*, *so*, *that*, and *too*:

(53)   a.   *John is [an *as good* driver].

b. *Gerald is [a *so creative* thinker].

c. *I didn't know we would be able to find [a *that good* singer].

d. *Joe is [a *too small*] linebacker.

What we get instead are structures in which the degree word and its adjective actually precede the indefinite article:

(54) a. John is [*as good* a driver].

b. Gerald is [*so creative* a thinker].

c. I didn't know we would be able to find [*that good* a singer].

d. Joe is [*too small* a linebacker].

One additional complication with regard to these structures is that they are only possible with the indefinite article *a(n)*. When any other kind of determiner or quantity structure is involved, neither the normal order shown in (51) nor the special order shown in (54) is possible.

(55) a. *Your friends are [some *as good* drivers].

b. *Your friends are [*as good* some drivers].

(56) a. *Fred is [the *too small* linebacker].

b. *Fred is [*too small* the linebacker].

In addition, examples with bare noun phrases are impossible:

(57) *Fred, Jerry, and Bill are [*too small* linebackers].

The very limited circumstances under which these degree words can be used with prenominal adjectives require us to state two unusually complicated rules. The first of these, given in (58), is a more restrictive version of the rule presented in chapter 10 for prenominal modifiers:

(58) A common noun phrase can consist of an adjective phrase followed by a smaller common noun phrase, with the following restriction: The adjective phrase must not include a complement and must not be introduced by *as*, *so*, *that*, or *too*.

The second special rule states the special way in which these four degree-words can be used:

(59) A noun phrase introduced by *a(n)* can be combined with a preceding adjective phrase introduced by one of the degree words *as*, *so*, *that*, and *too* to form a larger noun phrase.

Rule (59) gives the following structure for (54a):

(60)

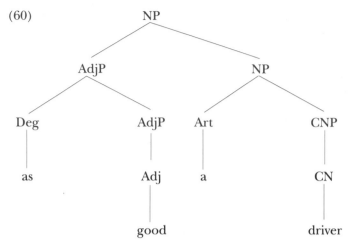

As with the prenominal structures given in chapter 10, this diagram does not itself give any idea of the extremely restricted circumstances under which an adjective phrase and a noun phrase can be combined in this way.

Another word can be used as a special degree modifier in noun phrases. This is the word *such*, which plays much the same role for common noun phrases that *so* plays for adjectives, adverbs, and quantity expressions. Its behavior is exhibited in (61) and (62).

(61)   a.   His relatives are [*such* idiots].
       b.   This article is [*such* rubbish].
       c.   Helen makes [*such* delicious pancakes].
       d.   Joe makes [*such* vile chowder].

(62)   a.   I've never before met [two *such* honest people].
       b.   If Bert makes [two more *such* stupid mistakes], Jones will fire him.
       c.   [One more *such* disastrous result] could ruin the company.

The examples in (61) and (62) suggest that *such* joins with common noun phrases. The examples in (62) further suggest that the result is itself a common noun phrase, a sequence that can combine with a preceding numeral to form a noun phrase. We thus are led to the rule in (63).

(63)   A common noun phrase can be combined with a preceding *such* to form a larger common noun phrase.

This rule gives the structures in (64).

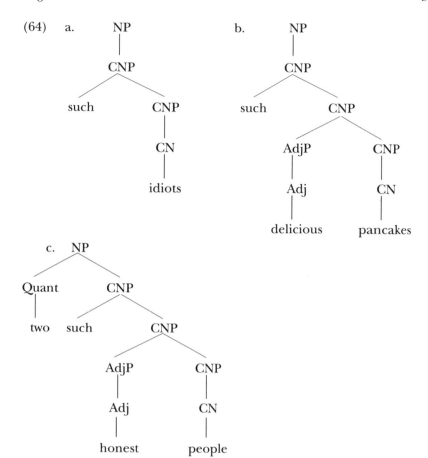

(64)   a.   NP
                    |
                   CNP
                  /   \
              such   CNP
                         |
                        CN
                         |
                       idiots

b.   NP
             |
            CNP
           /   \
       such   CNP
                /   \
            AdjP   CNP
              | |
             Adj   CN
              | |
          delicious pancakes

c.   NP
       /   \
   Quant   CNP
     | /   \
   two such   CNP
                /   \
            AdjP   CNP
              | |
             Adj   CN
              | |
           honest   people

So far, the syntax of *such* has been straightforward. However, with this word—as with several of the other words examined above—a special complication is induced by the indefinite article. Rule (63) would lead us to expect examples like the following:

(65)   a. *Alfred is [a such genius].
       b. *Frank drives [a such old car].

What are actually acceptable are examples in which *such* precedes the indefinite article:

(66)   a. Alfred is [such a genius].
       b. Frank drives [such an old car].

Because of the acceptable examples in (62), we are led to say that the ordinary place for *such* is right before a common noun phrase. Then, in order to account for the new examples in (66), we need to say that the indefinite article *a(n)* induces a leftward shift of *such*.

(67) a.

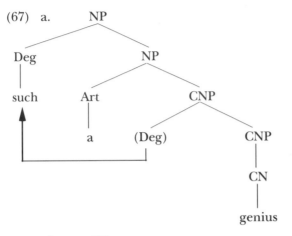

b.

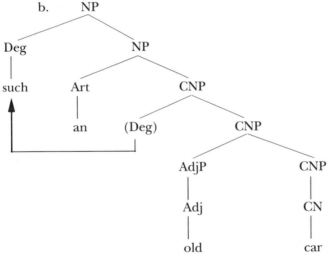

Finally, suppose that we want to use degree words such as *so*, *that*, and *too* with a noun like *genius* or *idiot*. Doing this depends on attaching these degree words to *much*:

(68) a.   Fred isn't [*so* much of a genius].
      b.   Nigel isn't [*that* much of an hothead].
      c.   Joe is [*too* much of a prima donna].
      d.   Jane isn't [*as* much of a composer].

As we might expect, we also have *more* in place of *more much, and *less* in place of *less much, and *enough* in place of *much enough:

(69)   a. *Harry is [*more* much of a hothead].
       b.   Harry is [*more* of a hothead].

(70)   a. *Harry is [*less* much of a hothead].
       b.   Harry is [*less* of a hothead].

(71)   a. *Harry is [much *enough* of an idiot.
       b.   Harry is [*enough* of an idiot].

Also possible are a small number of quantity expressions other than *much,* such as that in (72).

(72)   Horatio is [*a little bit* of a liar].

Again, this construction gives good results only in the singular, as we see when we try to construct corresponding examples with plurals:

(73)   a. *Fred and Greta aren't [*so* much of geniuses].
       b. *Nigel and Henry aren't [*that* much of hotheads].
       c. *Joe and Betty are [*too* much of prima donnas].
       d. *Jane and Robert aren't [*as* much of composers].
       e. *Harry and Joseph are [*more* of idiots].
       f. *Horatio and Jenny are [*a little bit* of liars].

These observations are summarized in the following rule:

(74)   A noun phrase can consist of a quantity phrase followed by an *of* phrase, where the object of *of* is a noun phrase introduced by *a(n)*.

Two of the structures that this rule yields are given in (75).

(75)   a.

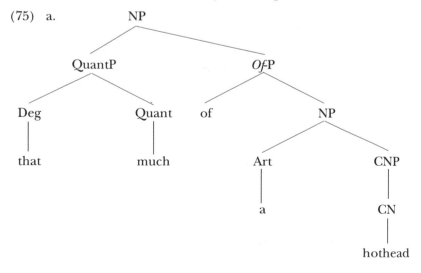

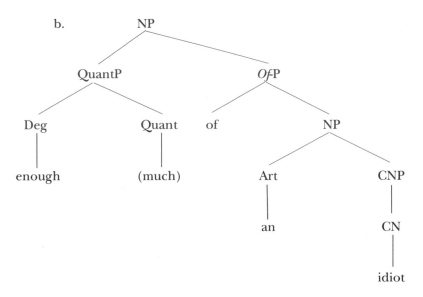

Exercises

1. Draw tree diagrams for the following noun phrases:
   a. two extremely fast runners
   b. as big a deficit
   c. this solemn a vow
   d. this devout an old man
   e. such long books
   f. such an ancient legend
   g. three such obnoxious children
   h. so much more of a bureaucrat

2. The bracketed noun phrase in the following sentence is ambiguous:

   Flora wants to read [more contemporary novels].

Our rules give two different structures, corresponding to the two separate interpretations of this noun phrase. Draw tree diagrams for these two structures.

12.5 Degree Modification with Verbs

Some verbs have scales associated with them, especially those denoting mental dispositions (for example, *love* and *admire*). On such scales, degrees are expressed indirectly through the use of quantity expressions—most of them involving *much*, as in (76).

(76)   William loves Brenda
$\left\{\begin{array}{l}\text{a. } [\textit{very} \text{ much}].\\ \text{b. } [\textit{this} \text{ much}].\\ \text{c. } [\textit{too} \text{ much}].\\ \text{d. } [\textit{as} \text{ much}] \text{ (as James does)}.\\ \text{e. } [\textit{so} \text{ much}] \text{ (that he wants to}\\ \qquad \text{move to Dayton)}.\end{array}\right\}$

As we would expect by this time, *more* and *enough* occur by themselves, without any accompanying *much*:

(77)   Jeff admires Lucy
$\left\{\begin{array}{l}\text{a. } *[\textit{more} \text{ much}].\\ \text{b. } [\textit{more}].\\ \text{c. } *[\text{much } \textit{enough}].\\ \text{d. } [\textit{enough}].\end{array}\right\}$

Once again, other quantity expressions are also possible:

(78)   Doris admires Arthur
$\left\{\begin{array}{l}\text{a. } [\text{a good deal}].\\ \text{b. } [\text{a little bit}].\\ \text{c. } [\text{quite a lot}].\end{array}\right\}$

A particularly simple rule will account for these examples:

(79)   A verb phrase can be joined with a following quantity phrase to make a larger verb phrase.

This rule gives a type of verb-phrase structure that we saw in chapter 11 with adverbial modifiers:

(80)

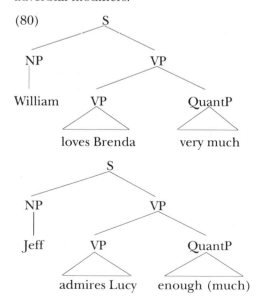

12.6 Clauses Associated with Degree Words

It is time now to discuss in detail the kinds of clauses that are often associated with particular degree words. For this purpose, we can divide the relevant degree words into two groups. The words in the first group (*so, such, too,* and *enough*) take following *result clauses,* whereas those in the second group (*as, more,* and *less*) take following *comparative clauses.* The syntactic properties of the clauses associated with these two groups are quite different, as are their interpretations. We will take up the result clauses first, since their syntax is more straightforward.

12.6.1 Result Clauses
The simplest form of result clause is that found with *so* and *such*:

(81) a. This book is *so* big [that it doesn't fit on the shelf].
     b. *So* many people stayed for lunch [that all the food was eaten immediately].
     c. Doris ate *such* a big lunch [that she fell asleep in class].
     d. Jerry writes *such* long articles [that his newspaper refuses to print them].

These clauses are clearly just finite *that* clauses, with no missing phrase or other complication. The *that* clause in each sentence just describes the result of a certain degree's being near the high end of some relevant scale.

With *too* and *enough,* clauses of a different type are used:

(82) a. The chicken is *too* hot [for you to remove from the package].
     b. The chicken is cool *enough* [for you to remove from the package].

In each of these sentences, an infinitival clause is associated with the degree word, and a careful inspection reveals a missing noun phrase:

(83) a. *You removed from the package.
     b. You removed *it* from the package.

Thus, *too* or *enough* can occur with an infinitival clause with a missing noun phrase. The identification of this missing noun phrase is like that for the *easy* construction studied in chapter 9: Whatever noun phrase is determined to be the subject of the adjective phrase also provides an identification for the missing noun phrase. In each of the sentences in (82), *the chicken* is interpreted as the subject of the adjective phrase and thus also identifies the missing noun phrase inside the *for* clause.

Another possibility also exists for *too* and *enough,* as the two examples in (84) show.

(84)   a.   Martha is *too* intelligent [to make that mistake].
       b.   Joel is old *enough* [to take care of himself].

In these examples, the infinitival constructions contain no missing noun phrases, and the subjects of the adjective phrases (*Martha* and *Joel*) are used to identify the subjects of the infinitive phrases rather than some missing noun phrase inside them.

12.6.2 Comparative Clauses
The kinds of clauses that go with comparative degree words are illustrated in (85).

(85)   a.   Joseph became *as* famous [*as* Thelma became].
       b.   Caspar spent *more* money [*than* Bernie spent].
       c.   Molly encountered *less* trouble [*than* Walter encountered].

In these examples we see pairings between *as* and *as*, between *more* and *than*, and between *less* and *than*. These pairings are the only ones possible, as (86) demonstrates.

(86)   a.   *John became *as* famous [*than* Thelma became].
       b.   *Caspar spent *more* money [*as* Bernie spent].
       c.   *Molly encountered *less* trouble [*as* Walter encountered].

These observations give us the following rule:

(87)   The words *more* and *less* can be associated with comparative clauses introduced by *than*; the word *as* can be associated with comparative clauses introduced by *as*.

Now let us examine the internal structure of the comparative clauses. If we look at the material after *than* and *as* in the bracketed sequences in (85), we find evidence of missing phrases:

(88)   a.   *Thelma became.
       b.   *Bernie spent.
       c.   *Walter encountered.

In each of these cases, what is needed to make an unacceptable sentence complete is a phrase of the same kind that is introduced by *as, more,* or *less*:

(89)   a.   Thelma became *famous*.   (adjective phrase—corresponds to *as famous*)
       b.   Bernie spent *money*.   (noun phrase—corresponds to *more money*)
       c.   Walter encountered *trouble*.   (noun phrase—corresponds to *less trouble*)

Let us refer to the phrases *as famous, more money,* and *less trouble* as *compared phrases*. In general, this category will include all the phrases in which we used *as, more,* and *less*:

(90) a. as intelligent, more intelligent, less intelligent (adjective phrases)
  b. as quickly, more quickly, less quickly (adverb phrases)
  c. as clever a fiddler, a more clever fiddler, a less clever fiddler (noun phrases)
  d. as much bread, more bread, less bread (noun phrases)
  e. as much of the bacon, more of the bacon, less of the bacon (noun phrases)
  f. as much of a problem, more of a problem, less of a problem (noun phrases)

With this concept in hand, we can give the following rule:

(91) A comparative clause consists of either *as* or *than* followed by a finite sentence with a missing phrase of the same type as the compared phrase.

For the particular bracketed constructions in (85), we have the structures illustrated in (92).

(92) a. (as famous)

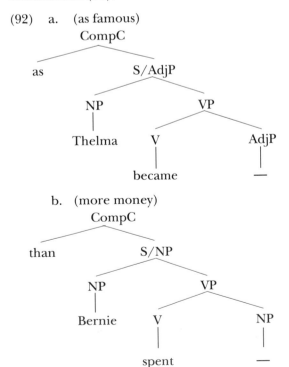

  b. (more money)

c.   (less trouble)

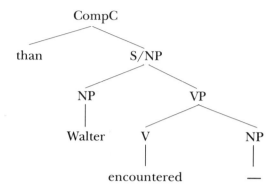

Where the compared phrase is an optional phrase in the sentence, we do not get a sensation of a missing phrase inside the comparative clause:

(93)   a.   Jane writes stories *more often* than she writes articles.
       b.   Joe proofreads footnotes *more carefully* than he proofreads text.

In these examples, the sequences of words after *than* sound like complete sentences in their own right:

(94)   a.   She writes articles.
       b.   He proofreads text.

Nevertheless, even for examples like these we will assume that there are missing phrases in the comparative clauses. In (93a), the missing phrase must be a frequency adverb, whereas in (93b) it must be a manner adverb—see the diagrams in (95).

(95)   a.   (more often)

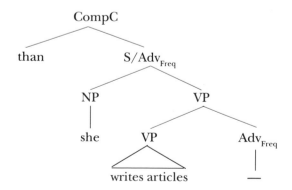

b. (more carefully)

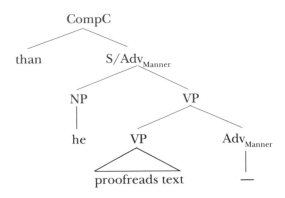

Exercise

1. In the following sentences, identify the compared phrase and say what type of phrase it is.

    a. Janet plays golf more often than she plays tennis.
    b. Janet plays more golf than she used to play.
    c. More people from Connecticut live in frame houses than live in stone houses.
    d. Jones wrote a better story than we expected him to write.
    e. Norma is more of a clown than Robert is.
    f. Barbara received more letters from Franklin than Joe received from Beth.
    g. Barbara read more letters from Franklin than Joe read.

12.6.3 Double-Scale Comparatives

All the comparatives discussed above have had the effect of comparing degrees on a single scale. Consider the interpretation of sentence (85a), which is repeated here as (96).

(96)   John became *as* famous [as Thelma became].

We can break the interpretation down into the following three parts:

(97)   a. John became famous to some degree x.
        b. Thelma became famous to some degree y.
        c. x is equal to y.

Since x and y here represent points on the same scale, the scale on which fame is measured, we can refer to this comparative construction as a *single-*

scale comparative. All the other comparatives that we have studied up to this point also have this property.

Now let us consider the following example:

(98)   David is *as* erudite [as he is creative].

Here the compared phrase consists of the adjective *erudite*, but we do not find a corresponding missing adjective phrase inside the comparative clause. What we find instead is another adjective phrase, one consisting of the word *creative*. Furthermore, when we think about the interpretation of (98), we realize that it has to be broken down as follows:

(99)   a.   David is erudite to degree *x*.
       b.   He is creative to degree *y*.
       c.   *x* is equal to *y*.

What this sentence expresses, then, is a situation that must be depicted with two scales instead of one:

(100)

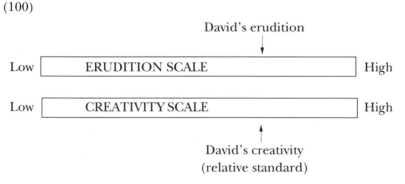

We will recognize the special interpretation of this comparative by calling it a *double-scale* comparative.

Double-scale comparatives are also found in which the compared phrase is a noun phrase. Here are two examples:

(101)   a.   More pigs eat corn than dogs eat hay.
        b.   Pigs eat more corn than dogs eat hay.

In (101a), the compared phrase is *more pigs*, which tells us that the first scale for this sentence will be "number of pigs." For the second scale, we have to look in the comparative clause for a phrase that will yield a scale that is comparable to the first. The clear answer for (101a) is "number of dogs," a scale provided by the subject noun phrase of the comparative clause. In (101b), scales are provided by the two direct objects. The compared phrase, *more corn*, sets up "amount of corn" as the first scale, and the corresponding noun phrase in the comparative clause is *hay*, which gives as the second scale "amount of hay."

One particular kind of compared phrase provides evidence that even double-scale comparatives contain a missing element:

(102)   Joe bought more of the records than he bought of the tapes.

In this sentence, the compared phrase is *more of the records*, which is clearly a noun phrase. The corresponding phrase in the comparative clause appears to be the prepositional phrase *of the tapes*. But this phrase appears with a verb that does not generally allow *of* phrases but does allow full noun phrases:

(103)   *He bought [$_{Of\text{-}P}$ of the tapes].
           He bought [$_{NP}$ a tape].

Thus, just from the environment in which *of the tapes* appears, we would expect it to be a noun phrase. One easy way to make it a noun phrase is to add a quantity word:

(104)   He bought [*many* of the tapes].

Such an addition, of course, is not possible within the comparative clause in (102), as (105) shows.

(105)   *John bought more of the records than he bought [many of the tapes].

We can make sense of these observations if we assume that the object of *bought* in (102) contains a missing quantity phrase—see (106).

(106)

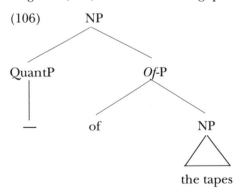

The structure for the entire comparative clause of this example, diagrammed in (107), will include a sentence with a missing quantity phrase.

(107)

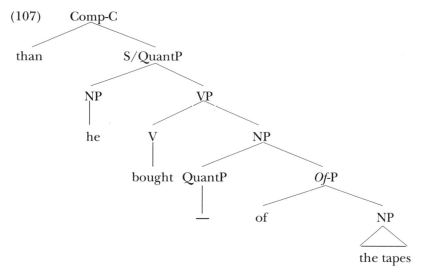

We also have a reason to extend an analysis like this to the other types of double-scale comparatives that we have seen. In each of the following examples (repeated from above), the phrase providing the second scale is italicized:

(108) a.   David is as erudite as he is *creative*.
       b.   More pigs eat corn than *dogs* eat hay.
       c.   Pigs eat more corn than dogs eat *hay*.

At first glance, the first of these phrases looks just like a normal adjective phrase and the second and third look like normal bare noun phrases. If they really were normal phrases of these two types, we would expect to be able to include a degree word in the adjective phrase and quantity phrases in the noun phrases, just as we can in the following simple sentences:

(109) a.   He is [*very* creative].
       b.   [*Many* dogs] eat hay.
       c.   Dogs eat [*much* hay].

However, such additions are impossible within the compared clauses in question:

(110) a.   *David is as erudite as he is *very creative*.
       b.   *More pigs eat corn than *many dogs* eat hay.
       c.   *Pigs eat more corn than dogs eat *much hay*.

The impossibility of such overt degree and quantity expressions is explained if every double-scale comparative clause must contain either a missing degree expression or a missing quantity expression.

This reanalysis gives the following structures for the comparative clauses in (98) and (101):

(111)   a.   Comp-C

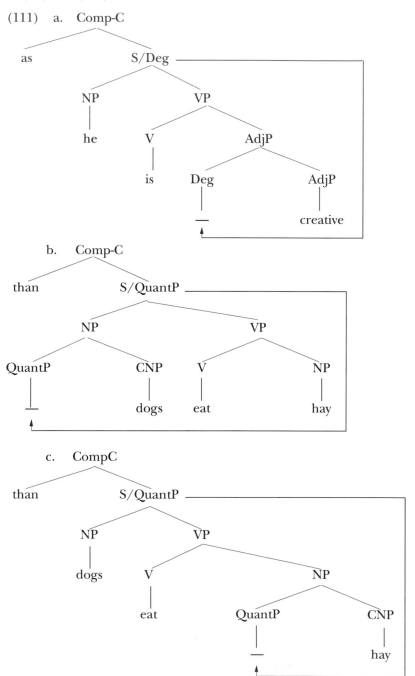

Exercise

1. Decide whether the comparative contained in each of the following sentences is single-scale or double-scale. If you think that it is double-scale, say what the two scales are.

    a.   More people drink coffee than drink tea.

    b.   More tigers live in zoos than bears live in the wild.

    c.   Bob eats pancakes more often than he eats bacon and eggs.

    d.   People are more careless than animals are.

    e.   Joe sent more letters to congressmen than he sent telegrams to the president.

    f.   The company sent more refrigerators to Siberia than it sent heaters to Kuwait.

12.6.4 Positioning of Clauses Associated with Degree Words

Clauses associated with degree words are generally found in one of two positions: either at the right side of the phrase that contains the associated degree word or at the end of the sentence. See the diagrams in (112).

(112)

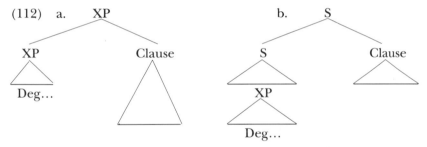

In a majority of the examples discussed earlier in this section, these two positions are indistinguishable, since the degree-modified phrase is itself at the end of the sentence. So let us look at some examples where a distinction can be made, in order to arrive at some conclusions about the behaviors of different varieties of clauses.

First let us examine some examples containing result clauses:

(113) a. ?**So* many minnows [that Martha lost her temper] were fed to the dog.

      b. *So* many minnows were fed to the dog [that Martha lost her temper].

(114) a. ?**Such* an upsetting meeting [that everyone resigned from the Budget Council] took place yesterday.

      b. *Such* an upsetting meeting took place yesterday [that everyone resigned from the Budget Council].

(115) a. *Too* many relatives [to pack into one house] landed on us on Memorial Day.

 b. *Too* many relatives landed on us on Memorial Day [to pack into one house].

(116) a. *Enough* ice cream [to keep the children happy] had been brought to the picnic.

 b. *Enough* ice cream had been brought to the picnic [to keep the children happy].

We see that, whereas a result clause introduced by *that* is really acceptable only at the end of its sentence, an infinitival clause associated with *too* or *enough* can stay in the phrase in which its degree word appears. Diagrams for two of these sentences—one with the result clause joined onto the sentence as a whole and the other with the result clause joined onto the subject noun phrase—are presented in (117).

(117) a.

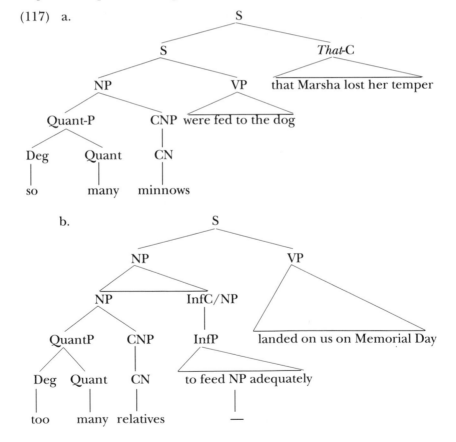

With comparative clauses, just as with infinitival result clauses, we find that both positions are possible:

(118) a.   [$_{NP}$ *More* books *than Pete will be able to read*] appeared on the history reading list.

   b.   [$_{NP}$ *More* books] appeared on the history reading list *than Pete will be able to read*.

(119) a.   [$_{NP}$ *As* much money *as John donated in Phil's name*] was donated in Brenda's name.

   b.   [$_{NP}$ *As* much money] was donated in Brenda's name *as John donated in Phil's name*.

These sentences show that, in general, the position of the comparative clause can be chosen freely. Two qualifications are necessary, however. The first is that double-scale comparatives are much better if the comparative clause is at the end of the sentence, as in (120).

(120) a.   *[$_{NP}$ More pigs *than dogs eat hay*] eat corn.

   b.   [$_{NP}$ More pigs] eat corn *than dogs eat hay*.

The second qualification is that the choice of location for the comparative clause affects the possibility of applying an optional deletion rule, as we will see near the end of subsection 12.6.5.

Exercise

1. For each of the following sentences, draw a tree diagram:

   a.   Jonah sent so many letters to the mayor that she stopped reading her mail.

   b.   Rita put enough money in her account to cover those three checks.

   c.   Alma gave more cookies to George than she gave donuts to Randy.

   d.   Jack told Irene how much richer than he was now he wanted to become in the future.

   e.   Jack told Irene how much richer he wanted to become in the future than he was now.

   f.   I'd like to know how many more people than Fred invited were allowed to stay for lunch.

   g.   I'd like to know how many more people were allowed to stay for lunch than Fred invited.

12.6.5 Deletion Rules for Comparative Clauses

Every one of the comparative clauses that we have examined so far looks very much like a complete sentence, except for containing a missing phrase that corresponds to the compared phrase. English also allows shortened versions of many comparative clauses. The shortened versions are brought about by two special deletion rules.

The first (and less drastic) of these two rules is illustrated in (121)–(124).

(121) a. Clara sends money to Houston more often than Joe sends money to Little Rock.
      b. Clara sends money to Houston more often than Joe does __ to Little Rock.

(122) a. James read the book more carefully than he read the play.
      b. James read the book more carefully than he did __ the play.

(123) a. Jock will serve more wine to them than he will serve beer to them.
      b. Jock will serve more wine to them than he will __ beer __ .

(124) a. Doris has given postcards to Pam more often than she has given stamps to Pam.
      b. Doris has given postcards to Pam more often than she has __ stamps __.

Each of the (b) sentences differs from the (a) sentence in two respects. In the first place, it shows a special-purpose verb. In the second place, all the material in the comparative clause that is identical to material in the main clause has been removed. The only phrase left standing after each special-purpose verb is some single phrase that is not identical.

Examples (125)–(128) show what happens when everything after the special-purpose verb is identical.

(125) a. Clara sends money to Houston more often than Joe sends money to Houston.
      b. Clara sends money to Houston more often than Joe does __.

(126) a. James read the book more carefully than Joel read the book.
      b. James read the book more carefully than Joel did __.

(127) a. Jock will serve them more wine than Alice will serve them.
      b. Jock will serve them more wine than Alice will __.

(128) a. Doris has sent postcards to Pam more often than Nora has sent postcards to Pam.
      b. Doris has sent postcards to Pam more often than Nora has __.

In these cases, everything after the special-purpose verb can be deleted.

The second deletion rule for comparative structures applies to sentences in which the comparative clause and the main clause are identical except for some single contrasted phrase, as in (129)–(132).

(129) a. *John* listens to music more often [than *Bill* listens to music].
b. *John* listens to music more often [than *Bill*].

(130) a. John listens *to folk music* more often [than he listens *to jazz*].
b. John listens *to folk music* more often [than *to jazz*].

(131) a. More people play *soccer* [than play *water polo*].
b. More people play *soccer* [than *water polo*].

(132) a. John gave more books *to Shirley* [than he gave *to Fred*].
b. John gave more books *to Shirley* [than *to Fred*].

We can derive the (b) sentences in (129)–(132) by applying the following rule to the (a) sentences:

(133) If the comparative clause is identical to the main clause except for a contrasted phrase, optionally remove everything from the comparative clause except for this contrasted phrase.

An important qualification on the operation of this rule is that it gives good results only when the comparative clause is at the end of the sentence. Leaving the comparative clause inside the phrase that contains the associated degree words yields strikingly unacceptable results, as in (134) and (135).

(134) a. ?[$_{NP}$ More people than play *water polo*] *play soccer.*
b. *[$_{NP}$ More people than *water polo*] play *soccer.*

(135) a. John gave [$_{NP}$ more books than he gave *to Fred*] *to Shirley.*
b. *John gave [$_{NP}$ more books *than to Fred*] *to Shirley.*

The one exception here is that the results are good when the comparative is a double-scale one and the single phrase remaining is the phrase that indicates the second scale, as in (136).

(136) a. [$_{NP}$ More people *than ducks*] play soccer.
b. [$_{NP}$ More pigs *than dogs*] eat corn.

This exception is surprising in view of the fact—noted above—that full double-scale comparative clauses are generally not acceptable inside the degree-modified phrases:

(137) a. *[_{NP} More pigs *than dogs eat hay*] eat corn.
       b. [_{NP} More pigs] eat corn *than dogs eat hay.*

Exercises

1. For each of the following sentences, say which of the two special deletion rules has been applied. For some of the sentences, the answer may be that neither rule has been applied. In sentences where one of the rules has applied, say what has been deleted.

    a.   Laura is reading more mysteries than she is epics.
    b.   More Northerners eat hominy than okra.
    c.   Joe ate as many cashews as he could.
    d.   Jack is buying more grapes from Bolivia than he is from California.
    e.   More people drink beer in restaurants than do in bars.

2. The following sentence is ambiguous:

        Martin makes Jack do more laundry than Fred does.

Explain as clearly as you can how this ambiguity arises.

12.7 The Superlative Construction

A special alternative to the comparative construction exists in English for cases in which we want to say that some degree on a scale is higher than any other corresponding degree. This alternative construction, the *superlative*, comes in two varieties. The first variety shows a very close syntactic and semantic correspondence to full-sentence comparatives; the second shows a semantic correspondence with comparatives inside relative clauses. The first of these two varieties in illustrated in the (a) sentences of (138)–(142); the (b) sentences are the corresponding comparatives.

(138) a. Jacob is [_{AdjP} *the most forthright* of all the children in the class].
       b. Jacob is [_{AdjP} *more forthright* than any of the other children in the class].

(139) a. Your uncle has improved [_{AdvP} *the most rapidly* of all the players on the team].
       b. Your uncle has improved [_{AdvP} *more rapidly* than any of the other players on the team].

(140) a. This problem required [_{NP} *the most work* of all of the problems in the chapter].
       b. This problem required [_{NP} *more work* than any of the other problems in the chapter].

(141) a   Gordon felt the shock [_QuantP_ *the most* of all the members of the family].

   b.   Gordon felt the shock [_QuantP_ *more* than any of the other members of the family].

(142) a.   Ned caught [_NP_ the biggest fish of anyone who was on the lake yesterday].

   b.   Ned caught [_NP_ a bigger fish than anyone else who was on the lake yesterday].

The superlative constructions in the above examples are almost like the corresponding comparative constructions. The main differences are these: The superlatives have *most* instead of *more*, the superlatives have a preceding definite article, and the superlatives have an *of* phrase instead of a comparative clause. Tree diagrams for the bracketed portions of (138)–(142) are given in (143).

(143) a.

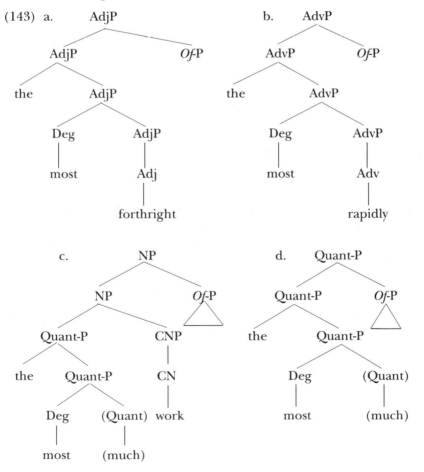

e.

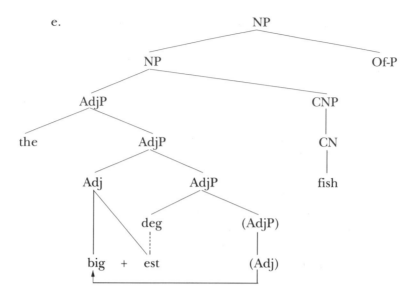

The one situation in which the parallel between comparatives and superlatives of this kind breaks down is with partitive structures, either those that are genuinely quantitative or those peculiar degree constructions discussed in section 12.4:

(144)   a. *Carol attended [$_{NP}$ *the most of the lectures* of anyone].
      b. Carol attended [$_{NP}$ *more of the lectures* than anyone else].

(145)   a. *Oliver is [$_{NP}$ *the most of a liar* of anyone].
      b. Oliver is [$_{NP}$ *more of a liar* than anyone else].

This particular variety of superlative receives its interpretation externally, in that we are comparing some set of individuals with one another, with the "first-place" member of the set being some individual referred to outside of the superlative construction itself. We can see this by building an interpretation for (138a), which is repeated here:

(146) Jacob is the most forthright of all the children in the class.

The first step is to construct a set of parallel sentences mentioning other members of the group to which Jacob belongs and their associated degrees of forthrightness:

(147)   Child$_1$ is x_1 forthright.
           Child$_2$ is x_2 forthright
           Child$_3$ is x_3 forthright.
           .
           .
           .

           Jacob is x_n forthright.

The second step is to make a claim of superiority for the degree associated with Jacob:

(148) x_n is greater than any of the other x's.

Similar interpretations are possible for the other superlatives given above.

Even with a domain of individuals identified, however, we can have ambiguities, as (149)–(151) show.

(149) John admires Carol [$_{QuantP}$ *the most* of all the persons in the class].

This sentence can have either of the following interpretations:

(150) a.   Person$_1$ admires Carol x_1 much.
          Person$_2$ admires Carol x_2 much.

            .
            .
            .

          John admires Carol x_n much.
       b. x_n is greater than any of the other x's.

(151) a.   John admires person$_1$ x_1 much.
          John admires person$_2$ x_2 much.

            .
            .
            .

          John admires Carol x_n much.

       b. x_n is greater than any of the other x's.

In spoken English, the ambiguity generally disappears; whichever noun phrase represents the position of the entities that are being considered one at a time generally gets stronger stress than the other. A pronunciation of sentence (149) with stress on the word *John* will yield the first interpretation, whereas stress on the word *Carol* will yield the second.

Let us turn now to the second kind of superlatives. With these, there is no *of* phrase to indicate a domain of comparison; the superlative is just an ingredient of an ordinary noun phrase:

(152) a.   Tom and Fred just succeeded in catching [the biggest bass in Eagle Lake].
       b.   Jonathan bought [the oldest house in Austin].

In (152a), we are not comparing Tom and Fred's bass with a bass that anyone else might have caught. Similarly, in (152b) we are not comparing this house with houses that other people bought; we are simply comparing it with other houses in Austin. Tom and Fred, and Jonathan, are not seen here as belonging to any domains of comparison. To the extent that these sentences can be paraphrased by sentences with comparatives, the comparatives are down inside relative clauses:

(153) a.   Tom and Fred just succeeded in catching [the bass in Eagle Lake *that was bigger than any other bass in Eagle Lake*].
       b.   Jonathan bought [the house in Austin *that is bigger than any other house in Austin*].

We have already seen two examples, (142a) and (152a), in which the superlative is expressed by a suffixed *-est* instead of a preceding *most*. As a general rule, the same adjectives and adverbs that take *-er* as a comparative suffix take *-est* as a superlative suffix, and those that can only have *more* in the comparative can only have *most* in the superlative:

(154) a.   the smartest   *the most smart
       b.   the shortest   *the most short
       c.   the highest   *the most high
       d.   the loveliest   the most lovely
       e.   the narrowest   the most narrow
       f.   the subtlest   the most subtle
       g. *the obesest   the most obese
       h. *the decentest   the most decent
       i. *the deviousest   the most devious
       j. *the intelligentest   the most intelligent

In addition, the same adjectives and adverbs that have irregular comparative forms also have irregular superlative forms:

(155) a.   good   *the goodest   the best
       b.   well (adverb)   *the wellest   the best
       c.   bad   *the baddest   the worst
       d.   far   *the farest   the farthest
       e.   little (quantity word) *the littlest   the least

Exercise

1. Draw a tree diagram for each of the following sentences:
       a.   Jesse made his statement the most concise.
       b.   Jesse made his statement the most concisely.
       c.   Harvey wrote the most complicated poem of all the people who entered the contest.
       d.   Dorothy regretted the mistake the most of any person in the group.

IV
Special Constructions

Chapter 13

Special Subject-Predicate Relations

In each of the sentences discussed in earlier chapters, the functions of the subject and the predicate can be roughly characterized by saying that the subject identifies some person or entity and the predicate describes it. This division of labor is evident in the following sentences:

(1)   **Identification**   **Description**
   a.   Thomas Jefferson   founded the University of Virginia.
   b.   My cat   is on the mat.
   c.   You   are fortunate.
   d.   What you are saying   makes very little sense.

For ease of reference, we will refer to sentences whose subjects and predicates exhibit this relation as *descriptive sentences*.

In the present chapter, we will consider some sentences that do not have an overall descriptive function of this kind. In section 13.1 we will examine the *existential construction*, which has a special syntax as well as an interpretation that asserts the existence of someone or something rather than asserting that a certain description applies to a subject. In section 13.2 we investigate a number of sentences that we will describe as *identificational* in function. In such sentences, the verb phrase serves to identify the subject instead of describing it. In section 13.3 we look at the *cleft construction*, an identificational construction that has the same kind of interpretation as the constructions discussed in section 13.2 but has some very marked syntactic peculiarities.

13.1 The Existential Construction

Two simple examples of the existential construction are given in (2).

(2)   a.   There is a fly in my soup.

        b.   There is a cat on the mat.

Each of these sentences has the word *there* as its subject. This subject is followed by *is*, a noun phrase, and a locative phrase, in that order. The noun phrases serve as the subjects of the locative phrases, in the same way that they would in the following nonexistential sentences:

(3)   a.   A fly is in my soup.

        b.   A cat is on the mat.

We will refer to the noun phrase that comes after BE in the existential construction as the *lower subject*, to distinguish it from the *there* that serves as the subject of the sentence as a whole. Thus, *a fly* and *a cat* are the two lower subjects in (2).

Not every English sentence beginning with *there* is an existential sentence. The sentences in (4) illustrate an entirely different English construction.

(4)   a.   Thére is Jones.

        b.   Thére is the picture of Fred.

        c.   Thére goes your brother.

In these sentences, the initial word *there* is a genuine locative phrase or motion phrase. As the accent marks indicate, it always receives a fairly heavy degree of stress when it is spoken. By contrast, the *there* of the existential construction is always spoken without any stress at all. In this chapter, we will focus our attention on existential constructions, excluding from consideration the sentences that begin with locative *there*.

13.1.1 The Basic Syntax of the Existential Construction

How might the existential construction be described by a rule? Suppose in particular that we wanted to describe it by giving a special environmental specification for the verb BE. The part of the specification that would describe the complement choice would say that BE could be followed by a noun phrase and a locative phrase, while the part that described its subject would require the word *there*. Thus, the specification as a whole would be as in (5).

(5)   *BE: there* [—NP LocP]

This kind of specification yields (6) as the tree for sentence (2a).

(6)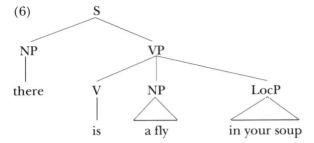

In the sentence just diagrammed, the second complement of the verb BE is a locative phrase. The rules of English also permit two other types of phrases as complements here: present-participial verb phrases and passive phrases. The two sentences in (7) illustrate these possibilities.

(7)   a.   There is a giraffe *standing on the porch.*
       b.   There was a purse *found at the library.*

These two configurations call for the additional complement specifications given in (8).

(8)   a.   BE: *there* [—NP VP$_{PresPart}$]
       b.   BE: *there* [—NP PassP]

In addition, it is possible to build an existential sentence in which there is no complement after the noun phrase:

(9)   There is a Santa Claus.

For this sentence, we need the following specification:

(10)   BE: *there* [—NP]

These last three environmental specifications give the following trees:

(11)   a.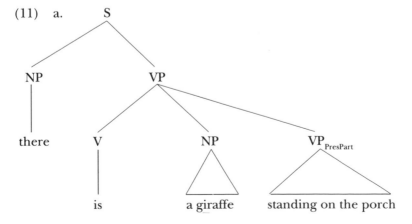

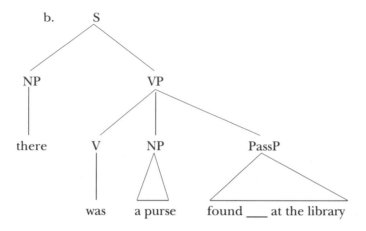

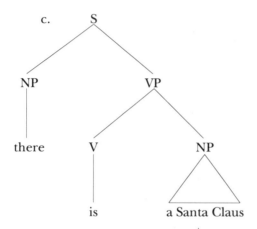

Exercise

1. Draw a tree diagram for each of the following sentences:
   a. There must have been a penny in the cupboard.
   b. There have been some mistakes made.
   c. There were four sailors sitting on the bench.
   d. John wants to know how many chairs there are at the table.
   e. Barbara told us where there were some glasses.

13.1.2 Number Agreement in Existentials

Many other languages besides English have an existential construction in which a key element is a substitute subject. In many if not most of these languages, the verb of the sentence is invariably singular, no matter what the number of the lower subject happens to be. Many nonstandard varieties of English also have this property, so that both examples in (12) are acceptable.

(12) a. There is a bat in the belfry.
      b. There is some bats in the belfry.

Standard English, however, requires a plural verb when the lower subject of the existential is plural, as in (13).

(13) a. There is a bat in the belfry.
      b. There are some bats in the belfry.

We can think of the word *there* as being invisibly marked with the number of the lower subject, and as passing its number on to the verb phrase with which it is joined. In some sentences, the word *there* is quite far away from the lower subject. Even in these sentences, a plural lower subject requires that *there*'s verb be plural:

(14) a. * *There* seems (singular) to have been *three explosions* on the boat.
      b. *There* seem (plural) to have been *three explosions* on the boat.

Although *three explosions* is several verb phrases down from SEEM, this noun phrase still manages to transmit its number to the highest verb. It appears to do this by way of its link to the upper subject *there*.

13.1.3 The Noun Phrase in the Existential Construction

Unlike most of the structures that we have studied in earlier chapters, the existential construction yields better results with some noun phrases than with others. We have already seen that phrases introduced by *a, some,* and *three* give satisfactory results. We also get acceptable existentials with noun phrases introduced by *a lot of, several, many,* and numbers of all sorts, as well as by noun phrases consisting of a plural or mass noun alone:

(15) a. There is *a lot of beer* in the refrigerator.
      b. There are *several manuscripts* in the desk.
      c. There are *many accidents* on Highway 183.
      d. There was *one can* in the cupboard.
      e. There were *ninety-nine bottles of beer* on the wall.
      f. There are *termites* in the foundation.
      h. There is *mildew* on the siding.

The results are much less natural with noun phrases of the type referred to as definite in chapter 5, as the examples in (16) demonstrate.

(16)   a. *There are *them* in the room.
        b. *There was *John* on the committee.
        c. *There are *these tomatoes* in the basket.
        d. *There was *my car* stolen by a burglar.

In addition, noun phrases that are introduced by "universal" quantity words are not acceptable, either:

(17)   a. *There is *every apple* on the table.
        b. *There is *each flower* in a pot.
        c. *There are *all guests* in the lounge.

For reasons having largely to do with the way in which existentials are interpreted, indefinite noun phrases are much more natural in this construction than members of either of the other two groups. Correspondingly, they are often less natural than definite and universal noun phrases in the position of subject:

(18)   a.   The chair is in the kitchen.
        b.   Every chair is in the kitchen.
        c.   ? A chair is in the kitchen.
        d.   ? Some chairs are in the kitchen.

Existential sentences in a variety of other languages seem to be especially hospitable to indefinite noun phrases, and, as in English, one of the primary functions of the existential in these other languages is to enable the speaker to avoid using an indefinite noun phrase as the subject of a sentence.

Definite noun phrases are acceptable in existentials in the special type of situation in which a question has been asked and the person answering wants to mention one or more alternatives. This type of situation is illustrated in (19) and (20).

(19)   Question: Who can we get to watch the children?
        Answer: Well, there's *John*.

(20)   Question: What can we read to them?
        Answer: Well, there's *this book*, and there's *the book about Snow White*, and there's *Fred's autobiography*.

Exercise
1. Should *most* be classified as a universal quantity word, or as an indefinite quantity word? Base your answer on its behavior in the existential construction, as determined by an experimental sentence that you construct.

13.1.4 The Existential Construction as a Test for Transparency

At the end of chapter 8, SEEM was mentioned as an example of a phrasal head that had the peculiar property of not really using its subject itself but merely passing it down to its complements. We noted that there are other phrasal heads with this property, and that there is a simple strategy for identifying them. We are now in a position to develop this strategy.

As was noted in subsection 13.1.2, it is possible to construct sentences in which the existential word *there* is quite far from the remainder of the existential construction. Our example was the following:

(21) *There* seem to have *been three explosions on the boat.*

In this example, SEEM and the perfect HAVE intervene. The verb BE and the adjective LIKELY show the same capacity:

(22) *There* is likely to *be an explosion on the boat.*

By contrast, many other verbs and adjectives give unacceptable results when they intervene between *there* and the remainder of the construction. Some typical examples are given in (23) and (24).

(23)   a. * *There* intends to *be an admiral on the committee.*
        b. * *There* hope to *be several hurdlers on the team.*

(24)   a. * *There* is reluctant to *be an admiral on the committee.*
        b. * *There* are eager to *be several hurdlers on the team.*

To understand the difference between the verbs and adjectives that can intervene and those that cannot, we need to recall the difference—noted at the end of chapter 8—between transparent heads and nontransparent heads. Transparent heads merely pass their subjects on to their complements, whereas nontransparent heads must use their subjects to identify some participant in the event or state that they themselves denote. What distinguishes words that can intervene is simply that they are transparent. They have no use of their own for a subject, and as a consequence they do not impose any restrictions on their subjects. This is the case with SEEM and LIKELY; when we ask how they use their own subjects, the answer is that they do not use them at all. Because of this, they can accept a subject like *there*, which has no interpretation of its own apart from the interpretation it receives by being linked to the remainder of the existential construction. By contrast, each of the words INTEND, HOPE, RELUCTANT, and EAGER depends on its subject to identify the animate being that has a particular mental state. These heads have something more pressing to do with a subject than merely to hold it for some lower predicate. Thus, a meaningless subject such as *there* fails to provide what these heads require for a complete interpretation of the phrase that they head.

This analysis implies that the *there* of existential sentences is significantly different from the *it* that occurs as a substitute for clauses. In the case of *it*, any verb or adjective that calls for a certain kind of clause as subject will be satisfied instead by an *it* linked to a clause of the appropriate sort. On the other hand, a verb or an adjective that calls for a certain kind of noun phrase is not satisfied by an occurrence of *there* that is linked to a noun phrase of the correct type. For instance, INTEND is a verb that requires a human subject. If a *there* linked to a human lower subject could satisfy this requirement, all the starred sentences in (23) and (24) would be acceptable. The fact that they are unacceptable indicates that these two constructions are fundamentally different from each other in the roles that their subjects serve.

These considerations have an important practical consequence. In chapter 8, it was suggested that there are two possibilities for the understood subject of a phrase with no expressed subject. The first possibility was seen with verbs like HOPE. With these verbs, the subject of the infinitival complement was an understood pronoun, which was coreferential with the subject of HOPE. The second possibility appeared with verbs like SEEM. With these verbs, the subject of SEEM served itself as the subject of the infinitival complement. Verbs and adjectives like SEEM were referred to as *transparent*, in recognition of the fact that they do not really use their subjects themselves but simply pass them down to their complement phrases.

When we want to know which of these two basic situations obtains for the complement of a certain verb or adjective, we can construct an experimental sentence in which we let that verb or adjective take *there* as a subject, with the remainder of the existential construction appearing in the complement. If the sentence is acceptable, then the word is like SEEM in that it does not really use its subject itself. On the other hand, if the sentence is unacceptable, then we have an indication that the verb or adjective had a need of its own for a subject, which the existential *there* was not able to satisfy. In such cases, the complement subject is like an understood pronoun, for which the upper subject serves as the antecedent.

Let us apply this test to the adjectives CERTAIN and WILLING, as they are used in the following examples:

(25)   a.   The doctor is *certain* to be in the stadium.
       b.   The doctor is *willing* to be in the stadium.

We now construct a sentence in which we split an appropriate existential:

(26)   There is a doctor in the stadium.

Here are the results:

(27)   a.   There is certain to be a doctor in the stadium.
        b. *There is willing to be a doctor in the stadium.

From this evidence we can conclude that *certain* is transparent, whereas *willing* is not.

This test can be used to show that a variety of other verbs and adjectives are transparent in the same way as SEEM, LIKELY, and CERTAIN. Here are some additional examples:

(28)   a.   There *appears* to be a spot on the rug.
        b.   There *happens* to be a fingerprint on the mirror.
        c.   There *must* be an apple in the refrigerator.
        d.   There *has* been an explosion in the factory.

(29)   a.   There is *apt* to be a shortage.
        b.   There is *sure* to be a revolver in the drawer.

Exercise

1. For each of the following verbs, construct an experimental sentence to determine whether it is transparent. The relevant sentences will contain verb phrases in which the verb is followed immediately by an infinitival phrase.
        a.   TRY
        b.   REFUSE
        c.   TEND
        d.   APPEAR
        e.   BEGIN
        f.   FORGET

13.1.5 Verbs That Do Not Use Their Objects

We have just seen a handful of verbs and adjectives that are transparent, in the sense that they do not use their subjects themselves but merely pass them down to their complement phrases. There is also a small group of verbs in English that treat their direct objects in the same way. A clear example is provided by the verb BELIEVE, as it is used in (30).

(30)   Katy believes the monkey to be on the merry-go-round.

The environmental specification that allows this sentence is given in (31).

(31) BELIEVE: NP [—NP InfP]

We can see right away that this sentence can be paraphrased by one in which BELIEVE takes a *that* clause:

(32) Katy believes that the monkey is on the merry-go-round.

This fact suggests the possibility that the object of BELIEVE in (30) is not really being used by BELIEVE but is merely being used to identify the subject of the infinitival phrase. This idea can be tested by using *there* as the object of BELIEVE, followed by an infinitival phrase. Here is a relevant pair of examples, the first a simple existential and the second a sentence in which this existential is used with BELIEVE:

(33) a.   There is a monkey on the merry-go-round.
      b.   Katy believes there to be a monkey on the merry-go-round.

The acceptability of (33b) provides confirmation that BELIEVE in this configuration does not really use its object itself. Another verb with the same property is CONSIDER:

(34) a.   There is a bug in this program.
      b.   George considers there to be a bug in this program.

In contrast to BELIEVE and CONSIDER, many verbs that take direct objects followed by infinitives do use their objects themselves. PERSUADE is one such verb; its object identifies the person whose mind was made up to carry out a certain action. The following pair of sentences shows the result of trying to use the existential *there* as a direct object of this verb:

(35) a.   There is a doctor in the stadium.
      b.   *Bill persuaded there to be a doctor in the stadium.

Another verb of this type is ASK:

(36) a.   There is a bailiff in the hall.
      b.   *The judge asked there to be a bailiff in the hall.

Exercise
1. Construct an experimental sentence to determine whether each of the following verbs uses its object. Be sure to use verb phrases of the form V+NP+InfP.
      a.   ALLOW
      b.   PERMIT
      c.   EXPECT
      d.   INSTRUCT

13.1.6 Other Verbs Occurring in Existentials

In each of the examples we have considered so far, the verb of the sentence has been some form of BE. We also find the same kind of construction with a small number of other verbs, chiefly those denoting existence or motion of some sort:

(37) a. There exists a smallest positive whole number.
      b. There came a man from Tennessee.
      c. There went out a decree from Caesar Augustus.
      d. There arrived three packages in the mail.

This kind of existential is substantially more marginal than the existential with *be*. However, it shares with it the same subject—*there*—and the same preference for indefinite noun phrases as lower subjects. Like the existential with *be*, this construction allows us to avoid using an indefinite noun phrase as the first noun phrase in a sentence. English is just one of many languages that seem to have special constructions for achieving this effect.

13.2 Identificational Sentences

13.2.1 Subjects and Predicates of Identificational Sentences

Among the descriptive sentences discussed in earlier chapters were some in which the verb phrase consisted of BE followed by a noun phrase, as in (38).

(38)

	Subject	**Description**
a.	I	am [$_{NP}$ a dentist].
b.	You	are [$_{NP}$ the person for whom the job was created].
c.	Your mother	is [$_{NP}$ one of Martha's friends].
d.	What Fred writes	is [$_{NP}$ unadulterated rubbish].

Many identificational sentences have a similar outward form. They consist of a subject noun phrase—typically a name or a description or even a pronoun—and a verb phrase consisting of BE following by another noun phrase. A first example of this type of sentence is given in (39).

(39) [$_{NP}$The inventor of the lightbulb] was [$_{NP}$Thomas Alva Edison].

Here the phrase that follows the verb does not describe the inventor of the lightbulb; instead, it identifies him. This sentence could, in fact, constitute an answer to a test question such as "Identify the inventor of the lightbulb." Some additional examples of identificational sentences are given in (40).

(40) a. [$_{NP}$The country that won the 1986 World Cup] was [$_{NP}$Argentina].

b. [$_{NP}$The guy who disrupted the meeting last night] was [$_{NP}$the guy who rents your basement apartment].

c. [$_{NP}$I] am [$_{NP}$Ronald Reagan].

d. [$_{NP}$The substance that you are putting on your meat right now] is [$_{NP}$sodium chloride].

e. [$_{NP}$Sodium chloride] is [$_{NP}$the substance that you are putting on your meat right now].

f. [$_{NP}$Sir William Jones] was [$_{NP}$the person who first postulated a common parent language for Sanskrit, Latin, and Greek].

g. [$_{NP}$The person who first postulated a common parent language for Sanskrit, Latin, and Greek] was [$_{NP}$Sir William Jones].

These sentences might serve as responses to the following utterances:

(41) a. Identify the country that won the 1986 World Cup.

b. Who was the guy who disrupted the meeting last night?

c. Who are you?

d. Can you name the substance that I'm putting on my meat right now?

e. Tell me what sodium chloride is.

f. Who was Sir William Jones?

g. Name the person who first postulated a common parent language for Sanskrit, Latin, and Greek.

As examples d–g show, the same phrase that serves as the identified phrase in one situation can serve equally well as the identifying phrase in a different situation.

In addition to identificational sentences in which BE is followed by an ordinary noun phrase, we find some in which BE is followed by a gerundive, an infinitive clause, or or a *that* clause:

(42) a. [$_{NP}$The thing that bothered Bill] was [$_{NP}$Molly's forgetting his name].

b. [$_{NP}$The project that John is working on now] is [$_{NP}$fixing the fence].

(43) a. [$_{NP}$The thing that Beth wants] is [$_{InfC}$for Grant to sail around the world].

b. [$_{NP}$Rhonda's most important goal] is [$_{InfC}$to finish college in three years].

(44) a. [$_{NP}$Bill's opinion] is [$_{That\text{-}C}$that we should try to arrange a truce].
      b. [$_{NP}$The thing that bothers Martha] is [$_{That\text{-}C}$that we haven't made a decision].

One particular kind of identifying sentence is the so-called *pseudocleft sentence*, illustrated in (45).

(45) a. [$_{NP}$What Bill put in the safe] was [$_{NP}$Marcia's necklace].
      b. [$_{NP}$What Jonah would like for you to bring back] is [$_{NP}$a pint of yogurt].
      c. [$_{NP}$What Carol approved of] was [$_{NP}$Bill's returning the trophy].
      d. [$_{NP}$What Barbara wants] is [$_{InfC}$for us to clean the chicken house].
      e. [$_{NP}$What Tom says] is [$_{That\text{-}C}$that he will call us from Philadelphia].

The subject of each of these sentences is a definite free relative clause of the sort we studied in chapter 7. The phrases that come after BE are of the same types as those in (40), (42), (43), and (44). Since a free relative clause is just a special kind of noun phrase, we can regard the pseudocleft sentence as nothing more than the particular version of the identificational sentence that is obtained when the subject happens to be a definite free relative clause. Thus, we will not treat it as a special construction in its own right.

13.2.2 The Interpretation of Identificational Sentences

As was noted above, the basic import of an identificational sentence is to give a description and then identify the individual or entity or substance that satisfies the description. While this characterization of these sentences may seem quite simple, it has some unexpected and interesting consequences. In particular, this characterization provides an explanation for some peculiar aspects of subject identification and pronoun interpretation in identificational sentences.

Let us begin by looking more closely at sentence (45a), which is repeated here:

(46) [$_{NP}$What Bill put in the safe] was [$_{NP}$Marcia's necklace].

The interpretation of the free relative clause in subject position can be roughly approximated as in (47).

(47) the x such that [Bill put x in the safe]

The verb phrase in (46) identifies this *x* as Marcia's necklace. In so doing, it implies the truth of the statement that we get by substituting *Marcia's necklace* for *x* in the small sentence in brackets:

(48)   Bill put *Marcia's necklace* in the safe.

These results may seem obvious. A more interesting situation arises in (49).

(49)   [$_{NP}$What Bill enjoys] is [$_{NP}$reading Cicero].

The interesting problem here is to determine how the subject of the gerundive *reading Cicero* is identified. Suppose that we just apply the rule given in chapter 8 for sentences in which the verb is followed by a gerundive. For the sentence in (50a), this rule gave us the subject identification shown in (50b).

(50)   a.   Jonah resents [working in an office].

b.

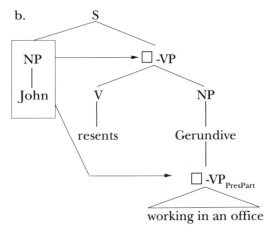

But applying the same rule to (49) picks out *what Bill enjoys* as the understood subject of *reading*. This result is clearly incorrect; the understood subject of *reading* is not *What Bill enjoys* but *Bill*.

Our interpretive idea concerning identificational sentences is useful here. The free relative clause is interpreted as in (51).

(51) the *x* such that [Bill enjoys *x*].

The verb phrase then identifies the *x* in question as *reading Cicero*. If we now substitute *reading Cicero* for *x* in the small sentence in (51), we arrive at the following:

(52) Bill enjoys *reading Cicero*.

With this structure as a basis for subject interpretation, the rule from chapter 8 does give the correct result:

(53)

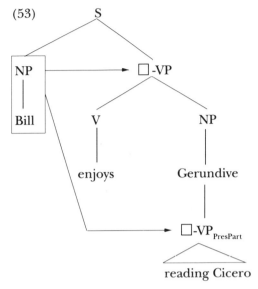

The central point here, then, is this: When we are dealing with an unexpressed subject in the verb phrase of an identificational sentence, the correct identification of that subject requires a computation based on a structure in which the identifying phrase has been substituted in the interpretation of the subject.

The contrast between subject identification in ordinary descriptive sentences and that in identificational sentences is illustrated in a surprising way by (54).

(54)   a.   What *John* enjoys is making *him* sick.
       b.   What *John* enjoys is making *himself* sick.

Both of these sentences are acceptable; the challenge is to explain why both the nonreflexive pronoun and the reflexive pronoun are possible as objects of *making*. From our discussion in chapter 8, we know that *him* should appear if the subject of *making* is not coreferential with the pronoun, and that *himself* should appear if the subject of *making* is coreferential with it.

In one of the structures that we have seen for verb phrases of the form *is* + present-participial phrase, the lower verb phrase serves as a complement of *is*. This is the structure that we need for (54a):

(55)

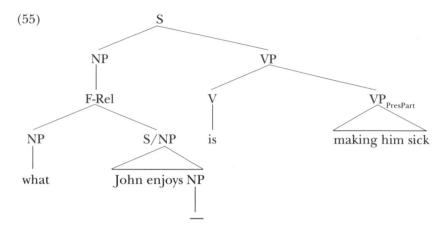

We can apply the subject-identification rules of chapter 9 to such a structure directly, with the following result:

(56)

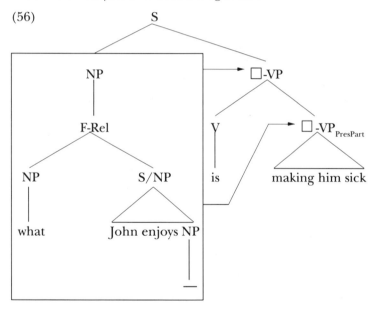

Here the subject of the sentence as a whole has provided the identification for the subject of the past-participial phrase. Since this subject is not coreferential with the object of *making*, the nonreflexive pronoun *him* is called for.

The other structure that we have seen for verb phrases of the form *is* + present-participial phrase is the kind of structure where the present-participial phrase is a gerundive in a predicate that identifies the subject:

(57)

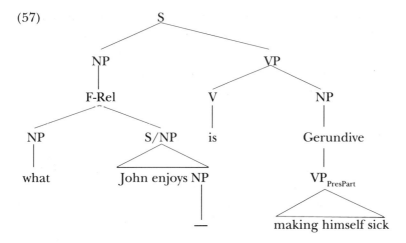

This is the structure that will call for a reflexive pronoun as object of *making*. Here the free relative clause is interpreted as in (58).

(58)   the *x* such that [John enjoys *x*]

Substituting the verb phrase *making himself sick* for *x* in the bracketed sentence, we obtain the sequence in (59a), whose structure is that given in (59b).

(59)   a.   John enjoys *making himself sick*.

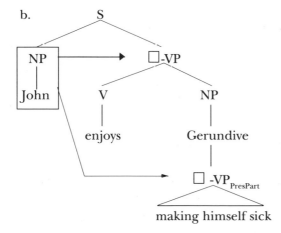

Applied to this structure, the rules of chapter 8 pick out *John* as the understood subject of *making*. Since *John* and the object pronoun are coreferential, the reflexive form is the correct choice here.

        Although the substitution idea works well with the last few examples that we have discussed, other examples can be found for which it is hard to see exactly how to apply this technique. One pair of sentences that resists such a treatment is much like the pair of sentences just considered:

(60)   a.   John's favorite activity is making *him* sick.
       b.   John's favorite activity is making *himself* sick.

For the first sentence, no problem arises. As with (54a), we treat the verb phrase as consisting of *is* plus a past-participial complement. The noun phrase *John's favorite activity* then becomes the understood subject of *making*. Because this noun phrase is not coreferential with the object of *making*, the nonreflexive *him* is the correct choice.

The problem arises with (60b). Here we clearly have an identificational sentence. However, the noun phrase *John's favorite activity* does not have a ready-made interpretation of the form *the x such that* [...]. Without an interpretation like this, we do not have a sentence with a blank into which we can substitute the phrase *making himself sick*. Consequently, we do not get *John* picked out as the understood subject of the gerundive. Here an explanation might possibly depend on some understanding of our unconscious mental definitions of words like *activity*. Suppose that such definitions themselves had blanks in them. For instance, *X's activity* might mean something like "thing that *X* indulges in ___." Then we might derive the interpretation of (60b) by the same kind of substitution that we used above:

(61) John indulges in [making himself sick].

Once again, the subject-identification rules given in chapter 8 have the effect of picking out *John* to identify the subject of *making*. The result is that the reflexive pronoun is the correct choice for the object of *making*.

One additional kind of identificational sentence that merits special attention is exemplified in (62).

(62)   a.   [$_{NP}$The thing that Beth wanted to do] was [$_{VP}$keep the flame burning].
       b.   [$_{NP}$What the teacher does] is [$_{VP}$grade on the curve].
       c.   [$_{NP}$What Roger did] was [$_{VP}$find the correct analysis].
       d.   [$_{NP}$What Bertram seems to have done] is [$_{VP}$solve the riddle of the Sphinx].
       e.   [$_{NP}$What Brenda is doing] is [$_{VP}$changing the oil].

In each of these sentences, the phrase after BE is a verb phrase. In addition, each of the subjects in these sentences contains an occurrence of the transitive DO found in simple-sentence verb phrases such as *do it* and *do something*. In each of the subjects this DO is followed by a missing direct object:

(63) a. The thing [$_{\text{B-Rel}}$ that [$_{\text{S/NP}}$ Beth wanted to do ___]]
     b. [$_{\text{F-Rel}}$ what [$_{\text{S/NP}}$ the teacher does ___]]
     c. [$_{\text{F-Rel}}$ what [$_{\text{S/NP}}$ Roger did ___]]
     d. [$_{\text{F-Rel}}$ what [$_{\text{S/NP}}$ Bertram seems to have done ___]]
     e. [$_{\text{F-Rel}}$ what [$_{\text{S/NP}}$ Brenda is doing ___]]

The verb phrase after BE is a bare-stem phrase in the first four of these sentences but a present-participial phrase in the fifth. These examples suggest is that there is a kind of matching in form between the DO inside the subject and the verb after BE. When the DO is a bare stem, a present tense, a past tense, or a past participle, then the verb after BE should be a bare stem. On the other hand, when the DO is the present-participle form *doing*, the verb after BE should be a present participle too.

In applying to these examples the kind of substitution that we used with earlier examples, we should note that the verb phrase after BE is substituted not for the blank alone but for DO plus the blank. Thus, from an example like (64a), we obtain the interpretation given in (64b). Then substitution of the verb phrase after BE for *do* plus the missing noun phrase gives (64c).

(64) a. [$_{\text{NP}}$What Nancy will do ___] is [$_{\text{VP}}$send a note to the teacher].
     b. the *x* such that [Nancy will do *x*]
     c. Nancy will *send a note to the teacher.*

Incidentally, the same kind of connection between a transitive phrase headed by DO and an ordinary verb phrase occurs in dialogues such as that in (65).

(65) a. Person A: Tell me what Nancy will [$_{\text{VP}}$do ___].
     b. Person B: She will [$_{\text{VP}}$send a note to the teacher].

Here again, *send a note to the teacher* takes the place not just of the missing noun phrase but of the full verb phrase consisting of *do* plus this missing noun phrase.

Exercises

1. The following sentence is ambiguous:

     What the president wants is to be taken seriously.

     a. Describe this ambiguity, making it as clear as you can what the two different interpretations are.

b.   On one interpretation of this sentence, the understood
     subject of *taken seriously* is *what the president wants.* On the
     other interpretation, the understood subject of this passive
     phrase is *the president.* Say how these quite different subject
     identifications come about.

2. Answer the corresponding questions concerning the following ambiguous sentence:

What the president is doing is leaving scars on the economy.

13.3 The Cleft Construction

We turn now to a construction that is specifically designed to serve an
identificational function. This construction, which is often referred to as
the *cleft construction,* is illustrated in (66).

(66)   a.   It was Velma [that you reported to the commissioner].
       b.   It must have been Tony [who(m) you sent to the commissary].

13.3.1 Two Plausible but Incorrect Analyses
A quick look at (66) might give the impression that the sentences
represent constructions with which we are already familiar. For this
reason, we will begin by comparing the cleft construction with two previously studied constructions to which it is superficially similar.

The first idea to consider is that the examples in (66) involve the *it* +
pseudocomplement construction described in chapter 4. Sentences exhibiting this construction have a substitute subject *it* taking the place of a
clause that serves as an understood subject. The clause itself then occurs
in the position of a complement. Two examples are given in (67).

(67)   a.   *It* is true [that Gordon discarded the ace].
       b.   *It* is obvious [whose car Pete borrowed].

In (67a) the pseudocomplement is a *that* clause; in (67b) it is an indirect
question. Turning back to the sentences in (66), we might think that (66a)
contains a pseudocomplement *that* clause and that (66b) contains an
indirect question.

Two major problems exist for this analysis. The first becomes apparent
as soon as we try to put the pseudocomplements back in subject position.
When we try to do this with (67) and then with (66), we get sharply
contrasting results:

(68) a. [That Gordon discarded the ace] is true.
    b. [Whose car Pete borrowed] is obvious.

(69) a. *[That you reported to the commissioner] was Velma.
    b. *[Who(m) you sent to the commissary] is Tony.

The second major problem arises specifically with the idea that the bracketed material in (66a) is a *that* clause. An examination of other examples reveals that what follows *Velma* in this sentence must contain a missing noun phrase. This fact is established by the contrast between (70), where missing-noun-phrase positions can be found, and (71), where there are none.

(70) a. It was Velma [that you took ___ to the meeting].
    b. It was Velma [that you talked to ___]

(71) a. *It was Velma [that you took Beth to the meeting].
    b. *It was Velma [that you talked to Fred].

This contrast provides solid evidence that the bracketed structure in (66a) cannot be a *that* clause but instead must be a missing-phrase construction of some kind.

The second idea that we might consider is one that would allow us to view the bracketed sequences as missing-phrase constructions. This idea is that the bracketed sequences in (66) are just ordinary relative clauses modifying *Velma* and *Tony*, respectively. The main problem with such an analysis is that it is not consistent with what we have established previously about relative clauses. If the bracketed sequence in (66a) actually were a relative clause, the *that* which introduces it would indicate that it was restrictive rather than nonrestrictive. But having this clause modify *Velma* would violate the prohibition against having proper nouns modified by restrictive relative clauses. In this example, it would force us to say that the sequence *Velma that you took to the meeting* could be a well-formed noun phrase. Sentence (72) confirms that in fact it cannot be.

(72)   *Velma that you took to the meeting returned your call.

13.3.2 The Structure of the Cleft Construction

Now that we have established that the cleft construction is separate from any we have discussed previously in the book, let us examine its structure, starting with the two sentences we considered at the beginning of the present section:

(73) a. It was Velma [that you reported to the commissioner].
    b. It must have been Tony [who(m) you sent to the commissary].

Each of these sentences has as its subject the word *it*, and each contains an occurrence of BE, a noun phrase, and a sequence that is strikingly similar in internal structure to a restrictive relative clause. In what follows, we will refer to the position of the noun phrase as the *focus* position, and to the clause that follows it as the *cleft clause*. Thus, the following diagram would be appropriate for example (73a):

(74)

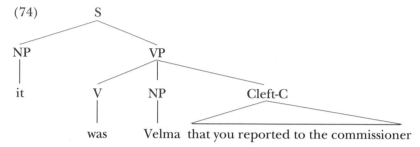

In what follows, we will want to address two general questions:

- What kinds of phrases can occur in the focus position?
- What are the characteristics of the cleft clause?

Let us start with the first of these questions. The two examples that we have seen so far have both had noun phrases in focus position. As the additional examples in (75) show, many other types of phrases are possible.

(75) a. It was *here* that Linda put the molasses.   (locative phrase)
      b. It was *to Boston* that they decided to take the patient ___.
          (motion phrase)
      c. It was *then* that the answer occurred to her __.   (time phrase)
      d. It was *with a great deal of regret* that I vetoed your legislation ___.
          (manner phrase)
      e. It was *by starting a fire* that the army avoided defeat __.   (means
          phrase)
      f. It was *three whole days* that the battle lasted ___.   (duration
          phrase)

Among the few types of phrases that cannot appear in focus position in standard English are adjective phrases and verb phrases of various inflectional forms:

(76) a. *It is *fond of Martha* that Harry seems to be __. (adjective phrase)
      b. *It was *to see his brother* that Harry tried ___.   (infinitival phrase)
      c. *It is *stealing apples* that Julia caught Frank ___.   (present-
          participial verb phrase)

In addition, individual adverbs such as *carefully* and *regretfully* are not acceptable in the focus position, even though prepositional phrases that express the same ideas are acceptable:

(77) a. *It was *carefully* that Donna removed the wrapping ___.
(Compare: It was *with care* that Donna removed the wrapping___.)
b. *It was *regretfully* that Joe fired Pete.
(Compare: It was *with regret* that Joe fired Pete.)

The examples presented in (75) show one striking characteristic of the cleft clause: Despite the fact that a wide variety of focus phrases occurred in these examples, the word *that* was always acceptable as an introducing element. Thus, the following rule accounts for a broad group of cleft clauses:

(78) A cleft clause can consist of the word *that* plus a sentence with a missing phrase.

The same rule can be expressed in diagram form as in (79), where XP stands for a phrase of any variety, just as it did in the discussion of indirect questions in chapter 4.

(79)   Cleft-C

that   S/XP

We do not need to put any special restrictions on the kind of missing phrase allowed, since any type that can appear as the focus can also be the missing phrase in a cleft clause introduced by *that*.

Cleft clauses may also be introduced by a few other elements, primarily *who, whom,* and *whose* plus common noun phrase:

(80) a. It was Smiley [*who* ___ spilled beer on this couch].
b. It must have been Dorothy [*who*(*m*) Fred was referring to ___].
c. It is Martha [*whose work* critics will praise ___].

Also acceptable are prepositional phrases containing these noun phrases:

(81) a. It was Smiley [*on whom* the sheriff placed the blame ___].
b. It is Margaret [*on whose shoulders* the burden will rest ___].

Surprisingly, though, other *wh* words that serve well in restrictive relatives are not as natural in clefts:

(82)   a. ? It is this car [*which* I want you to sell ___].
             (Compare: It is this car [*that* I want you to sell ___].)
        b. ? It was on Thursday [*when* the schedule was announced].
             (Compare: It was on Thursday [*that* the schedule was
             announced ___].)
        c. ? It was in Boston [*where* they held the tea party ___].
             (Compare: It was in Boston [*that* they held the tea
             party ___].)

Thus, we need the following additional rule for the formation of cleft
clauses:

(83)   A cleft clause can have as an introducing phrase either *who, whom,*
        or *whose* plus a common noun phrase. In addition, it can be intro-
        duced by a prepositional phrase containing one of these noun
        phrases. In the first case, the adjoined structure is a sentence with
        a missing noun phrase; in the second case it is a sentence with a
        missing prepositional phrase.

The two separate cases of this rule are shown in (84).

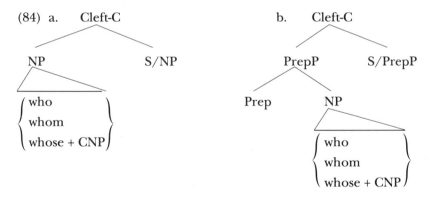

Exercise
1. Draw tree diagrams for the following sentences:
        a.   It must have been Harold who locked us on the deck.
        b.   Jones knows who it was that Smith wanted to interview.
        c.   It was Gordon whose canary the python swallowed.
        d.   It was on this desk that Nadine put the keys.

13.3.3 Interpreting the Cleft Construction

By now we have seen enough to suspect that the identificational function of cleft constructions is carried out in a way that mimics the process by which restrictive relative clauses are interpreted. As in the latter process, we have a structure (here a finite sentence) with a missing phrase. Just as there was an understood noun phrase provided to the restrictive relative clause, here an outside phrase is provided also (in this case, the phrase in focus position). This general situation is represented graphically in (85).

(85)

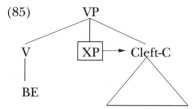

Just as with relative clauses, what happens at this point depends on whether the structure receiving the donated phrase is introduced by a *wh*-phrase. If it is not (if it is introduced either by *that* or by nothing), then the phrase is donated directly to the sentence with a missing phrase, which uses it to complete its meaning:

(86)

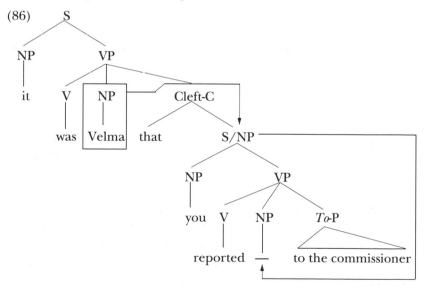

For the sentence pictured in (86), this process would yield an interpretation containing the sentence in (87).

(87)   You reported *Velma* to the commissioner.

On the other hand, if the cleft clause is introduced by a *wh* phrase, the interpretation proceeds in two steps instead of one. First the focused phrase replaces the *wh*-word in the introducing phrase; then this introducing phrase fills in the meaning of the missing phrase.

(88)

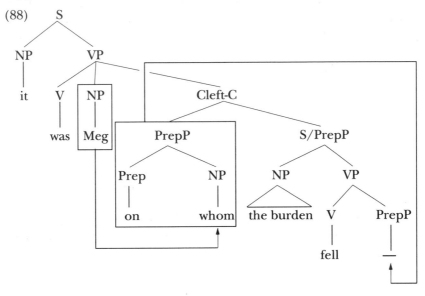

Thus, for a sentence like the one diagrammed in (88), we arrive at an interpretation that implies (89).

(89)   The burden fell on *Meg*.

Exercise
1. Take the tree diagrams that you drew for the exercise at the end of the preceding subsection and indicate the way in which each of the identifications is determined.

13.3.4 The Cleft Construction with Transparent Verbs

Earlier in this chapter, we noted that the existential *there* can be separated from the verb BE only by a transparent predicate—that is, only by a predicate that has no use of its own for its subject. Thus, (90a) is possible, since SEEM and HAVE are transparent, whereas (90b) is not.

(90)   a.   There seem to have been three explosions on the boat.
        b.   *There intends to be an admiral on the committee.

The cleft construction exhibits exactly the same property. The *it* and the BE can be separated, but only by a predicate that does not have a use of its own for its subject. Thus, although an ordinary noun phrase like *John* may serve as the subject of either a transparent predicate or a nontransparent one, the *it* of the cleft can only be the subject of a transparent one. We see this contrast in (91) and (92).

(91) a. John seems to own that house.
      b. John wants to own that house.

(92) a. It seems to be John that owns that house.
      b. *It wants to be John that owns that house.

Thus, just as was the case with existential *there*, the *it* of the cleft construction in no sense serves as a surrogate for a noun phrase that occurs in the focus position. In (92b), in particular, the verb WANT needs an animate subject, and the word *it* clearly fails to stand in for *John* as the subject of this verb.

In similar fashion, the *it* of the cleft construction can be an object only for a verb that does not use its object itself. Thus we see another contrast similar to the one in subsection 13.1.5:

(93) a. We believed it to be Smith who was leaving the message.
      b. *We persuaded it to be Smith who was leaving the message.

Exercise

1. Construct an experimental sentence to determine whether each of the following verbs and adjectives is transparent. The relevant sentences will contain verb phrases in which the verb is followed immediately by an infinitival phrase.

      a. ATTEMPT
      b. REFUSE
      c. TEND
      d. APPEAR
      e. APT
      f. EAGER

Chapter 14

Special Sentence Types

Up to this point in the book, we have been concerned solely with declarative sentences—that is, sentences that are used to make statements of various kinds. In this chapter, we will study some other types of sentences which are used for special purposes. The first group to be considered consists of direct questions. The second group consists of several kinds of exclamative constructions, which are similar to questions in form. The third group consists of imperatives.

14.1 Direct Questions

In chapter 4 we gave a good deal of attention to a special type of clause construction: the type traditionally referred to as the *indirect question*. These questions were used as subjects and objects of larger sentences. The present section deals with the corresponding constructions that function as independent utterances. Although the outward situation in which direct questions occur is extremely simple, their internal structure is actually more complex in one significant respect than the internal structure of indirect questions.

14.1.1 Yes-No Questions and Alternative Questions

The first group of direct questions that we will examine consists of "yes-no" questions. The contrast between ordinary affirmatives and yes-no questions can be seen in the following pairs:

(1) a. Jack *caught* the measles.
     b. *Did* Jack *catch* the measles?

(2) a. Chris *wants* a drink.
     b. *Does* Chris *want* a drink?

(3)   a.   The bankers *trust* Smith.
       b.   *Do* the bankers *trust* Smith?

We will give a special name to the kind of structure that these questions exhibit, referring to them as *inverted finite structures*. In addition to seeing them serve as direct questions, as in these examples, we will also see them serve as parts of other constructions. This is why we want to have a name for them that is different from *direct yes-no-question*. If we can determine how these inverted finite structures are formed, our rule for forming direct yes-no questions can then be stated very simply, as in (4).

(4)   A direct question can consist of an inverted finite structure by itself.

Let us look more closely, then, at these structures. As was the case with the emphatic construction discussed in chapter 3 and the *not* construction discussed in chapter 11, this new construction contains a tensed form of *do* (either *did*, *does*, or *do*) and a bare-stem verb. We clearly have another construction that has a special-purpose verb phrase as a basic ingredient. In addition, just as with the negative construction, a change in word order is required: The tensed *do* must be shifted to the left of the subject. Thus, a rule for inverted finite structures can be stated as in (5).

(5)   To form an inverted finite structure, use a special purpose structure and then shift the head verb to the left of the subject noun phrase.

With this rule in mind, we can think of inverted finite structures as being formed in the manner shown in (6).

(6)   a.   Jack did catch the measles.   (use special-purpose verb
                                            phrase)
       b.   Did Jack catch the measles?   (shift head verb to left of
                                            subject)

The effects of this derivation are represented in (7), where S_{Inv} is an abbreviation for an inverted finite structure.

(7)

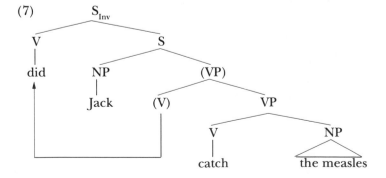

As the rules developed here would lead us to expect, the verbs that were odd in the way in which they entered into emphatic sentences are odd in the same way when they are used in inverted finite structures. Consider the examples in (8)–(10).

(8) a. John *has* gone to the library.
     b. **Does* John *have* gone to the library?
     c. *Has* John gone to the library?

(9) a. You *are* busy.
     b. *Do you *be* busy?
     c. *Are* you busy?

(10) a. Jack *can* play the fiddle.
     b. *Does Jack *can* play the fiddle?
     c. *Can* Jack play the fiddle?

The derivations of the three acceptable (c) examples, given in (11)–(13), show how the statement about exceptional special-purpose structures and the rule for inverted finite structures work together to give the right results.

(11) a. John *has* gone to the library.   (use special-purpose verb phrase)
     b. *Has* John gone to the library?   (shift head verb to left of subject)

(12) a. You are busy.   (use special-purpose verb phrase)
     b. Are you busy?   (shift head verb to left of subject)

(13) a. Jack *can* play the fiddle.   (use special-purpose verb phrase)
     b. *Can* Jack play the fiddle?   (shift head verb to left of subject)

The structures resulting from these derivations are illustrated in (14).

(14) a.

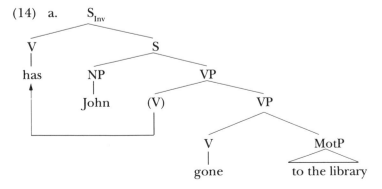

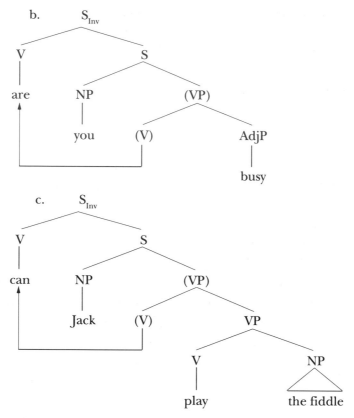

When we wish to indicate that an inverted finite structure is serving as a direct question, we can do it by adding the symbol DQ (for "direct question") to the top of the tree diagram. For the example in (13b), considered as a question, the tree would look like (15).

(15)

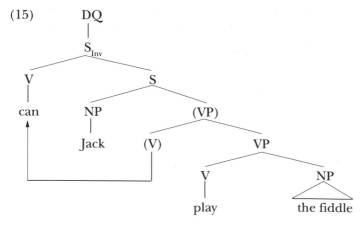

Just as the class of indirect questions includes alternative *whether* questions as well as yes-no *whether questions*, there are direct alternative questions that are close in their syntax to direct yes-no questions. The (a) sentences in (16) and (17) both have indirect alternative questions as complements, and the (b) sentences show the corresponding direct questions.

(16) a. We want to know [whether John sued Karen or Karen sued John].
      b. Did John sue Karen, or did Karen sue John?

(17) a. Harry didn't tell us [whether Sue played chess or Joe played bridge or Sam played poker].
      b. Did Sue play chess, or did Joe play bridge, or did Sam play poker?

In (16b) we have the conjunction *or* joining together two inverted finite structures. In (17b) the same conjunction joins three inverted finite structures. Thus, although we will not discuss conjunctions systematically until chapter 16, we can give a rough rule for this kind of question:

(18) A direct question can consist of two or more inverted finite structures joined by *or*.

The structure we would get for (16b) is shown in (19).

(19)

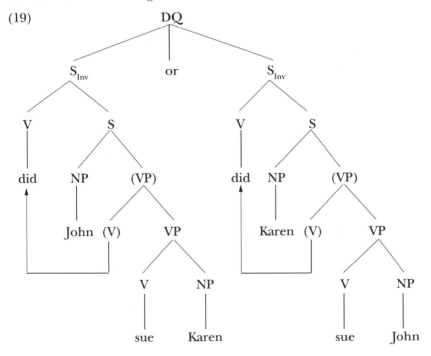

Exercises

1. For each of the following questions, draw a tree diagram:
   a.   Does your brother have a job?
   b.   Do these people know your cousin?
   c.   Has your car been washed?
   d.   Were the coats made in New York?
   e.   Did Sally see the doctor yesterday, or will she see him today?

2. Across various dialects of English, we find two different ways of negating and questioning sentence (i):
   (i)   John has the necessary money.
The two different questions are given in (ii), and the two different negative sentences are given in (iii):
   (ii)   a.   Does John have the necessary money?
          b.   Has John the necessary money?
   (iii) a.   John doesn't have the necessary money.
          b.   John hasn't the necessary money.
On the basis of these examples, give the simplest explanation you can think of as to how these two varieties of English differ. What should we say about the variety illustrated in the (b) sentences that we do not say about the variety illustrated in the (a) sentences?

14.1.2 Negative Yes-No Questions

The special-purpose head verbs with contracted *not* count as special-purpose verbs in their own right. Thus, they can themselves undergo the formation of inverted finite structures:

(20)   a.   Didn't Jack return the book?
       b.   Isn't Alice with Fred?
       c.   Hasn't George written his paper?

A detailed derivation for sentence (20a) is given in (21).

(21)   a.   Jack *not did* return the book.   (initial sequence with special-purpose verb phrase)
       b.   Jack *did not* return the book.   (shift of head verb to left of *not*)
       c.   Jack *didn't* return the book.   (optional contraction of *not* with *did*)
       d.   *Didn't* Jack return the book?   (shift of head verb to left of subject)

Steps a–c are those discussed in chapter 11. They result in the structure shown in (22).

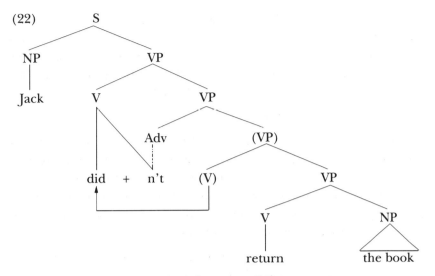

(22)

Shifting the finite verb to the left, we get (23).

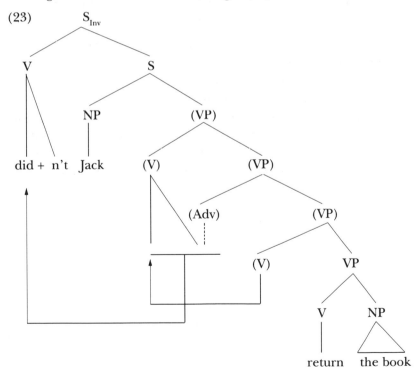

(23)

If this diagram seems more than ordinarily complex, it is because of the unusual complexity of the construction whose derivation it is representing.

Let us turn now to a different matter: the question of how negative yes-no questions are used. In circumstances in which either a positive or a negative answer is equally likely, such questions are never used. For instance, if we have no idea one way or the other whether Jack returned the book, the appropriate question is not (20a) but (24):

(24) Did Jack return the book?

By contrast, a question like (20a) might be asked in either of two special circumstances. The first is when the person asking the question is sure or virtually sure that the answer is affirmative, and wants to force the hearer into giving an affirmative answer. Thus, this type of question crops up frequently in courtroom cross-examination and in news conferences. Examples illustrating this effect are given in (25).

(25)   a.   Didn't it seem strange to you that your employer sent you home early on the night of the fire?
       b.   Didn't you state in your acceptance speech at the convention that you were strongly in favor of a tax cut?

In both of these cases, the questioner's implication is clearly that only an affirmative answer is appropriate.

The second circumstance in which negative questions are used is when the questioner has just discovered grounds for doubting the truth of something that had previously been taken for granted. For instance, suppose that Carol has been assuming all along that Henry paid the light bill for their apartment, but then they get a letter in which they are threatened with a cutoff of electrical service. It would then be natural for Carol to address the following question to Henry:

(26)   Didn't you pay the light bill?

Exercise
1. As was shown in this section, questions can be formed on negative special-purpose structures as well as on positive special-purpose structures.
       (i)   Didn't Janet open the package?
       (ii) Hasn't Fred made his bed?
Give complete derivations for these questions, showing all of the steps that have gone into their formation.

14.1.3 Tag Questions

There is one more special type of construction in English that belongs in a discussion of yes-no questions. This construction, which has the appearance of an abbreviated yes-no question, is commonly attached to the end of a declarative sentence. Instances of this construction are italicized in (27) and (28):

(27) a. John went to Villanova, *didn't he?*
  b. They know what is going on, *don't they?*
  c. George has spent a lot of money, *hasn't he?*
  d. This cake is quite rich, *isn't it?*
  e. Martha will graduate in May, *won't she?*

(28) a. John didn't go to Villanova, *did he?*
  b. They don't know what's going on, *do they?*
  c. George hasn't spent much money, *has he?*
  d. This cake isn't very sweet, *is it?*
  e. Martha won't graduate in May, *will she?*

While many languages have constructions which have the same function in conversation as this particular English construction, in few of these other languages is the construction so complicated.

In describing the "tag questions" in (27) and (28), we can begin by observing three properties of the construction. First, there is a pronoun subject, which in each case agrees with the subject of the preceding declarative. Second, in front of this subject is a special-purpose verb that matches the declarative verb in tense, number, and person—that is, for most verbs it will be a positive or a negative form of *do*, whereas for the exceptional verbs it will be a positive or a negative form of that verb. Finally, and most surprisingly, this special-purpose verb is negative if the declarative is positive, and positive if the declarative is negative. The former situation obtains in (27), the latter in (28). Thus, we might give the following rule for forming a tag question to go with a given declarative:

(29) To form the tag question that goes with a given declarative, use as the subject the pronoun that agrees with the subject of the declarative. To the left of this subject put a special-purpose verb that fits with the verb of the declarative sentence. If the declarative sentence is affirmative, make the special-purpose verb negative, and vice versa.

We can illustrate the operation of this rule by using it to derive a tag to go with the declarative given in (30).

(30)   Martin lives in Denver.

The first thing we need to determine is what pronoun is appropriate as a subject noun phrase. For *Martin,* the corresponding pronoun is *he.* The second question is what special-purpose verb corresponds with the verb *lives.* Here the answer is either *does* or *doesn't.* The final question is whether the declarative sentence is affirmative or negative. Since it is affirmative, we use the negative form *doesn't* in the tag. These three choices give us the correct result:

(31)   Martin lives in Denver, *doesn't he?*

Tag questions have two different functions in English, and the difference in use goes along with a difference in intonation contour. The first intonation pattern is one that rises on the tag:

(32)   Ruth knows about the meeting tomorrow, doesn't she?

This question would be asked with this intonation if a speaker suddenly felt insecure about a proposition that had not been questioned previously. Here the previously unquestioned assumption is just that Ruth knows about the meeting tomorrow. The utterance serves the function of asking for a confirmation of this proposition. Had the questioner not taken this proposition for granted previously, an ordinary yes-no question would have been much more appropriate:

(33)   Does Ruth know about the meeting tomorrow?

The other possible intonation on a tag question falls sharply at the end. We might hear this intonation in an utterance of the example in (34).

(34)   The weather's nice today, isn't it?

This utterance is clearly not intended to confirm anything about which the utterer is uncertain. Nor is it intended to convey information to the hearer. Instead, it is to be taken as an "invitation to agree." Such an utterance is often used to get a conversation going. In British English, the same construction with the same intonation can also be used as an invitation to concede a point, and thus can be used to terminate a conversation. The following is a possible British example:

(35)   Your plan would make it awfully difficult to keep our rivals out, wouldn't it?

This use is completely foreign to American English.

14.1.4 Direct Phrasal Questions

We now turn our attention to direct questions that are introduced by various sorts of questioned phrases. We saw a good many indirect questions of this sort in chapter 4, including the following:

(36) a. whose alligator the plumber located
      b. which goat George was shouting at
      c. how many employees Karen introduced to the visitors
      d. in which room George stayed
      e. how fond of chocolates the monkeys are
      f. when the concert will begin
      g. where his horse is

For each of these indirect questions, there is a corresponding direct question:

(37) a. Whose alligator did the plumber locate?
      b. Which goat was George shouting at?
      c. How many employees did Karen introduce to the visitors?
      d. In which room did George stay?
      e. How fond of chocolates are the monkeys?
      f. When will the concert begin?
      g. Where is his horse?

The direct questions are almost exactly like the indirect questions. The only difference is that the sentences on which the direct questions are based are finite inverted structures instead of ordinary sentences. That is, their verb phrases are special-purpose phrases, and the head verb has been shifted to the left of the subject. We can thus describe these questions by a relatively simple rule:

(38) To form a direct phrasal question, join a questioned phrase to an inverted finite structure with a missing phrase of the same type as the questioned phrase.

For the first of the questions in (37), this rule yields the tree diagram in (39).

There is one special case where rule (38) gives the wrong results. Among the structures that would surely count as an inverted finite structure with a missing noun phrase would be the structure shown in (40), in which the missing noun phrase is the subject.

(39)

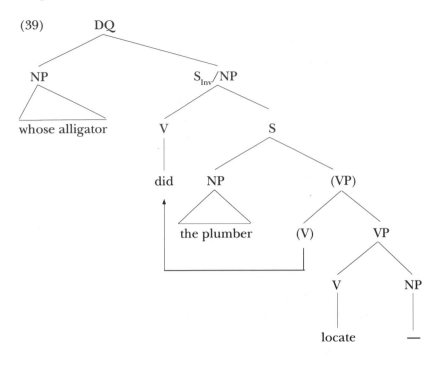

(40)

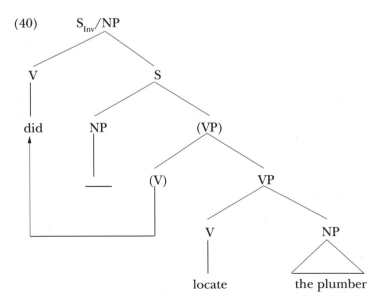

From this structure, rule (38) would allow the formation of the question diagrammed in (41).

(41)

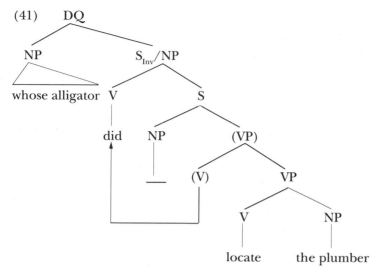

Unless we put emphatic stress on *did*, this is not an acceptable question. The actual question that we get instead is shown in (42).

(42)   Whose alligator located the plumber?

For this question we want an uninverted sentence, just as was the case with the corresponding indirect question:

(43)

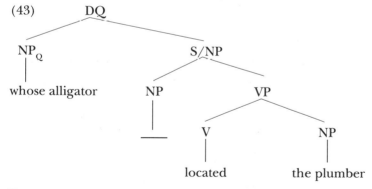

Because of this kind of question, we will amend rule (38) as follows, dividing it into two separate cases:

(44)   To form a direct phrasal question: If the questioned phrase is the subject of the question, then join the questioned phrase to an ordinary sentence with a missing noun phrase. Otherwise, join the questioned phrase to an inverted finite structure with a missing phrase of the same type as the questioned phrase.

Exercises

1. For each of the following direct questions, draw a tree diagram:
   a. Which coat did Edgar mend?
   b. What did Fred do with the rug?
   c. Why didn't you keep the change?
   d. How many patients wasn't the doctor able to examine?

2. The bracketed indirect question in the following sentence is ambiguous:

   I wonder [what Ruth had taken to the market].

Draw tree diagrams for the two structures that this indirect question can have. Then determine what the corresponding direct question is for each of the structures. Explain what it is that makes the ambiguity disappear when we change to the direct questions.

14.2 Exclamatives

The term *exclamatives* refers to a small class of English constructions whose special function is to express amazement. One of these constructions is illustrated in (45).

(45) a. Didn't John do a great job!
      b. Don't those twins look like their grandmother!
      c. Hasn't this been a terrible summer!
      d. Isn't Horton a jackass!

This construction is identical in every respect except one to negative yes-no questions. The one difference is that these sentences carry a falling intonation contour at the end instead of a rising contour. Although these utterances are not in any way requests for information, they are like questions in calling for some response from the hearer. The kind of response they solicit is an emphatically enthusiastic affirmative answer.

Another exclamative construction has the form of an affirmative yes-no question, except that the intonation is falling at the end instead of rising:

(46) a. Did I make a mess of that exam!
      b. Was Smith cross today!
      c. Has that kid grown!
      d. Can Ella sing!

These examples can be made slightly more natural by prefacing them with *boy* or some comparable interjection, and by inserting the word *ever* after the subject:

(47) a. Boy, did I ever make a mess of that exam!
     b. Damn, was Smith ever cross today!
     c. Man, has that kid ever grown!
     d. Jesus, can Ella ever sing!

Unlike the exclamatives that look like negative questions, these do not call for a particular type of response from the hearer.

Still other exclamative constructions are used to indicate a high degree of some quality. These constructions are exemplified in (48) and (49).

(48) a. *How tall* you have grown ___!
     b. *How soothingly* John reads his poems ___!

(49) a. *What a sullen fellow* Gordon seems to have become ___!
     b. *What a dope* Gordon seems to have become ___!
     c. *What beautiful paintings* you bought ___!
     d. *What masterpieces* you bought ___!
     e. *What tasteless furniture* you have piled ___ up!
     f. *What trash* you have piled ___ up!

These examples have three properties in common. The first is that they have an introductory phrase beginning with *how* or *what*. The second is that they contain corresponding missing phrases. These two properties they share with questions, both direct and indirect. The third common property is that all of them have a general-purpose verb and normal subject-verb word order, instead of having a special-purpose verb shifted to the left of the subject. This property has the effect of setting them very clearly apart from direct questions.

The rules for the introductory phrases of the above sentences are quite simple. The phrase can be an adjective phrase or an adverbial phrase starting with the degree word *how*. It can also be a noun phrase, which can have one of the following three forms:

> *what* + *a*(*n*) + singular count common noun phrase
> *what* + plural count common noun phrase
> *what* + mass common noun phrase.

The exclamative phrases formed with *what* show the same pattern as the noun phrases introduced by *such*, which were discussed in chapter 12:

(50) a. *what* a dope, *such* a dope   (singular count)
     b. *what* masterpieces, *such* masterpieces (plural count)
     c. *what* trash, *such* trash   (mass)

One final type of exclamatory utterance consists of an introductory exclamatory phrase by itself:

(51)   a.   How stupid!
        b.   What a ridiculous price!
        c.   What a bargain!
        d.   What beautiful dentures!
        e.   What idiots!
        f.   What beautiful music!
        g.   What garbage!

14.3 Imperatives

Our third special class of sentences, imperatives, are used primarily to give instructions, orders, commands, invitations, and suggestions for action.

14.3.1 Second-Person Imperatives

The most basic type of imperative consists simply of a verb phrase, with no overt subject preceding it:

(52)   a.   Eat your spinach.
        b.   Sign your name on this line.
        c.   Be patient.

In these examples, as in all the imperative examples we will see, the verb is in its bare-stem form. Example (52c) shows clearly that it is the bare-stem form and not the present-plural form that is required. If we had used the present-plural form of *be* in that example, we would have obtained the unacceptable sentence in (53).

(53)   *Are patient.

Although there is no overt subject in these examples, in each case there is an understood subject *you*. A rule for this type of imperative can thus be stated as follows:

(54)   An imperative may consist of a bare-stem verb phrase alone. Such a structure is interpreted as having an understood subject *you*.

A slightly more complex type of imperative exhibits an overt subject, as in (55).

(55)   a.   *You* sit down.
        b.   *Someone* call a doctor.
        c.   *Somebody* say something.
        d.   *Everybody* sit down.

The possible subjects in this construction do not go very far beyond *you*, *you guys, someone, somebody, everybody,* and so forth. This additional possibility is described in (56).

(56)   An imperative can consist of a subject (*you* or some larger noun phrase introduced by *you*; also *somebody, someone*) followed by a bare-stem verb phrase. The subject must be one that can refer to one or more people who are being addressed.

Rules (54) and (56) give the two basic possibilities for affirmative imperatives. For negative imperatives, we start with the same basic structures that are given by rules (54) and (56) and preface them with the word *don't*. This gives us the following sets of results, the first lacking subjects and the second showing them:

(57)   a.   Don't go away.
       b.   Don't be impatient.

(58)   a.   Don't you sit down over there.
       b.   Don't anybody say anything.

(The *anybody* and *anything* that we see in place of *somebody* and *something* are a result of the negative context here; this effect will be discussed in detail in chapter 15.) We can describe negative imperatives, then, as in (59).

(59)   A negative imperative can consist of *don't* followed by an overt or understood subject followed by a bare-stem verb phrase.

One additional possibility exists for forming a negative imperative: Instead of using *don't*, we can use *do not*, as in (60).

(60)   a.   Do not walk on the grass.
       b.   Do not post bills.

Unlike the word *don't*, the two-word sequence *do not* cannot be used with imperatives containing an overt subject:

(61)   a.   *Do not you sit down over there.
       b.   *Do not anybody say anything.

The rule we need for these imperatives must therefore be stated as follows:

(62)   A negative imperative can consist of *do not* followed by an understood subject *you* followed by a bare-stem verb phrase.

14.3.2 First-Person Imperatives

Besides the imperatives described above, which are generally used to elicit some sort of behavior from the person or persons being spoken to, English allows another sort. The primary purpose of these imperatives is to suggest a course of action in which the speaker is to be included. The simplest form is exemplified in (63).

(63)   a.   Let's go to the circus.
       b.   Let's be careful.

Each of these examples consists of the form *let's* followed by a bare-stem verb phrase. Although there is no overt subject, the understood subject is clearly *we*. We can also have first-person imperatives in which there is an overt subject, as in (64).

(64)   a.   Let's everybody take a deep breath.
       b.   Let's all five of us go in Fred's car.

In these examples, we have *let's* followed by a noun phrase followed by a bare-stem verb phrase.

The rule for making negative versions of these imperatives is simple: Merely use *let's not* instead of *let's*:

(65)   a.   Let's not go to the circus.
       b.   Let's not be careless.

(66)   a.   Let's not everybody talk at the same time.
       b.   Let's not all five of us try to crowd into Fred's car.

There is also an alternative negative form that is not standard for American English. In this form the sequence *don't let's* is used instead of *let's not:*

(67)   a.   Don't let's go to the circus.
       b.   Don't let's be careless.

(68)   a.   Don't let's everybody talk at the same time.
       b.   Don't let's all five of us crowd into Fred's car.

14.3.3 Imperatives with a Conditional Force

All the imperatives discussed so far have occurred in simple sentence structures. In addition to this basic use, they have a rather surprising additional use in which they are joined to a following declarative by a conjunction. The examples in (69) and (70) illustrate this use.

(69)   a.   *Eat your spinach,* and you can have some cake.
       b.   *Don't spill the beans,* and I'll let your parakeet live.

(70)   a.   *Eat your spinach,* or I'll give your cake to the dog.

        b.   *Don't spill the beans,* or your parakeet will get it.

The italicized sequences in these sentences look exactly like the imperatives that we saw above, with a bare-stem verb phrase in the (a) examples and a bare-stem verb phrase preceded by *don't* in the (b) examples. In addition, they strongly request a certain kind of action. The sentences in (69), containing *and,* can be paraphrased as in (71).

(71)   a.   If you eat your spinach, you can have some cake.
        b.   If you don't spill the beans, I'll let your parakeet live.

By contrast, the sentences in (70), which contain *or,* have paraphrases that contain *unless* instead of *if:*

(72)   a.   Unless you eat your spinach, I'll give your cake to the dog.
        b.   Unless you don't spill the beans, your parakeet will get it.

This use of imperatives is also possible when the imperative has a subject, as in (73).

(73)   a.   Somebody make a motion for adjournment, and we can all go home.
        b.   Don't any of you move, or this parakeet will get it.

The same use sometimes is found with first-person imperatives as well:

(74)   a.   Let's leave now, or we will get stuck in rush-hour traffic.
        b.   Let's leave now, and we will get home in time to watch the World Series.

V
Some Topics in the Semantic
Interpretation of English

Chapter 15

Negation

With one set of significant exceptions, almost all the sentences that we have examined so far in this book have been from the class of what are traditionally known as *affirmative* sentences. The one exceptional set was the set of negative sentences considered in chapter 11, several of which are repeated here in (1).

(1)   a.   Joe did not shave before breakfast.
        b.   I did not go to the post office.
        c.   Max has not vanished.
        d.   Smith is not a genius.

This construction, in which a special-purpose verb is placed to the left of *not*, provides a very basic means for expressing negative propositions. However, it is only one element in a surprisingly rich and complex system. In this chapter we will try to arrive at an overall view of this sytem.

By a *negative sentence*, we will mean roughly a sentence that contains any word from a certain list of words with negative meanings. This list will include some words that are clearly negative: *not, -n't, never, no, none, nothing, no one, nobody,* and *nowhere.* It will also include some that are not quite so obviously negative: *hardly, scarcely, seldom, rarely, little,* and *few.*

15.1 Logical Negations of Affirmative Sentences

A useful way to start out on this topic will be to make some informal comparisons between affirmative sentences and sentences that are interpreted as their *logical negations.* Sentence X expresses the logical negation of sentence Y if X is true when Y is false and X is false when Y is true. Thus, for example, (2b) expresses the logical negation of (2a).

(2)   a.   Smith understands Latin.
        b.   Smith does not understand Latin.

If the first of these two sentences is true, the second must be false; if the first is false, the second must be true.

The pair of sentences in (2) shows the relation in syntactic form that we studied in chapter 11. To see some examples illustrating a more complex relation, let us look at some affirmative sentences containing the word *some*.

(3) a. Jack saw *something*.
     b. Connie drank *some* beer.
     c. The president *sometimes* calls a meeting.
     d. Shirley *sometimes* gives *some* money to *some* of her friends.

The logical negations of these examples are most naturally expressed by the following negative sentences:

(4) a. Jack did *not* see *anything*.
     b. Connie did *not* drink *any* beer.
     c. The president doesn*'t ever* call a meeting.
     d. Shirley doesn*'t ever* give *any* money to *any* of her friends.

There are two chief differences in form between the affirmative sentences in (3) and their corresponding negatives in (4). The first is that the negative sentences contain *not* or *-n't* along with a special-purpose verbal structure. The second is that the negative sentences contain *any* and *ever* words in place of the *some* words in the affirmatives. In what follows, we will refer to the *some* words as *assertives* and to the *any* and *ever* words as *nonassertives*. The two sets of words are listed pairwise in (5).

(5) **Assertive**   **Nonassertive**
     some   any
     someone   anyone
     somebody   anybody
     something   anything
     somewhere   anywhere
     sometimes   ever

The negative sentences in (4) show one set of logical negations for the affirmative sentences in (3). As it happens, the rules of English allow another set of logical negations as well. The negative sentences of the first kind are repeated in (6), and the alternative negative sentences are listed in (7).

(6) a. Jack did *not* see *anything*.
     b. Connie did *not* drink *any* beer.
     c. The president doesn*'t ever* call a meeting.

   d.   Shirley does*n't ever* give *any* money to *any* of her friends.

(7)   a.   Jack saw *nothing*.
      b.   Connie drank *no* beer.
      c.   The president *never* calls a meeting.
      d.   Shirley *never* gives *any* money to *any* of her friends.

In this alternative group of negative sentences, there is no *not* preceded by a special-purpose verb. Instead, the first nonassertive word of the affirmative sentence (*anything, any, ever*) is replaced by a corresponding *negative word* (*nothing, no, never*). As the following unsuccessful modifications of (6) indicate, only the first nonassertive may be replaced by the corresponding negative word:

(8)   a.   *John *ever* gives *no* money to *any* of his friends.
      b.   *John *ever* gives *any* money to *none* of his friends.

For affirmative sentences with assertive words in their subjects, only the second variety of negative sentence is possible as their negation. We can see this by looking at the sets of sentences in (9)–(11).

(9)   a.   Someone is sleeping in my bed.
      b.   Some zebras can fly.
      c.   Something has happened to Bertram's optimism.

(10)   a.   *Anyone isn't sleeping in my bed.
       b.   *Any zebras can't fly.
       c.   *Anything hasn't happened to Bertram's optimism.

(11)   a.   No one is sleeping in my bed.
       b.   No zebras can fly.
       c.   Nothing has happened to Bertram's optimism.

Setting ourselves the task of comparing affirmative sentences with sentences that express their logical negations has provided us with some preliminary observations about negative sentences. It has also given us some useful concepts—specifically, the concepts *assertive, nonassertive,* and *negative*, which refer to important classes of English words. But so far, we have not tried to state any actual rules about negative sentences.

15.2 Some Additional Negative Sentences

At this point, it might seem natural to give a rule for negative sentences that would derive them by taking affirmative sentences and making some simple changes. In such an approach, we would construct (12b) by starting with (12a), inserting a *not*, and changing *something* to *anything*.

(12)   a.   The mole will see something.
       b.   The mole will not see anything.

Similarly, we would construct (13b) by taking (13a) and changing the first assertive word to a negative.

(13)   a.   Some of the guests signed the register.
       b.   None of the guests signed the register.

The weakness of this approach becomes apparent only when we look at some additional negative sentences.

   A first problematic example is given in (14).

(14)   Some of the guests did not sign the register.

From what affirmative sentence would this negative sentence be derived? It might at first glance appear that this sentence represents the logical negation of (15).

(15)   Some of the guests signed the register.

But in fact (15) is negated not by (14) but by (16).

(16)   None of the guests signed the register.

We can prove that (14) is not the logical negation of (15) by imagining a situation in which both sentences would be true at the same time. Let us suppose that ten guests are currently staying in a certain hotel, and that six have signed the register and four have not. Then both (14) and (15) are clearly true. Thus, (14) cannot be the logical negation of (15). This is not to say that (14) is not the logical negation of any affirmative sentence at all. In point of fact, it is the logical negation of (17).

(17)   All of the guests signed the register.

But these two sentences do not show the same correspondence in form that we saw in our earlier pairs of affirmative sentences and their logical negations.

   Another negative sentence that would be difficult to describe as the logical negation of a positive sentence is that given in (18).

(18)   Many of the voters did not vote for Carter.

This might at first glance appear to express the logical negation of (19).

(19)   Many of the voters voted for Carter.

Yet we can prove, by the same kind of reasoning as in the previous paragraph, that the meanings of (18) and (19) are not related in this way. In particular, it is easy to imagine circumstances in which both sentences are true at the same time. For instance, if anything over 50 million counts as "many" for the purposes of this discussion, and if 75 million voters voted for Carter and 100 million did not, then both of the sentences would be true. In fact, it is not at all unusual to hear sentences like (20), where both propositions are asserted at the same time.

(20)   Many of the voters voted for Carter, but many of them did not.

If we really want a sentence expressing the logical negation of the original affirmative sentence, we need to resort to (21).

(21)   Not many of the voters voted for Carter.

15.3 The Notion of Scope and the Left-to-Right Rule

As a first step toward understanding how these various kinds of negative sentences are constructed and interpreted, let us consider exactly what the difference in meaning is between (18) and (21). We can get some idea of the difference by giving each one in turn a rather awkward paraphrase in which the meaning is divided between several clause levels, as in (22) and (23).

(22)   a.   Many of the voters did not vote for Carter.
        b.   For *many* of the voters,
                  it is *not* the case that
                      they voted for Carter.

(23)   a.   Not many of the voters voted for Carter.
        b.   It is *not* the case that
                  for *many* of the voters,
                      they voted for Carter.

In (22b), the bottom two lines express a negative proposition, which the top line claims is true for many of the voters. In (23b), by contrast, the bottom two lines express a proposition to the effect that something is true for many voters, which the top line negates.

Differences of this kind in the meanings of two sentences are traditionally referred to as differences of *logical scope*. In (22b), *many* has a more dominant position that *not*, and we say that *many* has "wider scope" than *not*. In (23b), on the other hand, *not* has a more dominant position than *many*, so that *not* has the wider scope here.

The pair of sentences (24) exhibits an exactly parallel difference in meaning.

(24) a.   Calvin often doesn't call us.
      b.   Calvin doesn't often call us.

Here the relevant paraphrases are those given in (25).

(25) a.   It is *often* happens that
                it is *not* the case that
                    Calvin calls us.
      b.   It is *not* the case that
                it is *often* happens that
                    Calvin calls us.

In (24a) the frequency adverb *often* has wider scope than *not*; in (24b) this relative scope is reversed, with *not* having the wider scope.

One final pair of examples, a rather surprising one, will prove useful when we try to fashion a coherent set of rules:

(26) a.   Many of the members were not contacted by Carol.
      b.   Carol did not contact many of the members.

Although active sentences and their corresponding passives usually do not differ in their meanings, we can perceive a clear difference between (26a) and (26b). This difference is made explicit in the following paraphrases:

(27) a.   For *many* of the members,
                it was *not* the case that
                    they were contacted by Carol.
      b.   It was *not* the case that
                for *many* of the members,
                    Carol contacted *them*.

Again the critical difference is a difference of relative scope. In (26a) wider scope is assigned to *many*, whereas in (26b) it is assigned to *not*.

Let us now look for a general rule that will correctly determine relative scope in specific examples. A helpful observation to make here is that in all three of the sentences in which *often* or *many* had wider scope, these words occurred to the left of *not*:

(28) a.   *Many* of the voters did *not* vote for Carter.
      b.   Calvin *often* does*n't* call us.
      c.   *Many* of the members were *not* contacted by Carol.

By contrast, in the three sentences in which *not* had wider scope, it occurred to the left of *many* or *often*:

(29)   a.   *Not many* of the voters voted for Carter.
       b.   Calvin does*n't often* call us.
       c.   Carol did *not* contact *many* of the members.

With these examples in mind, then, let us tentatively adopt the following rule:

(30)   **Left-to-Right Rule**: In determining the relative scope of quantity words and negatives, assign scope on the basis of the left-to-right position in the sentence, starting with wider scope for whatever is found on the left.

The effects of this rule can be seen in the way that it applies to the active-passive pair mentioned above:

(31)   a.   *Many* of the members were *not* contacted by Carol.
            Wide   Narrow
       b.   Carol did *not* contact *many* of the members.
                      Wide   Narrow

In each of the pairs of examples considered in the last few paragraphs, the two negative sentences contained identical quantity words or frequency adverbs. It is now time to turn our attention once again to pairs of sentences in which the quantity words are not the same, one being assertive and the other being nonassertive. An initial example is provided by (32).

(32)   a.   William *sometimes* does*n't* answer his mail.
       b.   William does*n't ever* answer his mail.

These two sentences can be broken down into paraphrases as in (33).

(33)   a.   It *sometimes* happens that
                 it is *not* the case that
                      William answers his mail.
       b.   It is *not* the case that
                 it *ever* happens that
                      William answers his mail.

The major puzzle posed by this pair of sentences is what makes *sometimes* a good choice in (32a) and *ever* a good choice in (32b). Here we are really returning to the question of the essential difference between assertives like *sometimes* and nonassertives like *ever*. With this pair of examples in hand, we might hazard the following guess at a rule for nonassertives:

(34)   **Nonassertive Rule**: Nonassertive words are used in situations in which they fall within the scope of a negation, i.e., situations in which they have narrower scope than some negative word.

This rule clearly provides an account of why the two sentences in (32) both sound acceptable with their differing frequency adverbs. Beyond that, however, it provides an explanation for the fact that we cannot replace *sometimes* in (32a) by *ever.*

(35) *William *ever* does *n't* answer his mail.

The Left-to-Right Rule dictates that *ever* should be assigned wider scope than *n't*; however, this assignment violates the Nonassertive Rule, which requires that *ever* have narrower scope than some negation.

As a matter of fact, we now have an explanation for our earlier observation concerning the impossibility of having *not* as part of the verb phrase along with a nonassertive subject. Consider the examples in (36).

(36)   a. *Anyone isn't sleeping in my bed.
       b. *Any zebras can't fly.
       c. *Anything hasn't happened to Bertram's optimism.

The left-to-right order of words in these sentences dictates that the nonassertive words should have wider scope than the negatives, but this scope assignment violates the Nonassertive Rule. By contrast, no problems arise with the sentences in which the subject contains the corresponding negative word:

(37)   a.   No one is sleeping in my bed.
       b.   No zebras can fly.
       c.   Nothing has happened to Bertram's optimism.

These negative words are interpreted as if they were compounds of *not* plus the corresponding nonassertive:

(38)   a.   no one = 'not anyone'
       b.   no = 'not any'
       c.   nothing = 'not anything'

Applying the Left-to-Right Rule to sentence (37a), with *no one* broken up into 'not anyone,' we get the following result:

(39)   *Not*   *anyone* is sleeping in my bed.
       Wide   Narrow

This assignment of scope satisfies the Nonassertive Rule, which here requires that *anyone* fall within the scope of some negative word. In similar fashion, sentences (37b) and (37c) satisfy both the Left-to-Right Rule and the Nonassertive Rule.

The combination of the Left-to-Right Rule and the Nonassertive Rule does not strictly forbid the appearance of nonassertives in subject position.

We might expect them to appear in this position in any situation in which some negative element preceded the subject of the sentence. As a matter of fact, there are at least three such situations in English.

The first of these occurs when we build a phrasal question out of a negative special-purpose verb. The following question introduced by *why* provides a good example:

(40) Why have*n't any* of the books been returned?

Because of the inverted order of subject and special-purpose verb in this question, the Left-to-Right Rule assigns *n't* wider scope, which is just what is needed if the occurrence of *any* is to be permitted by the Nonassertive Rule. By contrast, the use of *any* would not be possible in an answer for this question, since here the Left-to-Right Rule would assign wide scope to *any*:

(41) *Any of the books have*n't* been returned because the library is closed.

The second situation in which nonassertives are possible in subject position arises in connection with a special construction which deserves attention in its own right. In this construction, a negative noun phrase or adverb appears at the beginning of a sentence, with a blank element left in its place. In addition, we find the same kind of inversion of subject and special-purpose verb that is found in questions. Here are three examples:

(42) a. *Nothing* have I seen ___ that would rival the pyramids.
      b. *Never* has Ferguson ___ written a book that was more astonishing than his new novel.
      c. *Not often* do we discover such a fine artist ___.

When we substitute nonassertives for the subjects in these sentences, the results are completely acceptable:

(43) a. *Nothing* has *anyone* seen ___ that would rival the pyramids.
      b. *Never* has *anyone* ___ written a book that was more astonishing than Ferguson's new novel.
      c. *Not often* does *anyone* ___ discover such a fine artist.

In each of these three sentences, the nonassertive subject is preceded by the negative word in the sentence. Consequently, the Left-to-Right Rule gives the scope assignment that the Nonassertive Rule requires. On the other hand, if we put the words into normal order, the occurrence of the nonassertives to the left of the negatives gives unacceptable results:

(44) a. *Anyone has seen *nothing* that would rival the pyramids.
      b. *Anyone has *never* written a book that was more astonishing than Ferguson's new novel.

  c. *Anyone does not often discover such a fine artist.

The third situation in which nonassertives occur in subject position arises in complex sentences such as those in (45).

(45) a. Karen doesn't think [that anyone will find the ring].
   b. Nobody believes [that anything can be done].

In each of these sentences, the nonassertive word serving as the subject of the lower clause falls within the scope of a negative word found in the main clause.

15.4 Nonassertives with Other Negative Words

Besides such obviously negative words as not, no, never, and nobody, there are a number of words whose negative-like interpretation allows nonassertives within their scope. One group of these words includes hardly, scarcely, few, little, seldom, and rarely. As the sentences in (46) show, nonassertives behave with them just as they did with the more obvious negatives.

(46) a. Hardly any of the citizens ever say anything.
   b. * Any of the citizens hardly ever say anything.
   c. Hardly ever do any of the citizens say anything.

(47) a. Few of the citizens ever say anything.
   b. * Anything is ever said by few of the citizens.

(48) a. Little time has he ever spent with his family.
   b. *He has ever spent little time with his family.

As before, the sentences that are acceptable in these examples are those in which every nonassertive falls within the scope of a negative word, with scope being determined strictly by the Left-to-Right Rule.

  There is a second group of words whose essentially negative meanings license nonassertives within their scope. These are verbs and adjectives like doubt, deny, inconceivable, and unlikely, which allow nonassertives in their object and subject clauses:

(49) a. We doubt [that anyone will ever say anything].
   b. Richard denied [that anyone had ever offered him any money].
   c. It is inconceivable [that any of the papers will ever be found].
   d. It is unlikely [that the Cubs will ever win any championships].

Here it makes good sense to view the scope of these verbs and adjectives as being their clausal subjects and objects. Thus, the appearance of nonassertives in these new sentences falls under the Nonassertive Rule as that rule was originally stated.

Exercises

1. Explain briefly why the second sentence is more acceptable than the first:

> *I think that anyone ever reads this magazine.
> I doubt that anyone ever reads this magazine.

2. Explain why the second sentence is more acceptable than the first:

> *This book is ever given to few readers.
> Few readers are ever given this book.

15.5 Other Environments for Nonassertives

There are several other special circumstances that allow nonassertives to be used. In the first place, they are allowed in yes-no questions, both direct and indirect:

(50)　a.　Did *anyone ever* meet George?
　　　b.　We are trying to determine [whether *anyone ever* met George].

In the second place, they are found in various conditional clauses, including those introduced by *if*, *whenever*, and so on:

(51)　a.　[*If any* of you *ever* see *any* flying saucers], you should report them to Freddy.
　　　b.　[*Whenever anyone* sees *any* flying saucers], Freddy gets very excited.

Finally, nonassertives show up regularly in the comparative construction:

(52)　a.　Jones walked farther [than *any* members of the club had *ever* walked before].
　　　b.　Rachel made more saves [than *any* goalkeeper had *ever* made before].

Thus, the rule given earlier for nonassertives needs to be extended as in (53).

(53)　Nonassertive words may be used in situations in which they fall within the scope of a negative word, a conditional word, or a comparative.

Exercise

1. For each of the italicized nonassertives below, say what it is that allows it in the sentence.

    a.   If *any* of you did not get a questionnaire, Fred will send one to you.

    b.   Whether *anyone* will read Joe's article is unclear.

    c.   John tried to leave the house without disturbing *any* of his neighbors.

    d.   Few people believe that Joe's investigation will result in *any* indictments.

    e.   Only once did Clara detect *any* sign of life.

15.6 Exceptions to the Left-to-Right Rule

In the past two sections, the Left-to-Right Rule has formed an important part of our explanation for the way in which nonassertives and negative words behave when they occur together. Despite its importance, this rule does have two major exceptions.

The first of these exceptions comes to light when we try to give a rule to regulate the behavior of assertive words like *someone* and *something*. Earlier in this chapter we examined two sentences that contained assertives in company with negative words:

(54)   a.   *Some* of the guests did *not* sign the register.
              Wide   Narrow

       b.   William *sometimes* does*n't* answer his mail.
                    Wide   Narrow

We noted that these assertive words had wide scope in these sentences, a fact that would follow from the Left-to-Right Rule. All that we would need to say about the assertive words themselves would be that, unlike nonassertive words, they are capable of occurring outside the scope of a negation. However, something more needs to be said, as the examples in (55) show.

(55)   a.   John did*n't* eat *some* of his pie.
       b.   Horace did*n't* speak to *some* of his friends.

These examples are at least marginally acceptable, and they call for interpretations in which the *some*s have wider scope than the negatives:

(56)   a.   For *some* of his pie
               it is *not* the case that
                    John ate *it*.

b. For *some* of his friends
       it is *not* the case that
          Horace spoke to *them.*

Despite the fact that these interpretations violate the Left-to-Right Rule, they are the correct ones for the sentences in (55). These new examples thus suggest the existence of the following two rules:

(57)   Assertives are interpreted as having wider scope than negatives.

(58)   The Left-to-Right Rule may be relaxed for assertive words.

Two other words that sometimes violate the Left-to-Right Rule are the universal words *all* and *every.* Unlike the assertives, these two words are perfectly capable of appearing within the scope of a negation, as in (59) and (60).

(59)   a.   Thelma did*n't* sell *all* of her books.
       b.   It is *not* the case that
               for *all* of her books
                  Thelma sold *them.*

(60)   a.   George did*n't* write to *every* senator.
       b.   It is *not* the case that
               for *every* senator
                  George wrote to *him/her.*

In these two examples, the scope relations are exactly those dictated by the Left-to-Right Rule.

The problem comes with examples in which the universal precedes the negative. Such examples are quite rare in formal English but are not unusual in spoken English. Two are given in (61).

(61)   a.   *All* of the packages did*n't* arrive on time.
       b.   *Everyone* did*n't* sign Connie's birthday card.

The Left-to-Right Rule would dictate the following interpretations for these sentences:

(62)   a.   For *all* of the packages
               it was *not* the case that
                  they arrived on time.
       b.   For *everyone*
               it was *not* the case that
                  he/she signed Connie's birthday card.

But these interpretations require the same states of affairs required by the sentences in (63).

(63) a. *None* of the packages arrived on time.
      b. *No one* signed Connie's birthday card.

These are not generally the interpretations intended when speakers of English use sentences like those in (61). Instead, the intended readings would be those in (64), which are clear violations of the Left-to-Right Rule.

(64) a. It is *not* the case that
              for *all* of the packages
                  they arrived on time.
      b. It is *not* the case that
              for *everyone*
                  he/she signed Connie's birthday card.

To accommodate the examples in (61), then, we need to make note of another exception to the Left-to-Right Rule:

(65) The universal words *all* and *every* may fall within the scope of a negative word even when they occur to its left.

This possibility for *all* and *every* may be related to another odd fact about them: Although they are capable of standing by themselves without any negation in their environment, they do not like to be assigned wider scope than a negation in situations where a negation is present. *All* with wide scope plus *not* with narrow scope should mean exactly the same thing as *not* with wide scope plus *any* with narrow scope. But only the *not* + *any* combination is really acceptable in situations in which both should be possible. We see this contrast in acceptability in the following pair of sentences:

(66) a. ?**All* historians do *not* revere Benedict Arnold.
      b. Benedict Arnold is *not* revered by *any* historians.

Exercise

1. The following two sentences might be used to describe exactly the same situation:

> Popeye didn't eat some of his spinach.
> Popeye didn't eat all of his spinach.

At first glance, it might appear that these two sentences should not be equivalent in meaning, since *some* and *all* do not mean the same thing, and there is no other visible difference in the two sentences. Explain how it is possible for them to be equivalent.

Chapter 16
Conjunction and Ellipsis

In this chapter we will study two extremely important classes of English rules: the rules that form *conjoined structures* (in which two or more smaller structures of some single type are joined together to form a larger structure that is itself of the same type) and the *ellipsis rules* (which spell out the conditions under which it is permissible to delete material that is identical to material presented earlier). The ellipsis rules are presented in the same chapter with the conjunction rules because conjoined sentences provide excellent opportunities to study various ellipsis rules and because at least one important ellipsis rule applies only in conjoined structures.

16.1 Conjoined Structures

16.1.1 Basic Possibilities
Conjoined structures are formed with the help of the so-called coordinating conjunctions of traditional grammar. In English, these words are *and*, *or*, *nor*, and *but*. For our initial examples of conjoined structures, we will start with some joined together by *and*. These examples, which are given in (1), illustrate the variety of different types of phrases that can be linked by a conjunction.

(1)   a.   I believe that *Trudy is in Atlanta* and *Bob is in Houston*.
           (conjoined sentences)
      b.   Smith *hit the ball* and *ran to first base*.
           (conjoined finite verb phrases)
      c.   The baby seemed *very tired* and *somewhat cross*.
           (conjoined adjective phrases)
      d.   *John* and *the man from Houston* share the same surname.
           (conjoined noun phrases)

 e.   Fred seems to have been *tied up* and *left in the garage.*
        (conjoined passive phrases)
 f.   We saw many *students of chemistry* and *doctors of medicine.*
        (conjoined common noun phrases).

In each of these examples, not only do we have two phrases of the same type joined by *and*, but in addition the larger phrase so formed acts as if it is itself a phrase of the same type. For instance, in (1a) the entire structure made from two conjoined sentences combines with a preceding *that* to make a *that* clause. In (1b), two finite verb phrases are conjoined, and the larger structure so formed is doing something that a finite verb phrase can do: serving as the predicate of an independent sentence. A similar point can be made about each of the remaining examples in (1). These observations are summed up in (2).

(2)   If two phrases are of the same type, then they can be joined together by *and*, and the resulting phrase is also of the same type.

This preliminary rule gives us structures of the form illustrated in (3).

(3)
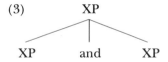

For examples (1a) and (1b), we have the following tree structures:

(4)   a.
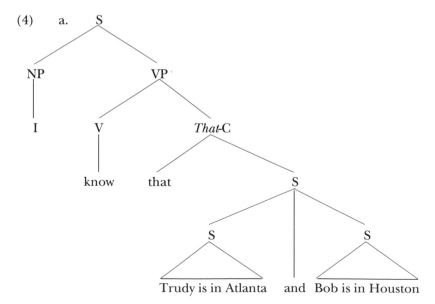

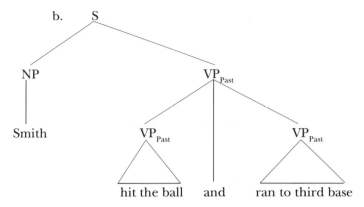

Now that we have a basic idea of how conjoined structures are built, let us look in more detail at the elements that can join their parts. We can illustrate the possibilities by examining the ways in which two adjective phrases can be joined:

(5) a. Joseph is [tired of Houston *and* eager to move back to Topeka].
     b. Joseph is [*both* tired of Houston *and* eager to move back to Topeka].
     c. Joseph is [tired of Houston *or* eager to move back to Topeka].
     d. Joseph is [*either* tired of Houston *or* eager to move back to Topeka].
     e. Joseph is [*neither* tired of Houston *nor* eager to move back to Topeka].

The same kinds of examples can be constructed with other types of phrases. General pictures of the possibilities are given in (6), where XP is again used as a symbol for a phrase of any type.

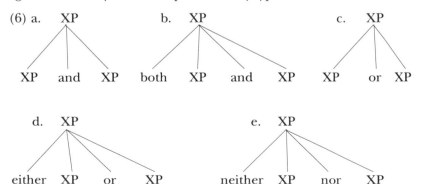

Each of these possibilities except for *both ... and* can work when there are more than two phrases being joined:

(7)   a.   Martha will [feed the cat *and* lock the door *and* turn off the lights].
      b.   * Martha will [*both* feed the cat *and* lock the door *and* turn off the lights].
      c.   Martha will [feed the cat *or* lock the door *or* turn off the lights].
      d.   Martha will [*either* feed the cat *or* lock the door *or* turn off the lights].
      e.   Martha will [*neither* feed the cat *nor* lock the door *nor* turn off the lights].

The failure of the *both ... and* combination can be attributed to the fact that *both* needs exactly two entities wherever it is used.

   The word *but* is somewhat more limited in its possibilities. It must join exactly two sequences:

(8)   a.   [Trudy is in Atlanta *but* Bob is in Houston].
      b.   Smith [hit the ball *but* failed to get to first base].
      c.   The baby seemed [quite energetic *but* somewhat cross].
      d.   We saw [many shrikes *but* no falcons].

(9)   a.   * [Trudy is in Atlanta *but* Bob is in Houston *but* Angela is in Dallas].
      b.   *Smith [hit the ball *but* failed to get to first base *but* kept on smiling].
      c.   *The baby seemed [quite energetic *but* somewhat cross *but* rather cooperative].
      d.   *Ted saw [many shrikes *but* no bluebirds *but* dozens of juncos].

The constraining factor here may not actually be syntactic in nature. A semantic condition on the acceptability of *but* structures is that the second conjunct must represent a clear reversal of expectation, given the first. Two successive reversals of expectation may simply be hard for listeners to keep track of. In what follows, then, we will assume that the difference in acceptability between two *and*s and two *but*s is attributable to a difference in the semantic properties of the two words, rather than to any difference in their syntax.

Exercises
1. In each of the following sentences, two sequences are joined to make a larger sequence of the same type. First decide what types of sequences are

conjoined, then draw a tree diagram for the sentence as a whole.

    a.   Gary is scrubbing the floors and repainting the woodwork.

    b.   Charles thinks that the king of England and his friends should write a book.

    c.   Bob wants Tony to keep the sweaters but return the books.

    d.   Martha has put chairs on the lawn and on the patio.

    e.   Neither Bruce nor his colleagues know how to restring a racket.

2. At first glance, it would appear that the two sentences below have virtually the same structure, differing only by the presence in the first of the word *that*:

    (i) Jones knows that Blake fries hamburgers and that Ali peels potatoes.

    (ii) Jones knows that Blake fries hamburgers and Ali peels potatoes.

A closer examination shows that the sequences that are joined in (i) are not of the same type as those that are joined in (ii). Draw tree diagrams for the two sentences that make the difference clear.

3. The following sentence is ambiguous:

    We know the men and the women know the children.

This ambiguity rests in part on the fact that the verb *know* is ambiguous and allows two different sorts of complements (noun phrases and clausal complements with omitted *that*). It also rests in part on the fact that several different kinds of sequences can be joined by conjunctions. Draw tree diagrams for the two different structures that this sentence can have.

4. Think of one or more sentences that show whether a past-tense verb phrase and a present-tense verb phrase count as "phrases of the same type" for the purposes of being conjoined. Then look for sentences that will answer the same question about bare-stem verb phrases and present-participial verb phrases after the verb SEE.

16.1.2 An Alternative Analysis of Conjoined Phrases

At this point, it might seem that a simpler analysis of conjoined structures is possible: one in which we conjoin sentences, and then optionally reduce them by keeping just one copy of the material in them that is the same in both conjuncts. For example, we would derive (10a) from (10b) by keeping just one copy of the two identical subjects and sharing it between the two conjuncts.

(10)   a.   Martha [fed the cat *and* locked the door].

            b.   [Martha fed the cat *and* Martha locked the door].

For another example, we would derive (11a) from (11b) by coalescing the two identical verb phrases into one.

(11) a. [Gordon *and* Shirley] missed the meeting.
      b. [Gordon missed the meeting *and* Shirley missed the meeting].

In each of the two cases given above, our analysis has the apparent virtue of deriving one sentence from a longer sentence that has exactly the same interpretation. Unfortunately, there are many instances in which deriving conjoined phrases in this way would require a source sentence whose meaning was quite different.

As a first example, sentence (12a) would have to be derived from (12b).

(12) a. Few people belong to the Assembly of God and drink bourbon.
      b. Few people belong to the Assembly of God and few people drink bourbon.

A moment's reflection reveals that these two sentences do not mean the same thing at all. In (12a) the claim is made that there are few people who belong to the Assembly of God and who at the same time drink bourbon, whereas (12b) claims that there are few people who belong to the Assembly of God and also that there are few people (not necessarily the same few people) who drink bourbon. We might represent these two different meanings as in (13).

(13) a. there are *few* people x such that (i) is true and (ii) is true:
          (i)   x belongs to the Assembly of God
          (ii) x drinks bourbon
      b. (i) is true and (ii) is true:
          (i)   there are few people x such that
                x belongs to the Assembly of God
          (ii) there are few people y such that
                y drinks bourbon

As these representations suggest, the difference in meaning between (12a) and (12b) is just a difference in scope, of the same general sort as the scope differences that we studied in chapter 15. The evidence provided by this scope difference is easier to account for if we derive conjoined verb phrases as such in their own right, rather than deriving them from conjoined sentences.

A problem of a different sort arises with conjoined subjects. Though it might not seem implausible to derive the conjoined noun phrase in (14a) from the conjoined sentence in (14b), a similar derivation is much less plausible for the conjoined noun phrases in (15a), (16a), and (17a).

(14) a. [Gordon *and* Shirley] missed the meeting.
      b. [Gordon missed the meeting *and* Shirley missed the meeting].

(15) a. [Joe *and* Billy] wear the same hat size.
      b. ? [Joe wears the same hat size *and* Billy wears the same hat size].

(16) a. [Hydrogen *and* helium] differ.
      b. ? [Hydrogen differs *and* helium differs].

(17) a. [Charles *and* Marie] embraced.
      b. ? [Charles embraced *and* Marie embraced].

The last three predicates all seem to be able to use conjoined subjects (in fact, plural subjects in general) in a way that treats them as a group rather than as separate individuals. Because of the existence of such predicates, we need to be able to create conjoined noun phrases directly, without deriving them from conjoined sentences. This is just what we did in our earlier analysis.

The two bodies of evidence considered above both provide arguments for maintaining the analysis with which we began this discussion rather than going to an alternative in which conjoined phrases are derived by way of conjoined sentences. For the remainder of this chapter, we will adhere to the original analysis and view conjoined phrases as just that.

16.1.3 Conjoined Sequences of Phrases
In addition to joining words or phrases with conjunctions, we may also join *sequences* of phrases. Three examples are given in (18).

(18) a. Martha went [to Austin] [on Thursday] *and* [to Dallas] [on Friday].
      b. We gave [doughnuts] [to Angela] *and* [cookies] [to Fred].
      c. Joe sent letters [to Greta] [yesterday] *and* [to Martha] [today].

In (18a), the two sequences *to Austin on Thursday* and *to Dallas on Friday* are clearly not single phrases, but instead are both sequences consisting of two phrases: a motion phrase followed by a time phrase. Likewise, *to Dallas on Friday* has to be analyzed as a sequence of two separate phrases rather than as a single phrase. A similar assessment holds for the two sequences *doughnuts to Angela* and *cookies to Fred* in (18b), and also for the two sequences *to Greta yesterday* and *to Martha today* in (18c).

For sentences of this sort, it is very difficult to suggest appropriate tree structures. We can get an idea of the problem by looking first at two plausible structures for the first conjunct in (18a):

(19)

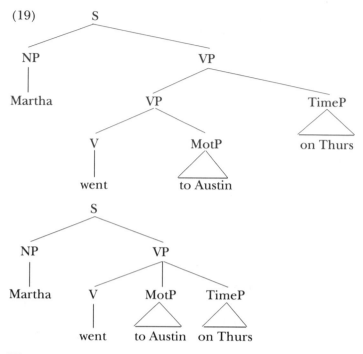

We can then consider the tree in (20) as representing the entire conjoined structure.

(20)

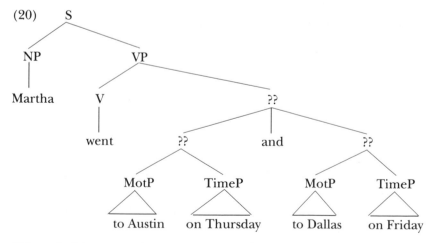

Although this tree conforms to our previous view that a conjunction such as *and* should join two phrases, the phrases in question are suspect. The reason is that in neither of the simple-sentence trees given in (19) do the motion phrase and the time phrase make up a larger phrase. Thus, the conjoined structure in (20) is not consistent with either of the simple-sentence structures in (19).

In sum, while the existence of sentences such as those in (18) needs to be acknowledged, there is currently no completely satisfactory analysis of these sentences within the general framework adopted in this book.

16.1.4 A Special Possibility for Conjoined Structures

A final kind of conjoined construction can be built from two conjoined sentences or phrases that end in an identical phrase on the right. Two such structures are shown in (21), with the shared phrase in each conjunct italicized.

(21)   a.   [[John likes *the night watchman*], but [Bill doesn't like *the night watchman*]].

      b.   Bob [[is married to *the Secretary of Transportation*], but [rarely eats lunch with *the Secretary of Transportation*]].

From such structures, we can extract the shared final phrase and put it at the right-hand end of the conjoined structure:

(22)   a.   [[John likes ___], but [Bill doesn't like ___]], *the night watchman*.

      b.   Bob [[is married to ___], but [rarely eats lunch with ___]] *the Secretary of Transportation*.

As the above examples show, there is a special comma punctuation used after each of the two conjoined nonidentical parts. These commas correspond to special intonation breaks in the spoken sentences.

For sentences like these, we will assume the sorts of structures illustrated in (23).

(23)   a.

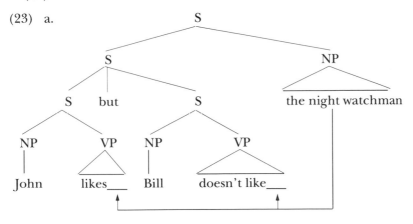

b.

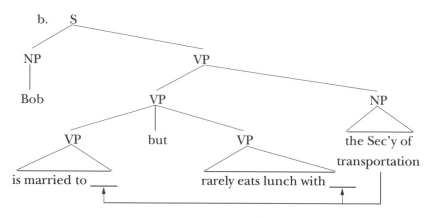

16.1.5 A Closer Look at Alternative Questions

In chapters 4 and 14, we had occasion to study a type of question closely related to yes-no questions. The indirect variety was exemplified by the sentence repeated here as (24a), and the direct variety by (24b).

(24)   a.   We want to know [whether John sued Karen or Karen sued John].
         b.   Did John sue Karen or did Karen sue John?

We are now in a position to consider these constructions in more detail.

Let us begin with the indirect question in (24a). We know that we have yes-no indirect questions beginning with *whether*. To such questions, exemplified in (25a), we assigned the structure shown in (25b).

(25)   a.   [whether Martha is leaving]
         b.

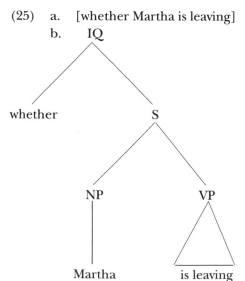

Suppose we also try to treat the indirect question in (24a) by the rule that analyzes it into *whether* and a following sentence. This step is possible now because we have made provisions for conjoined structures. Here is the structure that we would derive:

(26)

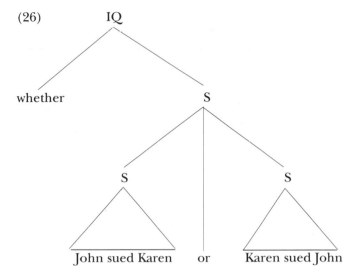

Now we might inquire as to whether alternative questions are possible in which sequences other than full sentences are joined together. As the following examples show, they definitely are.

(27) a. We want to know [whether you tried to hire [Martha *or* Harry]].
      b. Did you try to hire [Martha or Harry]?
      c. Sample answer: I tried to hire *Martha.*

(28) a. Please tell us [whether you consider him [reticent or arrogant]].
      b. Do you consider him [reticent or arrogant]?
      c. Sample answer: I consider him *arrogant.*

(29) a. George didn't say [whether he wanted Bill to [wash the windows first or sweep the floors first]].
      b. Did George want Bill to [wash the windows first or sweep the floors first]?
      c. Sample answer: George wanted Bill to *sweep the floors first.*

The general relation between question and alternatives can be seen with the help of diagram (30).

(30)

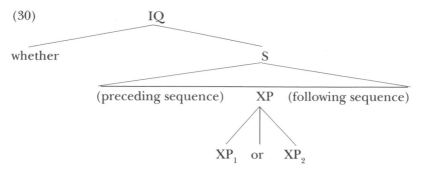

Here we have *whether* joined to a sentence that contains two smaller phrases of some type joined by *or*. We can calculate the two alternatives by leaving everything else in the sentence the same and replacing the conjoined phrase first by one of the smaller phrases and then by the other:

(31)   a.   (preceding sequence) XP$_1$ (following sequence)
        b.   (preceding sequence) XP$_2$ (following sequence)

Surprisingly enough, every one of the above *whether* questions has an additional interpretation in written English. Let us look again at the indirect question in (24a), which is repeated here as (32).

(32)   [whether John sued Karen or Karen sued John]

The interpretation that we have been assuming all along is one in which the question offers two alternative answers. However, it is also possible to interpret this as an indirect yes-no question. After all, sentence (33) is one that could be either true or false:

(33)   John sued Karen or Karen sued John.

On this interpretation, the question would have a positive answer if one or the other of the two sentences that made it up were true and a negative answer if neither were true.

We also get the same type of additional interpretation for (34).

(34)   [whether you tried to hire Martha or Harry]

On this second interpretation, this question has a positive answer if the conjoined sentence (35) is true and a negative answer otherwise.

(35)   You tried to hire Martha or Harry.

In spoken English, this ambiguity disappears by virtue of a sharp difference in intonation patterns. When we intend (34) as an alternative question, we put a sharply rising intonation at the end of the first conjunct and a sharply falling one at the end of the second:

(36)   [whether you tried to hire Martha or Harry]

By contrast, when we intend the same sequence of words as an indirect yes-no question, then the intonation is much flatter, falling slightly at the end:

(37)   [whether you tried to hire Martha or Harry]

One more fact about alternative questions, mentioned briefly in chapter 14, is that it is perfectly possible to give more than two alternatives:

(38)   a.   We want to know [whether you tried to hire [Martha or Harry or Katy].
        b.   Please tell us [whether you consider him [reticent or arrogant or indifferent]].
        c.   George didn't say [whether he wanted Bill to [wash the windows first or sweep the floors first or put away the chairs first]].

All of these, of course, have corresponding direct questions:

(39)   a.   Did you try to hire [Martha or Harry or Katy]?
        b.   Do you consider him [reticent or arrogant or indifferent]?
        c.   Did he want Bill to [wash the windows first or sweep the floors first or put away the chairs first]?

16.2 Ellipsis Rules

We now turn to an important class of syntactic rules that allow us to delete something that is identical to something else in the sentence or discourse. Such rules are generally called *ellipsis rules*. English has several important rules of this type. One of these rules, the first that we will discuss, applies only in conjoined sentences, whereas the other rules apply in a much wider variety of circumstances.

16.2.1 A Special Ellipsis Rule for Conjoined Sentences

The rule that applies specifically to conjoined structures has the effect of removing an identical middle part from sentences after the first in a series of conjoined sentences. Examples are given in (40) and (41).

(40)   a.   I *work* in a factory and Sam *works* in an office.
        b.   I *work* in a factory and Sam, in an office.

(41)   a.   Pete *must eat* meat, and Fred *must eat* bread.
       b.   Pete *must eat* meat, and Fred, bread.

We will refer to this rule as the *gapping rule*, and we can state it as follows:

(42)   When two or more sentences are joined together by conjunctions, and they are identical except for their subjects and a phrase at the end of the verb phrase, then the identical material can be optionally removed in all of the sentences after the first.

This rule can apply only when we have conjoined *sentences*. As (43) shows, there is even a contrast here between conjoined sentences and conjoined *that* clauses.

(43)   a.   Joe knows that [I *work* in a factory] and [Sam, in an office].
       b.   *Joe knows [that I *work* in a factory] and [that Sam, in an office].

In addition, the sentences to which this rule applies must be directly joined by *and*. That is, the rule cannot apply if either affected sentence occurs merely as a subordinate part of a conjoined sentence:

(44)   a.   [Pete likes meat], and I can guarantee that [Fred likes bread].
       b.   *[Pete likes meat], and I can guarantee that [Fred, bread].

(45)   a.   We had originally been told that [Sam nominated Pam], and we were later informed that [Willis nominated Phyllis].
       b.   *We had originally been told that [Sam nominated Pam], and we were later informed that [Willis, Phyllis].

The gapping rule does not work with words referred to in traditional grammar as "subordinating conjunctions," as (46) shows.

(46)   a.   Sam encouraged Pam because Willis encouraged Phyllis.
       b.   *Sam encouraged Pam because Willis, Phyllis.

The kind of unacceptable sentence given in (46b) provides us with one of many arguments for refusing to group these subordinating words together into a single class with the coordinating words *and, but, or,* and *nor.*

16.2.2 Long-Distance Ellipsis Rules

We turn now to a group of ellipsis rules that are much freer in their application. They can apply readily between conjoined sentences, and they can also apply in a variety of other circumstances. As one special case, they can apply between sentences uttered by two different speakers in a discourse. The formal property that unites them is that each specifies one or more left-hand contexts allowing deletion to take place.

16.2.2.1 Ellipsis after "Small Verbs," *To*, and *Not* The first such long-distance ellipsis rule is the one that allows for the deletion of the parenthesized material in the following sentences:

(47)   a.   John appears to be *fond of ice cream*, but I'm not sure that he really is (*fond of ice cream*).
   b.   We thought that Fred would be *working hard on the project*, but it turns out that he hasn't been (*working hard on the project*).
   c.   Whenever Martha has *drunk a beer*, Fred has (*drunk a beer*), too.
   d.   Carter said that he wouldn't *sign the bill*, but I bet that he will (*sign the bill*).
   e.   Martha once thought that George would soon be *the richest man in Texas*, but now it's doubtful that he ever will be (*the richest man in Texas*).

In each of the examples in (47), what we might refer to as a "small verb" serves as the left-hand context for the deleted material. These "small verbs" include forms of BE, perfect HAVE, and the modals. Deletions after the finite forms of the special-purpose verb DO constitute a special case of the same kind of ellipsis:

(48)   a.   Mabel *speaks French*, and Jerry *speaks French*, too.
   b.   Mabel *speaks French*, and Jerry does (*speak French*), too.

(49)   a.   Hal *perused the article*, and Nat *perused the article*, too.
   b.   Hal *perused the article*, and Nat did (*peruse the article*), too.

We can see how important these left-hand contexts are if we try to delete the same types of phrases when the left-hand contexts are not the same. Some illustrative unacceptable results are given in (50)–(53).

(50)   a.   John seems *fond of ice cream*, and Bill seems *fond of ice cream*, too.
   b.   *John seems *fond of ice cream*, and Bill seems ___, too. (deleted adjective phrase)

(51)   a.   Frank wanted Bill to *mow the lawn*, so we had him *mow the lawn*.
   b.   *Frank wanted Bill to *mow the lawn*, so we had him ___. (deleted bare-stem verb phrase)

(52)   a.   Beth believes that Fido should *go on a diet*, and we want to insist that the cat *go on a diet*, too.

b. *Beth believes that Fido should *go on a diet,* and we want to insist that the cat ___, too.   (deleted bare-stem verb phrase)

(53) a. Martha once thought that George would soon become *the richest man in Texas,* but now it's doubtful that he will ever become *the richest man in Texas.*

b. *Martha once thought that George would soon become *the richest man in Texas,* but now it's doubtful that he will ever become ___.   (deleted predicate noun phrase)

A similar kind of ellipsis is possible after the infinitive marker *to,* and also after an occurrence of *not* that accompanies a special-purpose verb:

(54) a. I'm not positive that John *knows the answer,* but he certainly seems to (*know the answer*).

b. If you ask Martha to *add your name,* I'm sure that she'll be glad to (*add your name*).

(55) a. James is *conscientious,* but Billy is not (*conscientious*).

b. Sandra will *read your reports,* but Harold will not (*read your reports*).

The above observations above are summarized in the following rule, which mentions specific neighboring elements.

(56) Optionally delete the second of two identical phrases if the second comes after one of the following elements:

(i)   BE
(ii)   perfect HAVE
(iii) modals
(iv)   special-purpose DO
(v)   the infinitive marker *to*
(vi)   a *not* associated with one of the verbs in (i)–(iv).

As was noted above, this particular rule is a "long-distance" ellipsis rule. The sentences in (57) show that the second occurrence of the phrase can be quite far away from the first.

(57) a. We were originally told that Sam had *nominated Pam,* but we were later informed that Willis had *nominated Pam.*

b. We were originally told that Sam had *nominated Pam,* but we were later informed that Willis had ___.

As a matter of fact, this pair of sentences is in all other respects very close in form to the pair given in (45), repeated here as (58).

(58)   a.   We had originally been told that [Sam nominated Pam], and
              we were later informed that [Willis nominated Phyllis].
        b.   *We had originally been told that [Sam nominated Pam], and
              we were later informed that [Willis, Phyllis].

Sentences (57b) and (58b) offer a striking demonstration of the difference between a long-distance ellipsis rule (ellipsis after a small verb) and
a "local" ellipsis rule (the gapping rule).

An ellipsis after a helping verb can actually occur not only within a single
sentence but also between two separate sentences uttered by different
speakers:

(59)   Speaker A: I'm not sure that Sheila has *read the poem*.
        Speaker B: It's clear that Martha has ___, though.

16.2.2.2 A Special Construction Involving Ellipsis after Special-Purpose
Verbs   English allows a special elliptical construction that we can treat as
an optional variant of the one just considered. Each of the (a) sentences
in (60)–(63) shows an ordinary ellipsis after a helping verb, while the (b)
sentences show the special new construction.

(60)   a.   David knows how much money was taken, and Bill does __, too.
        b.   David knows how much money was taken, and *so does Bill.*

(61)   Speaker A: Karen has exceeded the speed limit.

        Speaker B: { a. Bill has ___, too. }
                    { b. *So has Bill.* }

(62)   a.   James didn't erase the blackboard, and Bob didn't __, either.
        b.   James didn't erase the blackboard, and *neither did Bob.*

(63)   Speaker A: Nora won't remember the password.

        Speaker B: { a. George won't ___, either. }
                    { b. *Neither will George.* }

This new construction is described in terms of the old one in the following
rule:

(64)   a.   If a sentence has the structure
                    NP—special-purpose verb—*too,*
              then optionally substitute for it:
                    So—special-purpose verb—NP.

b. If a sentence has the structure
    NP—special-purpose verb + *n't*—*either,*
    then optionally substitute for it:
    Neither—special-purpose verb—NP.

One extra restriction must be put on this rule, as we can see by comparing the acceptable (b) examples in (60)–(63) with the unacceptable ones in (65) and (66).

(65) a. David knows how much money was taken, and I think that Bill does___, too.
      b. *David knows how much money was taken, and I think that *so does Bill.*

(66) a. George doesn't read Latin, and I am convinced that Joan doesn't ___, either.
      b. *George doesn't read Latin, and I am convinced that *neither does Joan.*

The restriction that we see here is one that limits the special *so* and *either* construction to independent sentences, or to independent sentences joined by conjunctions. What is specifically impossible is the use of this construction in complements and other subordinate clauses.

16.2.2.3 Ellipsis after Questioned Phrases   Another important ellipsis rule of English allows for the deletion of repeated material after a questioned phrase. This kind of ellipsis is found in direct questions:

(67) a. Speaker A: Someone is coming.
          Speaker B: *Who* (is coming)?
      b. Speaker A: McCarthy moved to Massachusetts.

$$
\text{Speaker B: } \left\{ \begin{array}{l} \textit{When} \\ \textit{Why} \\ \textit{How long ago} \end{array} \right\} \text{(did he move to Massachusetts)?}
$$

The same kind of ellipsis is also found in indirect questions:

(68) a. Someone is coming, but I don't know *who* (is coming).
      b. We know that McCarthy moved to Massachusetts, but we haven't been able to

$$
\text{determine } \left\{ \begin{array}{l} \textit{when} \\ \textit{why} \\ \textit{how long ago} \end{array} \right\} \text{ (he moved to Massachusetts).}
$$

A rule for this kind of ellipsis is stated in (69).

(69)   Optionally delete the part of the question that follows the ques-
        tioned phrase, if there is a sentence earlier in the discourse that
        duplicates the meaning of this second part of the question.

Does this kind of ellipsis occur only in questions, as rule (69) implies, or
does it apply generally in constructions introduced by *wh* phrases? The
contrast between an indirect question and an identical definite free
relative clause provides clear evidence that the former view is correct:

(70)   a.   John cooked something, but Betty didn't know [what John
             cooked].   (indirect question)
        b.   John cooked something, but Betty didn't know [what ___].

(71)   a.   John cooked something, but Betty didn't eat [what John
             cooked].   (definite free relative clause)
        b.   *John cooked something, but Betty didn't eat [what ___].

16.2.2.4 Ellipsis in Noun Phrases   A third kind of long-distance ellipsis in
English involves deletions that occur after one of a specified list of
elements that occur in noun phrases. This type of deletion is shown
in (72).

(72)   a.   Jack has two *pictures of Rockefeller Center*, and Martha has three
             (*pictures of Rockefeller Center*).
        b.   Many *animals* were saved, but many (*animals*) were lost.
        c.   Naturalist have spent many years searching for *ivory-billed
             woodpeckers*, but only a few (*ivory-billed woodpeckers*) have been
             sighted.
        d.   John's *house* is old, but Martha's (*house*) is new.

As is the case with these examples, the deleted material generally makes up
a common noun phrase. The left-hand elements that permit the deletion
include the numerals, quantity words (e.g., *some*, *many*, and *few*), and
genitive forms such as *John's* and *Martha's*.

For genitives that are related to pronouns rather than to full noun
phrases, we see the same kind of distinction that we observed in chapter
10. The examples in (73) show the differences.

(73)   a.   Karen read Bill's paper, and Bill read *my* paper (*mine* ___).
        b.   Nora fed her dog, and Danny fed *your* dog (*yours* ___).

In order to account for the elliptical versions of the above sentences, we
need to specify that what we earlier called the *strong genitive* be used as the
left-hand context for an ellipsis.

Exercise

1. For each of the following sentences, answer three questions:

    (i)   What types of phrases are conjoined? Are they single phrases, or sequences of phrases?

   (ii)   Has the "right-extraction" rule (described in subsection 16.1.4) applied?

  (iii)   Which ellipsis rules have applied, if any?

    a.   John should clean the shed, and Peter, mow the lawn.

    b.   I wanted to see your parents last week, but didn't get to.

    c.   George will, and Ruth might, take your course on dolphins.

    d.   They are able to make a contribution, but probably won't.

    e.   John could have been, but wasn't, watching his favorite program.

    f.   Brenda was the winner in 1971 and Robert in 1972.

    g.   Jack was given a railway set, and Jimmy, a baby giraffe.

    h.   It's cold in January in England but in July in New Zealand.

    i.   The suggestion made Alice angry and Marcia happy.

    j.   We discovered that John had been playing football and Alice, writing a letter.

    k.   George told us that he had discovered something interesting, but never told us what.

    l.   Several of John's jokes are as long as yours and as stale as Gordon's.

Chapter 17

Time Relations and Aspect

In this chapter we turn our attention to two additional sets of semantic rules for English. The rules in the first set affect our *temporal interpretations* of English sentences. The temporal interpretation of a sentence provides information about how the time of each state or event mentioned in the sentence is related to other times. The rules in the second group are concerned with what has traditionally been called *aspect*. The aspectual properties of a sentence determine the answers to such questions as whether a certain event happened just once or is repeated regularly, and whether a certain activity is to be viewed as completed at a certain time or as still going on. These two sets of rules are intimately related, in that we sometimes need to know the temporal interpretation of a given sentence before we can make a correct aspectual determination.

17.1 Time Relations

17.1.1 Temporal Interpretations of Simple Sentences.
We can begin our study of tense and time relations in English by looking at the time relations that are expressed in simple English sentences. At the beginning, what will be said will have the air of being so familiar that it hardly needs to be said at all. But in order to understand more complex and interesting cases, it is necessary to present some familiar examples in a clear light.

17.1.1.1 Temporal Relations Assigned by Individual Elements   Imagine that we hear the following sentences:

(1)   a.   Joseph was happy.
      b.   Joseph is happy.
      c.   Joseph will be happy.

Each of these sentences reports a state of being happy. When asked to consider each sentence in turn and say when the reported state was in effect, we might say that it was in effect in the past in (1a), in the present in (1b), and in the future in (1c). If we are pressed to say in more detail what we mean by these three familiar terms, we might begin by saying that all of them are understood with respect to the moment when the sentences are uttered. In what follows, we will refer to this basic point in time as *utterance time*. In (1a) the time of Joseph's understanding is earlier than utterance time, in (1b) it is identical with utterance time, and in (1c) it is later than utterance time. These relations are pictured in (2).

(2)

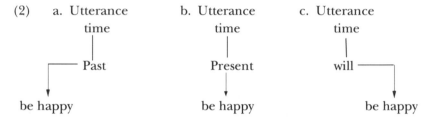

With examples like these in mind, we can give initial versions of general rules for interpreting past tense, present tense, and the modal *will*. Each of these rules will be an instruction concerning the way in which the time of an associated verb phrase is determined, and each of them will be accompanied by a diagram that expresses the rule in picture form. (For past tense and present tense, the "associated verb phrase" is just the verb phrase whose head is marked with the tense ending; for WILL, the "associated verb phrase" is the verb phrase that serves as a complement of WILL.)

(3)   Past tense can be interpreted as indicating that the time of the associated verb phrase is earlier.

(4)   Present tense can be interpreted as indicating that the time of the associated verb phrase is identical.

(5)   The modal WILL can be interpreted as indicating that the time of the associated verb phrase is later.

WILL ⌐————————⌐
                            ↓

In addition to these three basic linguistic elements, there are a number of other expressions which are interpreted as indicating a temporal relation. To begin with, the special verb USED takes complement infinitival phrases that express states or habitual actions and assigns to them an earlier time:

(6)   a.   John *used to* understand the problem.
      b.   Carol *used to* hang wallpaper.

(7)   USED indicates that the time of the associated infinitival phrase is earlier than the moment of utterance.

Another important temporal element is BE GOING, which gives us an extra way of assigning a time later than utterance time:

(8)   a.   John *is going to* leave for Europe tomorrow.
      b.   The weather *is going to* improve tomorrow.

(9)   The phrase *be going* plus infinitive is interpreted as assigning a later time to its associated verb phrase.

BE GOING ─────────────┐
                      ▼

Finally, we have three special constructions that can be interpreted as assigning a later time to a complement verb phrase:

(10) a.   John *is leaving* for Europe tomorrow.
      b.   John *is to* leave for Europe tomorrow.
      c.   John *leaves* for Europe tomorrow.

In constrast to the WILL and BE GOING constructions, these last three constructions are interpreted as "scheduled futures." We can see this most clearly when we try to use them to predict the future occurrence of an event that cannot really be scheduled. Meteorological events (raining, snowing, and so forth) fall in this category:

(11) a.   It will rain hard tomorrow.
      b.   It is going to rain hard tomorrow.

(12) a. ? It is raining hard tomorrow.
      b. ? It is to rain hard tomorrow.
      c. ? It rains hard tomorrow.

In each of the examples discussed so far, the relation of the time of a verb phrase to utterance time is expressed by some linguistic element that does not really do anything else in the sentence. We now turn to some examples of words whose contributions to the interpretation of a sentence are temporal and nontemporal simultaneously.

A first example is HOPE, a verb whose primary function is to denote a certain mental attitude. When we use this verb with a finite complement (a *that* clause), we find that it does not impose any temporal interpretation on what is hoped for. Instead, we are free to impose any of the three basic temporal relations on the complement by a choice of tense or modal within the complement itself, as in (13).

(13)   a.   John hopes that he *was* in the correct room. (earlier)
       b.   John hopes that he *is* in the correct room. (same time as)
       c.   John hopes that he *will be* in the correct room. (later)

By contrast, when we use this verb with an infinitival complement, the only possible interpretation is one in which the time of being in the correct room is *later*:

(14)   John hopes to be in the correct room.

Of the three sentences in (13), only (13c) is equivalent in meaning to (14). For this reason, we need the following temporal rule for HOPE:

(15)   HOPE assigns to its complement infinitival phrase a *later* time.

HOPE ─────────────┐
                  ↓

Other verbs that take infinitival complements have a different temporal effect. *Seem*, for instance, imposes an "identical" interpretation on its complement infinitival phrase:

(16)   John seems to be in the correct room.

Of the three sentences in (17), only the second is synonymous with (16).

(17)   a.   It seems that John *was* in the correct room.
       b.   It seems that John *is* in the correct room.
       c.   It seems that John *will be* in the correct room.

Thus, we need the following rule for SEEM:

(18)   *Seem* assigns its complement infinitival phrase an *identical* time.

SEEM
  ↓

The verbs HOPE and SEEM both insist on just one time assignment for their infinitival complements. With some adjectives, however, both "identical" and "later" times can be assigned to infinitival complements. CERTAIN provides a clear example:

(19) John is certain to be at home.

The three basic possibilities for finite clauses with CERTAIN are shown in (20), where it is indicated whether each can be paraphrased by (19).

(20) a. It is certain that John *was* at home.
          Cannot be paraphrased by (19).
      b. It is certain that John *is* at home.
          Can be paraphrased by (19).
      c. It is certain that John *will be* at home.
          Can be paraphrased by (19).

Thus, for CERTAIN the following rule is justified:

(21) CERTAIN can assign either an identical time or a later time to an infinitival complement.

Many English modals are similar to these verbs and adjectives in making a temporal as well as a nontemporal contribution to the interpretation of a sentence that contains them. The modal MAY, for instance, has several different nontemporal interpretations, one of which is 'possibility'. This is the interpretation that it has in the following two sentences:

(22) a. It may be raining in Mobile right now.
      b. It may be raining in Mobile tomorrow night.

These sentences show us that the MAY of possibility allows the time of its complement verb phrase to be either identical with or later than utterance time. The sentence in (23) shows that it clearly excludes an earlier event time.

(23) *It may be raining in Mobile yesterday afternoon.

For MAY, then, we need the following rule:

(24) MAY (under the interpretation 'logical possibility') assigns either an identical time or a later time to its complement verb phrase.

MAY (logical possibility)   MAY (logical possibility)⌐
        ↓   ↓

The modal MUST is another example of a word with several different senses, each one of which imposes a time relation on the complement verb phrase. One of the primary senses of MUST is something like 'logical necessity'. The sentences in (25) illustrate the kind of time interpretation that it imposes.

(25)   a.   It must be raining in Mobile right now.
        b. *It must be raining in Mobile tomorrow night.
        c. *It must be raining in Mobile yesterday afternoon.

These examples show that MUST is like MAY in excluding an 'earlier than' interpretation, but that it differs from MAY in that it also excludes a 'later than' interpretation. Thus, we need the following rule for the MUST of logical necessity:

(26)   MUST (under the interpretation of 'logical necessity') assigns an *identical* time to its complement verb phrase.

        MUST (logical necessity)
           ↓

On other interpretations, both MAY and MUST assign a later time. The interpretations in question are 'permission' (for MAY) and 'obligation' (for MUST):

(27)   a.   You may come to the meeting tomorrow (if you wish to).
        b.   You must come to the meeting tomorrow (whether you want to or not).

Other modals besides these two have time interpretations that vary according to which of their nontime interpretations we pick. To take one final example, we can observe a subtle distinction between a use of CAN indicating 'ability' and a use indicating 'possibility'. Along with this contrast goes a contrast in time interpretation. The 'ability' interpretation assigns an 'identical' time, whereas the 'possibility' interpretation assigns a later time. These facts are illustrated by the sentences in (28).

(28)   a.   Joe can do eighty pushups.   (ability)
        b. *He can't do eighty pushups at the end of next summer.
             (ability)
             (Compare: He won't be able to do eighty pushups at the end of next summer.)
        c.   Joe can return to his diet at the end of next summer.
             (possibility)

17.1.1.2 Combinations of Temporal Elements: The Time-Assignment Principle   We have now examined several English constructions in which a time of some sort is imposed on a verb phrase. In each of the particular example sentences considered so far, the relations such as 'earlier', 'identical', and 'later' have all been understood with respect to utterance time. When we look at slightly more complex examples, we see that the reference point with respect to which the basic time relations are calculated need not be utterance time. A good first example is provided by (29).

(29)   John hoped to win the election.

We have two basic intuitions about the temporal relations expressed in this sentence. The first is that the time of hoping to win is earlier than utterance time. The second is that the time of winning the election is later than the time of hoping, but not necessarily later than utterance time. There is a simple way to obtain this result from the rules that we have set up already. The past tense on HOPE pushes the hoping to an earlier time. When we then use HOPE's own rule and assign a later time to the winning of the election, we measure not from utterance time but from the time of hoping. The relations we want are expressed in diagram form in (30).

(30)

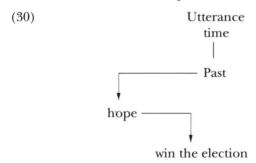

The general principles we have used here are stated in (31).

(31)   a.   When a rule assigns a time to a construction that serves as an independent utterance, it does so in relation to utterance time.

      b.   When a rule assigns a time to a complement phrase, it does so in relation to the time assigned to the larger phrase of which the complement is a part.

Principle (31a) serves to get a temporal interpretation started; principle (31b), which we will refer to as the *Time-Assignment Principle,* takes over once we move down past the first temporal assigner in a sentence.

Exercise

1. For each of the sentences given below, draw a time diagram indicating the temporal structure.

      a.   Florence is going to want to keep the notes. (Assume that WANT is like HOPE.)

      b.   George must intend to boycott the meeting. (Assume that INTEND is like HOPE.)

17.1.1.3 Perfect HAVE as 'Earlier'   We have seen above that a common means of expressing the 'earlier' relation is the past-tense inflection on a verb. As useful as the past tense is, there are several situations in English in which it cannot be used. As a first example, suppose that we want to use the modal *may* in a sentence in which we are asserting the possibility that it was raining yesterday. As was noted above, we cannot simply use *may* followed by *be raining*:

(32)   *It may be raining yesterday.

On the other hand, if we were to use *was* instead of *be*, we would violate the requirement that *may* be followed by a bare-stem verb phrase:

(33)   *It may *was* raining yesterday.

In situations of this sort, when English rules exclude the use of a past-tense verb, we have a second means of expressing the 'earlier' relation: use of *have* plus a past-participial verb phrase, as in (34).

(34)   It may *have been* raining yesterday.

Perfect HAVE substitutes for a forbidden past-tense form with a variety of other modals, and also in infinitival constructions:

(35)   a. *John should *took* the shirts to the cleaners yesterday.
       b. John should *have taken* the shirts to the cleaners yesterday.

(36)   a. *John must *took* the shirts to the cleaners yesterday.
       b. John must *have taken* the shirts to the cleaners yesterday.

(37)   a. *John might *forgot* to leave a message last Thursday.
       b. John might *have forgotten* to leave a message last Thursday.

(38)   a. *Harry appears to *took* the wrong bus last night.
       b. Harry appears to *have taken* the wrong bus last night.

(39)   a. *We believe Beth to *was* telling the truth this morning.
       b. We believe Beth to *have been* telling the truth this morning.

For this use of HAVE, we need the following rule:

(40)   HAVE can assign an earlier time to its complement past-participial
        verb phrase.

                                    HAVE

We can see how this rule for HAVE can be used with the other rules
proposed above by looking at the rather complex example (41).

(41)   Janet must have hoped to win the election.

By starting with utterance time and then using the rules for MUST, HAVE,
and HOPE in that order, we arrive at the diagram given in (42).

(42)   Utterance
                                   time

                                   must

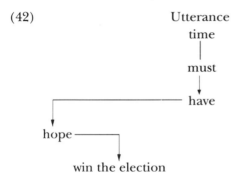

                                   have

                hope

                        win the election

The same use of HAVE occurs in the past-perfect construction found in
finite sentences:

(43)   a.   Joe had changed the oil just the day before.
        b.   Sue had payed for the ticket on the 20th.

Such sentences typically function as "flashback" sentences in discourses,
providing background information for the main narrative sequence. We
see an example of this function in the following simple discourse of three
sentences, where we have a past-perfect sentence sandwiched between two
past-tense sentences:

(44)   a.   Fred did not know why the oil light was flashing.
              (simple past tense)
        b.   The oil had been changed just three days ago.
              (past perfect)
        c.   He decided to stop at the Gulf station on his way home.
              (simple past tense)

In this discourse, two primary events are described (sentences a and c), both of them taking place on the same day. The sentence that occurs between them provides a description of a background event that occurred previously. The time of this background event is earlier than the time of the primary events, which are themselves earlier than the utterance time of the discourse. We can think of the past perfect as consisting of two parts: the past-tense inflection itself and HAVE. The past tense is interpreted as shifting the time of its verb phrase to an earlier time, typically the time of the primary events being narrated. We do not now have the option of using another past tense to shift the time even further back, since the rules of English word formation do not allow forms like *changeded* (CHANGE + Past + Past). Here HAVE makes its usefulness felt by imposing another shift in an earlier direction. By the rules suggested so far, then, we would derive the temporal structure given in (45b) for the past-perfect sentence in (45a).

(45)   a.   Martha had won the election.
       b.

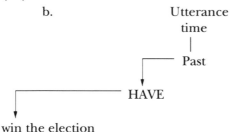

win the election

   The same use for perfect HAVE can be observed in certain situations that call for a present-participial verb phrase. One such situation is exemplified in (46).

(46)   Existing from week to week on bread and water, Joe is secretly fascinated with gourmet cooking.

Suppose that we want to indicate that the time of Joe's existing on bread and water was earlier than the time of his being fascinated with gourmet cooking. We cannot merely put an *-ing* suffix onto the past tense form *existed*, as in (47).

(47)   *Existeding* all through 1957 on bread and water, Joe is secretly fascinated with gourmet cooking.

Here, once more, perfect HAVE serves the desired purpose:

(48)   *Having existed* all through 1957 on bread and water, Joe is secretly fascinated with gourmet cooking.

Exercise

1. Draw time diagrams for the following sentences:
    a. Jones may have hoped to win the election.
    b. Jones had hoped to win the election.
    c. Maxwell seems to have promised to make the bed. (Assume that PROMISE imposes the same kind of time interpretation on its infinitival complement as HOPE does.)

17.1.2 The Time-Assignment Principle Applied to Finite Clauses

The preceding three subsections have provided a good working idea of how the relative positions of various times are determined in simple sentences, including those with nonfinite structures of various sorts. When we examine finite complements, we find the same interpretations for past-tense verbs, present-tense verbs, and modals. However, just as with the various time assignments calculated in the last several subsections, the time assignments imposed by tenses and modals in complements are generally understood in relation to the time of the larger phrase of which the finite complement forms a part.

To see how the temporal interpretation for a finite complement is calculated, imagine the following situation. It is now Monday, the day before an exam. We suspect that Joe will not come to the exam the next day, and we are already thinking about the excuse that Joe will make on Thursday for not having come to the exam. Here is a rough picture of the critical times involved in this situation:

(49)   Monday   Tuesday   Thursday
       (day we are talking)   (day of exam)   (day of Joe's excuse)

In this situation, we are entitled to utter the following sentence:

(50) Joe *will* tell everyone on Thursday that he *overslept* on Tuesday.

The main point of interest here is the interpretation of the past-tense form *overslept*. We clearly do not interpret it as earlier than the moment of utterance, since the time of the alleged oversleeping is in fact on the day after the moment of utterance. However, we can still view the past tense as expressing an 'earlier' relation. Instead of understanding this relation with respect to the moment of utterance, we need to understand it with respect to the time of the telling. Thus, (51) is the picture that we want for the temporal structure of this sentence.

(51)

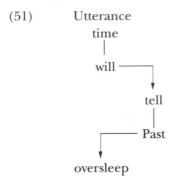

The absence of an arrow on the line below *tell* signifies that the verb does not impose any time assignment of its own on its finite complement but merely lends the complement its own time as a point of reference for interpreting whatever tense and modal forms the complement contains. In the present example, the past tense on *overslept* borrows the time of the telling and moves from that time to an earlier time.

A similar adjustment is required for interpreting present tense and *will* in the same context, as the following examples show.

(52)   a.   John will tell you on Thursday that he feels fine.
        b.   John will tell you on Thursday that he will write a letter.

In these examples, we again understand the time of John's telling as the reference point with respect to which the present tense and the *will* in the complements are interpreted. We interpret the present tense in the complement of (52a) as indicating a time identical with the time of telling. Likewise, we interpret the *will* in (52b) as indicating a time later than the time of telling. Here are the relevant diagrams:

(53)   a.   b.

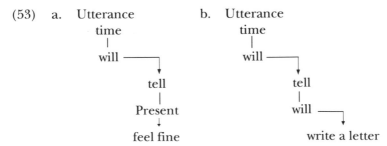

The basic principle governing the imposition of time assignments in complements is the same as that proposed above for nonfinite complements. We repeat it here as (54).

(54) **Time-Assignment Principle:** When a rule assigns a time to a complement phrase, it does so in relation to the time assigned to the larger phrase of which the complement is a part.

In the examples given above, this principle dictates that the time of each complement is calculated in relation to the time of the verb phrase headed by *tell* rather than in relation to utterance time.

It may be helpful here to observe an incidental effect of the Time-Assignment Principle as it operates in finite complements. In each of the examples considered above, the tense choice was exactly the same as the one that would have been found in the corresponding examples of quoted speech (often referred to as "direct speech"). We can see this parallel in (55)–(57). In each of these pairs, the first sentence contains reported speech and the second contains quoted speech:

(55) a. John will tell everyone on Thursday that he *overslept* on Tuesday.
 b. John will tell everyone on Thursday, "I *overslept* on Tuesday."

(56) a. Maxine will report that Joseph *feels* fine.
 b. Maxine will report, "Joseph *feels* fine."

(57) a. Martha will say tomorrow that she *will* write a letter.
 b. Martha will say tomorrow, "I *will* write a letter."

This parallel between the verb forms in quoted speech and the verb forms dictated by the Time-Assignment Principle for finite complements will give us a quick and efficient tool for recognizing situations where something beyond the Time-Assignment Principle is coming into play. Specifically, when we see pairs of examples in which the corresponding verb forms are not the same, we will know that the verb forms of the finite complements are not what would be predicted by the Time-Assignment Principle acting alone. In such cases, we will be led to look for some additional rule or principle.

Exercise

1. For each of the following sentences, draw a time diagram.
 a. Martha will want to know whether anyone called. (Assume that WANT imposes the same kind of interpretation on an infinitival phrase as HOPE does.)
 b. Fred is certain to say that he doesn't know the answer.

17.1.3 The English Past-Harmony Rule

In each of the examples in the preceding subsection, the main clause itself was in the future tense and contained the modal *will*, and the Time-Assignment Principle gave exactly the correct results by itself. Correspondingly, tense choice in finite complements turned out to be exactly the same as tense choice in quoted speech.

In many languages, the same degree of simple regularity is found when the main-clause verb is in the past tense. English is different in this regard, as we can see by comparing quoted speech and reported speech after the past-tense form *told*:

(58) a.   When I saw him two years ago, John told me, "I *am* enjoying my first-semester syntax class."
      b.   When I saw him two years ago, John told me that he *was* enjoying his first-semester syntax class.

(59) a.   John told me last April, "I *will* graduate in May" (but he didn't graduate after all).
      b.   John told me last April that he *would* graduate in May (but he didn't graduate after all).

Using nothing but the Time-Assignment Principle, we would have expected the following reported-speech sentences rather than those in (58b) and (59b):

> *When I saw him two years ago, John told me that he *is* enjoying his first-semester syntax class.
> *John told me last April that he *will* graduate in May (but he didn't graduate after all).

As a careful examination of the diagrams in (60) will show, the Time-Assignment Principle yields perfectly reasonable temporal structures for these two unacceptable sentences.

(60)

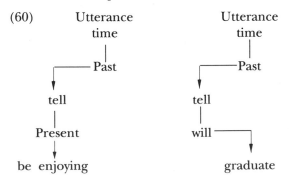

Thus we see that in past-tense contexts the tense choices depart from what the Time-Assignment Principle would lead us to expect.

17.1.3.1 Differences between Expected and Occurring Verb Forms   We have just seen two pairs of sentences in which there is a difference between the verb form of a direct quotation and the verb form in the corresponding finite complement. Some additional examples in which there is a contrast are given in (61)–(63).

(61)   a.   Yesterday afternoon, Dewey said, "Dora *hears* something in the chimney."

   b.   Yesterday afternoon, Dewey said that Dora *heard* something in the chimney.

(62)   a.   Karen said, "William *is* going to attend the meeting," but in the end he didn't.

   b.   Karen said that William *was* going to attend the meeting, but in the end he didn't.

(63)   a.   Last night at the play, Fred said, "Nelda *can't* see the stage."

   b.   Last night at the play, Fred said that Nelda *couldn't* see the stage.

The contrasts that we have found are listed in the following table:

(64)

Predicted by Time-Assignment Principle	Actually occurring
hears	heard
is	was
will	would
is going	was going
can't	couldn't

The difference between the predicted forms and the actually occurring forms is just that the latter look like past-tense forms whereas the former look like non-past-tense forms. In the cases of *hears* vs. *heard*, *is* vs. *was*, and *is going* vs. *was going*, we see clear examples of a simple contrast between present tense and past tense. The *will-would* contrast and the *can-could* contrast may be treated in the same way. That is, contrary to the analysis of chapter 2, we have grounds here for analyzing *would* as the past-tense form of *will* and *could* as the past-tense form of *can*. Thus, where the Time-Assignment Principle would lead us to expect a present-tense form, we simply find the corresponding past-tense form. In what follows, the actually occurring forms will often be called "past-harmonic versions" of the expected forms. So, for instance, we would say that *heard* is the past-harmonic version of *hear(s)*, that *would* is the past-harmonic version of *will*, and so on. More generally, we can give the following rule:

(65)   The past-harmonic version of a non-past-tense verb form is just the corresponding past-tense form.

There is one more unexpected form of complement verb that can be induced by a past tense. Consider the following sentence:

(66)   Yesterday John told me "I returned the book on Tuesday."

The temporal situation in this sentence is diagrammed in (67), where the quotation marks indicate quoted speech.

(67)

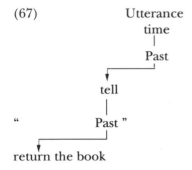

The main clause here has a past event time, and this past event time itself serves as a reference point for the 'earlier than' relation of the event time in the complement. One relatively informal way of expressing this message in reported speech is the following:

(68)   Yesterday John told me that he returned the book on Tuesday.

Here the verb in the complement is the same as that in the corresponding direct quotation in (66). The above statement about a correspondence between expected non-past-tense forms and actually occurring past-tense forms would not be relevant here, since the expected complement verb is already past. Leaving the quoted-speech form unchanged gives a result that is correct for this variety of English. However, in a more formal variety of English the same content would be expressed by a sentence containing a past-perfect form in the complement:

(69)   Yesterday John told me that he *had returned* the book on Tuesday.

This additional sentence thus requires us to add that where the Time-Assignment Principle would call for a past-tense form, we find instead a past-perfect form. In other words, the past-harmonic version of a past-tense form is a past-perfect form.

One particular word of English has no past-harmonic version and thus cannot be used in complements of past-tense sentences. The word is the modal *must*, as we can see when we try to report a past utterance of the sentence in (70a).

(70)   a.   Yesterday Ann said, "Karen must finish the paper within two hours."

      b.   *Yesterday Ann said that Karen must finish the paper within two hours.

The problem here is that *must* does not have a past-tense form. That is, there is no word in English that does for *must* what *was* does for *is* or what *would* does for *will*. The strategy that English speakers use when they are faced with situations of this sort is to look for some verbal element that means the same thing and that does have a corresponding past-tense form. In the case of *must*, a natural choice is *have to*:

(71)   a.   Yesterday Ann said, "Karen *has* to finish the paper within two hours."

      b.   Yesterday Ann said that Karen *had* to finish the paper within two hours.

17.1.3.2 Formulation of a Past-Harmony Rule   In the preceding subsection, we focused exclusively on determining the past-harmonic versions of various English verb forms. We need to turn back now to the question of the exact circumstances under which these forms are induced.

In each of the examples given in the preceding paragraphs, it is an actual past tense on a verb such as SAY or TELL that forces the use of past-harmony forms in the complements below it. As it happens, the past tense does not necessarily have to appear on these verbs of saying, as we see in the following examples:

(72)   a.   Rachel *intended* to tell us, "I *won't* be able to attend the meeting."

      b.   Rachel *intended* to tell us that [she *wouldn't* be able to attend the meeting].

(73)   a.   John *hoped* to be able to say, "Peter won't swallow any more goldfish."

      b.   John *hoped* to be able to say that [Peter *wouldn't* swallow any more goldfish].

(74)   a.   Karen *used* to tell us, "Cornelius *doesn't* know what he *is* doing."

      b.   Karen *used* to tell us that [Cornelius *didn't* know what he *was* doing].

With regard to the sentences in (74), it is reasonable to classify the special form *used* as a past-tense form even though there is no corresponding present-tense form that we can point to.

Beyond past tenses, though, there is one additional word that induces exactly the same past-harmony effects in complement clauses. This is the perfect HAVE, in its 'earlier' interpretation:

(75) a. Mary seems to *have* told Fred, "John *will* attend the party."
      b. Martha seems to *have* told Fred that [John *would* attend the party].

Taken as a group, examples (72)–(75) suggest that past-harmony effects in complements are induced whenever there is an 'earlier' time assignment associated with a phrase higher up, whether this 'earlier' shift is expressed by a past-tense form or by perfect HAVE.

A single 'earlier' element high up in a structure can make its presence felt all the way down through a chain of finite complements. Some idea of the extensiveness of this effect can be gained by noting the difference between the tenses found in the quoted speech in (76a) and those found in the corresponding reported speech in (76b).

(76) a. Phyllis *wanted* to tell Arthur, "John *doesn't* think that he *will* ever find out whether anyone *knows* when his baggage *will* arrive."
      b. Phyllis wanted to tell Arthur that [John *didn't* think that he *would* ever find out whether anyone *knew* when his baggage *would* arrive].

Here it is the past-tense form *wanted* that induces the past-harmony effects, and it induces them all the way down into the lowest complement, with no help from any other 'earlier' shift along the way.

With all of the preceding discussion in mind, we are now in a position to give a comprehensive formulation of the Past-Harmony Rule:

(77) **Past-Harmony Rule:** In the portion of a temporal structure that lies below an 'earlier' element, replace every form predicted by the Time-Assignment Principle with its corresponding past-harmonic form.

This rule says, in effect, that a past-tense form or a HAVE makes the entire structure below it a "past-harmony domain" in which changes of the indicated type must take place. This domain can easily be expressed graphically. The diagrams in (78) represent the temporal structures of the two sentences with which we began our discussion.

(78)   a.   John told me that he *was* enjoying his first-semester syntax course.

        b.   John told me last April that he *would* graduate in May.

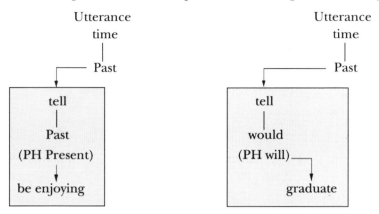

Here the shaded areas indicate the borders of past-harmony domains, and "PH Present" and "PH will" stand for past-harmonic versions of present tense and *will.*

Exercise

1. For each of the following sentences, draw a time diagram:
     a.   George seems to have thought that Bill would win the competition.
     b.   We were sure that Carol would insist that David was competent.
     c.   George will assume that Fred forgot that Susan was in Toledo.
     d.   Carol must know that Ralph told Frank that Alice would feed the monkeys.
     e.   Jane should have realized that George did not understand the problem.

17.1.3.3 Usurpation and the Nonapplication of the Past-Harmony Rule
There is one special group of situations in which the past-harmony rule does not apply. Under special circumstances, the past time of some lower clause can be "usurped" by a nonpast time from the clause above it. To see a concrete situation of this sort, we can begin by looking at the example of quoted speech in (79).

(79)   John *told* me on Sunday, "Marsha *doesn't* like the plan."

By the rules that we have developed, the corresponding reported-speech sentence would be contained in a past-harmony domain:

(80)   John *told* me on Sunday that Marsha *didn't* like the plan.

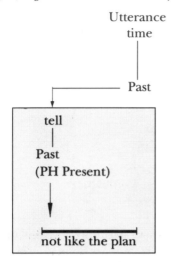

Yet under certain circumstances, we can also report this utterance of John's as in (81).

(81)   John *told* me on Sunday that Marsha *doesn't* like the plan.

Our intuition about this sentence is that Marsha's not liking the plan is a state of affairs that exists not only at the time when John is speaking but also at utterance time. The temporal structure of sentence (81) is represented in (82).

(82)

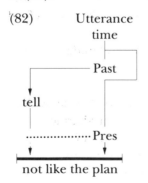

The essential ideas expressed in (82) are the following: The state of not liking the plan extends far enough through time to include utterance time as well as the earlier time of telling. In this situation, utterance time can usurp the rights of the left-hand branch of the temporal structure. Time relations of complements are then calculated with respect to utterance time rather than with respect to the time of telling. A major consequence is that the verb of the complement does not show any past-harmony marking, since it is no longer connected to an 'earlier' shift in the structure above it.

In the situation that we described with sentence (81), the state of not liking the plan extended from at least the time of John's speaking through utterance time. Had this state of affairs terminated before utterance time, then usurpation would not have been possible, and the past-harmony rule would thus have been applied. We can see the impossibility of usurpation here by adding something to sentences (80) and (81) to indicate that Marsha changed her mind at some point between John's speech and our speech:

(83)   a.   *John *told* me on Sunday that Marsha *does* not like the plan, but she seems to have changed her mind.
       b.   John *told* me on Sunday that Marsha *did* not like the plan, but she seems to have changed her mind.

The corresponding picture here is that given in (84).

(84)

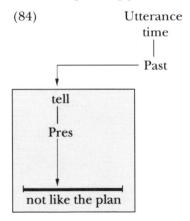

In this situation, the relation to the time of telling ('identical') is different from the relation to utterance time ('earlier'). Thus, the utterance time cannot usurp the 'earlier' branch in this diagram as it did in the case where the time of not liking the plan had a longer span. The 'earlier' branch remains dominant, and thus a past-harmony domain is created.

A similar possibility for usurpation arises in connection with events that are later than utterance time as well as later than the time of telling. Suppose that it is now Wednesday, and that the Monday and Friday in (85) are in the same week.

(85)   On Monday John told me "I will come to the meeting on Friday."

If we express this as reported speech and do not take the option of having utterance time usurp, we get sentence (86).

(86)   On Monday John *told* me that he *would* come to the meeting on Friday.

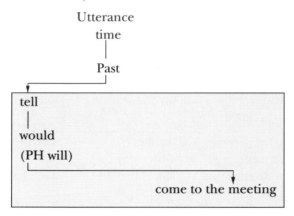

On the other hand, if we do take the usurpation option, we get sentence (87), with the temporal structure shown.

(87)   On Monday John told me that he will come to the meeting on Friday.

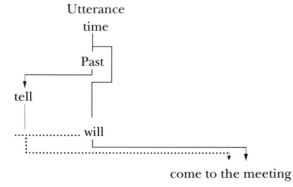

Again, as with the structure in (82), we no longer have conditions that create a past-harmony domain. As a consequence, the complement contains *will* instead of *would*.

Exercises

1. Draw time diagrams for the following sentences:
      a.   John said that George will find a solution.

    b.   Barbara told us that Harry will claim that he didn't think that he would see the letter.

2. Study the following pair of sentences:
    (i)   John said that he will come to the picnic, and I'm sure that he will come.
    (ii)   * John said that he will come to the picnic, and I'm sure that he did come.

Explain as clearly as you can why the first one is acceptable and the second one is not.

17.1.4 Special Uses of Present Tense and Past Tense

In the subsection just concluded, we saw a clear case of a complication in the relationship between syntactic tense marking and semantic temporal relation. In particular, we saw instances of past tense that were not interpreted as 'earlier' but instead were interpreted as past-harmonic versions of present tense. There are several additional situations in English in which syntactic past-tense and present-tense markings do not have their ordinary interpretations. The purpose of this subsection is to provide a quick survey of these situations.

17.1.4.1 Present with 'Later' Interpretation: Temporal Clauses   One important situation of this type is illustrated by the sentences in (88), each of which contains a subordinate clause serving as a temporal modifier.

(88)   a.   [Before Aaron *leaves* for Akron tomorrow], Joe *will* introduce him to you.
        b.   [After the party *is* over], Fred *will* drive Sam to the airport.
        c.   [When Sue *arrives* at the airport], someone *will* give her a ticket.
        d.   [While Marsha *is* interviewing Fred], you *will* be interviewing Alice.

In each of these sentences, the main clause contains the verb *will*, which indicates that the time of the accompanying verb phrase is later than utterance time. By contrast, none of the adverbial subordinate clauses contain *will* or any other verb imposing a shift in a later direction. Yet we understand the event reported in each of these clauses as occurring later than utterance time. For these cases, then, we need the following special rule:

(89)   If a present-tense sentence occurs in a clause introduced by a temporal word (*before, after, when, while*), and if the main clause has a future interpretation, then the present tense can be given the interpretation 'later'.

17.1.4.2 Present with 'Later' Interpretation: Conditional Clauses We find additional instances of present tenses with future interpretations when we look at subordinate clauses that have a conditional interpretation. The most obvious examples are clauses introduced by *if*:

(90) a.   [If Geraldine *asks* us to help her], we *will* call you.
      b.   [If I *am* not here when you call], Dorothy *will* write down your message.

However, there are many other examples of the same sort in which the conditional meaning, though less apparent, is no less real:

(91) a.   [Whoever *crosses* the line first] *can* adopt this orphaned rabbit.
           (*If X* crosses the line first, *X* can adopt this orphaned rabbit; likewise for *Y* and so on.)
      b.   We *will* award the prize to the person [who *submits* the best essay].
           (*If* person *X* submits the best essay, we will award the prize to *X*; likewise for person *Y* and so on.)
      c.   [Whether or not Shirley *agrees* with tomorrow's vote], she *should* abide by the decision of the group.
           (*If* Shirley agrees with tomorrow's vote, she should abide by the decision of the group; *if* she does not agree with it, she should still abide by the decision of the group.)
      d.   Bill *is going* to be difficult to work with during the summer, [no matter how many new employees are hired next month to help him].
           (Bill is going to be difficult to work with during the summer *if* *X* employees are hired; likewise *if* *Y* employees are hired, and so on.)

These examples require us to add the following rule:

(92) If a present-tense form occurs in the subordinate part of a conditional sentence or in a subordinate clause that is understood in a similar way, and if the main clause is in the future tense, then the present-tense form can be given the interpretation 'later'.

17.1.4.3 Past-Tense Forms Interpreted as Present-Tense: Hypothetical Conditionals Let us turn now to an additional situation in which past-tense forms are interpreted as if they were in the present tense. This situation involves what are often referred to as "hypothetical" conditionals, which are closely related in meaning to the ordinary conditionals of the sort that we examined above. Sentence (93a) is an ordinary conditional, and sentence (93b) is a hypothetical conditional that has the same temporal interpretation.

(93)   a.   If you *miss* class tomorrow, you *will* not hear Professor Grant's elucidation of Hugo's metaphors.

       b.   If you *missed* class tomorrow, you *would* not hear Professor Grant's elucidation of Hugo's metaphors.

Despite the differences in their verb forms, the two sentences in (93) share identical temporal structures, with both the subordinate clause and the main clause moving toward the future. To the extent that there is any difference in meaning, it is in a greater feeling of hypotheticality about (93b). These observations suggest that the past-tense form in the subordinate clause is to be interpreted as a hypothetical version of the present-tense form. Furthermore, since the present-tense form in a conditional can have a 'later' interpretation, we now have an explanation for the fact that the past-tense verb can come to assign a 'later' relation to the verb phrase to which it is attached. The steps in the interpretation are summarized in (94).

(94)   a.   A past-tense form can be interpreted as the 'hypothetical' version of the present-tense form.

       b.   A present-tense form, in the subordinate clause of a conditional, can be interpreted as 'later'.

It is also necessary to state rules for the verb forms that can occur in the main clause of a hypothetical construction. In (93b) we saw *would*, itself a past-tense form of *will*. The two other possibilities are *could* and *might*:

(95)   a.   If Alfred *wanted* to leave after midnight, he *could* catch a ride with Mark.

       b.   If Alfred *wants* to leave after midnight, he *can* catch a ride with Mark.

(96)   a.   If you *went* to the station early, you *might* catch a glimpse of the senator.

       b.   If you *go* to the station early, you *may* catch a glimpse of the senator.

We have just noted the use of special hypothetical verb forms in what we have referred to as "hypothetical" contexts. Now we need to say something more about what a hypothetical context actually is. We can get some important clues by examining the longer discourse in (97).

(97) If John *decided* not to return next year, we *would* have several problems. When we *went* to the president to ask permission to replace him, we *would* have to argue in writing that the position *needed* to be filled. After we *received* permission, we *would* need to find an acceptable replacement. The replacement that we *hired* *would* find a great deal of rebuilding work to be done.

This discourse begins with a subordinate clause introduced by *if*. This clause asks us to imagine that a certain future event (John's deciding not to return next year) has materialized. In the remainder of that sentence, and in all the sentences that follow, consequences of that imaginary future event are spelled out. The past-tense forms throughout the discourse indicate that the original supposition is still being assumed.

In order to calculate the time relations in (97), we use exactly the same rules that we used for individual hypothetical sentences. We take each past-tense verb to be a hypothetical version of a corresponding present-tense verb, and each *would* to be a hypothetical version of *will*. The effect of these rules is to make the time relations in (97) exactly like those in the nonhypothetical discourse (98).

(98) If John *decides* not to return next year, we *will* have several problems. When we *go* to the president to ask permission to replace him, we *will* have to argue in writing that the position *needs* to be filled. After we *receive* permission, we *will* need to find an acceptable replacement. The replacement that we *hire* *will* find a great deal of rebuilding work to be done.

The present tenses in this nonhypothetical discourse are interpreted as follows:

(99) a. *decides*: present tense in a conditional, interpreted as 'later'
b. *go*: present tense in a temporal clause, interpreted as 'later'
c. *needs*: present tense in a complement clause, interpreted as 'same time'
d. *receive*: present tense in a temporal clause, interpreted as 'later'
e. *hire*: present tense in a clause understood as an implicit conditional, interpreted as 'later'.

Thus, the past-tense forms in the hypothetical discourse in (97) get exactly the same temporal interpretations, once we apply the simple rule that says to treat them as special versions of present-tense forms.

17.1.4.4 Past-Tense Forms Interpreted as Present-Tense: Counterfactual Conditionals We turn now to a second type of conditional that induces some special verb forms. Conditionals of this new type are defined by the fact that the speaker presupposes the proposition expressed in the *if* clause to be false. Here are some examples:

(100) a.   If you *lived* in Dallas now, you could drive home in half a day.
            (Presupposition: You *do* not live in Dallas now.)
       b.   If Joe *knew* how to sing, he would have a job at the Metropolitan Opera.
            (Presupposition: Joe *does* not know how to sing.)

Again, as was the case with hypothetical conditionals, we see past-tense verbs receiving a time interpretation that in simple sentences is expressed with present-tense verbs. Thus, in both of the sentences in (100) the past-tense form appears to express counterfactuality rather than the 'earlier' relation, and the rule that we need to state here is that the past-tense form can serve as the "counterfactual" version of the present-tense form.

When we want to have a counterfactual clause in which an 'earlier' relation is imposed, we go a step further and resort to the past-perfect construction:

(101) a.   (Presupposition: You *were* not here yesterday.)
            If you *had been* here here yesterday, you would have met Marsha.
       b.   (Presupposition: You *did* not see the movie last night.)
            If you *had seen* the movie last night, you would be laughing, too.

Thus, in counterfactual *if* clauses, past-perfect forms are interpreted as counterfactual versions of ordinary past-tense forms.

The verb forms that we find in the main clauses of counterfactual conditionals are *would* and *could* as special versions of present tense, and *would have* and *could have* as special versions of past tense:

(102) a.   If Geraldine suspected that the money had been spent, she *would* be upset.
       b.   If there weren't so many clouds in the sky, you *could* see the mountains from here.

(103) a.   If Geraldine had suspected that the money had been spent, she *would have* been upset.
       b.   If there hadn't been so many clouds in the sky, you *could have* seen the mountains from here.

Just as was true of hypothetical conditionals, a counterfactual conditional may create a "counterfactual context" in a larger discourse. The discourse in (104) provides an example.

(104) If Jacob *lived* in Boston, he *would* go to watch the Boston Celtics several times each week during the winter. When the Celtics *won* he *would* celebrate, and when they *lost* he *would* weep. Every winter, the money that he *paid* for tickets *would* add up to several hundred dollars.

We can get some idea of the way in which these verb forms correspond to noncounterfactual forms by imagining the form that a comparable discourse would take if Jacob did live in Boston:

(105) Since Jacob *lives* in Boston, he *goes* to watch the Boston Celtics several times each week during the winter. When the Celtics *win* he *celebrates*, and when they *lose* he *weeps*. Every winter, the money that he *pays* for tickets *adds* up to several hundred dollars.

In this discourse, the present-tense forms are interpreted not as 'later' but as 'same time'. This is likewise the interpretation of the corresponding past-tense forms in the counterfactual discourse (104).

In every sentence discussed so far in which a counterfactual presupposition came into play in a sentence or a discourse, it arrived as part of a conditional sentence. English provides another major means for initiating counterfactual discourses, which is illustrated by (106):

(106) a. Joe *returned* that book. We wish that he *hadn't* returned it.
      b. Janice *doesn't* live in Texarkana. Caleb wishes that she *did* live there.

As a matter of fact, noncounterfactual complements are unacceptable with *wish*:

(107) a. *We wish that Joe *didn't* return that book.
      b. *Caleb wishes that Janice *lives* there.

Just as with counterfactual *if* clauses, a counterfactual complement of *wish* may introduce an entire counterfactual discourse:

(108) Caleb wishes that Janice *lived* in Texarkana. She *would* be able to get messages to his parents, and the replies that they *sent* through her *would* give him an idea of how well they *were* getting along.

Again, we can compare this discourse with one in which Janice's living in Texarkana is not contrary to fact:

(109) Caleb is glad that Janice *lives* in Texarkana. She *is* able to get messages to his parents, and the replies that they *send* through her give him an idea of how well they *are* getting along.

One small addition needs to be made to our statements about counterfactual forms: In the vast majority of cases, the counterfactual version of a present-tense verb is just the corresponding past-tense form. However, under certain circumstances, the counterfactual version of *am* and *is* is *were* rather than the expected *was*. These circumstances are illustrated in (110).

(110) a. If I *were* (*was) you, I would be happy about the outcome of the election.
   b. If he *were* (?*was*) here now, he would be objecting to everything that we are doing.
   c. If I *were* (*was) to raise an objection, I would be overruled.

These occurrences of *were* are little more than frozen relics of an earlier "subjunctive" form that was once used in counterfactuals. They are less natural than *was* when the subject is something other than a pronoun, and they are totally impossible when they appear outside of the immediate vicinity of the *if*:

(111) a. If the book that Connie wrote *was* (?*were*) still in print, we would assign it to our students.
   b. If someone lived in the house now, whoever it *was* (*were) would have many unwelcome problems with termites.

Our general rule, then, will be that *was* is the counterfactual version of *am* and *is*. We will then add a very narrow special rule to say when *were* is called for instead:

(112) Use *were* as a replacement for the counterfactual form *was* when it is the main verb of a clause introduced by *if*. This replacement is obligatory in the expression *if I were you* and is preferable in the case where the subject is a pronoun. The degree of acceptability falls when the subject is not a pronoun. When used in some other way than as the main verb in the *if* clause, the normal form *was* must be used.

Exercises
1. Below are two sentences with the past-tense form *went*. Say what the single common interpretation is for the past tense here.
   (i) John *went* home early.
   (ii) If John goes home early tomorrow, Bill will tell everybody the next day that John *went* home early.

2. Below are two more sentences containing a past-tense verb form.
   (i) If Joe *lived* in Boston, he would be skiing instead of playing
        tennis.
   (ii) If Joe *lived* in Boston, he must know about the swan boats.
These two past-tense forms are not interpreted in the same way. How is
each one interpreted, and how do you knew which interpretation to
assign?

17.1.5 Two Additional Uses for HAVE

As we have seen, the HAVE + past participle construction is often used to
express the 'earlier' relation, particularly in circumstances in which no
past-tense inflection is possible or in circumstances in which the past tense
expresses something else. This construction is also used with two other
interpretations. These interpretations can be seen most clearly in the
present tense of the perfect construction.

The first use is illustrated in (113).

(113) a.   Joe has lived in Austin for sixteen years.
       b.   The Smith brothers have sold groceries since 1968.

Both of these sentences assert that a certain state of affairs has existed for
a period of time that begins at some point in the past and goes up to and
includes the moment of utterance. This interpretation is represented
graphically in (114).

(114)   Utterance
               time

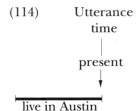

For this situation, neither the simple present tense nor the simple past
tense is appropriate. With the present tense, the results are simply
unacceptable:

(115) a. *Joe lives in Austin for sixteen years.
       b. *The Smith brothers sell groceries since 1968.

If we use the past tense instead of the perfect HAVE in (129a), we get an
acceptable sentence as a result:

(116) Joe lived in Austin for sixteen years.

However, this sentence is appropriate only if Joe no longer lives in Austin—that is, if the state being referred to has ended by the moment of utterance. Sentence (116), then, would have to be represented as in (117).

(117)   Utterance
                          time

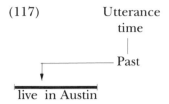

live in Austin

If we try to replace the present perfect in (113b) by the past tense, the result is again ill-formed:

(118) *The Smith brothers sold groceries since 1968.

The unacceptability of (118) can be analyzed as arising from a conflict between the past tense (which puts the state of affairs completely in the past) and the phrase *since 1968* (which means 'from 1968 to the present time'). Thus, this use of the present perfect is one that is not duplicated in English by either the present tense or the past tense.

The second additional interpretation for the present perfect is illustrated in (119).

(119) a.   Joe has written you a letter today.
       b.   Kasparov has asked for a postponement.
       c.   Marsha has accepted the position.

At first glance, these sentences might appear to have the same 'earlier' interpretation as the occurrences of HAVE that we saw in the examples of subsection 17.1.1.3. In particular, it might seem that these sentences are interpreted in exactly the same way as the corresponding sentences containing past-tense forms in place of the present-perfect forms:

(120) a.   Joe wrote you a letter today.
       b.   Kasparov asked for a postponement.
       c.   Marsha accepted the position.

A careful examination of many examples, however, indicates that the present perfect is much more restricted than either the simple past tense or the nonpresent forms of perfect HAVE. The following three-sentence sets illustrate some of the situations in which there is a clear contrast in acceptability:

(121) a.   Alice finished her dissertation yesterday.
      b.   Alice must have finished her dissertation yesterday.
      c. *Alice has finished her dissertation yesterday.

(122) (asked at some point after Truman's death)
      a.   Did you ever talk with Truman?
      b.   Should you ever have talked with Truman?
      c. ? Have you ever talked with Truman?

(123) (asked of a person who has nearly been run down by a reckless
      driver who immediately left the scene)
      a.   Did you see the guy's license number?
      b.   Shouldn't you have seen the guy's license number?
      c. ? Have you seen the guy's license number?

(124) a.   Did you hear that explosion?
      b.   Shouldn't you have heard that explosion?
      c. ? Have you heard that explosion?

What all the inappropriate (c) examples in (121)–(124) have in common can be made clear if we make use of a new concept, which we can call the "potential period of occurrence" of a certain kind of event. It will be useful to contrast (119c), one of the acceptable present perfects, with (124c), one of the unacceptable ones. In (119c), the type of event with which the statement is concerned can roughly be referred to as "Marsha's accepting the position." The period during which such an event could occur presumably includes part of the past, but also extends to the present and beyond. We can diagram this potential period of occurrence as a rectangle that begins at some point in the past and includes utterance time. Making the statement in (119c), then, involves the claim that an event of this type actually did occur prior to the moment of speaking:

(125)   Utterance
                            time

                          Present

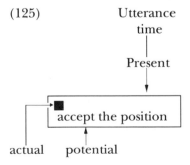

What is important here is that the potential period of occurrence for this event includes the moment of utterance.

The situation with regard to (124c), where the central event is "your hearing that explosion," is quite different. Here the potential period of occurrence is extremely short and actually terminates before the moment of utterance

(126)   Utterance
                            time
                             |
                          Present
                             |
                             ▼

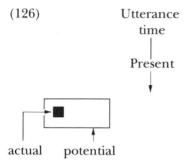

actual   potential

The strangeness of the present perfect here can be explained by noting the failure of the potential period of occurrence to include the moment of utterance. For reasons that vary from one example to another, the inappropriateness of the present perfects in (120)–(123) can be explained in the same way.

It is worth paying particular attention to the way in which this account of the present perfect excludes adverbs like *yesterday* while allowing *today*. Let us look again at the two examples above in which this difference shows itself:

(127)   Joe has written you a letter today.

(128)   *Alice has finished her dissertation yesterday.

In the first of these examples, the event is "Joe's writing you a letter today"; the period during which this event could occur includes the moment of utterance, since this latter point falls within the boundaries of the time period designated by today. In the second example, the event is "Alice's finishing her dissertation yesterday." The potential period of occurrence for this event is the period designated by *yesterday*, a stretch of time that fails to include the moment of utterance.

We see the same contrast in another light when we examine a time adverb like *this morning*, comparing its behavior in a past-tense context and in a present-perfect context:

(129) a.   Joe wrote you a letter this morning.
       b.   Joe has written you a letter this morning.

In (129a), we can understand the time adverb *this morning* as referring either to a time period that includes the moment of utterance or to a time period that ended earlier the same day. In (129b), only the first of these interpretations is possible. Thus, (129b) would be an appropriate utterance at 11:30 A.M. but not at 2 P.M. This limitation on the present perfect in (129b) follows from our requirement that the potential period of occurrence for the event "Joe's writing you a letter this morning" include the moment of utterance.

These two special interpretations of the present-perfect construction are sometimes available for a single sentence, so that the sentence is ambiguous. Consider (130).

(130) Joe has stood on his head for thirty seconds.

On one interpretation, this sentence can be understood as asserting that a certain action has been going on from some moment in the past up to and including the time of speaking:

(131)   Utterance
                           time
                            |
                         Present
                            ↓
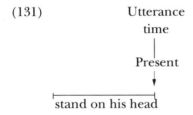
stand on his head

On the other interpretation, this sentence says something about a certain kind of event—"Joe's standing on his head for thirty seconds." The potential period of occurrence includes the moment of utterance, and the sentence asserts that at least one event of this type took place prior to the moment of speaking:

(132)   Utterance
                                           time
                                            |
                                         Present
                                            ↓
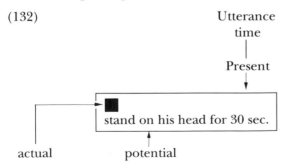

actual   potential

The ambiguity of this sentence thus provides evidence that these two interpretations really are distinct, and are not merely special cases of a more general rule of interpretation.

We have now studied in some detail the two interpretations that are possible for the present-tense form of the perfect HAVE construction. Are these same two interpretations available for the other forms of the perfect HAVE construction? In the case of the first special interpretation—that involving a period of time beginning in the past and continuing up through the moment of speaking—the answer is clearly Yes. Evidence for such an interpretation is provided by sentences such as those in (133).

(133) a. Jane may have lived in Austin since 1968.
b. Having lived in Austin since 1968, George knows many people at City Hall.

With regard to the second interpretation—that requiring a potential period of occurrence that extends through the moment of speaking—it is harder to give a clear answer. What we need for a clear test is a verb phrase that sounds more natural in present-perfect form than in simple past form.

Verb phrases containing the adverb *yet* appear to be slightly more acceptable in the present perfect than in the past tense, at least in fairly formal English:

(134) a. John hasn't opened the letter yet.
b. ? John didn't open the letter yet.

We can take this as a small piece of evidence that the word *yet* does not go well with an 'earlier' interpretation. When the *have* construction appears in bare-stem form with a modal, the *yet* is perfectly acceptable:

(135) John may not have opened the letter yet.

Sentence (135), then, provides a small piece of evidence in favor of the view that the bare-stem HAVE construction, like the present-tense form of HAVE, allows the interpretation involving a potential period of occurrence.

To summarize, the perfect HAVE construction has a total of three separate interpretations. In each of the forms except the present perfect, all three interpretations are possible. In the present perfect, by contrast, the 'earlier' interpretation that is shared with the simple past tense is not available. This restriction is one of the more troublesome for foreign learners of English to master. Given the 'earlier' interpretation found in nonfinite perfects like (136) and past perfects like (137), it is natural to believe that (138) should be possible as well:

(136) a.   John must have completed his studies in May.
       b.   John appears to have completed his studies in May.
       c.   John regrets having completed his studies in May.

(137)   John had completed his studies in May.

(138)   *John has completed his studies in May.

This restriction against using the present form of the perfect HAVE construction to mean 'earlier' is the major restriction to be remembered in connection with this construction.

17.2 Aspect

So far in this chapter, our concern with time has been restricted to time *relations*—that is, to the manner in which the times of various events in sentences were related to the time of utterance and to other times. In the present section we turn to *aspectual* properties of sentences, which involve a completely different way of looking at time. Subsection 17.2.1 provides an initial idea of what is meant by an aspectual property. In subsection 17.2.2 four basic aspectual classes of verb phrases are distinguished. The rules in which these distinctions play a role are set forth in subsection 17.2.3.

17.2.1 The Nature of Aspect

When we examine the aspect of a sentence, we stop looking at the relations between the time of an event or state and some other time and focus on the way in which the event or state itself, considered in isolation, spreads out in time. The difference between the temporal relations expressed in a sentence and the aspectual properties of the sentence can be illustrated with the help of two pairs of examples.

Examples (139a) and (139b) exhibit different time relations but the same aspectual structure.

(139) a.   Joan wrote a sonnet.
       b.   Alfred will eat a peach.

Joan's writing a sonnet and Alfred's eating a peach are placed in different positions relative to the time of utterance by virtue of the past tense in the first sentence and the modal WILL in the second. However, the aspectual properties of these two sentences are exactly the same. Both assert the existence of an event that progresses through a series of intermediate stages and has a natural endpoint. In (139a) the natural endpoint occurs when the fourteenth line of the sonnet is written down; in (139b) the natural endpoint is when the last bite of the peach disappears. If we justified the truth of these two sentences by showing movies of them, we would see these successive stages quite clearly as both the unwritten portion of the sonnet and the uneaten portion of the peach got smaller. Both the differing relational properties and the identical aspectual properties of these sentences are captured in (140).

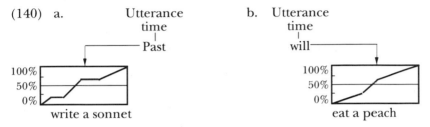

(140) a. Utterance time — Past — write a sonnet
b. Utterance time — will — eat a peach

Here we have represented the aspectual structure of the two verb phrases by showing a graph of the portion of the task that has been completed at successive times, with 0 percent at the beginning of the interval and 100 percent at the end of the interval.

Our second pair of examples consists of two sentences that exhibit identical time relations (both being earlier than the time of utterance) but quite different aspectual properties:

(141) a. Joan wrote a sonnet.
b. Roger had a rash.

As noted already, sentence (141a) asserts the existence of an event that progresses through a sequence of stages to a natural endpoint. Sentence (141b), by contrast, asserts the existence of a certain state, one that does not involve an idea of steady progression or successive stages. Although Roger's doctor might as a matter of fact notice different stages associated with Roger's rash, there is nothing inherent in the meaning of the sentence that would imply such a succession. These similarities in time relations and differences in aspectual properties are summarized in diagram form in (142).

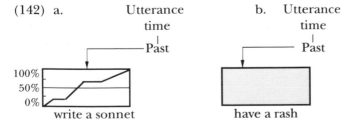

(142) a. Utterance time — Past — write a sonnet
b. Utterance time — Past — have a rash

At first glance, aspectual properties of sentences may seem much more subjective than the time relations that were the topic of discussion in section 17.1. Yet there are several important kinds of English rules in which aspectual properties of sentences play a definite role:

- rules governing the appearance of certain aspectual adverbials
- rules governing the interpretation of time adverbs
- rules governing the availability and interpretation of the simple present tense
- rules governing the availability and interpretation of the progressive construction (BE plus present-participial verb phrase).

In subsection 17.2.3 we will discuss these rules in detail. Meanwhile, though, we can get an initial glimpse of the kinds of differences involved, using just the two verb phrases in (141). Here are some contrasting examples that show the effects of these four kinds of rules:

(143) a. ? Joan wrote a sonnet *for fifteen minutes*. (The *for*-phrase adverbial is unnatural.)
       b. Roger had a rash *for three days*. (The *for*-phrase adverbial is natural.)

(144) a. When Sam arrived for a visit, Joan wrote a sonnet. (The time of writing the sonnet follows the time when Sam arrived.)
       b. When Sam arrived for a visit, Roger had a rash. (The time of having the rash includes the time when Sam arrived.)

(145) a. *Joan writes a sonnet. (The simple present tense is unacceptable.)
       b. Roger has a rash. (The simple present tense is acceptable.)

(146) a. Joan is writing a sonnet. (The progressive is acceptable.)
       b. *Roger is having a rash. (The progressive is unacceptable.)

17.2.2 Four Basic Aspectual Classes

This section will introduce four major aspectual classes. Distinguishing these four classes will greatly simplify the job of stating the rules that account for the kinds of contrasts that we saw immediately above. Intuitive descriptions and a few examples will be given here. Then, in the natural course of studying the rules in which these classes play a role, we will develop some experimental tests that will help us to determine what class a given verb phrase belongs to.

17.2.2.1 States The first aspectual class is the class of *states*. Some examples of sentences that report states are given in (147).

(147) a. Roger had a rash.
     b. Karen felt happy.
     c. Jonah owned a horse.
     d. Fred's grandfather weighed two hundred pounds.
     e. This tree is dead.
     f. Thor has a tumor on his toe.
     g. Nora liked the book.

As was noted above, states characteristically are interpreted as being rather uniform throughout an interval; consequently, they do not have natural endpoints. In addition, they generally do not involve any action on the part of their subject.

17.2.2.2 Activities The aspectual class consisting of activity sentences is one whose members, at first glance, look very much like states. Here are some examples:

(148) a. Karen talked to Martha.
     b. Jonah pestered the cat.
     c. Mavis snored.
     d. Martin wandered around.

As their name implies, activities are in general more "active" than states. However, they are similar to states in not having any natural endpoints. For instance, there is no point at which an episode of "talking to Martha" would necessarily come to a conclusion, as "eating a peach" would have to.

17.2.2.3 Accomplishments The next aspectual class of verb phrases is generally referred to by the term *accomplishment*. In contrast with states and activities, accomplishments have natural endpoints. We have already seen two examples of accomplishment verb phrases: *write a sonnet* and *eat a peach*. Other accomplishment verb phrases occur in the following sentences:

(149) a. Ron peeled the carrot.
     b. Jody repaired the toaster.
     c. Dorothy built a house.
     d. Heifetz performed the Third Partita.
     e. Georgia wrote a sonnet.
     f. A man traveled from Jerusalem to Jericho.

In each of these, there is also a definable endpoint for the event denoted by the verb phrase: the point at which the carrot is completely peeled, the point at which the toaster works again, the point at which the house is finished, and so on.

17.2.2.4 Achievements   The final aspectual class of verb phrases consists of achievements. Verb phrases of this class are like accomplishment verb phrases in having a clear natural endpoint. Yet, as we will see more clearly below, they differ from accomplishments in attaching much greater importance to the endpoint than to any earlier point. Several examples are given in (150).

(150) a.   Linda finished her thesis.
      b.   Joel arrived at the meeting.
      c.   Fred's goldfish died.
      d.   Carol got to Boston.

17.2.3 Rules in Which the Aspectual Classes Play a Role

In (143)–(146) we got a glimpse of the effects of several rules in which aspectual properties of sentences play a role. Having identified the four major aspectual classes, we are now in a position to undertake a more systematic examination of these rules.

17.2.3.1 Rules Concerning Aspectual Adverbial Phrases   Two kinds of adverbial phrases are commonly used to indicate the duration of a state or event. One kind is headed by *in*, the other by *for*.

As a preliminary matter, we need to observe that phrases such as *in four minutes* can be used in two distinct ways, only one of which is relevant in what follows. These phrases can indicate how long a certain event goes on, or they can indicate how long it is before a certain state or event begins. Both readings are possible in the following ambiguous sentence:

(151) Roger Bannister will run a mile in four minutes.

On one reading, the sentence means that the task of running a mile will require four minutes from start to finish. On the other reading, the sentence means that the running of the mile is scheduled to begin four minutes after the moment of utterance. The former interpretation is aspectual in nature, having to do with the time internal to the event itself, whereas the latter interpretation is relational, having to do with the time of the event relative to another time. In what follows, we will be interested exclusively in the aspectual interpretation.

We turn now to the matter of primary concern. *In* phrases are most acceptable in situations in which natural endpoints exist (accomplishments and achievements):

(152) a. Ron peeled the carrot $\begin{Bmatrix} \textit{in three minutes.} \\ \textit{?for three minutes.} \end{Bmatrix}$ (accomplishment)

     b. Linda finished her thesis $\begin{Bmatrix} \textit{in three months.} \\ \textit{?for three months.} \end{Bmatrix}$ (achievement)

By contrast, *for* phrases are most natural in situations in which such endpoints do not exist (states and activities):

(153) a. Roger had a rash $\begin{Bmatrix} \textit{for three days.} \\ \textit{?in three days.} \end{Bmatrix}$ (state)

     b. Karen talked to Martha $\begin{Bmatrix} \textit{for thirty minutes.} \\ \textit{?in thirty minutes.} \end{Bmatrix}$ (activity)

The above discussion affords a practical dividend that merits special attention: The differing hospitality to *for* phrases and *in* phrases provides an effective means for distinguishing between activities and accomplishments. For instance, suppose that we want to determine the class membership of the following two sentences.

(154) a. Simon treated Roger's rash.
     b. Simon healed Roger's rash.

When we add aspectual adverbials of these two kinds to the two sentences, we get a clear result:

(155) a. Simon treated Roger's rash for three weeks (*in three weeks).
     b. Simon healed Roger's rash in three weeks (*for three weeks).

We conclude from this experiment that treating Roger's rash is an activity, whereas healing Roger's rash is an accomplishment.

Applied to a variety of verb phrases, this test yields some surprises. In particular, we find many examples in which two verb phrases are headed by the same verb but nevertheless have to be placed in different classes. One group of examples is illustrated in (156) and (157).

(156) a.   Brenda *drove to San Francisco* in an hour (*for an hour).
      b.   Brenda *drove toward San Francisco* for an hour (*in an hour).

(157) a.   Gordon rowed two miles in an hour (*for an hour).
      b.   Gordon rowed for an hour (*in an hour).

The contrast between (156a) and (156b) derives from the fact that only in the former is a specific goal attained. Similarly, (157a) asserts that a definite distance was covered, whereas (157b) does not. These examples, then, can be accounted for by the following rule:

(158) Motion verb phrases in which a definite goal is reached or a definite distance is covered count as accomplishments, whereas motion verb phrases in which neither of these conditions holds count as activities.

   The examples in (159)–(162) illustrate another contrast between accomplishment and activity.

(159) a.   Freddy *ate a pancake* in two minutes (*for two minutes).
      b.   Freddy *ate pancakes* for two hours (*in two hours).

(160) a.   Linda *drank a glass of beer* in thirty seconds (*for thirty seconds).
      b.   Linda *drank beer* for thirty minutes (*in thirty minutes).

(161) a.   Frances read a story in thirty minutes (*for thirty minutes).
      b.   Frances read stories for three hours (*in three hours).

(162) a.   Grant wrote a poem in three weeks (*for three weeks).
      b.   Grant wrote poetry for three months (*in three months).

In each of these pairs of examples, the first sentence involves some definite unit or amount of something, whereas the second does not. These examples can be accounted for by the following rule:

(163) If a certain verb phrase has a direct object that denotes a definite number or amount, and the verb phrase is an accomplishment, then a corresponding verb phrase in which the object denotes an indefinite number or amount will count as an activity.

Exercise
1. Use the *for*-versus-*in* test to decide whether the verb phrases in the following sentences should be classified as accomplishments or as activities. Some may be classifiable as both.
   a. Joe walked around the block.   c. We ate Joe's biscuits.
   b. Your father built this house.   d. Nelda will tell John the story.

e. The soup cooled.

f. The squirrels disappeared.

g. Jody finished your sentence.

h. Smith managed the company.

17.2.3.2 Interpretation of Time Adverbs   The four basic aspectual classes that were described above show marked differences in the manner in which they require ordinary time adverbs to be interpreted. Some of these time adverbs denote individual points of time (*at three o'clock yesterday afternoon, right at that moment*), whereas others denote intervals of time (*yesterday, last year, on Tuesday*). The major differences in interpretation concern the question of where the state or event in question has to lie in relation to the time span denoted by the adverb.

States are the most permissive of the four classes in this regard, as we can see clearly by considering a simple situation. Suppose that Roger had a rash yesterday from noon until eight o'clock in the evening. Suppose also that Beth came to see him at three o'clock that afternoon. Under these circumstances, both of the sentences in (164) are completely acceptable.

(164)   a.   Roger had a rash *yesterday.*

b.   Roger had a rash *when Betty came to see him at three o'clock.*

The relation between the period of the rash and the time spans denoted by these two adverbs is represented in (165).

(165)   a.   have a rash   b.   have a rash

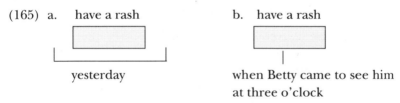

yesterday   when Betty came to see him
at three o'clock

In the first case the time adverb denotes a period that includes the state, whereas in the second case the time adverb denotes a point that is itself included in the period in which the state is in effect.

In the case of activities and accomplishments, the possibilities of interpretation are more limited:

(166)   a.   Karen talked to Martha *yesterday.*

b.   Karen talked to Martha *at three o'clock.*

(167)   a.   Joan wrote a sonnet *yesterday.*

b.   Joan wrote a sonnet *at three o'clock.*

Sentences (166a) and (167a) are interpreted in the same manner as the state sentence (164a). Again, the time span denoted by *yesterday* can include the interval during which the event was going on. But the interpretations of sentences (166b) and (167b) are different from that of the state sentence (164b). Here *at three o'clock* cannot be just some point within the interval in which the talking or the writing took place; it can only indicate the moment at which these events started. Thus, the following interpretations are the ones that we get for activities and accomplishments:

(168)   a. talk to Martha   b. talk to Martha

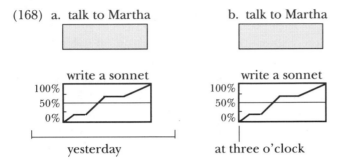

We get still another interpretation for achievement sentences. In contrast with activities and accomplishments, the only requirement for achievements is that the time span of the adverb cover the final moment of the achievement. The contrast between achievements and accomplishments in this regard is particularly striking:

(169)   a.   John spent several years finishing his dissertation. He finally finished it on July 4, 1987 (at three o'clock in the afternoon). (achievement)

        b.   *John spent several years writing his dissertation. He finally wrote it on July 4, 1987 (at three o'clock in the afternoon). (accomplishment)

(170)   a.   Carolyn spent several days getting to Boston. She finally got there at three o'clock (at three o'clock this afternoon). (achievement)

        b.   *Carolyn spent several days driving to Boston. She finally drove there at three o'clock (at three o'clock this afternoon). (accomplishment)

Even though achievements, like accomplishments, can be described as taking a long time, we are entitled with achievements to use any time adverb that covers the final moment, without regard to all the time that went before that moment. This requirement is pictured for sentence (169a) in (171).

(171) finish his dissertation

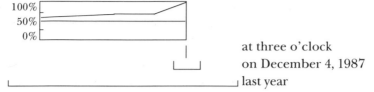

at three o'clock
on December 4, 1987
last year

As examples (169b) and (170b) show, this kind of interpretation, one in which the time adverb does not include the entire event, is completely impossible for accomplishments.

Exercise

1. Use some time adverbs to test whether each of the following sentences contains an accomplishment verb phrase or an achievement verb phrase.

    a. Edison invented the phonograph.
    b. Sequoyah developed an alphabet.
    c. David noticed the bug.
    d. Frankenstein created a monster.
    e. Harold relinquished his claim.
    f. Katy let go of the rope.
    g. Columbus discovered America.
    h. Nancy won the race.

17.2.3.3 Possibilities for Verb-Phrase Interpretation The third area in which the basic aspectual classes described above play a role is in determining the possibilities for two contrasting interpretations for verb phrases. These interpretations, which are themselves aspectual in nature, can be referred to as *punctual* and *habitual*. A verb phrase with a punctual interpretation refers to a state or event that occurs either once or some definite number of times. By contrast, a verb phrase with a habitual interpretation denotes a state or event that recurs with some degree of frequency. The following pairs of sentences illustrate these two interpretations:

(172) a. Roger had a rash last week. (punctual state)
     b. Roger occasionally had a rash. (habitual state)

(173) a. Jonah pestered the cat last night. (punctual activity)
     b. Jonah pestered the cat every day. (habitual activity)

(174) a. Alfred ate a peach yesterday. (punctual accomplishment)
     b. Alfred ate a peach three times a year.
       (habitual accomplishment)

(175) a.   Carol discovered a new problem on Thursday.
            (punctual achievement)
       b.   Carol discovered a new problem several times a month.
            (habitual achievement)

Now let us turn to the question of the external circumstances under which these two interpretations are available. For habituals, the anwer is simple: So long as the verb phrase itself is of a form that makes sense with a habitual interpretation, then that interpretation is allowed. The sentences in (176) give some idea of the range of the environments that permit a habitual interpretation.

(176) a.   Cora *had a headache every day.*   (past tense)
       b.   Nora *writes a novel every year.*   (present tense)
       c.   Joe's son will *write a letter every week.*   (bare stem as complement of WILL)
       d.   *Eating a peach three times a year* is good for you.
            (present participial)
       e.   Sharon appears to have *finished an essay every month.*
            (past participial)

With the punctual interpretation, the possibilities are more limited. The most readily apparent restriction concerns the possibility of such an interpretation for simple sentences in the present tense. The sentences in (177) show the possibilities for the four basic aspectual classes.

(177) a.   John can't talk on the phone now. He *has a headache.*   (state)
       b.   Flora is busy right this minute. *She *plays the piano.*   (activity)
       c.   Max will see you in a minute. *Right now he *writes a letter.*
            (accomplishment)
       d.   Sarah will be free in just a second. *Right now she *finishes her breakfast.*   (achievement)

The following rule represents an initial attempt at expressing this limitation:

(178) When it occurs in the simple present tense, a nonstate verb phrase cannot receive a punctual interpretation.

A consideration of additional examples reveals that this interpretive restriction needs to be stated in a more general form. We find the same effects with nonfinite verb phrases when the event time and the current reference point are the same. A clear example is given in (179), where the intended interpretation of the modal MUST is 'logical necessity'.

(179) *John must take a bath right now.

This sentence with this interpretation is just as unacceptable as (180), in which *take a bath* appears in the present tense.

(180) *It must be the case that John takes a bath right now.

These examples, then, suggests that the statement in (178) should be replaced by one that does not refer specifically to the present tense:

(181) If the event time is the same as the current reference point, a nonstate verb phrase cannot receive a punctual interpretation.

We have here a rule in which a matter concerning aspect (the availability of a punctual interpretation) is determined by a combination of a basic aspectual property (whether the phrase denotes a state) and a property of time relations (whether the event time and the current reference point are the same).

Exercises

1. If we were to examine a great many verb phrases with a view to determining whether they could qualify for a habitual interpretation, we would find that some verb phrases seem to require a frequency modifier whereas others do not. Here are some examples from both of these groups:

    a. Jack eats grasshoppers.   Jack eats grasshoppers quite frequently.

    b. ? Jane makes a mistake.   Jane rarely makes a mistake.

    c. ? Peter drinks three beers.   Peter drinks three beers every Saturday.

    d. ? Norbert attends a concert.   Norbert attends a concert every Sunday.

    e. Ida eats peas with a knife.   Ida occasionally eats peas with a knife.

    f. Kathleen watches television.   Kathleen often watches television.

    g. ? Barry sells a truck.   Barry sells a truck about once a week.

    h. Norma drives a truck.   Norma drives a truck about once a week.

Give a simple statement that distinguishes between the verb phrases that need a frequency modifier in order to have a habitual interpretation and those that do not.

2. As was noted earlier in this chapter, MAY can have two interpretations (logical possibility and permission), and MUST can also have two (logical necessity and obligation). We see both interpretations for MAY in (i) below, and both for MUST in (ii):

    (i)   John may eat lunch at his office.

    (ii)   John must eat lunch at his office.

Now look at the following sentences:

    (iii)   John may destroy this letter.

    (iv)   John must destroy this letter.

In (iii), MAY has the same two interpretations that it had in (i). However, MUST in (iv) has only the 'obligation' interpretation. Explain why the logical-necessity interpretation is allowed in (ii) but not in (iv).

3. In subsection 17.1.3, which dealt with past harmony, it was noted that in informal speech a past tense in quoted speech is matched with a past tense in the corresponding reported speech:

    (i)   Carol said "Janice *collected* the money."

    (ii)   Carol said that Janice *collected* the money.

In addition, of course, the past-harmony rule sometimes dictates a matchup between a present tense in quoted speech and a past tense in reported speech:

    (iii)   Carol said "Janice *collects* the money."

    (iv)   Carol said that Janice *collected* the money.

In the following sentence, we have a past tense in the subordinate clause that can be interpreted as 'earlier' but not as a past-harmony present:

    (v)   Carol said that Janice *married* Phil.

Explain why this subordinate past tense can only be interpreted as 'earlier'.

17.2.3.4 Availability and Interpretation of the Progressive   A final area in which the four basic aspectual classes are differentiated involves the progressive construction, which consists of BE plus a present-participial verb phrase. We will begin by describing how it is interpreted with activities and accomplishments, since its interpretation here is the most straightforward.

    In our general discussion of the activity and accomplishment sentences, we noted that they were interpreted as taking place during an interval. As was observed in subsection 17.2.3.2, a time adverb that refers to a single moment can only be taken as indicating the point at which this interval begins. Thus, sentences such as (182a) and (182b) could have only the interpretations in which *at three o'clock* identifies the beginning time of the event.

(182) a.   Karen talked to Martha at three o'clock.

at three
o'clock

b.   Joan wrote a sonnet at three o'clock.

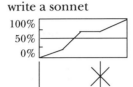

at three
o'clock

It is precisely here that the progressive construction fills a gap. It takes a particular complement verb phrase that by itself would stand for an entire activity or accomplishment stretched over an interval, and creates a larger verb phrase that stands for a slice of an activity or accomplishment—a slice that can be as small as a single moment:

(183) a.   Karen was talking to Martha at three o'clock.

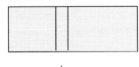

at three
o'clock

b.   Joan was writing a sonnet at three o'clock.

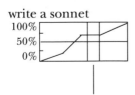

at three
o'clock

With achievements, the progressive has a similar though not identical effect, as can be seen in (184).

(184) a. On June 18, Linda was finishing her thesis.
     b. When the clock chimed eight, Joel was arriving at the meeting.
     c. At the time when the phone rang, Fred's goldfish was dying.
     d. At five o'clock, Carol was getting to Boston.

As was noted earlier, a single-moment time adverb with an achievement generally denotes the endpoint of the event. However, when we use such an adverb with an achievement verb phrase in a progressive construction, the adverb marks out the time of a prefinal slice of the event. The contrast between a simple achievement and an achievement in a progressive construction is depicted in (185).

(185)   a. finish her thesis   b. be finishing her thesis

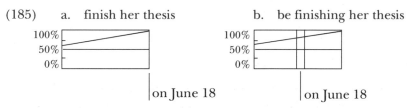

Progressives associated with activities, accomplishments, and achievements serve to fill the gap that we noted in the preceding subsection. Although the examples with the simple present tense in (186) are not acceptable, the corresponding progressive examples in (187) are.

(186) a. *Right now, Georgia plays the piano. (activity)
     b. *Right this minute, John takes a bath. (accomplishment)
     c. *At this point, Karen finishes her thesis. (achievement)

(187) a. Right now, Georgia is playing the piano. (activity)
     b. Right this minute, John is taking a bath. (accomplishment)
     c. At this point, Karen is finishing her thesis. (achievement)

In addition, the logical-necessity reading of *must*, which was impossible with *take a bath*, is readily available with the corresponding progressive:

(188) a. *John must take a bath right now.
     b. John must be taking a bath right now.

Thus, the restriction that nonstates cannot have an event time identical with the current reference point applies only to nonprogressive verb phrases.

    Let us turn now to the fourth basic class, the class of states, and see how phrases of this type behave with the progressive construction. As a general rule, state verb phrases are unacceptable with the progressive:

(189) a. *I am knowing the answer to your question.
            (Compare: I know the answer to your question.)
       b. *Joan is owning two cars.
            (Compare: Joan owns two cars.)
       c. *This bar of soap is costing fifty cents.
            (Compare: This bar of soap costs fifty cents.)
       d. *The manager is weighing two hundred pounds.
            (Compare: The manager weighs two hundred pounds.)

This fact might be connected to the fact—noted in subsection 17.2.3.2—
that state verb phrases can be asserted for individual "interior points" as
well as for intervals. The relevant example is repeated in (190).

(190)   Roger had a rash when Betty came to see him at three o'clock.

             have a rash

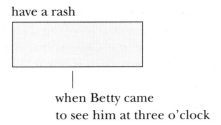

             when Betty came
             to see him at three o'clock

Since the major effect of the progressive construction is to create a
predicate with this possibility, and since states already have it, the progressive would be superfluous with them.

   In several special cases, however, state verbs can occur in the progressive
construction:

(191) a.   Karen understands this proof.
       b.   Karen is understanding this proof.

(192) a.   I really like this performance.
       b.   I am really liking this performance.

(193) a.   Donald finds your accusations ludicrous.
       b.   Donald is finding your accusations ludicrous.

The acceptability of the present tense in the (a) examples shows that these
really are state verb phrases. Both the (a) and the (b) sentences appear to
assert the existence of a judgment of some sort concerning an individual
entity or a set of entities. The (a) sentences suggest that the judgment is
a final and total judgment. The (b) sentences, by contrast, imply that the
judgment is an intermediate one based on only part of the available
evidence. Sentence (191b) would typically be used if Karen was only partly

done going through the proof, (192b) would be appropriate at an intermediate point in the performance, and (193b) would be used if Donald had heard only some of the accusations.

Another type of situation in which an apparent state verb phrase appears in the progressive construction is illustrated in the (b) sentences of (194)–(196).

(194) a. Jeffrey *resembles his brother.*
 b. Jeffrey is *resembling his brother more and more.*

(195) a. Dana *knows the answer.*
 b. Dana is *knowing more and more of the answers as the course progresses.*

(196) a. The manager *weighs two hundred pounds.*
 b. The manager is *weighing more and more.*

Each of the italicized phrases in the (b) sentences denotes a state that is changing in some way, rather than a state that is staying the same. Thus, the use of the progressive here may be the same as that illustrated in examples that contain change-of-state verbs such as COOL and SOFTEN:

(197) a. The soup is cooling.
 b. The wax is softening.

One final observation about the progressive concerns its interpretation with habitual verb phrases. Some contrasts between the simple present and the present progressive can be seen in (198)–(200):

(198) a. Jonah pesters the cat a lot.
 b. Jonah is pestering the cat a lot this year.

(199) a. Tony goes to Austin every Saturday.
 b. This fall, Tony is going to Austin every Saturday.

(200) a. Lorna proposes a new topic every two weeks or so.
 b. This spring, Lorna is proposing a new topic every two weeks or so.

The difference between the (a) sentences and the corresponding (b) sentences is a subtle one. Each of the (a) sentences seems to assert a permanent habitual state of affairs, whereas the corresponding (b) sentence implies that the habitual state of affairs may be only temporary.

Exercises

1. The English verb HAVE has a large number of different meanings, and can be used to head a variety of different kinds of verb phrases. Several verb phrases headed by HAVE are listed below. For each one, construct an

experimental progressive sentence that will indicate whether the verb phrase in question should be classified as a state verb phrase or as a verb phrase of some other kind.

a.	have a good time	e.	have some lunch
b.	have a headache	f.	have an interview with Fred
c.	have a heart attack	g.	have Hal mow the lawn
d.	have her hat on backwards	h.	have two chickens in the pot

2. In this discussion of aspect, we have assumed that there are four basic aspectual classes of verbs, and that any habitual verb phrase is related to a nonhabitual verb phrase from one of these four classes. An alternative viewpoint would be that at least some English verbs give rise to phrases that are inherently habitual. One verb for which such an analysis might be adopted is the verb LIVE, as used in the sentence *Quentin lives in Boston*. Using the behavior of the progressive with such a phrase, decide whether *live in Boston* should be classified as a state verb phrase or as an inherently habitual verb phrase.

Index